Botanical Medicine

Efficacy, Quality Assurance, and Regulation

Herbal Medicine -- legislation & jurisprudence -- congresses 7
Herbal Medicine -- economics -- congresses 7

Botanical Medicine

Efficacy, Quality Assurance, and Regulation

Editor **Daniel Eskinazi, D.D.S., Ph.D., L.Ac.**
The Richard and Hinda Rosenthal Center
  for Complementary & Alternative Medicine
Department of Rehabilitation Medicine
Columbia University College of Physicians &
  Surgeons, New York, New York

Associate Editors **Mark Blumenthal**
American Botanical Council, Austin, Texas

Norman Farnsworth, Ph.D.
University of Illinois at Chicago

Chance W. Riggins
American Botanical Council, Austin, Texas

Mary Ann Liebert, Inc. publishers
www.liebertpub.com

Copyright © 1999 by Mary Ann Liebert, Inc., 2 Madison Avenue, Larchmont, NY 10538

ISBN: 0-913113-83-2

All rights reserved.

No part of this book may be reproduced, stored in a retrieval system, or transmitted in any form or by any means, electronic, mechanical, photocopying, microfilming, recording, or otherwise, without written permission from the publisher.

Cover drawing of *Sambucus nigra* (elder) by Eric Yarnell, N.D.

Printed in the United States of America.

Preface

The 1992 legislative language creating the Office of Alternative Medicine at the National Institutes of Health clearly reflects a strong Congressional interest in the "investigation and validation" of alternative medicine. To achieve the mandated goals, the Office of Alternative Medicine, in cooperation with the Food and Drug Administration, has begun to address several regulatory issues under the aegis of the FDA. These issues may affect the research into, and availability of, products and devices that are relevant to alternative medicine.

One of the "alternative" approaches that falls within the purview of the Office of Alternative Medicine is that of botanical medicine. Indeed, the last decade has seen a resurgence of interest in the use of botanical products for medicinal purposes. This interest may have been kindled by factors such as inadequate treatments of chronic conditions, and other perceived shortcomings of the conventional health care system. Also, an increasing number of articles in the lay and scientific press have touted the virtues of these products, and the concerns about maintaining their availability in their natural habitat.

The role of botanicals is a rather complex one from a regulatory standpoint. These products fall within more than one regulatory category in the United States: they may be considered foods, dietary supplements, or drugs, chiefly depending on their intended use as defined by the products' labeling.

In 1994, the Office of Alternative Medicine invited the Food and Drug Administration to assist in the planning of a conference on botanical products. The "Symposium on Botanicals: A Role in US Health Care?" was organized in cooperation with the FDA, and brought together academia, industry, the United States Pharmacopeia, and agency and government officials, both from the United States and abroad, to discuss the role and regulation of botanical products in US health care.

The symposium was composed of five panels. Each panel was given the task of answering specific questions:

- "What are botanicals and how are they currently used?" This panel discussed the use of botanical medicines in foreign countries, and the most common uses in the United States.
- "How can we know that botanicals work?" This panel discussed the relative advantages and limitations of the traditional controlled clinical trial, as well as other methodological approaches, including single case studies and outcomes research.

- "How can we know that these products are safe?" This panel discussed methods for assessing potential adverse events resulting from the use of botanical products.
- "How can we ensure that botanical preparations will be reliable and of good quality?" This panel discussed the necessary steps to ensure the product's quality, purity, and reliability.
- "How do regulations affect the marketplace and impact the cost of health care?" This panel addressed two issues: (1) the economic factors impacting on the development of botanical medicine in various countries, including Europe and the United States; and (2) the legal and regulatory issues that are relevant to the marketing of these products.

This symposium was held in Washington D.C., in December, 1994. It was attended by more than 450 participants, many of whom viewed it as a historic event, as it brought together for the first time, in a cooperative atmosphere, the various parties directly interested in this set of issues. The meeting aided in identifying and defining the relevant issues. Follow-up meetings, such as several recent conferences sponsored by the Drug Information Association, have discussed many of the issues presented at the symposium in greater detail. In addition, the FDA has formed several internal working groups to discuss policy issues, which might result in new regulatory considerations for botanical products.

Although the material presented here has not been significantly updated since the workshop, it is still current and relevant, as the issues raised are still being debated in the same terms, and little further substantive progress has been made to date.

—Daniel P. Eskinazi, D.D.S., Ph.D., L.Ac.
Former Deputy Director
Office of Alternative Medicine

Contents

Contributors	xi
Acknowledgments	xv
Opening Comments From the Department of Health and Human Services *Devra Lee Davis, Ph.D., M.P.H.*	1

PART I:
WHAT ARE BOTANICALS, AND HOW ARE THEY CURRENTLY USED?   5

Overview	7
An Introduction to the Medicinal Use of Botanicals *Varro E. Tyler, Ph.D., Sc.D.*	13
Twenty-Seven Major Botanicals and Their Uses in the United States *Mark Blumenthal*	17
Types of Botanical Products Used in the United States *Robert S. McCaleb*	27
Herbal Use by Health Care Providers *J. Jamison Starbuck, J.D., N.D.*	33

PART II:
HOW CAN WE KNOW THAT BOTANICALS WORK?   37

Overview	39
Botanical Efficacy in the Clinical Setting *Andrew T. Weil, M.D.*	43
Evaluating an Ancient Kampo Prescription by Modern Methods *Peter Goldman, M.D.*	45
A Methodologic Case Study: Effect of a Proprietary Herbal Medicine on the Relief of Joint Pain in Arthritis *Simon Y. Mills, M.A., F.N.I.M.H.*	49
Databases Containing Information Pertaining to Botanical Medicine *Norman R. Farnsworth, Ph.D.*	55
Evaluation of Herbal Efficacy: Alternatives to the Randomized Controlled Trial *Richard L. Kravitz, M.D., M.S.P.H.*	59
Synthesis of Evidence: Examples From the Agency for Health Care Policy and Research *Vic Hasselblad, Ph.D.*	65

Establishing Consensus
John H. Ferguson, M.D. 75

Controlled Clinical Trials for Botanicals: Available, Possible, Necessary?
Dr. Joerg Gruenwald 77

Summary and Conclusions
Ka Kit Hui, M.D., F.A.C.P. 79

PART III:
HOW CAN WE KNOW THAT THESE PRODUCTS ARE SAFE? 81

Overview 83

The Safety of Botanicals: A Historical Perspective
Ryan J. Huxtable, Ph.D. 87

The Information Base for Safety Assessment of Botanicals
Dennis V.C. Awang, Ph.D., F.C.I.C. 103

Safety Monitoring of Botanicals by Government Agencies
Lori A. Love, M.D., Ph.D. 107

Safety Monitoring of Medicinal Plants in Europe (With Special Reference to Germany)
Barbara Steinhoff, Ph.D. 109

Safety of Herbal Remedies: Surveillance in the United Kingdom
Virginia S.G. Murray, M.Sc., M.F.O.M., Debbie Shaw, and Christine Leon 111

PART IV:
HOW CAN WE ENSURE THAT BOTANICAL PREPARATIONS WILL BE OF GOOD QUALITY? 115

Overview 117

Good Botanical Practices
Michael J. Balick, Ph.D. 121

Quality of Botanical Preparations: Environmental Issues and Methodology for Detecting Environmental Contaminants
James D. McChesney, Ph.D. 127

Domestication and Production Considerations in Quality Control of Botanicals
James E. Simon, Ph.D. 133

Shipping, Handling, Receipt, and Short-Term Storage of Raw Plant Materials
Trish Flaster 139

The Processing of Botanicals
Werner Busse, Ph.D. 143

Worldwide Harmonization of Botanical Standards: A Pharmacopeial View
Lee T. Grady, Ph.D. 147

PART V:
HOW DO REGULATIONS AFFECT THE MARKETPLACE AND IMPACT THE COST OF HEALTH CARE? 169

Overview 171

CONTENTS

The Economics of Botanicals: The European Experience
Melville K. Eaves — 175

The Economics of Botanicals: The U.S. Experience
Peggy Brevoort — 183

The Botanical Agenda, Science, and Incentives for Research
Ted J. Kaptchuk, O.M.D., C.A. — 193

Industry Views on Plant Monographs
Hubertus Cranz, M.D. — 195

Dietary Supplement Legislation
Stephen H. McNamara, Esq. — 199

Regulatory Models for Approval of Botanicals as Traditional Medicines
Mark Blumenthal — 205

Summary of Principal Findings and Policy Initiatives — 213

Summary of the Conference
Loren D. Israelsen — 215

Index — 217

Contributors

Dennis V.C. Awang, Ph.D., F.C.I.C.
President
MediPlant
P.O. Box 8693
Station T
Ottawa, Ontario KIG3JI Canada

Michael J. Balick, Ph.D.
Director and Philecology Curator of
  Economic Botany
Institute of Economic Botany
The New York Botanical Garden
Bronx, NY 10458-5126

Mark Blumenthal
Founder and Executive Director
American Botanical Council
P.O. Box 144345
Austin, TX 78714

Peggy Brevoort
Chief Executive Officer
East Earth Herb, Inc.
P O. Box 2802
4091 West 11th Avenue
Eugene, OR 97402

Werner Busse, Ph.D.
Head, Regulatory and Scientific Affairs
Dr. Willmar Schwabe GmbH and Co.
International Scientific Services
P.O. Box 410925
D-76209 Karlsruhe
Germany

Ke Ji Chen, M.D.
Professor of Clinical Cardiology and Geriatrics
Xiyuang Hospital
China Academy of Traditional
  Chinese Medicine
Beijing 10091
People's Republic of China

Hubertus Cranz, M.D.
Director General
European Proprietary Medicines Manufacturers'
  Association (AESGP)
7, Avenue de Tervuren
B-1040 Brussels
Belgium

Devra Lee Davis, Ph.D., M.P.H.
World Resources Institute
Washington, DC

Melville K. Eaves
Dr. Willmar Schwabe GmbH and Co.
P.O. Box 410925
D-7500 Karlsruhe-41
Germany

Daniel Eskinazi, D.D.S., Ph.D., L.Ac.
Richard and Hinda Rosenthal Center for
  Complementary and Alternative Medicine
Columbia University College of Physicians
  & Surgeons
630 West 168 Street, Box 75
New York, N.Y. 10032

Norman R. Farnsworth, Ph.D.
Research Professor of Pharmacognosy
  and Senior University Scholar
College of Pharmacy
University of Illinois at Chicago
833 South Wood Street
M/C 877
Chicago, IL 60612

John H. Ferguson, M.D.
Director
Office of Medical Applications of Research
National Institutes of Health
Bldg. 31–Room B103
9000 Rockville Pike
Bethesda, MD 20892

Trish Flaster
Chief Executive Officer
Botanical Liaisons
1180 Crestmoor Drive
Boulder, CO 80303

Peter Goldman, M.D.
Professor of Health Sciences
Department of Nutrition
Harvard School of Public Health
665 Huntington Avenue
Boston, MA 02115

Lee T. Grady, Ph.D.
Vice President and Director, Division of
  Standards Development
U.S. Pharmacopeia
12601 Twinbrook Parkway
Rockville, MD 20852

Dr. Joerg Gruenwald
PhytoPharm Consulting
Institute for Phytopharmaceuticals
Olafstrabe 6 D-13467
Berlin, Germany

Vic Hasselblad, Ph.D.
Associate Research Professor
Duke Clinical Research Institute
2024 West Main Street
Ste. A201
Durham, NC 27705

Ka Kit Hui, M.D., F.A.C.P.
Director, UCLA Center for East-West Medicine
University of California, Los Angeles
School of Medicine
Department of Medicine
200 UCLA Medical Plaza 16-8524-Ste. 420
Los Angeles, CA 90095

Ryan J. Huxtable, Ph.D.
Professor
Department of Pharmacology
College of Medicine
University of Arizona Health
  Sciences Center
Tucson, AZ 85724

Loren D. Israelsen
Executive Director
Utah Natural Products Alliance
1075 East Hollywood Avenue
Salt Lake City, UT 84105

Ted J. Kaptchuk, O.M.D., C.A.
Associate Director
Center for Alternative Medicine
  Research
Beth Israel Deaconness Medical Center
330 Brookline Avenue
Boston, MA 02215

Richard L. Kravitz, M.D., M.S.P.H.
Associate Professor of Medicine
University of California, Davis
Sacramento, CA 95616

Lori A. Love, M.D., Ph.D.
Office of Special Nutritionals (HFS-452)
Center for Food Safety and Applied
  Nutrition
U.S. Food and Drug Administration
200 C Street, SW
Washington, DC 20204

Robert S. McCaleb
President and Founder
Herb Research Foundation
1007 Pearl Street, Ste. 200
Boulder, CO 80302

James D. McChesney, Ph.D.
Vice President, Natural Products Chemistry
  and Development
Napro BioTherapeutics, Inc.
6304-A Spine Road
Boulder, CO 80301

Stephen H. McNamara, Esq.
Hyman, Phelps and McNamara
700-13th Street, NW, Ste. 1200
Washington, DC 20005

Simon Y. Mills, M.A., F.N.I.M.H.
Centre for Complementary Health
  Studies
University of Exeter
Exeter, Devon EX4 4RJ
United Kingdom

Virginia S.G. Murray, M.Sc., M.F.O.M.
National Poisons Unit
Guy's and St. Thomas Hospital Trust
Avonley Road
London SE14 5ER
United Kingdom

CONTRIBUTORS

James E. Simon, Ph.D.
Professor
Center for New Crops and Plant Products
Purdue University
Horticulture Building
West Lafayette, IN 47907-1165

J. Jamison Starbuck, J.D., N.D.
Attorney-at-Law
Naturopathic Physician
210 North Higgins, Ste. 222
Missoula, MT 59802

Barbara Steinhoff, Ph.D.
Bundesfachverband der Arzneimittel-Hersteller
Ubier Strasse 71-73
D-53173 Bonn
Germany

Varro E. Tyler, Ph.D., Sc.D.
Dean and Distinguished Professor Emeritus,
of Pharmacognosy
School of Pharmacy and Pharmacal Sciences
P.O.B. 2566
Purdue University
West Lafayette, IN 47996-2566

Donald P. Waller, Ph.D.
Department of Pharmaceutics and
Pharmacodynamics, M/C 865
College of Pharmacy
University of Illinois at Chicago
833 South Wood Street
Chicago, IL 60612

Andrew T. Weil, M.D.
Director, Program for Integrative Medicine
School of Health Sciences
University of Arizona
Tuscon, AZ 85724-5153

Acknowledgments

Many individuals contributed to the success of this symposium. However, we wish to give my special thanks to Freddie A. Hoffman, M.D., of the Food and Drug Administration, and to Adriane Fugh-Berman, M.D., and Andrew Parfitt, Ph.D., L.Ac., of the National Institutes of Health, who participated in the organization of this conference. Without their efforts the symposium could simply not have taken place. In addition, we wish to acknowledge the expert editorial assistance of Ms. Marion Brandis, and the careful corrections by Ms. Anne Paulus who generously donated her time.

Funds to assist in the editorial aspects of the preparation of this book, for which the editors are grateful, were provided by the following organizations:

INDENA USA, Inc., Seattle, Washington
The Moody Foundation of Galveston, Texas
Nature's Herbs of Orem, Utah
Nature's Way of Provo, Utah

Opening Comments From the Department of Health and Human Services

DEVRA LEE DAVIS, Ph.D., M.P.H.

Thank you, and my compliments to all who worked on this meeting: It is really an extraordinary opportunity. I want to thank you for making me part of this important event. This conference really is the first time that the government has brought together, in one place, such a diverse group of people concerned with complementary medicine.

We are here today, truly determined to broaden our areas of agreement and narrow our areas of disagreement and move forward to forge a scientific agenda, which will allow us to pursue important research questions regarding the issues of the use of botanicals in modern medicine. Given this task, the conference has remained scientific, not political. We are seeking to devise an agenda for future studies and collaborations.

Now, many in this room might well wonder what took us so long, while others are certainly questioning whether we really have enough information to have such a meeting. The purpose of this conference is really to address both of these concerns by bringing together skeptics and true believers to discuss freely the range of necessary scientific and regulatory goals that must be met.

How are we going to get there? I think a story from a very rich man, who recently died, might be helpful. Sam Walton was a multi-multi-millionaire, in fact a billionaire, and he was once asked: "Mr. Walton, how do you explain your success?" Being a man of few words he said: "Good decisions." He was then asked: "Well, how do you get to make good decisions?" And he replied: "Experience." He was asked then: "How do you get experience?" He replied: "Bad decisions."

We can quarrel about what bad decisions might have been made in the past. But I think the best decision that the Office of Alternative Medicine (OAM) and the Food and Drug Administration (FDA) have made is to bring us all together here today. I am here to express a commitment to and support for this meeting from the highest levels of the Department of Health and Human Services. We want to see the scientific assessment advance. In fact, the Department fully supports the National Institutes of Health (NIH) and FDA efforts to construct a valid symposium as this.

Assistant Secretary of Health Phil Lee came to us from San Francisco. San Francisco is a city that manages to be on the cutting edge of both biomedicine and complementary medicine. Dr. Lee understands how important it is to expand the search for effective methods to prevent disease and promote health, including the use of botanicals and related products. The Department has a sincere desire to cooperate with industry and foreign governments as well and to facilitate the process of assessing the usefulness and safety of botanicals scientifically.

It should be quite clear why we have to take a broader perspective on prevention and treatment of disease. A number of diseases have proven resistant to conventional medical treatments. Some of the work that my colleagues and I have recently published in the *Journal of the American Medical Association* is relevant. We found that, even when you adjust for smoking and aging and approved diagnostic technology, there is a real increase in cancer today that cannot be explained. Moreover, there has been no fundamentally new treatment for any of the major forms of cancer in more than three decades. We have had spectacular successes with the relatively rare cancers in children and young adults, such as leukemia and testicular cancer, but for the

---

World Resources Institute, Washington, DC.

most common forms of cancer—lung, colon, stomach, breast, and prostate—no fundamentally new treatment has been devised. As a consequence, we have to look with renewed interest to the possibility that some botanicals may be useful. The government has a pretty hard job in this area because there are many health care professionals with strongly held views on this subject, some of you are in this room today.

I want to recount a true story about what I was told about one of the first scientific studies of acupuncture. (We are not going to talk about acupuncture today, but I think it is relevant: The story relates what happens when an untested alternative therapy first appears on the scene.) In the 1930s a group of doctors brought an acupuncturist, Chang Hai, to a hospital in Paris to treat a very grave case. It was something they thought was one of the most serious diseases that could ever affect a man: impotence. The acupuncturist said he could cure this dreaded affliction. He proceeded to insert needles at different points in the patient's body and, every hour a group of 10 residents would come by and lift up the sheets to see if they had had success. After six hours, they declared that the experiment had been a clear sign that acupuncture did not work. That was the standard for clinical science at that time.

Over the next three days, you will hear what we have to do now to evaluate botanical product use in the arena of U.S. health care using the best scientific methods. In some sense, we are trying to push the bus in which we are also riding. Some estimates are that as many as one in three Americans today is using some form of alternative medicine. And we are now asking how we can assess a process scientifically that is already underway. The challenges are substantial, but I know that the crew who put this meeting together can tackle this.

In countries where Western medicine is not available and in countries where traditional remedies provide the chief means of treatment, botanical products are really the mainstay of medicine, as they have been for hundreds, and sometimes thousands, of years. But in modern countries today, in growing numbers, botanicals are also being used as supplements or sometimes instead of standard treatment. This interest in botanicals is primarily fueled by intense public interest. Many of you have seen articles in women's magazines, newspaper cover stories, television pieces on the use of botanicals, and recent advertising campaigns.

Let us define briefly what we mean by botanicals. Botanicals are labeled products that contain ingredients of vegetable matter or its constituents as finished products. Such vegetable matter may include either whole plants or plant parts. It might also include algae or macroscopic fungi and similar products or combinations of products. Plant material can include juices, gums, fatty oils, scent oils, and any other substances of this nature. For the purposes of this conference, we will not be considering yeast, bacteria, or microscopic organisms previously approved for drug use or accepted for food use in the United States. Nor will we be considering homeopathic products, even though many are derived from botanical sources. Botanicals may fit into more than one category in the United States, where a product is characterized by its intended use as defined in the Federal Food Drug and Cosmetic Act. Intended use is determined by labeling.

The major initial objective of the OAM and the FDA has been accomplished. We are here. Congratulations. The next step is to really try to have a frank exchange of the differing viewpoints, to bring together the experts and address the growing issues in order to take botanicals off the front pages of magazines and move them into clinical trials and ultimately into doctors' offices. And that, in fact, is the goal of this meeting. In this symposium, we must figure out how botanicals will fit within the current system of medical practice in the United States and what needs to be done to provide the kind of evidence that will be scientifically useful so that we can move forward. This meeting has given us an opportunity to examine different perspectives and establish an ongoing dialogue to develop the kind of information that will change the way medicine works today. The Department of Health and Human Services is here in a listening mode.

In the first panel, we will learn how botanical products have traditionally been used and how they are currently being used in our multicultural nation and in other countries. We will also examine different therapeutic formulations. In the second panel, we will hear about outcomes from clinical studies of botanical products and will learn what kinds of database exists and what needs to be developed. In the third panel, we will examine the safety of these plant products and how our industry and our federal agencies, such as the FDA and the Centers for Disease Control and Prevention, currently handle the reports of side effects and adverse events. Here, we especially welcome input from representatives of other countries who have dealt with this issue, including the United Kingdom, Germany, and Asia. The fourth panel will feature botanical experts and chemists from a number of agencies to examine some of the current controversies in plant nomenclature, and how we can go about reaching a consensus with respect to developing quality control guidelines. Panel five will look at the challenging legal, scientific, and regulatory issues that must be addressed.

Much of the public discussion on U.S. health care has focused on the questions of efficiency and equity of services delivered. There are areas of this country where a black woman who presents with breast cancer has, on average, twice the rate of metastatic disease when first diagnosed as a white woman. In fact, in Harlem Hospital in one 10-year period, half of the women diagnosed were metastatic when they first presented. This is clearly an inequity that we have to address; no one questions that. But we also know that no matter how efficient we may become in delivering health care, we also have to do a better job of reducing the demand for medical care by keeping people from developing disease in the first place. Many botanical products are relevant to the effort of promoting health and preventing disease. Recent analyses done by my colleagues and me have shown that cancer patterns in the United States and elsewhere vary significantly. This variation suggests that there might be opportunities for reducing the cancer burden if we could properly identify underlying factors. In addition, we know that some natural botanical products, such as some soy products, appear to be beneficial in promoting the reduction of cancer. We need to do a better job of identifying these materials and promoting their use.

At a time when our health care dollars are stretched to the limit, the mandate for looking at botanicals is clear and strong. And this meeting is a very important first step. It is not the first interaction between alternative medicine and the FDA, although it may well be the most public and one of the best attended. Based on the various medical traditions represented here today, the number and scope of botanical products we can examine is really staggering. We have to be able to look at both the adverse consequences as well as the benefits of botanicals, and do so within a framework that will be of some scientific value.

Botanicals are very, very important, but there are complicating issues, not the least of which is how to go about testing these materials as whole products, rather than as distilled ingredients. Many of you know that the FDA looks at data on such things as aflatoxin and sets standards for contamination. The Cancer Institute has studied heterocyclic amines, which are byproducts of cooking animal protein. And, in each of those studies, the extract of the pure principle is viewed in a cell culture for a whole animal and it is determined whether there is an increase in tumors. In fact, there may be a fundamental flaw with that approach when it is applied to testing botanicals. In the case of aflatoxin, you can increase the rate of tumors in animals exposed to it. However, when we eat aflatoxin in peanuts, for example, we are eating aflatoxin along with iron, zinc, selenium, manganese, fiber, and vitamin A in those peanuts at the same time. And the net result for human health of being exposed to aflatoxin in its common natural form at low levels may be negligible. In fact, the data on humans strongly suggests that nutritional status and exposure to other viruses are very important cofactors for whether or not aflatoxin really does produce cancer in humans. The same applies to heterocyclic amines: Extremely minute quantities of these materials are produced when protein is cooked. In animals and human cell cultures, they are potent carcinogens. But when we eat heterocyclic amines, we often eat them in whole foods that contain a lot of anticarcinogens, antioxidants, and the like. As a consequence, the net effect of our exposure may well be negligible. Again, botanicals could be very important, but we have got to come up with the scientific framework for studying them. They provide special challenges precisely because their components exist in these complex mixtures.

We are here today as scientists. The Department is interested in having everyone speak frankly and tell the truth about what you know and what your experiences are with these botanical materials. We must remain, in some sense, apart from politics, though politics is part of why we are here. We are aware that many of these products have biologic effects, some good and some bad. And we have to do a good job of finding out what these effects are and putting them in a context that will move medicine forward scientifically. Ten years from now, we will all look back on this meeting as a start of a very important process, the success of which depends on complete and frank exchange from all of you.

Part I

What Are Botanicals, and
How Are They Currently Used?

Overview

Norman R. Farnsworth, Ph.D., Research Professor of Pharmacognosy at the University of Illinois at Chicago, moderated a panel discussion that served to set the stage for the duration of the conference. On the panel were two Food and Drug Administration (FDA) physicians who were forthright when fielding the many sharp questions but were frequently compelled to qualify their views as personal, rather than as statements of formal FDA policy. Nonetheless, their openness and willingness to find a constructive common ground on which to debate these questions set the tone for the entire conference. It was this sort of constructive candor that transformed what started as a cross examination of government policy into a meaningful and collaborative exploration of the issues.

Botanical use in the United States is problematic and complex. The scientific and regulatory guidelines embodied by the FDA oversight of food and drugs are in place for a clearly useful purpose. In discussing the role of the FDA and possible future options and enabling mechanisms for change, the first panel discussion revolved around the central question: Is it feasible for government to regulate the safety and efficacy of botanicals without undermining the rights of consumers and the rapidly growing dietary supplement industry?

THE CURRENT STATUS AND ROLE OF THE FOOD AND DRUG ADMINISTRATION (FDA)

It is not the mandate of the FDA to analyze the problems and devise solutions to the marketing of botanicals in the United States

Robert Temple, M.D., of the FDA's Center of Drug Evaluation and Research, responded to the panel presentations by suggesting that several myths need debunking. One of those myths is that "everybody at the FDA hates the idea of botanicals." As a clinician and researcher, he appreciates that sometimes in science something "irregular works better than people think it will." It is the FDA's job to evaluate data that comes to it, not to seek out and make judgments on new therapies. But most of the information and data on botanicals do not come to it in part, because the herbal industry has been willing to proceed without making overt health claims, and thus does not need to register its products. The FDA is neither funded nor authorized to initiate inquiries proactively.

The situation is somewhat different in other countries. In Germany, for example, Commission E actively collects data and, thus, a database has been developed that is driven more by substantive issues than by marketing pressures. Dr. Temple was urged to consider adopting the results of this research. That would be problematic, he responded, because the standards of scholarship and publication requirements would then need to be reconciled. The rigor and methodology developed over the agency's history establish a de facto standard that may not, in many cases, be met by the Commission E data.

The current FDA system and standards were not developed with botanicals in view

The FDA system reflects the American scientific emphasis on empirical inquiry. "We at the FDA don't care where good things come from. If they come out of botanicals and funny mixtures, that's just fine." The problem is that current FDA standards were developed in the context of over-the-counter (OTC) drugs and require that a given product's therapeutic claim be consistently reproducible. This feature assures that the completed studies and testing have some relevance to the product's health claim and the government's endorsement. Dr. Temple believes that the central purpose of such testing is, in fact, to see if something works. To put the imprimatur of the government and American science behind a health claim, he believes, is a meaningful step. As a doctor and a scientist, he is not prepared to waive the rigor and experience that medical and scientific testing traditions bring to the questions of safety and efficacy in the case of botanicals. Many conferees disagreed, citing what amounts to the "force of common law": Millions of people over thousands of years have been using botanical substances; that experience should be factored into the FDA's evaluative process, as it is with the German Commission E monographs and with other countries' official positions, especially China and Japan. Such thinking, believes Dr. Temple, is unduly influenced by another myth, namely that "when something's been used for a very long time, it must be okay. That's not true for herbals, I'm sure, and it definitely isn't true for standard medicine." He cited, among dozens of possible examples, a couple of articles recently published in the medical literature, in which general responses based on common sense and conventional therapies were completely overturned by reexamining the facts in the light of rigorous scientific scrutiny. One adverse consequence of essentially exempting dietary supplements from this scientific scrutiny would be to permit the proliferation of possibly dangerous substances, such as in the recent epidemiologic disaster in Belgium, where some 50 women suffered serious damage to their kidneys.

The FDA is beginning to alter its policies, however, to make it easier to get studies under way. The FDA will also consider long-term use of a botanical product in diet as an indication that so-called "feeding studies" may not always be necessary. The agency will also take into account the history of marketing a product outside the country as part of the evidence required for the next step of moving into clinical trials. Similarly, some of the requirements for proving the actual effect of every component of a substance may not be applicable to botanicals, for which it is not uncommon to have dozens of ingredients in a compound. Dr. Temple conceded that analyzing the individual effects of separate components was a standard developed in the context of mixtures containing fewer than half a dozen elements.

However, Dr. Temple still believes that appropriate clinical trials, and the scientific framework that they bring to the complex question of biological effects, are vital to a rational approach to botanicals. His repeated admonition, even when asked about prune juice and bananas, was that "dose matters!" He believes that all sorts of side effects and contraindications could be masked by the weight of "common sense" and generations of "apparently successful" use of a substance. The dietary supplement framework in effect now allows such evidence to be considered. Dr. Temple stated his opposition to any stronger endorsement by the government through the FDA: Such a trend would undermine the value of systematic scientific testing and empirically based health claims.

"The system isn't broken, so why change it?" Botanicals as a special case; the cost of meeting clinical trial requirements

The cost of bringing a drug to market in the American regulatory system has been said to run approximately to $350 million. Even if such funds could be raised, the applicant could not be granted exclusivity with plant-based products. Dr. Temple concedes that current market and economic conditions make "the drug game an expensive one to play," but he calls the $350 million number "absurd." He reports that the drug industry puts out that figure to explain how expensive it is to stay in business and that it includes the average total cost of all research and development for U.S. companies, including all the false starts, all of their synthetics laboratories, and all of the things they do to screen compounds. These costs are then corrected for the "cost" of money (because new drug development begins 10 or 12 years before the compound is actually marketed), and then divided by the number of drugs they get into the marketplace. Thus, he concluded, the "$350 million number" reflects a political rather than an economic reality.

By contrast, he cites the example of Charles Pak, a physician from the University of Texas who, along with a colleague developed "all of the treatments of kidney stone disease that have been marketed to date—four separate new molecular entity compounds. They were all worked up without any drug company support, with some NIH [National Institutes of Health] grants— I don't know the amounts of them but they are not many millions of dollars— and having established they could treat kidney stone disease of various kinds, they found a drug company to make the product. These are two guys, without a lot of backing, with a zealous approach to kidney stones. Dr. Pak's mission in life was to eliminate all kidney stones."

But Dr. Temple did not say exactly how it is that many of these corners could be cut and these savings could be realized. When Varro E. Tyler, Ph.D., Sc.D. (Lilly Distinguished Professor of Pharmacognosy, Department of Medicinal Chemistry and Pharmacognosy, Purdue University, West Lafayette, IN) conceded that, even if the original cost estimates for testing were 2 or even 20 times too high, the cost would still be prohibitive because the primary incentive for protection from competition in the marketplace was missing. Some applications may be protected by orphan drug exclusivity if the products are used to treat a rare condition, and others may earn partial shielding under Waxman-Hatch provisions; however, the dilemma of insufficient economic incentive remains when trying to figure out how to find the funding to test the efficacy and safety of botanical substances.

Millions of people and thousands of practitioners believe in and use botanicals. Shouldn't the FDA adjust to that reality?

As Dr. Davis pointed out in her keynote remarks, conventional Western medicine and therapy is not a cure-all and millions of reasonable people are using botanicals for a variety of reasons, not least of which is a belief that botanicals work. J. Jamison Starbuck, N.D., J.D., a practitioner in Missoula, MT, reminded the conference attendees that she and her collegues all over the country need to be able to continue practicing this type of medicine. What will happen between now and the time when the FDA conditions have been satisfied? Dr. Temple replied that things will go on as before: This commerce and this medicine are even further protected by the new legislation.

However, many people believe that the use of botanicals is already so widespread that for the government to essentially wash its hands of regulatory responsibility fails to address an important need: Safety precautions tailored to the unique setting in which this type of medicine is practiced are needed now. Some people contend that false therapeutic claims are rampant and misunderstandings arising from nonuniform labeling are inevitable. Dr. Farnsworth told a frightening anecdote about observing a woman buying "pregnancy tea" in a health food store in Chicago, where the product labeling did not make clear to the user whether it would aid or end her pregnancy. His own analysis of the label on the product made him wonder whether the fetus might have been damaged unintentionally. Even certified practitioners are stymied by the current patchwork of federal and state laws regulating the practice of herbal and alternative medicine. In many situations, a person is discouraged from reporting adverse side effects. Many retailers and some manufacturers are known to be engaging in ill-advised practices, but would-be reformers voice frustration over what seems to be the government's "all or nothing" position. They perceive the stated position to be something like: "Do it our way, with all of these costs and details (which were designed for and have evolved in the context of the multi-billion-dollar drug industry), or just settle for the existing dietary supplement designation."

POSSIBLE REGULATORY CHANGES

Assuming that the status quo is *not* good enough and that better regulation and control of the industry would actually promote economic growth as well as enhance good medical practice, where can the botanical community go from here? Conferees revisited two possible answers over and again: Work within the present system, or adopt a system like the German system.

Move forward on promising opportunities within the context of the present FDA system

Dr. Temple repeated his belief that the results of scientific scrutiny promote maximum credibility; thus he was reluctant to accept wholesale the German (or some other) system about which he and his colleagues may have reservations regarding scientific rigor and regulation. He does, however, believe that a number of plant-derived substances could have efficacious benefits, especially for diseases and conditions for which conventional therapies and medicines have proven to be inadequate.

Earlier in the week, Simon Y. Mills, M.A., F.N.I., M.H., University of Exeter, Exeter, United Kingdom, previewed his presentation to Panel II. He presented a list of conditions and complaints in the British medical system that are most often treated by herbal remedies. The list ranged from general complaints, such as functional gynecologic disorders and recovery from long-term disability, to specific complaints, such as migraine. Dr. Temple reemphasized the example of Dr. Pak and his treatments for kidney stones, and suggested that a promising strategy would be to target a health problem for which results could be demonstrated more easily: memory or migraine, for example. He advised would-be researchers to think first about the characteristics of the disease/condition and the track record of conventional therapies in dealing with it.

He expressed the strong belief that major financial and drug company interest might follow preliminary positive results in such areas. Some of the therapeutic products from botanicals could have major commercial value: For example, according to Dr. Temple, "it's hard to imagine that a major drug company wouldn't be interested in a nonbenzodiazepine, nonbarbiturate, non–everything-else hypnotic. That would be a big deal, especially if it outperformed antihistamines."

The costs are still high and the economic incentives are low, however, in a system in which exclusivity may not be guaranteed, Dr. Tyler pointed out. The United States should consider the German model, he suggested, as a rational way to move forward that would bring a number of herbs and plant-based products under immediate federal scrutiny.

The German model as a basis for changing the system in the United States

Barbara Steinhoff, Ph.D., from the German Nonprescriptions Drug Manufacturers Association, Bonn, Germany, sat on Panels I, II, and III in order to bring to the discussion some firsthand experience with the German system and the Commission E monographs. But many of the American advocates for change already agreed with Dr. Tyler that the German criterion of "reasonable effectiveness"—based, in part, on the long recorded history of use, as well as on clinical trials—was a well-founded and practical avenue to follow in order to establish a foundation inside the American scientific/regulatory system.

The original objective of Germany's Commission E was to register herbal remedies and phytomedicines without facing the formidable task of running exhaustive clinical trials for each product. The Commission established a list of potential medicines based on volume of use and began to compile quality dossiers around the issues of safety and efficacy. In the process, the Commission developed a set of general criteria to describe medicinal plants, preparations, dose, risks, indications, and so on. A provider wanting to claim a special indication had to perform clinical studies, which were also required when the experts in the Commission judged that the existing data were insufficient.

According to Dr. Tyler, the many scientific concerns expressed by Dr. Temple—quality, dosage, side effects—are all adequately addressed in the German system. The American Botanical Council, Austin, TX, is in the process of translating all of these 400-odd reports on 320 plants into English and plans to publish them sometime within the next few years, according to its executive director, Mark Blumenthal.

Some of the botanists and pharmacognosists at the FDA may have begun looking at this information as well as other published international information. But how they will evaluate and judge the validity of such data remains to be seen. FDA scientists have an admitted bias toward rigor; they also have more experience with Canadian and Western European drug testing than they do with work from, say, Eastern Europe. The regulations say that all published, peer-reviewed data are equal, but the FDA has found that sometimes the procedures behind data collection and publication do not match their claims. Unless the data are extremely redundant and consistent, the FDA would be unlikely to accept the results with no further scrutiny.

A FOUNDATION FOR CHANGE

How can the process be moved to the next step, to encourage the necessary political and scientific work? We have already mentioned several elements that could develop into a plan. The translation of the Commission E monographs would clearly move the consideration and evaluation of data onto another level. And, notwithstanding the practicality of Dr. Temple's suggestions about targeting research strategies to medical conditions that seem to respond in an easily demonstrable way but are not adequately addressed by conventional therapies and drugs, Dr. Tyler has, for years, been urging botanical product producers to recycle some of their profits back through universities and research and development laboratories. But this has not yet happened.

OVERVIEW

Robert S. McCaleb, President and Founder of the Herb Research Foundation, Boulder, CO, is tracking such phenomena and suggests that the reason research has been haphazard is that the United States regulatory system is just too forbidding. Look at the record, he advised: No significant new plant-based drug has made it all the way through the drug approval process at the FDA in 30 years. He believes that the regulatory system could be redesigned to provide manufacturers with real incentives to do outcomes research. Until this happens, and notwithstanding all of the doubts American scientists may have about procedures and results from abroad, the significant work will be done in Germany, Japan, France, and elsewhere.

And as to whether "the system really is broke," Dr. Farnsworth concludes that, in terms of getting valuable (as well as reliable) information to the public, the system undeniably is "broke." It comes down to the question of standards, he insisted. The FDA seems to think that anything short of its present standard is inadequate if the government is to endorse health claims. Many professional scientists and practitioners believe that the European (and particularly the German) approach reflects a more practical, yet scientifically acceptable, way to proceed. As long as the perceived cost of voluntarily entering the regulatory system is so high and the burden is on the producer to meet it, it is not going to happen. As a consequence, the possible dangers and benefits to the American public of these widely used products will remain a matter of confusion and controversy.

An Introduction to the Medicinal Use of Botanicals

VARRO E. TYLER, Ph.D., Sc.D.

DRUG THERAPY IN THE UNITED STATES

Mrs. John Q. (Jane) Public had a terrible cold. As a matter of fact, it was a severe case of influenza. Both her head and her joints ached. She had a fever, her eyes were watery, and her nose felt as if there were a cork in each nostril—that is, when it was not dripping. Her throat was sore and she had a hacking cough.

Emulating thousands of her fellow Americans, Jane dragged herself into the neighborhood pharmacy to seek relief. The attentive young woman behind the prescription counter looked at, and listened to her symptoms; then she recommended ibuprofen for the aches and pains, phenylephrine spray to make breathing easier, and a syrup containing guaifenesin and dextromethorphan for the cough.[1]* None of these preparations would cure the virus causing Jane's misery, but they did make her feel much better. At dinner that evening, she commented to her husband John about the miracles of modern chemistry that made such wonder drugs possible.

Of course, Jane was absolutely correct in praising the synthetic ibuprofen, phenylephrine, guaifenesin, and dextromethorphan that ameliorated her symptoms. But, like most Americans, she also had praises for the wonderful plastic jugs of milk that she purchased at the supermarket and the convenient aluminum cans of beer that made a six-pack easy to carry home. Although she had seen pictures of cows in magazines and had heard the word "brewing" on TV, she knew little about the origin or composition of either milk or beer. And again, like most Americans, she knew absolutely nothing of the natural prototypes that served as models for the synthetic drugs she valued so highly.

If she had, she would have realized that ibuprofen had really been developed by scientists who knew that salicylic acid has the ability to fit certain receptor sites on enzymes in the body, thereby inhibiting the biosynthesis of prostaglandins E and F, thus producing both analgesic and anti-inflammatory effects. Some acidic compounds modeled after salicylic acid, having a benzene ring, a terminal carboxyl group, a flat molecular configuration, and solubility in both water and lipids, are even more effective prostaglandin inhibitors. Ibuprofen is one of these.[2] Its structure and effects were discovered approximately 30 years ago and it was introduced to the American market in 1974.[3] However, its nonsteroidal anti-inflammatory and analgesic actions are essentially those of salicylic acid, which, in the form of its precursor salicin (found in willow bark) has been used therapeutically for centuries.[4] So, ibuprofen really owes its existence to knowledge derived from the physiologic effects of willow bark.

Similar cases can be made for the decongestant phenylephrine and its derivation from ephedrine, the active principle of the ancient Chinese herb ma huang; for the expectorant guaifenesin, a modification of guaiacol originally found in guaiac resin; and, of course, for dextromethorphan, a cough sedative modeled after the narcotic codeine (from the opium poppy). If one examines any of the other drugs widely used today, it becomes apparent that, almost without exception, they are modeled after other similar drugs of plant origin, many of which were, and/or continue to be, used in medicine in the form of various extracts of herbs, a term that is scientifically synonymous with plant drugs.

Although some plants have been used as medicines for centuries, even millennia, most have never

---

Dean and Distinguished Professor Emeritus of Pharmacognosy, School of Pharmacy and Pharmacal Sciences, Purdue University, West Lafayette, IN.

*See Ref 1, tables on pp. 672–710.

been proven to be safe and effective by the very high standards currently required in the United States. At least one drug company reports that those standards require an average investment of $350 million per new chemical entity to finance the requisite scientific and clinical studies.[5] Obviously, such an investment will not be made in the older plant drugs for which patent protection is unlikely. Therefore, herbs are sold in the United States today, not as drugs but as dietary supplements, without any label or packaging information regarding their therapeutic utility. When one considers the abundant misinformation regarding the herbs and phytomedicinals found in the popular advocacy literature, it becomes obvious that the current regulatory system in this country is unsatisfactory.

Drug therapy in Germany

Consider now the case of Frau Johann (Johanna) Q. Staatlich, a resident of Germany where a more enlightened system of herbal regulations prevails. If she had suffered from the same symptoms as her American cousin, upon entering the *Apotheke* she probably would have received recommendations for drugs similar, if not identical, to those received by Mrs. Public. However, it is very likely that, in addition, Johanna would have been given a tincture prepared from the fresh juice of the above-ground portion of the plant *Echinacea purpurea* (L.) Moench. She would also have received a package insert, and probably oral instructions as well, concerning its use as a nonspecific immunostimulant. It is highly probable that use of this product would have shortened the duration of her viral infection and its associated discomfort.[6]

People who are knowledgeable about the history of drugs might well ask: "How is it that the native American herb echinacea, widely known and used by the Indians of the Great Plains and also used in this country as a conventional medicine for some 50 years, can be sold as a drug with complete instructions for use in Germany but is available only as a dietary supplement and is sold without the instructions necessary for proper therapeutic use in the United States?" In my opinion, the answer is relatively simple. It is a matter of both attitude and knowledge on the part of the regulatory agencies in the two countries.

Differences in attitudes toward phytomedicinals

In Germany, plant drugs have a long tradition of use and are highly valued by the public. The regulatory agency, the *Bundesgesundheitsamt*, recognizes this and has made a special effort to evaluate them, not as new chemical entities, but as classic plant drugs that have a long history of use.[7] A special expert committee, the Commission E, has been at work since 1978 and has now studied and published its findings on approximately 300 herbs. Some 200 of these have been found to have a favorable risk–benefit ratio and are currently approved for sale as drugs. Commission E was proactive in its determination of safety and efficacy.[8] Its standards were those of absolute certainty of safety and reasonable proof of efficacy. The judgments it has rendered are basically sound, and the Commission E monographs published in the *Bundesanzeiger* comprise the best information currently available on the therapeutic use of herbs and phytomedicines.[9]

Unlike the *Bundesgesundheitsamt*, the United States Food and Drug Administration (FDA) has done little to meet these special interests of the public it serves. There is no one currently at a policy-making level in the FDA who is knowledgeable about herbal medicine, and the agency has consistently denied requests to form panels of experts. The agency has also continued to insist that classic plant drugs be evaluated for safety and efficacy by exactly the same costly process required for new chemical entities, yet the FDA must know that no company will invest the requisite sum in a drug for which market exclusivity is almost certainly unattainable. In addition, FDA officials at the highest levels have made disparaging remarks about the use of phytomedicinals, apparently based on limited observations of the actions of a few irresponsible persons or organizations that are not representative of rational herbalism.[10]

As a result, only a very few herbs have been approved for sale as drugs in the United States. Most of these herbs are laxatives, such as senna and cascara. Others include such insignificant products as slippery elm bark, a demulcent, and witch hazel extract (Hamamelis Water). The latter produces an astringent effect, not because of its herbal content, but because of the 14 percent alcohol added to the tannin-free aromatic distillate.

Truly significant herbs of real therapeutic utility,

such as the aforementioned echinacea tincture, as well as *Ginkgo biloba* extract, enteric coated, carefully dried garlic powder, chamomile, valerian, feverfew, saw palmetto extract, and the like, remain as unapproved drugs in this country.[11] While they may be sold as dietary supplements, these products are deficient in labeling, opening the way for exaggerated claims in the advocacy literature. Quality control is also often deficient for such unregulated products.[12]

It seems to me that these deficiencies alone make a strong case for implementing sensible herbal regulations in the United States. The right of the public to purchase a quality product with reasonable assurance of efficacy and with full knowledge of the drug's utility should override all other regulatory considerations.

Advantages of phytotherapy

At this point, some people might well ask: "Why is herbal medicine necessary? Are not our present medications sufficient?" There are several answers. We have already found one of them when we discussed the different treatments recommended for both Mrs. Public's and Frau Staatlich's influenza. Clearly, the proper use of phytomedicines can add a dimension currently lacking in the United States in the treatment of certain diseases and syndromes. For example, the use of echinacea to ameliorate symptoms of colds and influenza might reduce the often improper use of antibiotics in such conditions, thus minimizing the possibility of developing resistant strains of microorganisms.

Cost control is another important consideration in medical care, and herbal medicines have a distinct advantage over most synthetic drugs. Studies have shown that benign prostatic hyperplasia is treatable either with finasteride at a cost of about $1.75 per day or with saw palmetto extract at $0.40 per day. Migraine headache prophylaxis with feverfew costs $0.10 to $0.25 per day and with propanalol or methysergide, from $2.00 to about $8.00 per day. Reduction of hypercholesterolemia may be effected with enteric-coated garlic tablets for about $0.15 daily; similar reduction obtained with a bile-acid sequestrant, such as cholestyramine, costs up to $4.00 daily.[13,14] In this age of intense concern with the cost of health care, we literally cannot afford to overlook the savings to be realized from the use of phytomedicinals for treating certain diseases or syndromes.

Although I have only given a few examples here, there are probably at least 150 classic plant drugs that fall into this category. Many of them were formerly listed in the official compendia. Most gradually ceased to be used some 50 years ago, not necessarily because they were ineffective, but because they were replaced by patented single-chemical entities that afforded a greater profit to their manufacturers. Research on these classic remedies would almost certainly pay dividends, both to the organizations undertaking it and to consumers. However, the lack of patentability is a problem, and will remain so, as long as such ancient remedies are held to the same standards of proof of utility required for new chemical entities. Pharmaceutical manufacturers are interested only in the novel, exotic plant drugs, such as those from the Brazilian rain forests, because these manufacturers do see the possibility of obtaining market exclusivity for them. The classic plant drugs, with even greater potential utility, are neglected in the United States.

Proposed solution to the regulatory problem

There is a solution to the problem and it is a cheap and rapid one at that. Simply adopt the present German system. I favor that approach over the creation of a special class of folkloric drugs that can be marketed without any proof of safety or efficacy. The latter system does now exist in England and France, but it is too subject to abuse through hyperbolic claims and it would probably be totally unworkable in the litigious climate now existing in the United States. The German system, requiring reasonable proof of efficacy and absolute proof of safety, is far better and should serve worldwide as the ideal example for the regulation of herbs and phytomedicines.

Just because a single plant part contains several active ingredients that complement one another to produce a desirable therapeutic effect is no reason to prevent that plant from entering the materia medica. Yet this attitude is currently taken by the FDA with respect to plant extracts. The German system considers such an extract as a single drug and allows it to be evaluated as such. This is an important corollary to the philosophy of requiring only reasonable proof of efficacy for classic plant drugs.

Evaluating each of the hundreds of constituents in such a preparation separately—as currently required by the FDA—when an extract can be evaluated and standardized as a whole, is simply not a reasonable regulatory philosophy.

Need for adequate regulation of botanicals

Even a casual observer of the American scene will recognize that things in this country definitely go in cycles. The hirsute countenances that were so popular in the 1890s have returned in the 1990s after being anathematized for nearly a century, except, of course, for artists and other eccentrics. And so it is with the common drugs that provide relief for many self-limiting syndromes. Peppermint and chamomile for indigestion, valerian and hops for insomnia, psyllium seed and senna leaves for constipation, and many, many other remedies have regained their popularity as useful drugs; and a multitude of people are desirous of obtaining quality products and knowing how to use them properly.[15]

The wine growers in the Mosel Valley of Germany have a saying that, roughly translated, goes like this: "Trust is wonderful, but regulation is better." I think this motto is eminently applicable to herbs and phytomedicines. Surely the FDA can find some reasonable way to regulate these products as the drugs they are. (And do not try to tell me that special consideration cannot be given to any particular class of drugs, or I shall shout the words "homeopathic preparations" in your ear!) The Germans have already developed a system that works well. All of the expertise in the entire United States is at the FDA's beck and call. I can only conclude, reluctantly, that if the FDA cannot develop a suitable regulatory system for herbs and phytomedicines, it is simply because it is unwilling to undertake this task. In essence, that would mean it is unwilling to serve the public it was organized to protect. Let us hope the FDA's future actions will prove this not to be the case.

REFERENCES

1. Bryant BG, Lombardi TP. In: Covington TR et al., eds. *Handbook of Nonprescription Drugs*, 10th ed. Washington, DC: American Pharmaceutical Association, 1993, pp. 89–115.
2. Meacham R Jr. *Hazleton Laboratories Pharmaceutical Newsletter*. 3(2):5, 1992.
3. Nicholson JS. Ibuprofen. In: Bindra JS, Lednicer D, eds. *Chronicles of Drug Discovery*, vol. 1. New York: John Wiley & Sons, 1982, pp. 149–172.
4. Krantz JC Jr. *Historical Medical Classics Involving New Drugs*. Baltimore: Williams & Wilkins, 1974, pp. 37–41.
5. Tyler VE. The herbal regulatory dilemma. *Herbs of Choice: The Therapeutic Use of Phytomedicinals*. New York: Pharmaceutical Products Press, 1994, pp. 17–31.
6. Bräunig B, Dorn M, Knick E. Echinacea purpureae radix: zur Stärkung, dur körpereigenen Abwer bei grippalen Infeletures. *Zeitschrift für Phytotherapie*. 13:7–13, 1992.
7. Schilcher H. The significance of phytotherapy in Europe. *Zeitschrift für Phytotherapie*. 14:132–139, 1993.
8. Keller K. Legal requirements for the use of phytopharmaceutical drugs in the Federal Republic of Germany. *J Ethnopharmacol* 32:225–229, 1991.
9. Tyler VE. Phytomedicines in Western Europe. In: Kinghorn, AD, Balandrin, MF, eds. *Human Medicinal Agents from Plants: ACS Symposium Series 534*. Washington, DC: American Chemical Society, 1993, pp. 25–37.
10. Brimelow P, Spencer L. Just call me "Doc." *Forbes 1993* 152(12):108–110.
11. Blumenthal M. FDA declares 258 OTC ingredients ineffective. *HerbalGram* 23:32–35, 49, 1993.
12. Casteñeda-Acosta J, Fischer NH, Vargas D. Transformations of parthenolide. *J Nat. Prod.* 56:90–98, 1993.
13. *1994 Red Book*. Montvale, NJ: Medical Economics Data Production Company, 1994.
14. *Rote Liste:1992, Bundesverband der Pharmazeutischen Industrie e.V.* Aulendorf/Wurttemberg, Germany: Editio Cantor, 1992.
15. Tyler VE. *The Honest Herbal*, 3rd ed. New York: Pharmaceutical Products Press, 1993.

Twenty-Seven Major Botanicals and Their Uses in the United States

MARK BLUMENTHAL

INTRODUCTION

Herb usage among consumers and health professionals is increasing in the United States. However, there are no solid data available that measures the U.S. commercial herb market accurately, either by individual herb sales or aggregate sales for the entire industry. Twenty-seven herbs in popular usage are herein discussed.

It is a well-established fact that consumers in the United States are using herbal products in ever increasing numbers. Although the herb market has been difficult to measure, the current conventional wisdom holds that the total retail sales for herbs in the United States in 1994 will probably be in excess of $1.5 billion. The American Herbal Products Association (AHPA) lists 550 herbs in its *Herbs of Commerce*, an index of preferred common and Latin names.[1]

The following list of herbs represents my selection of some of the most widely used medicinal herbs in the United States. Unfortunately, there currently exists no hard econometric data on the total tonnage of each individual herb sold in the U.S. marketplace, although the AHPA, the leading industry trade association, is currently conducting an industry tonnage survey that will eventually produce statistics on the size of the U.S. herbal market, both as an aggregate and by individual herb.

Several natural food industry trade publications have published surveys of opinions by herbalists and industry leaders as to which herbs are the largest sellers. However, the various opinions given are usually not based on hard data but on personal preference and market observations. Accordingly, some people may include herbs as being widely sold that do not appear on the following list. However, this list is not altogether arbitrary; it represents my 20 years of experience in the herb industry as well as interviews with industry leaders. Criteria for inclusion are based on the projected total tonnage sold and/or the appearance of the most popular herbs self-selected by consumers for health and therapeutic intent in the United States.

1. ALOE—*ALOE VERA* (L.) N.L. BURM. [LILIACEAE]

The widespread use of *Aloe vera* in cosmetic and personal care preparations is evidence of the common public perception of this herb as a plant with beneficial properties. Aloe's acceptance by the public is so complete that many practitioners forget to consider it as a medicinal herb. It is a common ingredient in numerous hand, body, and sun lotions; shaving creams; shampoos; and the like. Unfortunately, some of these commercial cosmetic and personal-care products probably contain more aloe on the labels than they do inside the containers as active ingredients; the products are sold on the marketing power and consumer recognition of the aloe name.

The benefits of aloe derive from two different types of products from differing parts of the leaf. To pharmacists, aloe generally refers to the stimulant laxative-producing anthraquinone compounds found in the leaf material. These aloe anthraquinones are approved as over-the-counter (OTC) drug ingredients in the United States and in many other countries and have been official in the United States Pharmacopeia (USP). However, to the gen-

---

Founder and Executive Director, American Botanical Council, Austin, TX.

eral public, aloe usually refers to the gel of the leaf that, when applied topically, produces almost immediate benefit for minor burns, sunburn, skin irritations, and wound healing. Aloe gel is also processed into various flavored and unflavored drinks that are ingested with the belief that this thin liquid will impart various gastrointestinal (GI) cleansing activities. Scientific research on aloe gel is currently focusing on the complex carbohydrates (mannans, particularly one called Acemannan), which have also shown immunostimulating activity. One Dallas-based pharmaceutical firm is currently engaged in clinical trials on aloe mannans for this purpose.

2. ASTRAGALUS—*ASTRAGALUS MEMBRANACEUS* BUNGE [FABACEAE]

Astragalus has become one of the most popular herbs from Traditional Chinese Medicine, being used for its well-known immunostimulant properties. The herb's primary use by laypersons in American herbalism is for treating colds and flus. Astragalus is also being experimentally used with other tonic herbs from Traditional Chinese Medicine as adjunct therapy for patients undergoing chemotherapy for cancer and AIDS, as the herb presumably helps to offset the adverse effects of chemotherapy by increasing overall immune system response. Research in the 1980s confirmed the immunostimulating activity of a high-molecular-weight polysaccharide from astragalus as having antitumor activity when combined with 10 percent of the normally effective dosage of interleukin-2.[2]

3. CASCARA SAGRADA—*RHAMNUS PURSHIANA* DC. [RHAMNACEAE]

The bark of this tree, which is native to northern California and the Pacific Northwest, has long been used as a stimulant laxative. Its extract and anthraquinone compounds, called cascarosides, are currently approved as OTC drug ingredients in the United States. Cascara bark has long been official in the USP and is employed in many herbal formulas intended for use as laxatives. Cascara is considered to be the most gentle of the anthraquinone laxatives.[3]

4. CAPSICUM—*CAPSICUM* SPP. [SOLANACEAE]

Cayenne, or red pepper, is a spice commonly used in American folk medicine. Unofficial use in the United States includes the combination with other herbs in various formulas for colds and for cardiovascular benefits. Capsicum is also used as an adjuvant herb for its heating properties in formulas; herbalists believe it spreads and activates the actions of other herbs. The oleoresin from cayenne is used for its counterirritant property in numerous OTC liniments for sore muscles and arthritic pain. The active ingredient capsaicin in the oleoresin is approved in the United States in topical preparations for relief of pain from shingles. In Germany, the Commission E has approved the low cayenne capsaicin (paprika) for use as an adjuvant in cardiovascular therapy and as a digestive aid.[4]

5. CHAMOMILLE—*MATRICARIA RECUTITA* L.; *MATRICARIA CHAMOMILLA* L. [ASTERACEAE]

The flowers from this daisy-like plant have been a traditional ingredient in teas and medicines in Europe for millenia. One of the most popular ingredients in herbal teas here, chamomile is well documented for its carminative, anti-inflammatory, and antispasmodic activity.[3] In Germany, chamomile is approved by the Commission E for internal use for similar actions as well as for a mouthwash for minor mouth and gum infections.[3,4] Chamomile has been monographed by the European Scientific Cooperative for Phytotherapy for inclusion in the European Pharmacopoeia, with indications suggested for both external and internal use.[5] Chamomile was the medicinal plant of the year in Germany in 1987.[3]

6. DONG QUAI—*ANGELICA SINENSIS* (OLIV.) DIELS [APIACEAE]

This herb is one of the five most commonly used herbs in Traditional Chinese Medicine. Sometimes referred to inappropriately in the popular literature as "ginseng for women," it has long been associated with its benefits for women's genitourinary complaints. It is used in numerous formulas for its analgesic, antispasmodic, and anti-inflammatory actions through the primary mechanism of regulation of PGE$_2$ levels.[6] Clinical trials in China appear to support its use for the treatment of dysmenorrhea, especially treating uterine and other muscle contraction and pain, although its reputation for use in premenstrual syndrome and menopause are not as well documented. (S. Dharmananda, personal communication, October 12, 1994).[7–10]

7. ECHINACEA (PURPLE CONEFLOWER)— *ECHINACEA PURPUREA* (L.) MOENCH; *E. ANGUSTIFOLIA* DC. [ASTERACEAE]

A native American botanical, this herb is by far one of the most popular medicinal herbs in general usage in the United States today. This was one of the herbs most widely used by American Indians in the Central Plains area for a wide variety of conditions, especially for its anti-inflammatory action. Research in Germany since the late 1930s has documented the antiviral, anti-inflammatory, and immunostimulating activity of various compounds found in all parts of the plant—roots, leaf, flower, and seed. In addition, clinical trials conducted in Germany indicate the herb's benefit in shortening the severity and duration of colds and flu.[10] The leading German product, on which most research is based, is made from the fresh-expressed juice from the leaves of *E. purpurea.* Echinacea is approved by the Commission E for "supportive therapy for colds and chronic infections of the respiratory tract and lower urinary tract." External use for healing sores and wounds is also approved.[4] Some pediatricians in the United States are reportedly beginning to use echinacea with success in treating otitis media in children.[11] An extensive review of echinacea's history, research, and uses is available in a paperback book devoted solely to this subject.[8]

8. FEVERFEW—*TANACETUM PARTHENIUM* (L.) SCHULTZ-BIP. [ASTERACEAE]

This herb has gained popularity in the United States in the past 10 years because of the publication of two clinical studies in British medical journals, documenting its efficacy in treating and preventing migraine headache. Historically used as an antispasmodic and analgesic for menstrual cramps (hence its species name *parthenium* from the Greek *parthenos*, "virgin"), British herbals of the seventeenth century mention its use for headache.[11,12] Feverfew is approved in Canada as a traditional herbal medicine in the OTC drug category for migraine prophylaxis with the condition that products contain a minimum of 0.2 percent parthenolide (the sesquiterpene lactone marker compound) to qualify for such claims.[13]

9. GARLIC—*ALLIUM SATIVUM* L. [LILIACEAE]

The primary reason Americans use garlic medicinally is for its highly touted ability to lower cardiovascular risk factors. In Germany, garlic is one of the largest selling nonprescription drugs because of the approval by the Commission E for its well-established ability to lower low-density protein cholesterol.[4] Such activity has been demonstrated in numerous clinical trials using garlic in both food and dietary supplement forms.[14] Two meta-analyses have been published confirming this activity, one in a leading U.S. medical journal.[15] There is no counterpart for this activity in the U.S. OTC drug monographs—that is, no such monograph exists for hypocholesteremics or agents that reduce other cardiovascular risk factors. According to the U.S. Public Health Service, approximately 690,000 Americans died in 1993 because of cardiovascular disease. Thus, the availability of safe, low-cost, natural products with long histories of food use, that can aid in prevention of primary risk factors associated with heart disease is all the more necessary as is the reasonable and proper labeling for such products. Additionally, epidemiologic research conducted by the National Cancer Institute in China suggests that consumption of garlic and other related members of the *Allium* genus can have a chemoprotective effect, especially in cases of stomach cancer.[16] This study has stimulated additional research on the potential chemopreventive activity of garlic.

10. GINGER—*ZINGIBER OFFICINALE* ROSCOE [ZINGIBERACEAE]

Ginger has enjoyed a surge in popularity in the past decade owing to a highly publicized clinical study in 1982 indicating that the popular root can prevent motion sickness when as little as one grain (approximately two average-sized capsules) of the dried powdered plant is ingested orally.[17] Additional studies also suggest antinauseant properties.[18] The growing popularity of ginger is evidenced by a recently published paperback book reviewing the historical and scientific information on ginger.[19] There is probably reasonably sufficient clinical evidence to qualify ginger for consideration for OTC drug approval for motion sickness.

11. GINKGO—*GINKGO BILOBA* L. [GINKGOACEAE]

A standardized extract of the ginkgo leaf has become the most widely used phytomedicine in Europe, with sales in 1989 exceeding more than $500 million. The cardiovascular activity of ginkgo extract is well documented as a stimulant of peripheral circulation, for anti–platelet activating factor activity and particularly for age-related disorders including senile dementia and short-term memory loss. A meta-analysis of 10 "well conducted controlled trials" on ginkgo extract was published in *The Lancet* in 1992:[20] The efficacy of ginkgo extracts for such conditions as absent-mindedness, difficulty in concentrating, memory difficulties, lack of energy, and other factors was discussed. In another meta-analysis, the same authors reviewed 40 clinical studies on ginkgo concluding, among other things, that the extract was safe.[21] Based on popular press accounts of such well-documented benefits, ginkgo has become increasingly popular in the United States as a dietary supplement. Although many claims for the cardiovascular benefits are well documented, unfortunately some marketers have exaggerated ginkgo's effectiveness when including it as a treatment for Alzheimer's disease. [Subsequent research has provided new data to suggest a possible use for ginkgo in this area.[22]]

12. GINSENG—*PANAX GINSENG* C.A. MEYER; *P. QUINQUEFOLIUS* L. [ARALIACEAE]

Ginseng is the best-selling herb in the United States, being the number-one selling herb in drugstores. Considered the king of tonic herbs in China and Korea, various types of ginseng root have been subjected to pharmacologic and clinical studies in both Asia and Europe. European research has focused on an extract standardized for ginsenoside content, a group of saponins to which most of ginseng's biologic activity is attributed. As is the case with a number of herbs, there are no FDA approved conventional OTC medications that are counterparts to natural products that exhibit an adaptogenic or "tonic" activity.

Because of the traditionally high cost of both the wild and cultivated ginseng roots, substitution and adulteration have often plagued the ginseng industry. A study conducted in 1979 found that 13 of 54 analyzed commercial ginseng products were mislabeled.[23] The American Botanical Council is currently engaged in a comprehensive review of more than 300 commercial ginseng products sold in North America. Products are being tested in two university laboratories for the presence of ginsenosides (for *Panax* species) or eleutheroside E (for products purporting to be *Eleutherococcus senticosus*, so-called "Siberian ginseng"). Test results on a product-specific basis will be published.[24]

13. GOLDENSEAL *HYDRASTIS CANADENSIS* L. [BERBERIDACEAE]

Goldenseal root, a botanical native to the Eastern United States, is used primarily for its action in catarrhal conditions in colds and flu, despite any modern scientific research to confirm its benefits. Formerly, it was widely used by residents of the Appalachian and neighboring areas. Unfortunately, a portion of goldenseal sales in the United States are based on the mistaken notion that ingestion of the herb will mask the presence of illicit drugs or their metabolites in human urine. This notion is drawn from a novel written in 1900 by John Uri Lloyd, of the Lloyd Brothers Pharmacy in Cincinnati, a leading authority on botanical medicine at the time. Because of his stature in pharmacy at the time, several letters were written to pharmacy journals discussing this putative property of goldenseal root. It is these references that have led to the myth of goldenseal's abilities.[25]

14. HAWTHORN—*CRATAEGUS* SPP. [ROSACEAE]

The fruits, flowers, and leaves of these common plants contain various flavonoids. The fruits have been made into jams and jellies for centuries while they have also been utilized in herbal medicine for their cardiotonic and hypotensive properties.[26] Hawthorn dilates the coronary artery, has a mild hypotensive effect, and increases blood flow and contractility of the coronary muscle. The herb is widely used by German physicians to treat arrhythmias and angina and is sometimes used in conjunction with digoxin and digitoxin.[26] Today, standardized extracts of these plant parts are widely used in Europe, especially in Germany, for their well-documented cardiotonic properties.[4] Despite the fact that there are no known adverse reactions to hawthorn, some authorities do not recommend it for self-medication, as cardiac conditions are too serious to be treated without professional assistance.[27] Nevertheless, hawthorn enjoys such a positive reputation among consumers that many use it prophylactically to avoid future cardiac difficulties.

15. HOPS—*HUMULUS LUPULUS* L. [MORACEAE]

In sheer tonnage, hops would have to qualify as a leader among the top 27 medicinal herbs, due to use in the brewing industry originally as a preservative, and now as a flavor ingredient. Hops is widely used for its sedative properties, although it is not as popular as valerian root (see below), with which they are often combined in herbal formulas.

16. LICORICE—*GLYCYRRHIZA* SPP. [FABACEAE]

This herb merits inclusion in this list simply for the tonnage that is imported to the United States; however, the primary use for about 90 percent of imported licorice and its extracts in this country is as a flavor additive in tobacco products. Contrary to public perception, almost all licorice candy sold in the United States is actually flavored with anise oil. Real licorice candy is made in Europe. From a medicinal perspective, licorice is one of the top five most commonly used Chinese herbs. It is widely used for its demulcent action in chest and throat irritation as well as an adrenal-gland stimulant or tonic. The compound glycyrrhizin, about 50 times sweeter than sucrose, is responsible for licorice's sweet taste. However, it is also responsible for the adverse effects associated with overconsumption of licorice, which can produce a condition known as pseudoaldosteronism, a result of excessive secretion of the adrenal cortex hormone aldosterone.[27] Deglycyrrhizinated licorice extract is used for gastric and duodenal ulcers in Europe and is gaining in popularity in the United States.[28]

17. MA HUANG—*EPHEDRA SINICA* STAPF [EPHEDRACEAE]

Ma huang, or ephedra, has become one of the most popular herbs in the marketplace because of its ability to stimulate the central nervous system (CNS) and suppress appetite. Thus, the herb is found in a plethora of energy products for athletic workouts and general activity as well as in weight-loss products. The herb's effects are due to the presence of the ephedra alkaloids, notably ephedrine and pseudoephedrine. These alkaloids and their salts are approved by the FDA as ingredients in OTC decongestant and bronchodilator drugs. The interest in ephedra for weight loss has been linked to the process of thermogenesis, the production of heat by dietary intake and reduction of fat.[29] The sale of this herb in dietary supplements has prompted a recent rash of regulatory activity on state and federal levels as well as an herb industry policy statement recommending appropriate precautions prior to use and restricting use by children under 13, which may be amended soon to children under 18 years of age.

18. MILK THISTLE—*SILYBUM MARIANUM* (L.) GAERTN. [ASTERACEAE]

This herb has surged in popularity in the United States in just the past 5 or 6 years. Previously, it was virtually unknown to the American herb market. Based on approximately 20 years of European clinical research conducted on a standardized extract of the seeds, people have begun to use this product as a liver tonic to help restore and maintain optimum liver function in cases of exposure to industrial pollutants, alcohol, and/or drugs. In Germany, the extract standardized to 70 percent flavonolignans is approved by the Commission E for various liver disorders, including cirrhosis. There are no known adverse side effects associated with short-term or long-term use.[30] Milk thistle provides yet another example of a safe and effective natural product that has no OTC or prescription drug counterpart.

19. PEPPERMINT—*MENTHA* × *PIPERITA* L. [LAMIACEAE]

Peppermint leaf is one of the most widely used of all herbal teas, both for its flavor and for its well-documented digestion-enhancing property, to which after-dinner mints owe their origin. Well known for its carminative action, peppermint in its distilled volatile oil form is one of the primary flavor ingredients used for candies, chewing gums, toothpastes, and mouthwashes. Enteric-coated peppermint oil capsules are used in Europe for the treatment of irritable bowel syndrome; such treatment is just recently being promoted to American health consumers.[31]

20. PSYLLIUM—*PLANTAGO OVATA* FORSSK. [PLANTAGINACEAE]

The market value of psyllium sold as a bulk laxative has been estimated to be $200 million or more annually. Approved as an OTC drug ingredient, the bulk laxative action of psyllium is responsible for its being included in a number of herbal products intended for "internal cleansing" programs. Additional use in appetite suppression products is based on the swelling action of its seed husk mucilage when combined with moisture, thereby increasing a sense of fullness in the gut.

21. SARSAPARILLA—*SMILAX* SPP. [LILIACEAE]

Sarsaparilla has been a common ingredient in soft drinks since the late 1800s. The New World medicinal root has also been used as a diuretic and tonic for centuries and was originally introduced into European medicine as a promising cure for syphilis, for which it is not effective.[32] Much of the increase in popularity of sarsaparilla over the past 10 years is due to its use in various herbal formulas intended for athletes and body builders. Marketers of these products have sometimes claimed that sarsaparilla contains testosterone or that it is a natural replacement for illegal androgenic steroids. The sarsaparilla steroids can in fact serve as precursors for the production of some steroidal drugs.[3] However, contrary to assertions by overzealous marketers, there is no evidence that this herb contains testosterone. So-called "Indian sarsaparilla," *Hemidesmus indicus*, a member of the Asclepiadaceae or milkweed family imported from India, is suspected of being substituted commercially for sarsaparilla, most of which comes from either Honduras, Mexico, Ecuador, or Jamaica.[33]

22. SAW PALMETTO—*SERENOA REPENS* (W. BARTRAM) SMALL [ARECACEAE]

The fruits of this small palm, native to the coastal regions of the Southeastern United States, were used as a foodstuff by the Seminole Indians of Florida. The partially dried, ripe fruits were used for various urogenital ailments before World War II. Saw palmetto was an official drug in the USP from 1906 to 1926 and in the National Formulary (NF) from 1926 to 1950.[33] The fruits yield a liposterolic fraction that is probably responsible for the activity of saw palmetto and have made it the most popular herbal remedy used by men for reducing the symptoms of benign prostatic hyperplasia (BPH). Clinical studies indicate that saw palmetto extracts increase urine flow, increase ease in commencing micturition, reduce the frequency of urination, and reduce the volume of retained urine.[3] Anti-inflammatory and anti-edema activities have been noted in the berries, presumably due to inhibition of the arachidonic acid cascade.[3] Placebo-controlled, double-blind clinical studies carried out on more than 2000 BPH patients in Germany have confirmed the effectiveness of a saw palmetto extract in such conditions.[3] Accordingly, the German Commission E approves saw palmetto preparations for use in BPH.[4] M. Murray cites 11 clinical studies indicating the efficacy of saw palmetto in various parameters associated with BPH.[28]

Articles in the consumer literature are beginning to compare saw palmetto to Proscar® (finasteride), asserting that the herb is not only more safe with no known adverse effects, but costs one third to one fourth as much as the recently approved synthetic pharmaceutical.[28,33] In 1990, the FDA reclassified all products, including saw palmetto, formerly sold OTC for prostate conditions, to prescription drug status. This was based on the premise that prostatic enlargement is neither self-diagnosable nor self-limiting, thereby not meeting two conditions of nonprescription drug use.[34] However, once a patient has received a proper medical examination and diagnosis of BPH, it would seem reasonable, to allow OTC sale of powdered saw palmetto capsules or saw palmetto extracts for the treatment of *symptoms* associated with BPH.

23. SENNA—*CASSIA ACUTIFOLIA* DELILE, ALEXANDRIAN SENNA; *C. ANGUSTIFOLIA* VAHL, TINNEVELLY SENNA = *CASSIA SENNA*) [FABACEAE]

The leaf and fruit of these Middle Eastern and Indian plants have been the source of laxative drugs ever since they were introduced by Islamic medicine centuries ago. Senna and its anthraquinones are approved OTC laxative ingredients. According to Tyler, "while senna is not as mild in its action as cascara, producing more smooth muscle contractions with attendant cramping, it is nevertheless more widely used because it is considerably cheaper. Bulk lots of the herb are only about one half the price of cascara."[3] Senna leaf has become a major ingredient in some popular herbal teas that have been marketed as "weight loss" products. This activity is presumably based chiefly on the laxative action of the senna.

The use of senna as a major ingredient in some herbal teas has lately become controversial; the ABC News show "Prime Time Live" ran a segment in November 1994 about several deaths that have been attributed to the use of a diet tea containing senna leaf as the first ingredient. Unfortunately, the marketer of the tea did not include laxative warnings on its labels. The safety labeling guidelines from AHPA—intended to become a set of industry-promulgated labeling guidelines that provide consumer access to safety information on various commercial herbal products—contains laxative warnings for senna.[35]

24. SIBERIAN GINSENG (ALSO CALLED ELEUTHERO GINSENG)— *ELEUTHEROCOCCUS SENTICOSUS* (RUPR. ET MAXIM.) MAXIM. [ARALIACEAE]

First introduced by the former Soviet Union in the mid-1970s, Eleuthero or Siberian ginseng was promoted as a tonic or "adaptogen," especially after the work of the Russian pharmacologist I.I. Brekhman, who helped to pioneer adaptogenic research. Brekhman's research indicated that use of the extract of Eleuthero helped the body to develop nonspecific resistance to various physical and even psychologic stressors. Promotion in the 1970s claimed that Soviet cosmonauts and Olympic team members used the product daily. The herb quickly caught the public's attention as a less expensive tonic than Asian ginseng (*Panax ginseng*) and became known as a stress tonic without the stimulation associated with ingestion of some types of red Asian ginseng.[36]

The scientific community and herbal industry have long had reason to believe that a significant proportion of the "Siberian ginseng" sold in the U.S. market is adulterated, most likely with Chinese Silk Vine (*Periploca sepium*), a member of the milkweed family (Asclepiadaceae), which, for many years, has been an adulterant for *Eleutherococcus*. In order to address this problem, the American Botanical Council has initiated its Ginseng Evaluation Program to analyze commercial ginseng products in North America. (For more on this project, see "Ginseng," above.)

25. SLIPPERY ELM—*ULMUS RUBRA* MUHL.; *U. FULVA* MICHX. [ULMACEAE]

The inner bark of this North American tree contains a mucilaginous substance that has been used for more than 100 years as a demulcent for throat and GI irritation. Slippery elm is still an approved OTC drug ingredient in lozenges sold for throat irritation.

26. VALERIAN—*VALERIANA OFFICINALIS* L. [VALERIANACEAE]

Valerian, the aromatic root of a European plant, has been listed for centuries in official drug compendia in Europe and was formerly an official entry in the USP and NF. Valerian has become America's favorite unofficial sedative and sleep aid. European research continues to confirm the safety and efficacy of the root as a sedative. It is not known to be habit forming and, unlike barbiturates, does not have synergy with alcohol. Research indicates that the sesquiterpenes valerenic acid and valeranone, plus compounds known as valepotriates in the volatile oil, are most likely responsible for the root's CNS sedative activity; however, only the crude extract containing all fractions, and not individual fractions, yielded such activity.[3,37,38] The German Commission E approves valerian as a calmative and sleep-inducing agent useful in treating cases of unrest and anxiety-produced sleep disturbances.[3,4] Valerian has been monographed by ESCOP (European Scientific Cooperative on Phytotherapy) for possible adoption by the European community.[39,40]

27. WITCH HAZEL—*HAMAMELIS VIRGINIANA* L. [HAMAMELIDACEAE]

If one considers the hundreds of thousands, or possibly millions, of bottles of witch hazel water sold in U.S. pharmacies each year, then it would be proper to include this herb in the list of major herbs. The leaves, twigs, and bark of this North American tree are widely used for their astringent properties. Hamamelis extract and water were formerly official entries in the USP and NF until 1955. Various liquid witch hazel preparations are produced by either stream distillation with alcohol added or, in Europe, by alcohol extraction. The latter preparation supposedly contains appreciable levels of tannins while the former does not. Although some witch hazel preparations are used in Europe to treat varicose veins, in the United States witch hazel is almost always used topically for its astringency, much of which may be due to the presence of alcohol at 14 percent.[41]

REFERENCES

1. Foster S, ed. *Herbs of Commerce.* Austin: American Herbal Products Assn., 1992.
2. McCaleb R. Immune system stimulation from astragalus. *HerbalGram.* 17:24, 1988.
3. Tyler VE. *Herbs of Choice: The Therapeutic Use of Phytomedicinals.* New York: Pharmaceutical Products Press, 1994.
4. Blumenthal M, Busse WR, Goldberg A, et al. The Complete German Commission E Monographs: Therapeutic Guide to Herbal Medicines. Austin, TX: American Botanical Council; Boston, MA: Integrative Medicine Communications; 1998.
5. ESCOP (European Scientific Cooperative on Phytotherapy). Monograph on Matricariae Flos. Meppel, The Netherlands. Reprinted in *HerbalGram* 24:44–45, 1990.
6. Chang HM, But PPH. *Pharmacology and Applications of Chinese Materia Medica,* vol. 2. Hong Kong: World Scientific, 1987.
7. Foster A. *Echinacea: Nature's Immune Enhancer.* Rochester, VT: Healing Arts Press, 1991.
8. Foster S. *Echinacea, The Purple Coneflowers.* Botanical Series No. 301. Austin: American Botanical Council, 1991.
9. Hobbs C. Echinacea: A literature review. *HerbalGram* 30:33–48, 1994.
10. Blumenthal M. Echinacea highlighted as cold and flu remedy. *HerbalGram* 29:8–9, 1993.
11. Foster S. *Feverfew,* Tanacetum parthenium. Botanical Series No. 310. Austin: American Botanical Council, 1991.
12. Hobbs C. Feverfew: *Tanacetum parthenium. HerbalGram* 47:20:26–35, 1989.
13. Awang DVC. Feverfew fever: A headache for the consumer. *HerbalGram* 29:34–36,66, 1993.
14. Foster S. *Garlic,* Allium sativum. Botanical Series No. 311. Austin: American Botanical Council, 1991.
15. Warchafsky S, Kramer R, Sivak S. Effect of garlic on total serum cholesterol: A meta-analysis. *Ann Int Med* 1993;119(7):599–605.
16. You WC, Blot WJ, Chang YS, et al. Allium vegetables and reduced risk of stomach cancer. *J Natl Cancer Inst* 81:162–164, 1989.
17. Mowrey DB, Clayson DE. Motion sickness, ginger and psychophysics. *Lancet* 1(8273):655–657, 1982.
18. Fischer-Rasmussen W, Kjaer SK, Dahl C, Asping, U. Ginger treatment of hyperemesis gravidarum. *Eur J Obstet Gynecol Reprod Biol* 38(1):19, 1991.
19. Schulick P. *Ginger: Common Spice or Wonder Drug?* Brattleboro, VT: Herbal Free Press, 1993.
20. Kleijnen L, Knipshild P. *Ginkgo bilboa. Lancet* 340(8828):1136–1139, 1992.
21. McCaleb R. Latest on ginkgo. *HerbalGram* 29:20–21, 1993.
22. Le Bars PL, Katz MM, Berman N, et al. A placebo-controlled, double-blind, randomized trial of an extract of *Ginkgo biloba* for dementia. *JAMA* 278(16):1327–1332, 1997.
23. Liberti L, Der Marderosian A. Evaluation of ginseng products. *J Pharm Sci* 67:1487–1489, 1978.
24. Blumenthal M, Awang DVC, Fong HH, et al. Analysis of North American commercial ginseng: American Botanical Council's ginseng evaluation program. In: Bailey WG, Whitehead C, Proctor JTA, Kyle JT, eds. *The Challenges of the 21st Century: Proceedings of the International Ginseng Conference—Vancouver 1994.* Burnaby, BC: Simon Fraser University; 1995, pp. 109–111.
25. Foster S. *Goldenseal,* Hydrastis canadensis. Botanical Series No. 309. Austin: American Botanical Council, 1991.
26. Hobbs C. Hawthorn: A literature review. *HerbalGram* 22:19–33, 1990.

24. Blumenthal M, Awang DVC, Fong HH, et al. Analysis of North American commercial ginseng: American Botanical Council's ginseng evaluation program. In: Bailey WG, Whitehead C, Proctor JTA, Kyle JT, eds. *The Challenges of the 21st Century: Proceedings of the International Ginseng Conference—Vancouver 1994.* Burnaby, BC: Simon Fraser University; 1995, pp. 109–111.
25. Foster S. *Goldenseal*, Hydrastis canadensis. Botanical Series No. 309. Austin: American Botanical Council, 1991.
26. Hobbs C. Hawthorn: A literature review. *HerbalGram* 22:19–33, 1990.
27. Tyler VE. *The Honest Herbal*, 3rd ed. New York: Pharmaceutical Products Press, 1993.
28. Murray M. *Natural Alternatives to Over-the-Counter and Prescription Drugs.* New York: William Morrow, 1994.
29. Mowrey D.B. *Fat Management: The Thermogenic Factor.* Lehi, UT: Victory Publications, 1994.
30. Foster S. *Milk Thistle*, Silybum marianum. Botanical Series No. 305. Austin: American Botanical Council, 1991.
31. Foster, S. Peppermint, *Mentha x piperita.* Botanical Series No. 306. Austin: American Botanical Council, 1991.
32. Hobbs C. Sarsaparilla: A Literature Review. *HerbalGram* 17:1,10–15, 1988.
33. Whitaker JM. Shrink enlarged prostate without drugs or surgery. *Health and Wellness Today.* Autumn:6, 1994
34. Blumenthal M. FDA reclassifies OTC prostate products to Rx status. *HerbalGram* 23:35, 1990.
35. McGriffin M, Hobbs C, Upton R, Goldberg A. *American Herbal Product Association's Botanical Safety Index.* Boca Raton, FL: CRC Press, 1997.
36. Foster S. *Siberian Ginseng*, Eleutherococcus senticosus. Botanical Series No. 302. Austin: American Botanical Council, 1991.
37. Foster S. *Valerian*, Valeriana officinalis. Botanical Series No. 312. Austin: American Botanical Council, 1991.
38. Hobbs C. Valerian: A literature review. *HerbalGram* 21:19–34, 1989.
39. ESCOP (European Scientific Cooperative in Phytotherapy). Monograph on Valerianae Radix. Meppel, The Netherlands, 1990.
40. Blumenthal M. European scientific cooperative for phytotherapy symposium: European harmony in phytotherapy. *HerbalGram* 24:41–43, 1991.
41. Tyler VE, Brady LR, Robbers JE. *Pharmacognosy.* 8th ed., Philadelphia: Lea & Febiger, 1981.

Types of Botanical Products Used in the United States

ROBERT S. McCALEB

INTRODUCTION

The American botanical products market is quite diverse, encompassing culinary herbs and spices and crude drugs as starting materials for extraction and for semisynthesis of modern pharmaceuticals; herbs used for conventional foods; "functional foods" with health benefits; dietary supplements; and botanical medicines. Botanical medicines include traditional medicines, the use of which may be based on historical, cultural, or philosophical rationales. Many of these botanicals are sold as approved medicines in other modern nations. In addition, some American dietary supplements are identical in formulation to conventional botanical medicines that are sold elsewhere, especially in Europe. In the United States, regulatory obstacles and years of neglect have driven most botanicals from the pharmacy into the health food market. The range of products and their applications is reviewed in this article.

A wide variety of products make up the botanical marketplace. Definition of the marketplace is difficult, which creates difficulties in characterizing or measuring the size and growth of the industry. The diversity of products has also made government regulation of botanicals contentious and challenging. Some segments of the "botanicals industry" have no connection to or discourse with others. In other cases they are linked, buying from the same sources or selling through the same channels of distribution. The entire field, if one could even speak of so many industries as one field, comprises a range from the least processed—dried plant parts sold as culinary herbs or "crude drugs"—to more sophisticated products—herbal teas, blended traditional medicines, powdered herbs in capsules or tablets, liquid extracts, essential oils, oleoresins, and semipurified or highly purified plant extracts, including pure plant chemicals. The various products are sold as conventional foods, natural foods, dietary supplements, and over-the-counter and prescription medicines and as food, cosmetic, and drug ingredients sold as raw materials for manufacturing. This article will focus on those products that are used for "health benefits." This, too, bears definition, because many such benefits are within the realm of foods while others are therapeutic in nature.

DIMENSIONS OF THE U.S. BOTANICAL MARKET

It is not the primary focus of this paper to deal with statistics on the economic significance of the botanicals market nor to predict dollar value market potential. The following information is presented to provide basic information about the current value and distribution of the botanicals market in the United States.

Spices

Spices are rarely thought of as being medicinal plants, with some notable exceptions. However, the spice industry and the international market in spices as well as the technology for shipping, processing, and packing them, is similar to that used for crude drugs. Spices are imported from many of the same countries as medicinal herbs. According to the American Spice Trade Association (ASTA), U.S. consumption of spices in 1991 was 821,198,000 pounds. ASTA would not venture a guess as to the economic value of those spices at retail prices. How-

President and Founder, Herb Research Foundation, Boulder, CO.

ever, even when spices are sold in bulk form by the pound, American spice retail sales are probably in excess of $10 billion per year.

Orthodox drugs

The source of 25 percent of all prescription drugs dispensed from community pharmacies alone in the United States between the years 1959 and 1980 was active principles prepared from plants. In 1980 consumers paid more than $8 billion for these plant-derived medicines.[1]

Herbs as supplements and as traditional medicines

Regulatory and economic obstacles have driven most botanical crude drugs, and even sophisticated semipurified extracts, from the pharmacy and into the natural foods store in the United States. The American Herbal Products Association (AHPA)—a trade association for manufacturers and distributors—estimated in an industry survey that 1991 sales of herbal products were $1.3 billion. Growth of the industry since then has been at a level of 9 to 15 percent annually. (These figures are estimated totals.) There is no reliable information of the sales of herbs by individual categories, largely because the major companies in the industry are privately held and because of a lack of marketing research at the retail level. However, reportedly, there is growth in every category from flavor-based herbal teas as coffee substitutes to high-technology, standardized antioxidant concentrates. Some of the reasons for this dramatic growth are:

1. A growing fascination with "alternative" medicine
2. A desire for self-care, using natural products to improve health
3. Concern about the toxic side effects of potent chemical medicines
4. Concern for the environment and its dwindling resources
5. A growing respect for knowledge gleaned by centuries of herb use in the past
6. The health care cost crisis in modern medicine

The trend is expected to continue, with rapid increases in publicity about botanicals and increasingly larger and more sophisticated companies entering the market. This is especially apparent in the mass market, as herb sales are among the fastest growing product categories in pharmacies and groceries.

Range of botanical products

Any attempt to assess the research or regulatory needs of a category of products must address the range of products involved, and the purposes for which they are sold. A description of the major product categories in the botanicals market can be found in Table 1.

Categories of herbs in the U.S. market

Categorization of herbal products is more difficult than one might imagine. In fact, the continuing debate about dietary supplements underscores the problem of drawing a line between food, drug, and dietary supplement products based on any consistent criteria: consumer perceptions, label and marketing claims, or the nature of the products involved. Nearly all generalizations break down in attempting to categorize natural products for regulatory purposes.

Classification schemes

Following is an outline of possible classification schemes.

Pharmacologic effects

1. Mild to strong—pharmacological effect and/or toxicity
2. Crude to sophisticated—how different are the more purified versus crude products?
3. Simple to complex—phytochemicals, purified and semipurified extracts, unprocessed herbs, complex formulas
4. Traditional to orthodox
5. Food to drug—convential food, dietary supplement, traditional medicine, OTC drug, R_x drug

Reasons for botanical use

1. Health promotion—structure/function such as digestives, antioxidants, antiaging agents, adaptogens, immune stimulants
2. Lifestyle enhancement—performance, diet, aphrodisiac, stimulant, sedative
3. Disease prevention—cancer, heart disease, liver disease

TYPES OF BOTANICAL PRODUCTS USED IN THE UNITED STATES

TABLE 1. CATEGORIES OF BOTANICAL PRODUCTS

Botanical Category	Description	Examples
Minimally processed herbs		
Bulk herbs, culinary (including spices)	Whole, cut and sifted, or powdered herbs, leaves, roots, bark, flowers, seeds, and fruits	Oregano, cloves, cinnamon, nutmeg, parsley, garlic powder
Bulk herbs, medicinal	Whole, cut and sifted, or powdered herbs, leaves, roots, bark, flowers, seeds, and fruits	Slippery elm bark, senna leaf and pod, psyllium seed
Bulk herbs, general	Whole, cut and sifted, or powdered herbs, leaves, roots, bark, flowers, seeds, and fruits	Alfalfa leaf, goldenseal root, ginseng root, eucalyptus leaf, ma huang herb, gotu kola herb
Herbal teas	Bulk or tea-bagged plant parts, often with natural flavors for beverage use	Hibiscus, chamomile, chicory, peppermint, rose hips, orange peel, lemon grass
Medicinal herbal teas	Herbal teas, as above, with medicinal uses	*Ephedra*-based cold care teas, senna-based laxative teas
Potpourri	Plant parts for decorative or fragrance use	Pine cones, tea roses, eucalyptus leaves, senna pods, bougainvillea
Dietary supplements	Powdered crude herbs in capsules or tablets for health maintenance or functional attributes (e.g., antioxidant)	Goldenseal, dong quai, ginseng, garlic tablets
Extractives		
Dietary supplements	Herb extracts for concentrates in capsules or tablets, valued for "health maintenance" or functional attributes (e.g., antioxidant)	Bilberry, echinacea, standardized ginseng, garlic tablets, saw palmetto
Essential oils	Volatile oils for fragrance or medicinal use	Rose geranium, lavender, orange, tea-tree oils
Oleoresins	Extracted fat-soluble components for flavor or color	Oleoresins of cassia (cinnamon), paprika
Hydroalcoholic extracts	Extracts, concentrated or not, for health or flavor use, internal or external	Arnica extract (external)
Medicinal plants		
Conventional medicines, R_x	Purified plant chemicals for prescription drug use	Vincristine, reserpine, digitoxin, morphine
Conventional medicines, OTC[a]	Medicinal plants in crude form, standardized crude drug products, and purified plant chemicals for OTC[a] drug use	Senna, cascara sagrada, sennasides, ephedrine, atropine, peppermint oil, chlorophyll
Phytomedicines	Semipurified, standardized extracts of plants for health promotion or medicinal use	Milk thistle extract, bilberry extract, standardized ginseng, *Ginkgo biloba* extract
Preventive medicines	Botanicals for prevention of disease	See dietary supplements
Traditional medicines		
Asian	Traditional medicines with historical use in Asia	Traditional Chinese Medicine, Ayurvedic medicine
European	Many botanicals have long histories of use in Europe and are widely used in the United States as traditional herbal medicines	Valerian root, gentian root, chamomile flowers, fennel seed, raspberry leaf, linden flowers

TABLE 1. CATEGORIES OF BOTANICAL PRODUCTS (CONT'D)

Botanical Category	Description	Examples
Traditional medicines (cont'd)		
North American (including Canadian, Mexican)	Traditional medicines with historical use by Native Americans, Canadians, and Mexicans/Hispanics	Echinacea, goldenseal, devil's club, Labrador tea, gordo lobo, yerba santa, yerba buena
Other		
Cosmetic ingredients	Herb extracts used for body and hair care	Chamomile, rosemary, rose, lavender, evening primrose oil, castor oil
Pesticides and repellents	Plant-derived pesticides	Pyrethrum flowers, neem oil, citronella
Industrial products	Plant-derived products for industry	Castor oil, vernonia oil

[a]OTC, over-the-counter.

4. Symptomatic relief—antinausea, decongestant, analgesic
5. Disease treatment or cure—tinnitus, athlete's foot

Types of botanical products

1. Ethnic medicines within and outside ethnic community
   a. Traditional Chinese Medicine
   b. Indian Ayurvedic and Unani medicines
   c. Native American medicines
   d. Mexican traditional medicines
   e. Middle Eastern traditional medicines
   f. European herbalism
   g. American folk medicine
2. Foreign conventional
   a. European phytomedicines
   b. Canadian DIN (Drug Indentification Number) products
3. Domestic conventional
   a. Crude drug OTCs
   b. Sophisticated plant-derived OTCs
   c. Prescription
4. Alternative

Modality of use

1. Self-care—OTC conventional and traditional medicines
2. Practitioner mediated
   a. Licensed versus unlicensed
   b. Conventional versus alternative

THE NEED FOR PROFESSIONAL GUIDANCE OF POLICY

It should be apparent from the disparate products that make up the botanicals marketplace that public policy should be guided by people with expertise in specific fields related to botanicals such as pharmacognosists, ethnobotanists, food technologists, and practitioners of both conventional and traditional medical systems. Scientific research, public and professional education, and public policy all need to address the full range of current and future uses of botanicals. Without adequate financial incentives, companies will not fund adequate research or education; neither have meaningful levels of public funding yet been available for these. A serious effort in this area will become increasingly important to public health, because: (1) the public will continue to seek alternative medicines and natural products for diverse uses; (2) increasing publicity encourages this curiosity; (3) marketing efforts both create and follow public interest; and (4) botanical remedies have documented benefits that are worth exploring.

The newly passed Dietary Supplement Health and Education Act (DSHEA) provides for a review mechanism to evaluate claims for dietary supplements. This, however, only scratches the surface of the botanical market. A review and evaluation process is needed to encompass a much broader range of products than just those that can be characterized and labeled as dietary supplements. Such a process, the Botanical Ingredient Review (BIR), was proposed by the Herb Research Foundation and AHPA to bring professional expertise to the evaluation, categorization, and regulation of natural products.

SUMMARY

Botanical products have a vast range of uses. Even excluding products not expected to provide any physiologic effect, there is a huge range of features, products, and target markets. There is a growing need for research, education, and realistic public policy reform. There are significant regulatory challenges to be addressed and an urgent need to focus on public safety and health both in terms of benefits and of risks. This should guide our research, education, and policy in natural product medicine.

REFERENCE

1. Farnsworth NR, Akerele O, Bingel AS, et al. Medicinal plants in therapy. *Bull WHO* 63(6):965–981, 1985.

Herbal Use by Health Care Providers

J. JAMISON STARBUCK, J.D., N.D.

Herbs have been used as medicines for as long as human life has existed on earth. Prior to their recorded use in the Papyrus Ebers predating 1500 BC, plants and plant drugs were the primary and most widely used therapeutic modality among healers, physicians, midwives, and mothers until the mid-twentieth century. During this century, the development of effective pharmaceuticals, combined with the fact that whole-plant medicines usually cannot be patented, has resulted in a shift in medical emphasis in much of the developed world away from crude plant extracts toward quantifiable, isolated active compounds. Many of these compounds are plant extracts purified to a single, active component; often these compounds are synthetically derived.

Although by 1960 medical doctors in the United States had moved away from the study of pharmacognosy—medical botany and the dispensing of plant drugs—in favor of brand-name pharmaceuticals, herbal and botanical medicines continue to be used. The World Health Organization estimates that 80 percent of people in developing countries (65 percent of the Earth's population) still rely on traditional medicine. Plant medicines continue to be studied and used by traditional healers; Ayurvedic doctors; Traditional Chinese Medicine doctors; naturopathic physicians; Tibetan, Vietnamese, Korean, Japanese, and other Asian doctors; Native American healers; African-American healers; midwives, Unani and other Middle-Eastern doctors; Mexican-American curanderos; certain American religious groups; and the Amish.

By the mid-twentieth century in the United States, conventional medical doctors only were considered to be in the mainstream of medicine. Advances achieved by medical establishments, medical researchers, and pharmaceutical manufacturers overshadowed therapeutic work being done by other healers. Information on the actual numbers of non-M.D. medical practitioners and healers has never been compiled; statistics on their use of botanical medicine, patient loads, and the conditions treated remain unknown. However, what is known is that botanical medicines are already in the doctors' offices. Thousands of health care practitioners utilize plant medicines in their daily treatments of diseases; fully one third of the American population uses "alternative" medicine in managing their health care. Botanicals are among those medicines. What is also known about carefully administered medicinal plants is that they are generally believed to be safe and effective and can complement mainstream medicine in the treatment of disease.

A variety of medical professionals—including primary care physicians, acupuncturists, related allopathic providers, naturopaths, chiropractors, and other practitioners—utilize botanical medicine in their daily work with patients. Training in herbal medicine, scope of botanical knowledge, and range of use of herbs in the treatment of disease is variable among health care providers.

Among licensed primary care physician providers, naturopathic physicians (N.D.s) are best trained in the therapeutic use of Western botanical medicines. Naturopathic medicine has been a distinct medical profession in the United States since 1894. Herbal medicine is a cornerstone of naturopathic treatment. N.D.s are specifically trained in the precise utilization of botanical medicine for the broad spectrum of disease. Plant extracts are used to treat most medical conditions, including such common illnesses as hypertension, gastritis, insomnia, otitis media, arthritis, and asthma. Herbs are used alone or in conjunction with homeopathic remedies, nutritional support, physical modalities,

---

Attorney-at-Law, Naturopathic Physician, Missoula, MT.

and lifestyle counseling. Naturopathic physicians also frequently use botanical medicines as appropriate concurrent treatment to conventional patient management.

Naturopathic physicians are currently the only primary care physician providers in the United States whose medical school training unilaterally includes required and elective courses in herbal medicine. There are three naturopathic medical colleges in the United States. Bastyr University, Bothell, WA, requires 132 academic hours in botanical training for an N.D. degree; National College of Naturopathic Medicine, Portland, OR requires 88 hours; and Southwest College of Naturopathic Medicine, Tempe, AZ requires 134 hours. Mandatory course work includes introductory pharmacognosy, basic botany, plant taxonomy, and botanical medicine, including knowledge of medicinal properties and key active constituents of plants, materia medica, toxicology and contraindications, dosage, compounding, specific indications, and clinical uses. A sample of elective courses include "Botanicals for Management of GI [gastrointestinal] Problems," "Botanicals for Managing Pediatric Problems," "Advanced Topics in Botanical Medicine," "Nutrition and Herbs," and "Natural Products, Preformulated, Encapsulated and Packaged Products." The naturopathic medical curriculum also includes two years of supervised clinical hours during which much of the provided patient treatment includes botanical medicine.

Forty-five percent of the clinical portion of the national licensing examination for naturopathic physicians is comprised of botanical materia medica. Pharmacognosy is also tested on these examinations. State licensing laws specifically allow naturopathic physicians to use and prescribe botanical formulations. Information about herbal medicine predominates in required yearly continuing-education courses.

Licensed acupuncturists comprise another profession for which training usually includes botanical medicine although the training is specifically in Chinese herbology. Of the 25 accredited schools of acupuncutre in America, 15 have required courses in Chinese herbology. Five of those that do not require Chinese herbology offer elective classes in the subject. Hours offered vary from 22 to 364. In 1994, the National Commission for the Certification of Acupuncturists (NCAA) began to offer a certification in Chinese herbology. Candidates must submit verification of experience and pass a national examination to earn the title "Diplomate of Chinese Herbology (NCCA)."

Legislation regarding the licensing of acupuncturists has advanced recently to include specific mention of botanical medicine. Of the 27 states that currently license acupuncturists, nine have licensing legislation that specifically allows acupuncturists to practice Chinese herbology. Other states tolerate acupuncturists' use of Chinese herbs presumably because side effects and complaints have been minimal or nonexistent. Virginia was the only state that specifically prohibited the use of herbal medicine by acupuncturists.

Chinese medicinal herbs are most often imported from Asia and delivered to patients in tea, pill, or tablet form. Practitioners utilize Chinese herbs to treat the full spectrum of disease. Usually herbs alone, or herbs and acupuncture, are the only treatment.

Other licensed health care professionals who utilize botanical medicine include medical doctors, osteopaths, massage therapists, chiropractors, nurses, dentists, midwives, and physical therapists. According to current information, none of the schools that graduate these professionals offer any course work in botanical medicine. In fact, in some of these professional schools, botanical medicine is maligned and students are strongly discouraged from pursuing any information about the medical use of herbs.

In clinical practice, it is estimated that less than 1 percent of practicing medical doctors prescribe herbal medicines. The numbers are similar for other allopathic health care professionals. Those who do utilize botanicals are trained outside their recognized institutions. These individuals learn by apprenticing, often with a naturopath or an herbalist, through independent course work or by spending time in an ethnic community that has a collective understanding of the use of herbal medicine.

These licensed practitioners use herbs in various ways, depending on their training, their environments, and their medical philosophies. Often allopathically-trained professionals use botanical medicines as an adjunct to drug therapy, prescribing herbs along with pharmaceutical prescription drugs. Many allopathic practitioners who utilize botanical medicines are subject to strict scrutiny from their licensing boards; some providers have been sanctioned, have lost their licenses, have been asked to leave the state in which they have practiced, and have been otherwise penalized for using plant medicines.

A third group of health care providers who use botanical medicines is lay herbalists. The number of lay herbalists is estimated to be between 5000 and 10,000. This group includes individuals who act as herbalists within communities that have strong histories of using plant medicines, people with multigenerational family histories of herb use, and individuals with particular interests in herbal medicine. These providers have learned what they know about botanical medicine through apprenticeship, through variable training programs that do not lead to licensure, through family and community education, and through self-teaching.

Many of these individuals consider themselves to be adjunctive therapists; they do not diagnose disease but work in conjunction with licensed providers or with individuals who have working diagnoses from licensed providers. Lay practitioners sometimes offer information about botanical medicines in order to augment medical prescriptions. In other instances, the herbal information is utilized when medical options are ineffective or side effects are intolerable.

Lay practitioners utilize a broad array of botanical plants, from Western, Asian, South American, African, and European traditions. Lay practitioners treat all manner of illnesses, from simple acute conditions to life-threatening illnesses, such as cancer.

Fully trained herbalists, whether they be naturopathic physicians, acupuncturists, lay practitioners, or others, are aware of the subtleties of plant actions. Thorough training in botanical medicine can result in careful, appropriate prescribing and effective treatment. In a manner similar to the way a skilled cardiologist selects the cardiac glycoside best suited for an individual patient, so a meticulous naturopathic physician selects the specific plant medicine best indicated for a patient's particular presentation of asthma, bronchitis, or hypertension, for example. Careful selection includes decisions about formulation, delivery mode, dosing regimen, and duration of treatment.

Health care professionals who utilize botanical medicines cannot afford to indulge in a clinically ineffective ideology; they use botanical medicines because they work. To cite some simple examples: Shiitake mushrooms and echinacea have a documented positive effect on white blood cell numbers and the immune system; deglycyrrhizinated glycyrrhiza (licorice) is more effective than Tagamet in the treatment of gastritis; and Zingiber (ginger) is as effective as Dramamine in the management of motion sickness. Carefully selected, specifically indicated plant medicines, when prescribed for patients by trained practitioners, can be highly effective and safe in the therapeutic management of disease. Crude plant and whole-plant extracts work differently in the body than single constituent pharmaceuticals.

In conclusion, I would submit that there is no need for a question mark at the end of this conference's title. The reemergence of plant medicines has an integral role in U.S. health care. This is a role that is currently separate but certainly equivalent to the role played by pharmaceuticals. Herbal medicines, although underrecoginized and underutilized, offer vital answers to the quest to reduce the pain and suffering engendered by disease and to promote optimal health. The hope offered by botanical medicines is worthy of further attention through significant and substantial research. As we proceed in exploring and regulating herbal medicine, I recommend that we call upon and utilize the clinical work, clinical facilities, and opportunities for viable outcomes already present in doctors' offices and health care facilities across the United States.

Part II

How Can We Know That Botanicals Work?

Overview

Ka Kit Hui, M.D., FACP, Director of the Center for East–West Medicine at the University of California, Los Angeles (UCLA) School of Medicine, chaired the panel discussion on the effectiveness of botanicals. Although the presentations concentrated primarily on efficacy and oversight, the open panel produced a more far-reaching discussion about scientific standards of experimentation and how they might be applied to the real world of botanicals. A central question seemed to recur: "Because people all over the world are using plant-derived products, can't the U.S. government devise a more flexible role for itself in advising consumers?" As Dr. Hui put it, "our patients are desperate, they need useful information as they look for guidance and help. At UCLA, a mecca for health care in the West, many patients who come to us are using herbal medicines, and actually taking their lives into their own hands."

The debate revolved around the question of whether the current "gold standard" for such experiments, the double-blind, randomized clinical trial (RCT) that is controlled, could or should be supplemented with other levels of analysis and other kinds of data to provide a useful guide to the millions of people in the United States alone using botanical medicines.

Looking at the current status of the industry, the panel debated the practicality and merits of the RCT, reflected on how practical and sufficient various kinds of data and experience might be, and agreed that the issues go beyond merely defending or supplanting the gold standard.

As to possible changes, the experience in Europe and Asia suggests that herbal medicines might reasonably be divided into different levels according to use and thus treated differently by regulators. Also, the Food and Drug Administration (FDA) might change its own standards in order to embrace some of the standards developed elsewhere in the world to deal with this problem. Finally, several specific suggestions were given as to how this move might be facilitated.

THE SCIENTIFIC CONTEXT FOR EVALUATING BOTANICALS

A closer look at the randomized controlled trial

Robert Temple, M.D., of the FDA stated that properly controlled, randomized trials are the best way to develop reliable conclusions about efficacy. Furthermore, to encourage the use of other methods than RCTs to reach such conclusions would tend to undermine the small incentive that now exists to undertake RCTs. If manufacturers could make claims of efficacy based on data other than from RCTs, the positive pressure to develop solid scientific data on therapeutic modalities would disappear. Hence, Dr. Temple defended the current standard. On the other hand, given how few trials are being conducted, he agreed that the FDA should perhaps try to remove any impediments or disincentives to do them.

In this context, several observations were made about the practicality of RCTs. The Belgian physician Amory has demonstrated the value of randomized withdrawal studies, which remove the ethical dilemma associated with keeping potentially needy patients on placebo. But here, as with all crossover studies, including the $N = 1$ studies, the danger is in losing the double-blind feature of the trial in both patient and experimenter. Dr. Temple conceded that randomized trials could be more "real world," more naturalistic, than they currently are. He also indicated that it is not true, as critics contend, that they disallow subjective measures.

But are RCTs practical? Robert S. McCaleb, President and Founder, Herb Research Foundation, Boulder, CO, asked the group to consider the time and cost to evaluate the reduction of risk of cardiovascular disease consequent to taking a cholesterol-lowering product. Is a human clinical trial practical for demonstrating prevention in such cases? Dr. Temple believes the answer is "yes." A number of trials have demonstrated the efficacy of heart therapies, including a class of drugs called HMG co-A reductase inhibitors; beta blockers; thrombolytic agents; and aspirin. In Germany, an ongoing 4-year trial that is placebo-controlled is examining the effect of garlic on atherosclerotic plaque development in the carotid artery.

"Vaccine trials of course have been successful, though they can involve massive numbers of people," claimed Dr. Temple. "There have been attempts, even, to show that antioxidant vitamins combat the consequences of smoking; that trial didn't work, but it might have. They can be done, and they're less expensive than you might think, because the number of observations can be comparatively small. With the large simple trial, as many as 50,000 patients can be randomized in a relatively short time to get answers to important questions and detect modest but still valuable benefits. There are ways of approaching these things that a small botanicals manufacturer may see as daunting," Dr. Temple concluded, "but they are possible."

What is crucial, Dr. Temple emphasized, is the level of effect that can be discerned by the RCT. He concedes that epidemiologic trials can show dramatic results such as an eightfold change, but fail to prove anything at more subtle and ambiguous levels. A disagreement flared up over just such an example. Joerg Gruenwald, Ph.D., Medical Scientific Director at Lichtwer Pharma GmbH in Berlin, Germany, reported that a trial of the antidepressant hypericum (St. John's Wort) compared to standard antidepressants produced "good clinical evidence in double-blind, controlled studies." Dr. Temple's first reaction was that, "you can't do comparative trials on antidepressants" because the placebo effect can be as much as 50 percent; Dr. Gruenwald replied that, in this case, the results were closer to 80 percent, and therefore still statistically significant when the placebo effect was factored out.

Nonetheless, Dr. Temple saw no reason that botanicals should get a special exemption; that is, why "the method of testing must differ with the method of healing. Homeopathic remedies can be tested using RCTs and I don't understand why there aren't more of these. That's how to show your method works in a credible way to everyone. Principles of controlled trial have nothing to do with the theory or method of testing."

How this view fits into the real world and the value of other kinds of data

The fact remains that few legitimate RCTs have been conducted—or are even contemplated—for most botanicals. The reasons for this were already addressed in Panel I: Such experiments are sometimes impractical and commercially unrewarding. On the other hand, enlarging the focus of what might be considered as useful data provides an altogether different and more helpful picture.

Proponents of an abbreviated registration system refer to the significance of "historical usage." They invoke common sense to suggest that there are literally thousands of natural experiments making up the anecdotal record and that the very use of botanicals by so many people for so long should be taken into account as scientific evidence. But it is just this sort of vagueness that concerned Dr. Temple and many of the conference attendees. Plants can be deadly—especially so when dose is ignored; almost anything is toxic at some level. Dr. Temple pointed out that in 1962 the FDA, by legislative mandate, began to examine the hundreds of drugs and therapies that had been approved before that time. They often failed to identify any hard evidence of efficacy.

Nonetheless, there is a significant and growing body of "less hard data" on botanicals, as Norman R. Farnsworth, Ph.D., Research Professor of Pharmacognosy, College of Pharmacy, University of Illinois at Chicago, demonstrated in his overview. John H. Ferguson, M.D., Director, Office of Medical Applications of Research, National Institutes of Health (NIH), Bethesda, MD, pointed out that the National Library of Medicine at the NIH has just added more than 20,000 RCT experiments collected by a British team and labeled retroactively into the U.S. database. Moreover, increasingly sophisticated methods of evaluating anecdotal and historical data on botanicals from an epidemiologic perspective are now available. While these methods may not address concerns about claims for clinical efficacy from a scientifically rigorous viewpoint, many people at the conference believed that they were able to evaluate other important parameters such as unacceptable risk or adverse effects. These attendees maintained that failing to make the best use of this unique historical record would be unwise.

But Dr. Temple continued to maintain the importance of rigor. "Anecdotes and experiences are a wonderful way to find out what to do next and I wouldn't dismiss them, but they aren't credible evidence." He urged everyone to read a recent report from the Office of Technology Assessment on the usefulness of databases, which "is quite discouraging. It isn't that they're [databases] always wrong, it's that you can't discriminate between right and wrong because of the details and they have a fairly poor track record for noticing even modest side effects."

What else contributes to the clinical appreciation of botanicals?

Several physicians on the panel demonstrated that the debate is not a strictly academic one regarding standards. While guidance about efficacy from a reliable, authoritative source is invaluable, the practice of medicine will continue as it always has; sensitive medical practitioners will bring everything of any perceived value, however "soft" or suggestive it may be, to the treatment of their patients. It was pointed out that millions of Americans self-treat using botanicals, irrespective of the dangers inherent in this: "Health care is more than a biological outcome," said Ted Kaptchuk, O.M.D., C.A., a Research Associate at Beth Israel Medical Center in Boston, MA. Practitioners and clinicians report that people are looking for ways to be healed, and that botanicals fill an important psychologic niche in that search.

Andrew T. Weil, M.D., Associate Director of the Division of Social Perspectives in Medicine at the University of Arizona College of Medicine, Tucson, is sympathetic to the rigorous standards that regulators and researchers might want to invoke, but as a practitioner he faces practical problems that he described in his presentation. He wants to be able to rely on concentration, purity, and other data to be able to prescribe medicinal botanicals, but as of now he gets no help from "the system." He also champions the value of case reports, which the argument for RCTs tends to disparage. He finds case reports enormously suggestive and valuable for generating testable hypotheses about the still mysterious practice of medicine.

Peter Goldman, M.D., Professor of Health Sciences in the Department of Nutrition, Harvard School of Public Health, Boston, MA, brought a practical background to the discussion, because he teaches medical students how to evaluate data and literature. There is a great deal of analysis and judgment that can be brought to bear at the early phases of an inquiry, before the definitive RCTs are undertaken. Thus, even if the RCT remains as the gold standard, in the real world of medicine, many other types of information are used all the time. It is not a question of either/or, he explained, but rather how to put each kind of data to the best use.

APPROACHING AN ALTERNATIVE SYSTEM FOR EVALUATION

Is there a way to move beyond the debate over the RCTs and perhaps find a system that could realistically be implemented sooner?

Reexamine the use of botanicals and devise categories to reflect practical priorities

Ke Ji Chen, M.D., Professor of Clinical Cardiology and Geriatrics, Xiyuang Hospital of the China Academy of Traditional Chinese Medicine, reported that Chinese herbs have a long history of use and are included in the mainstream of medicine there. In 1985, basic law was established to provide guidance in the evaluation of herbs.

The German experience is similar; four of five doctors prescribe what are classified as phytomedicines: Garlic, *Ginkgo biloba*, hypericum, echinacea, all in widespread use, have been accepted by regulators as being "highly proven," and RCTs have provided only part of the rationale. European Community Directive 65/65 and another 1975 regulation mandated rating of as many of the major herbs as possible for quality, safety, and efficacy. To do this, all sources of bibliographic data were subjected to meta-analyses. For the well-known substances, dossiers have been compiled that are inclusive and substances that showed no reported adverse effects were licensed with a "probable" efficacy. The nature of the claim also was reflected in the required proof: Claims of effectiveness against minor disorders or for prophylactic use were permitted this lesser standard; treatments for major or life-threatening diseases still required the stricter standards, such as full RCTs. Several hundred substances and the products derived from them have thus begun to accumulate a legitimate regulatory history, which will inevitably facilitate future reporting and data collection on these substances.

Consideration of different standards within the FDA system

What might this experience suggest for the United States? The new law provides 2 years for the FDA to examine and report back to Congress approaches to the regulation of botanicals. Thus, an active dialogue with the agency, well begun by the time of this conference, might help to guide the United States in adopting more sophisticated regulations. Dr. Temple's concern about therapeutic claims is not going to be tested during that time, because dietary supplements do not make such claims. However, it was agreed that "the more interaction between the FDA and would-be claimants, the better." A number of possibilities have been considered or begun.

First, Freddie Ann Hoffman, M.D., Deputy Director Medicine Staff, Office of Health Affairs, is the FDA liaison to the NIH's Office of Alternative Medicine (OAM) and is also the person who fields inquiries for the agency. She stated her goal as putting industry in touch with the offices and people in her system who would process companies' applications to enhance dialogue and foster a smoother and more efficient application process. The pre-IND [Investigational New Drug] meeting is one way to accomplish this dialogue. In addition, the FDA has also shown, with some well-known substances, the willingness to reduce some of the chemistry and toxicology requirements in the early stage of testing in order to make it more cost efficient to move further into the testing process. Another way the FDA might facilitate testing is by recognizing the complex nature of most botanicals and the fact that "treatment programs" and combinations of agents are routine features of this kind of medicine. It may be that some of the categories and procedures developed to deal with pharmaceutical drugs will need to be revised to suit the biology of these kinds of medicinals. Finally, the nature and validity of clinical studies remains as a sticking point in the debate, although there is a category in the FDA's regulations called "well-controlled studies," whereby the agency has some discretion to determine greater or lesser validity in historical and published data. The industry might focus its efforts on demonstrating the value of such data, providing experts and evidence about the solid science behind some of the European and Asian work.

But, Dr. Hui remarked, if full RCTs were required for all of the botanicals in widespread use in the United States, this would take centuries to accomplish—and this does not address who would pay for such work. It was agreed that trials should be done, but that "we cannot wait for them to guide us in helping patients in the meantime."

PRACTICAL STEPS

The International Conference on Harmonization

Kiichiro Tsutani, M.D., Clinical Consultant in Acupuncture to the NIH, echoed one of the presenters in advocating adoption of the International Conference on Harmonization (ICH) standards as a way to get the United States caught up with the rest of the countries that are using botanicals. The goal of the ICH was to universalize the way regulators would judge the evidence, and, it is hoped, reduce animal and human tests that might be redundant, thereby saving some lives and making the drug development process more efficient and standardized. This process produces information on quality, safety, and efficacy and also requires standardization of all relevant terminology. Because the FDA has a wealth of biostatisticians and epidemiologists on staff, compared to many other countries' comparable organizations, the ICH and U.S. efforts might well benefit from fruitful collaboration and dialogue.

Dr. Temple is skeptical about such bureaucratic progress, however, because the European community operates under fundamentally different laws and regulations.

Developing a consensus

Should the government, perhaps through the OAM, fund studies that are likely to yield positive results? Dr. Temple admits "a bias for clinical trials," and thinks that "this is a comparatively good way to spend federal funds." If "the track record" of demonstrable results with botanicals could be improved, he believes that considerable funds might be allocated for more research in this area. Thus, a larger momentum may be generated inside the pharmaceuticals industry that could change the entire prospect for botanicals.

Dr. Goldman urged the group to consider what might be the next practical step after the conference to make something like this happen. He suggested that a widely used substance, such as garlic or ginkgo, might become the focus of a consensus conference. Dr. Ferguson then described the structure of the NIH consensus conferences that occur periodically. Dr. Goldman suggested that this exercise be more focused: Bring in experts and have them consider the published data and hypothesize how they would actually proceed to regulate and label that botanical drug, based on available evidence. In addition, consider the types of questions that might have to be answered to develop confidence in the claims that the manufacturers might want to make. He thinks that such an exercise might prove to be of enormous heuristic value and could perhaps provide a new context for negotiating with the FDA about a regulatory approach.

Botanical Efficacy in the Clinical Setting

ANDREW T. WEIL, M.D.

As a practicing physician with a degree in botany, I am in a very small minority. For the past 12 years I have practiced natural and preventive medicine in Tucson, AZ, using botanical remedies as one modality of treatment. I estimate that, for every prescription I write for a pharmaceutical drug, I give out 30 recommendations for botanicals. I get good results with these remedies and have seen no significant adverse reactions to them. Patients who consult me come from all over the country. They tend to be intelligent and well-educated, and many say they have given up on conventional medicine after it failed to help them attain better health. Acceptance of botanical remedies is high in this group.

Here are the advantages I see in practicing this kind of medicine.

1. Patients want it. There is great demand for natural therapies, especially from M.D.s. One of the commonest complaints from patients about conventional doctors is: "All they have to offer is drugs."
2. It is inherently safer. Medicinal plants contain relatively low concentrations of active principles. Botanical remedies are dilute forms of drugs and greater dilution equates with lower toxicity.
3. It is effective in some areas in which pharmaceutical medicine is not. Some botanicals have unique effects in conditions for which conventional medicine has little or nothing to offer. Examples are milk thistle (*Silybum marianum*) used to protect the liver from toxins and schizandra (*Schisandra chinensis*) used as a treatment for chronic hepatitis.
4. It is more cost effective than comparable standard treatment. As an example, compare the cost of lowering cholesterol with the Ayurvedic herb extract guggul (*Commiphora mukul*) to that of using currently available hypocholesterolemic drugs.

In my experience, it is difficult to talk to most physicians and pharmacologists about botanical medicine, more because of prejudice and emotional reaction than because of any lack of scientific data. Many doctors assume that all reported benefits of treatment with medicinal plants are "anecdotal," when, in fact, many good published studies exist. Few medical doctors read or even know of the existence of journals such as *Planta Medica* in which these reports appear. I have requested a number of representative studies to be distributed to this group; they concern the therapeutic efficacy of ginkgo (*Ginkgo biloba*) as an enhancer of blood circulation, of feverfew (*Tanacetum parthenium*) as a prophylactic treatment for migraine, of garlic (*Allium cepa*) for cardiovascular benefit, of stinging nettle (*Urtica dioica*) as a symptomatic treatment for allergic rhinitis, and of cranberry (*Vaccinium macrocarpon*) as a treatment for bacterial cystitis.

A major obstacle to expanded use of botanicals in clinical practice is the Western medical fixation with reductionistic approaches to natural products. It is simply not true that the actions of medicinal plants are reproduced by their isolated dominant constituents. Whenever I have had a chance to compare the therapeutic effect of a whole plant to the therapeutic effect of its isolated active principle, I have found important differences. One example I have written about in great detail is coca leaf (*Erythroxylum coca*) versus isolated cocaine. In Chinese medicine, not only is there great emphasis on synergisms of all constituents of single plants, there is also re-

---

Director, Program for Integrative Medicine, School of Health Sciences, University of Arizona, Tucson, AZ.

luctance to attribute the efficacy of a compound botanical remedy to any one component species.

As a practitioner my first concern is to follow Hippocrates' most famous admonition: *Primum non nocere*—first, do no harm. In my selection of medicinal plants to recommend to patients I make sure not to use harmful species. My next concern is efficacy and the availability of products that preserve the desired therapeutic effect, such as standardized extracts. I also follow Hippocrates' advice to revere the *Vis Medicatrix Naturae*—the healing power of nature. The intent of my botanical prescriptions is to take advantage of the body's own healing mechanisms. Both my patients and I are very satisfied with this kind of medicine and would like to see it become more available.

Evaluating an Ancient Kampo Prescription by Modern Methods

PETER GOLDMAN, M.D.

A major purpose of this conference is to find ways by which to prove that medicines derived from plants can fulfill the Congressional mandate that drugs sold in the United States must be safe and effective for the claimed indications for use. In this context, I have been asked to describe how a clinical trial was initiated in the United States to test the effectiveness of a Kampo drug for the treatment of rheumatoid arthritis (RA).

What are Kampo prescriptions?

Kampo is a system of medicine derived from Traditional Chinese Medicine that was the only form of medicine in Japan until approximately 100 years ago when the Meiji government replaced it with our system of Western medicine. Kampo prescriptions, like those of Traditional Chinese Medicine, are complex mixtures consisting of as many as a dozen crude herbs. Following the Meiji period, the use of Kampo medicines gradually declined and the teaching of this system of medicine almost completely disappeared. Recently, however, Kampo medicines have returned to popularity in Japan, although they are still prescribed almost entirely within the context of a Western-style medical system. Thus, ancient Kampo prescriptions are now produced on a large scale by modern methods in Japan and are dispensed in a spray-dried form that makes these prescriptions more convenient to take than traditional teas. The result is that the majority of Japanese physicians, all of whom are trained in conventional Western medicine, prescribe Kampo medicines in addition to Western drugs.

Arranging a clinical trial for a Kampo prescription

Almost 10 years ago, Tsumura and Company, Japan's largest producer of Kampo medicines, asked my advice about the possibility of gaining FDA approval to market Kampo medicines as prescription drugs in the United States. This certainly was an unconventional idea because at that time, few physicians had any interest in alternative medicine and the public's interest in such therapies had not yet been revealed to the medical profession. I was intrigued, however, by the challenge of trying to evaluate traditional medicinal plants, from which so many valuable modern drugs have been derived. Furthermore, the people at Tsumura recognized that their goal would not be achieved easily and that commercial success, if it occurred, might be many years in the future. I thought it was reasonable, therefore, to accept Tsumura's proposal to offer advice on how to sponsor a clinical trial for a Kampo drug in the United States.

Choosing a Kampo prescription to test

The initial task was to select a specific Kampo drug for the first clinical trial. We agreed that a good drug candidate would be one that promised benefit for diseases not already adequately treated by currently available therapies. Results with such a drug would certainly attract the most interest and, in addition, increase the possibility of ultimate commercial success. It would also be desirable if the drug were used for a disease that was fairly prevalent in order to facilitate the recruitment of patients for a

Professor of Health Sciences, Department of Nutrition, Harvard School of Public Health, Boston, MA.

study of adequate size. Furthermore, the disease being studied should have well-accepted clinical endpoints by which to measure therapeutic success. It would also be desirable if the study could be conducted in an outpatient environment in order to minimize costs.

Among the drug candidates considered was TJ-114, Tsumura's brand of the Kampo drug *sarei-to*, an ancient mixture of 12 herbs used for thousands of years in both China and Japan to treat pain and swelling and now used in Japan for the treatment of RA. Because RA is a fairly common disease for which therapy can be monitored in the outpatient environment by well-accepted clinical endpoints, it seemed to be a good disease to study.

Selecting a clinic

The next step was to find a group of clinical investigators who would be interested in conducting an appropriate trial and, in addition, be capable of carrying it out. Several herbal medical practitioners in the United Sates expressed an interest in participating in such a trial, but unfortunately the number of patients in their practices with RA was so small that it was uncertain whether these practitioners could enroll a sufficient number of patients. At that time it was also difficult to find among herbal practitioners those who were sensitive to all the requirements necessary to conduct a credible clinical trial. We seemed, therefore, to be faced with a paradox: Those practitioners who were most sympathetic to the potential benefits of herbal medicines were unable to conduct a trial that might prove their safety and effectiveness.

It seemed that the alternative would be equally paradoxical. This would be to find investigators who were knowledgeable about clinical trials and experienced in carrying them out, but who had little interest in applying these talents to the evaluation of a crude herbal preparation. We were fortunate, therefore, to gain the interest in this project of Dr. John Ward, a leading authority on RA, who had served for many years as the director of the Cooperative Systematic Studies of Rheumatic Diseases group supported by the NIH. Dr. Ward's background made him ideally qualified to apply contemporary standards of therapeutic trials in RA to the problem of evaluating an ancient drug.

On a visit to Tsumura's manufacturing facilities outside of Tokyo, both Dr. Ward and I, as well as our colleague Dr. Dwight Marble, were impressed with the quality of the methods used in producing TJ-114. We also learned that animal toxicity studies with TJ-114 had been carried out according to the standards of Good Laboratory Practices and that the manufacture of TJ-114 conformed to Good Manufacturing Practices. Furthermore, Tsumura could obtain evidence of human safety both from the Japanese medical literature and from its own records.

Designing an appropriate clinical trial

Dr. Ward proposed a rather novel design for the first U.S. investigation of TJ-114, a phase I-II trial with the purpose of obtaining a preliminary estimate of whether the drug was active or not. His proposal was based on a trial design developed in collaboration with Drs. Harold E. Paulus, Marlene I. Egger, and H. James Williams from a retrospective analysis of data gathered during previous trials conducted by the Cooperative Systematic Studies of Rheumatic Diseases group. This group had developed a standardized set of endpoints of arthritis severity, for example, measurements of morning stiffness, joint swelling, and joint tenderness, as well as overall assessments of disease activity by both patient and physician. These endpoints had been used in previous randomized, placebo-controlled clinical trials to evaluate such well-known disease-modifying antirheumatic drugs (DMARDs) as gold sodium thiomalate, methotrexate, and D-penicillamine. The response in terms of these endpoints was then compared for active drugs and the placebos used in the same studies. On the basis of this retrospective analysis, the cooperative arthritis study group proposed criteria that might be useful in distinguishing between an active disease-modifying antirheumatic drug and a placebo.[1]

Obtaining an IND

Dr. Ward proposed the use of this approach to analyze an open-label study and therefore applied for an investigator's IND, which the FDA granted. The study was then carried out on patients at centers of the Cooperative Systematic Studies of Rheumatic Diseases, which were located at the University of Utah and University of California, Los Angeles, in collaboration with Drs. Borigini, Paulus, Egger, and Williams. The study has now been completed and the results, I believe, will soon be submitted for publication.[*,2]

---

[*]Since this talk was presented, the results have been published. See Ref. 2.

SOME OF THE ISSUES RAISED BY THIS PROJECT

Having recounted some of these events, let us now take a closer look at some of the issues raised by this project to evaluate an ancient herbal remedy by modern methods.

The relationship between ancient and modern medical systems

The goal of this project was to test the feasiblity of using a remedy developed within an ancient system of medical diagnosis and treatment for use in our own system of medical diagnosis and treatment. We assume, therefore, that "pain and swelling" in the Kampo system of diagnosis includes the diagnosis of what we call "RA." Yet, RA is probably not a single disease. What if TJ-114 actually worked very well on only one of these diseases now lumped together as RA? Would it be appropriate to expect this ancient remedy to meet or exceed criteria established by a DMARD, which we may consider to be successful because it is effective for several of these diseases? This is a philosophical issue, however, and is probably less important to this audience than the pragmatic issue of finding drugs that satisfy the current food and drug laws.

Product characterization

The oldest food and drug law specified that a drug must be "pure," which, in a modern context, means that the drug is well enough characterized that it can, with confidence, be prepared reproducibly and, thus, that the results of a clinical trial will be applicable to the drug as it is used in practice. Ironically, the topic of drug purity or characterization is as important for many modern products of biotechnology as it is for ancient crude herbal formulas, but this topic is dealt with in more detail later in the conference. Suffice it to say at this point, however, that the FDA has shown itself willing to accept adequate documentation of the *process* under which a drug is produced when complete chemical characterization is clearly not feasible.

Safety

Before the FDA can grant permission to carry out clinical trials with a new drug, it must have sufficient evidence to provide reasonable assurance that a drug is safe. Although an herbal remedy such as sarei-to is a "new drug" in the context of the regulatory process, it differs from the usual new drugs introduced by the pharmaceutical industry, which are totally new molecules never previously administered to a human subject. Such new molecular entities generally require extensive animal testing, the rationale for such tests being that animal toxicity is a good predictor of human toxicity. An herbal medicine such as sarei-to, however, has been used for thousands of years and has been taken by hundreds of thousands of patients. Such human experience is potentially more valuable for assessing safety than routine animal toxicity studies, if the human experience is subjected to adequate surveillance for adverse drug reactions. Unfortunately, herbal practitioners and manufacturers at times become so convinced that an herbal medicine is safe that they fail to obtain formal evidence to document their opinions.

The results of this project convinced me that clinical studies to learn more about the value of herbal medicines can be set up within the context of the current regulations. This is not to say, however, that such studies can be set in motion easily or inexpensively. Nor does it mean that all herbal medicines offer sufficient promise on the basis of current evidence to justify the cost and effort of carrying out a clinical trial.

REFERENCES

1. Paulus HE, Egger MJ, Ward JR, et al. Analysis of improvement in individual rheumatoid arthritis patients treated with disease-modifying antirheumatic drugs, based on the findings in patients treated with placebo. *Arthritis Rheum* 33:477–484, 1990.
2. Borigini MI, Egger MJ, Williams HJ, et al. TJ-114 (Sarei-to), an herbal medicine in rheumatoid arthritis: A preliminary "Go-No Go" clinical trial. *J Clin Rheumatol* 2:309–316, 1996.

A Methodologic Case Study: Effect of a Proprietary Herbal Medicine on the Relief of Joint Pain in Arthritis. The Preparation of a Double-Blind Study with a Report of a Pilot Survey of Users of a Self-Prescribed Medication for Arthritis

SIMON Y. MILLS, M.A., F.N.I.M.H.

This article considers some of the practical issues involved in conducting rigorous clinical studies of the use of self-prescribed herbal remedies in the context of broader medical care. In my experience, the study that best encapsulates the issues is still under way. This means that there are no efficacy outcomes to report as yet and also, because of confidentiality issues, few details of the remedy can be provided. This presentation is, therefore, based on both the protocol* submitted for review to the local District Research Ethics Committee and on a detailed report of an initial study of potential users of over-the-counter (OTC) remedies for arthritis.

The protocol from which the methodologic details are taken follows the guidelines for Good Clinical Practice for trials on medicinal products adopted by the Committee for Proprietary Medicinal Products of the EC [European Community] on July 11, 1990, and the Declaration of Helsinki by the World Medical Association (June 1964; amended October 1975, October 1983, and September 1989).

The most common prescriptions for arthritis are anti-inflammatory agents. However, there are many products available for sale at pharmacies and retail outlets that patients can choose for themselves. Some of the now OTC drugs were originally prescription drugs that have gone through conventional medical routes of scrutiny. Others, such as the fish oils, arose out of very long popular tradition: Their use has been supported by clinical studies or by the identification of active anti-inflammatory agents within them. Finally, some drugs are available with less rationale.

Apart from those drugs with a history of clinical research from their previous use as prescription drugs, the use of remedies in the public domain raises serious questions about evaluation: How should these remedies be tested? The use of natural remedies in particular is increasing markedly in the United Kingdom, a trend given new impetus by the decision of the leading pharmacy chain there to promote herbal and homeopathic remedies in its OTC displays. A physician could justifiably ask that more information be made available as to whether or how these remedies might work and what impact they might have on the use of prescription drugs.

However, as medical supervision is by definition preempted, research into such treatments will have to rely on the subjects' own recognition of their conditions at least as much as independent clinical observations. Provided that relatively mild or stable cases are chosen for study, no critical medication is otherwise being prescribed, and general practitioners are fully consulted, then ethically satisfactory research into such OTC treatments should be possible.

This study uses both clinical and self-assessment measures to monitor the effects of a licensed herbal medicine sold OTC containing natural salicylates and other anti-inflammatory constituents. The self-assessment instrument used is the revised Arthritis Impact Measurement Scale (AIMS2), evolved from a popular, validated, and sensitive measure of self-

---

Centre for Complementary Health Studies, University of Exeter, Exeter, Devon, UK.
*The protocol has been published as follows: Mills S, Jacoby R, Chacksfield M, Willoughby M. Effect of a proprietary herbal medicine on the relief of chronic arthritic pain: A double-blind study. Br J Rheumatol 1996;35(9), 874–878.

reported arthritic symptoms.[1–11] It is supported by clinical observations, based on the Ritchie Index,[12] a recommended and validated tool in rheumatology,[13,14] at the start and completion of the trial.

From a population of subjects who are suffering joint pain from nonadvanced arthritis, recruited at OTC outlets in and around Exeter, two groups are randomly assigned to either treatment or placebo for a total of three months. Both the subjects and those in direct contact with them are blind to the assignment. There will be no crossover of treatment.

STUDY OBJECTIVES AND PARTICIPANTS

The study sets out to measure the degree of relief for sufferers of joint pain on the basis of three observations: (1) self-administered AIMS2 questionnaires filled out by each subject each month of a 3-month trial; (2) clinical application of the Ritchie Index at the start and completion of the trial; and (3) subject diary reports of concomitant use of analgesics.

The investigator will be responsible for the overall design and supervision of the project, for liaising with subjects' family doctors, for distributing the remedies, and for preparing the final report. The clinical supervisor will be a consultant physician who is responsible for confirming screening procedures, for the supervision of the clinical assessments, and for liaising with family doctors. The study coordinator will be responsible for the day-to-day running of the project and for the handling and supervision of patient treatment and correspondence. The clinical assessor is a metrologist who is responsible for providing a consistent rating using the Ritchie score at the outset and conclusion of the trial. And a senior medical statistician will be responsible for advising on design and random assignment as well as for data analysis.

OVERALL DESIGN AND PLAN OF STUDY

Pilot study

Because there has been very little information on the general health status of arthritis sufferers opting for OTC remedies and almost none for patients choosing natural OTC remedies, a substantial study was undertaken to build up the necessary baseline data while, at the same time, recruiting subjects for the study we are currently conducting. This entailed packaging AIMS2 questionnaires and information sheets in envelopes marked to appeal to arthritis sufferers and placing these envelopes prominently in the largest pharmacy and in two health food shops in central Exeter. Of 330 packages circulated, a total of 96 completed questionnaires were returned, a response rate of 29 percent. The relative rates for individual stores was 24 percent for the health food shop clients and 38 percent for the pharmacy.

Subjects were invited to provide their names and addresses if they wished to be approached for involvement in the eventual clinical trial; 87 (90 percent) did so. After analysis of the returned questionnaires, it was established that overall the client group were elderly (average age 60); female (78 percent); suffering arthritis for a long time (average duration 15 years); suffering pain as the main complaint; and were a self-reliant group with minimal functional disturbance (except in undertaking vigorous exercise, walking, and bending), good mental and emotional health (except a moderate degree of tension and a tendency to isolate from friends and relatives), and good mobility. The majority (84 percent) were taking medication prescribed by their doctors.

In most respects, there was very little difference in scores over the wide range of AIMS2 categories between the client groups at the pharmacy and health food shops. This was unexpected because, in the former case, respondents would have included people visiting the pharmacy to collect prescribed medicines from their doctors, rather than being primarily OTC customers. Furthermore, there is a tendency for the health food shop clients to complain of more pain (mean score: 5.74; SD 2.66 versus mean: 4.71; SD 2.09). One explanation might be a lesser use of stronger and prescribed analgesics and anti-inflammatories than people in the pharmacy sample. However, comparison of the use of all medication in the two samples shows the opposite trend, with the subjects in the health food shops' group taking significantly more medication than the subjects in the pharmacy group. There was also relatively little difference in comorbidity. It may thus be concluded that the health food shop customers were, in fact, both taking more prescribed medicines for their arthritis and had marginally more pain symptoms.

An alternative scenario, that the health food customer is more emotionally vulnerable, perhaps with a lower pain threshold and/or a neurotic reliance on medication, is not borne out by a comparison of scores for mood and tension. There was almost no difference in mood scores and there was a nonsignificant trend toward an increased level of tension in the health food shop clientele. In fact, emotional or psychologic distress scores were low in both groups. One possible suggestion is that the health food shop attracts more clients who have needed and tried conventional medicines for their arthritis and who are thus looking more desperately for alternatives.

There is also little difference in the age of the two groups and in the length of time they had suffered the arthritic symptoms. There is a slight preponderance of females in the health-food shops' group compared with those in the pharmacy sample, although both groups of respondents were already primarily female. This may not reflect the actual clientele base precisely: There is evidence from other questionnaire studies that females respond more often than males.

Finally, it is fascinating to note the extent of OTC preparations, health food supplements, and natural medicines used by each client group. The results show that there were relatively few (approximately 16–18 percent) multiple users in each store, that is, those taking more than four such remedies, again discounting the assumption that health food shop customers might be more attached to such remedies. In terms of product delivery to their clients, the pharmacy had the lead for cod liver oil, vitamins, and homeopathic remedies, but the health food shops had clear leads for garlic, oil of evening primrose, and mineral supplements. Other herbal product use was at a low level in both groups.

Those subjects who volunteer their names and addresses and who appear not to suffer any exclusion criteria are approached. Each application is additionally vetted by postal administration of an entry form, patient information sheet, consent form, a diary, and a second shorter version of the AIMS2 questionnaire; the family doctor is also contacted and asked to comment on suitability for admission into the trial. The condition of those subjects who are initially acceptable is then clinically assessed, using a standardized proforma and Ritchie score to record the levels of disability, joint damage, pain, and wider distress. Responders are finally randomly assigned, after stratification by age, gender, and clinical state, into two matched groups. Neither the study coordinator nor any clinical staff are aware of the details of the assignment or subsequent treatment.

Subjects in each group will receive medication for an initial 2 months, one group receiving the test compound, the second group a placebo. Each subject will also receive a second diary and a third (shorter) AIMS2 questionnaire with instructions to complete this at the end of the first month and return it to the investigator. After the final month's treatment, fourth (shorter) and fifth (full-length) questionnaires will then be sent out. At the end of 3 months, each subject will be requested to report back for a second clinical appraisal using a second version of the initial proforma and Ritchie score. Analysis will be conducted of both the self-assessment questionnaires and the clinical results to compare the changes in both populations.

Full study

Study population. Primary condition: Arthralgia (joint pain).

Inclusion criteria: Ambulant sufferers of either osteoarthritis (OA) or rheumatoid arthritis (RA) scoring pain scores on the entry AIMS2 questionnaire of three or more.

Exclusion criteria: Concurrent prescription of salicylate and other anti-inflammatory medication; joint pain from known pathologies other than stated elsewhere; severe joint damage; constant use of prescribed analgesics; severe cardiovascular disease; use of prescription antithrombotics, insulin, or digoxin; known salicylate sensitivity; mental incapacity; liver, kidney, or neurologic disease; malignant disease; or pregnancy and lactation.

Subject section: Subjects were recruited by display of initial questionnaires in pharmacy and health store outlets in Exeter and Devon, through an article in the local evening newspaper, and via an earlier item in a national women's magazine. Ability to reach the clinic for assessment was a preliminary criterion. Initial screening concentrated on applying inclusion and exclusion criteria from returned questionnaires and is confirmed through contacts with family doctors. Clinical assessment will complete this screening, with the Functional Classification of the American Rheumatism Association being the final arbiter in differentiating types of arthritic pain.

Method of subject assignment: After screening and selection, subjects are stratified into groups on the basis of gender, age, and the nature of the arthritis, before random assignment and codification by the statistician.

Remedies, dosage, adverse events, and duration of treatment. Test remedy: The test product is a mixture of herbs, some of which contain natural salicylates, marketed with a reviewed full product license for sale directly to the public as a "traditional herbal remedy for the symptomatic relief of rheumatic aches and pains. . . ." Because the trial is still in progress, the exact formulation of the tablets will not be mentioned here. However, each ingredient is provided in the protocol with references to pharmacopoeia standards and to literature citations for pharmacological activity.

Toxicology of test remedy: All constituents are on the General Sale List under the terms of the Medicines Act 1968; the product has been reviewed and full product license granted by the UIC Medicines Control Agency. A full literature search yielded no toxicologic reports for any of the plant constituents of the test remedy. Salicylate poisoning is well known but toxic levels are most unlikely to be reached with the test remedy. It is, however, possible that individuals with salicylate sensitivity might be prone to reactions, and this is an exclusion criterion.

Placebo: An identical tablet is produced containing only calcium phosphate.

Supply, packaging, and labeling: Bottles of treatment and placebo, each containing 150 tablets, are obtained from the sponsor. The container is a standard tracer pack bottle with tamper-evident seal and child-resistant top. Each bottle has on its label:

Centre for Complementary Health Studies,
<u>University of Exeter.</u>
For Clinical Trial
(the patient's name)
Two tablets to be taken twice a day after
breakfast and after the evening meal
(one of two code numbers)

Storage accountability and return of remedy: The cartons, fully assembled in stamped envelopes, with questionnaires and self-addressed envelopes included, are received at the University directly from the supplier, in two boxes, marked on the outside with code numbers. They are stored at the Centre in secure premises. The code is sent under separate cover to the statistician, to be held securely throughout the trial. Each subject is allocated to a code group, and he or she is sent two cartons from the appropriate box, each of which will last for four weeks. The investigator retains responsibility for stock control.

Duration of treatment: Both placebo and treatment groups will take medication for a total of 3 months.

Concomitant treatment: Subjects are instructed to maintain their current levels of self-prescribed medication throughout the trial. They are permitted to take as necessary any usual OTC analgesics but are asked not to start new brands. They are asked to record all use of analgesics, other remedies, and supplements in their diaries. Medical practitioners remain free to alter prescribed medication but they are asked to keep the trial in mind in such judgments, particularly in that the prescription of anti-inflammatory drugs would lead to withdrawal from the study. If there are any necessary changes in concomitant treatment, these are noted in the monthly reports and the question of possible withdrawal from the study would be addressed in consultation with the medical supervisor. Family doctors are informed and are given the Centre's number for further information if they wish to pursue inquiries. If any clinical change occurs necessitating the breaking of the code for that patient, the doctor will be referred to the investigator. The clinical supervisor is available to oversee all clinical decisions.

Adverse events and the premature termination of treatment: Subjects keep diaries for the trial and are asked to record any effects, both positive and negative, in their monthly reports. The subjects will additionally be provided with a contact number for more urgent inquiries. Any adverse event that can be clearly linked to the trial and is judged to be significant by the clinical supervisor will lead to that patient's withdrawal from the trial. Any adverse event that appears to be caused by the treatment will be classed as an adverse reaction and, if considered by the clinical supervisor to be severe, may lead to the termination of the whole project.

General ethical considerations (including warnings and precautions): No adverse reactions from taking treatment or placebo are expected and, after a preliminary question on any known salicylate sensitivity, no precautions or warnings are given to subjects beyond the general request to report any event that may arise. Initial screening will be directed to detecting exclusion criteria.

Pretrial procedures. Instructions to subjects: Each subject who volunteers to take part in the study is sent, with a stamped envelope for return, an information sheet; an entry form to complete, including demographic details, a health history, other current medical treatments, and the name of the family doctor; a second, shortened version of the AIMS2 questionnaire and other questions designed to pick out exclusion criteria; and a diary in which to record medication taken, daily symptom changes, and notable events. This first mailing will also ask subjects to indicate which of several appointment slots they could schedule for clinical assessment in Exeter. Subjects are asked to send these to the study coordinator, who will contact family doctors for any relevant clinical details and conduct an initial screen of returned forms. Each subject who complies with the appropriate criteria is sent a second letter with an appointment. Subjects are asked to present so that their symptoms can be clinically assessed before their treatment commences.

Observations and measurements: At the initial clinical screening and measurement, subjects are seen by the clinical assessor, who will confirm the inclusion criteria and note the presence of any exclusion criteria, taking clinical measures of the degree of pain, through oral responses. This process is overseen by the clinical supervisor. Each volunteer is also asked to complete the consent form at the clinic.

Trial procedures. Intervention: Subjects who pass assessment successfully have their charts sent to the study coordinator, who takes over all contact with the subjects for the duration of the trial. Each subject receives 2 months' worth of either treatment or placebo as well as two additional AIMS questionnaires, one to be filled out immediately, the second after 1 month. With the second questionnaire, the subject will also send out a standard request for the third month's tablets and a choice of appointment days for the last clinical assessment. Two self-addressed envelopes will also be included, clearly marked with timing instructions. With the third month's tablets, there will be a final AIMS2 and an appointment card confirming when the subject will be expected for a final assessment.

Compliance: The early involvement of the subjects in returning completed forms and taking the trouble to attend clinical assessment sessions will reduce the high level of drop-out, one of the main problems with distance trials. It is expected that with such elaborate requirements the level of noncompletion from those subjects eventually chosen for the trial should not exceed 30 percent. Subjects are issued more tablets than necessary for each month's treatment and are asked to return all containers for counting on the final clinical assessment day. In perfect compliance, there should be 26–30 tablets remaining in each container. Compliance will be considered acceptable if up to 60 tablets remain.

Handling of records: Questionnaires and all other records are sent directly to the study coordinator and stored securely at the Centre for Complementary Health Studies. Subjects' names will not be divulged to anyone outside the project and will not appear in any report.

Post-trial procedures. Observations and measurements: There will be no formal posttrial measures. Subjects will be advised about where to go for advice and how to obtain long-term treatment with the product under study if it were to prove successful.

Evaluation of efficacy: Efficacy will be assessed through the AIMS2 questionnaire, the Ritchie index, and diary records of the number of other OTC analgesics taken during the study. In the AIMS2 questionnaire, the critical measure will be the Pain scale, with clinical improvement judged as a global reduction in scoring across all four items. Mood, Tension, Dexterity, and Physical Activity scales will also be assessed. A clinically important change in pain score after treatment would be an average change of at least two units. Clinical assessment using the Ritchie score, will be a second measure noting changes in global scoring. Reported changes in parallel analgesic consumption will be compared to baseline levels recorded in diaries during the pretreatment phase. In all three measures, clinically significant ratings of efficacy will be calculated with regard to baseline values and variability as assessed in the pilot study.

Data processing and analysis. Result of sample-size estimation: For the selected group, the initial mean Pain score was 7.12 with a standard deviation of 1.43. Two-sided significance tests will be carried out. Taking a type II error of 0.05 (that is, a power of 0.95) and a more conservative requirement that a treatment effect of 15 units be detected, this gives an overall number of 50 to complete the study. Allowing for 30 percent fall out and a hedge against contingency, this suggests that a total of 75 participants be recruited.

Publication of data: In addition to providing a full report to the sponsor, and regardless of outcome, the results of the trial will be submitted for publication in a refereed medical journal. Interim reports on the profile of the subject population may be prepared both for publication and for the sponsor and those people who cooperate with recruitment.

Investigator's regulatory obligations

Ethics committee. Ethical review is provided by the Exeter Medical Research Ethics Committee.

Informed consent. At the outset of the project, subjects are provided with a full explanation of the trial and its objectives, potential benefits, inconveniences (there being no known risks), and the participant's rights and responsibilities in accordance with the Declaration of Helsinki. Only then will subjects be asked to confirm in writing their willingness to participate, and to allow their records to be used for date verification.

Licensing. The test remedy has a full medicine license under the terms of the Medicines Act 1968 and the EC Directive 65/65/EEC. Because the trial is being carried out according to the order of the product license holder and is in accordance with the licensed claims, no clinical trial certificate or exemption is required under the terms of the Medicines Act 1968 (Guidance Notes on Applications for Clinical Trial Certificates and Clinical Trial Exemptions, HMSO 1984: ISBN 0-11-21004-3. Ref. The Medicines [Exemptions for Licenses] [Clinical Trials] Order 1981 [SI 1981 No 164]).

Insurance. Insurance coverage for the trial is provided jointly by the University of Exeter and the supplier's product liability coverage. The sponsor has provided a written statement that he accepts the current *Guidelines of the Association of the British Pharmaceutical Industry* as far as they apply to a phase IV trial.

Confidentiality. The Centre for Complementary Health Studies is registered through the University of Exeter under the terms of the Data Protection Act.

REFERENCES

1. Meenan RF, Mason JH, Anderson JJ, et al. AIMS2: The content and properties of a revised and expanded Arthritis Impact Measurement Scales Health Status Questionnaire. *Arthritis Rheum* 35(1):1–10, 1992.
2. Hill J, Bird HA, Lawton CW, et al. The Athens impact measurement scales: An anglicized version to assess the outcome of British patients with rheumatoid arthritis. *Br J Rheumatol* 29(3):193–196, 1990.
3. Bell MJ, Bombardier C, Tugwell P. Measurement of functional status, quality of life, and utility in rheumatoid arthritis. *Arthritis Rheum* 33(4):591–601, 1990.
4. Mason JH, Anderson JJ, Meenan RF. Applicability of a health status model to osteoarthritis. *Arthritis Care Res* 2(3):8993, 1989.
5. Selman SW. Impact of total hip replacement of quality of life. *Orthop Nurs* 8(5):434, 1989.
6. Wallston KA, Brown GK, Stein MJ, et al. Comparing the short and long versions of the Arthritis Impact Measurement Scales. *J Rheumatol* 16(8):1105–1109, 1984.
7. Papageorgiou AC, Badley EM. The quality of pain in arthritis: The words patients use to describe overall pain and pain in individual joints at rest and on movement. *J Rheumatol* 16(1):106 IZ, 1989.
8. Thompson PW. Functional outcome in rheumatoid arthritis. *Br J Rheumatol* 27(Suppl 1):37–43, 1988.
9. Spitz PW, Fries JF. The present and future of comprehensive outcome measures for rheumatic diseases. *Clin Rheumatol* 6(Suppl 2):10911, 1987.
10. Potts MK, Brandt KD. Evidence of the validity of the Arthritis Impact Measurement Scales. *Arthritis Rheum* 30(1):934, 1987.
11. Meenan RF. The AIMS approach to health status measurement: Conceptual background and measurement properties. *Rheumatology* 9(5):785–788, 1982.
12. Ritchie DM, Boyle JA, Mcinnes JM, et al. Clinical studies with an articular index for the assessment of joint tenderness in patients with rheumatoid arthritis. *Q J Med NS* 37:393–406, 1968.
13. Lequesne M. European guidelines for clinical trials of new antiarthritic drugs. *EULAR Bull* (Suppl) 9:171–175, 1980.
14. Prevoo ML, Kuper IH, van't Hof, MA, et al. Validity and reliability of joint indices: A longitudinal study in patients with recent onset rheumatoid arthritis. *Br J Rheumatol* 32(7):S89–S94, 1993.

Databases Containing Information Pertaining to Botanical Medicine

NORMAN R. FARNSWORTH, Ph.D.

Several types of information are pertinent to the decision-making process for assessment of the safety and/or efficacy of any herbal product identified for potential human use. These are:

1. Ethnomedical use (ancient and/or recent)
2. Pharmacologic/biochemical assessment of the herb and extracts of the herb
3. Clinical studies (number and quality)
4. Secondary chemical constituents in the herbal product, distribution in the plant, and levels present
5. Pharmacologic/biochemical assessment of the secondary constituent
6. Quality control data necessary for reproducing results and for determining any extraneous contaminants
7. The degree to which cross cultural understanding of the disease process for which the herbal product is intended is important in determining safety and efficacy.

All of these kinds of information are available from on-line computer sources, with the exception of items 6 and 7. Ideally, any herbal product considered for human use should meet the following criteria: a history of ethnomedical use for the claims being made; correlation of these with the pharmacologic/biochemical test results from experimental animal or in vitro studies, and further correlation with results from clinical studies. If secondary metabolites have been identified in the plants pharmacologic/biochemical profiles that also correlate with the final medical application of the herbal product, this would represent powerful evidence for approval of the product. However, in some cases, while not all of the mentioned earlier data are available, few people would doubt the appropriateness of approving the herbal product—for example, prune juice for constipation. In this case, that prune juice is an effective laxative if taken properly, overwhelming long-term ethnomedical claims are available and well known, especially by the lay public. Limited experimental data on animals exist indicating that prune juice has laxative effects, yet, to the best of my knowledge, the active principle has not yet been discovered and clinical trials have not been carried out. The long-term use of prune juice for this effect in the United States, coupled with an absence of untold side effects (with the exception of diarrhea in humans if excessive amounts are ingested), would seem to obviate the necessity of identifying the active principle(s), running clinical trials, and performing pharmacokinetic and long-term feeding studies in laboratory animals. However, the purpose of my presentation is not to suggest criteria for approval of herbal products as medicines. Rather, this conference hopefully will sort out the many problems associated with a scientific and common-sense methodology for the development of regulatory procedures and recommendations.

ON-LINE DATABASES

To the best of my knowledge the following on-line databases can provide information of the biologic and/or chemical properties of plants (includ-

---

Research Professor of Pharmacognosy and Senior University Scholar, College of Pharmacy, University of Illinois at Chicago, Chicago, IL.

ing those used as medicines). Most of these databases do not cover literature prior to 1970. Therefore, reliance only on database searching to gain a full picture of the biologic and chemical properties of herbal remedies is not advised.

Medline

Medline is a service of the National Library of Medicine; it provides information pertinent to the life sciences and medicine, in the form of abstracts and literature citations. Medline seems to be the most complete and useful source of information on clinical studies of herbal products. Medline extracts data from more than 3000 journals worldwide.[1]

CA Search

CA Search, a product of Chemical Abstracts Services, is one of the largest and most widely distributed bibliographic databases in the world, covering most life and physical sciences from 1965 to the present. Data prior to 1965 are also retrievable, but coverage is not systematic. Literature coverage includes input from more than 14,000 journal titles and results in a computerized file made up of 72 percent journal articles; 16 percent patent information; 10 percent monographs, published proceedings of meetings, or theses; and 2 percent government documents. Subject retrieval is carried out using uncontrolled keywords, which may appear in the article title or in its abstract, subject headings, and/or word strings.[1] Very few reports involving clinical studies of herbal remedies are found in this database; rather, animal and in vitro experimental biologic test results on plant extracts and their secondary metabolites are included.

NAPRALERT

NAPRALERT is an acronym for Natural Products Alert. It is available on-line through the Scientific and Technical Network (STN) of Chemical Abstracts Services, but was developed by, and is currently maintained in, the Program for Collaborative Research in the Pharmaceutical Sciences, College of Pharmacy, University of Illinois at Chicago. Additionally, one can access the database directly through our program in Chicago over Bitnet, Internet, Compuserve, and other similar computer systems. NAPRALERT differs from the above on-line systems in that it is a third-form normal relational database that specializes only in natural products, primarily plants. It covers the global literature on the ethnomedical uses, experimental pharmacology, and biochemistry of extracts of living organisms; the occurrence of secondary metabolites in the organisms; and the pharmacology/biochemistry of these secondary metabolites, including human studies. Both positive and negative biologic test results are entered into the NAPRALERT system. Currently, there are data in NAPRALERT on more than 47,000 species of organisms, including more than 27,000 species of higher plants, derived from more than 120,000 scientific articles. About 70 percent of the data have been derived from a systematic search of the global literature since 1975; the remaining 30 percent are from retrospective searches of the literature on more than 500 genera of higher plants from 1900 to the present.[1,2]

Other on-line databases

Several other on-line databases are available that cover experimental data on plant extracts and secondary metabolites from them, but do not usually include clinical studies. These are TOXLINE, CANCERLINE, EMBASE, FSTA (Food Sciences and Technology Abstracts), AGRICOLA (formerly CAIN and produced by the U.S. Department of Agriculture), and BIOSIS, among others.[1] It should be emphasized that all of these on-line computer services present limited data and that original articles cited from these services must be acquired and analyzed for scientific value.

Examples of database searches

In order to give an indication of the value of database searching in the area of clinical studies of medicinal plants, Melchart and coworkers[3] searched the literature from 1966 to mid-1994 in an attempt to evaluate all published controlled clinical trials for immunomodulatory efficacy of Echinacea preparations. Medline, EMBASE, and PHYTODOK (a private database on clinical studies of phytomedicines located in Munich, Germany) were searched with the search terms "ECHINAC*," "Double-blind method," "Human," "Random Allocation," and others. By this means, a total of 26 controlled clinical trials on Echinacea preparations was located, including 34 test treatment groups. Of these, only 22 were deemed to be valuable. Statistical evaluations of several criteria in each study were carried out. It was concluded that the clinical efficacy of Echinacea preparations as immunomodulators was real but deficiencies in clinical protocols raised questions as to dosage and dosing regimens to be used. In other words, it is possible to retrieve substantial information from on-line and off-line databases that can be subjected to rigorous scientific evaluation.

A search of Medline from 1991 through 1994, using as search parameters "GINKGO" and "Clinical," produced 10 citations of clinical studies of extracts of *Ginkgo biloba*, two "Letters to the Editor," and five reviews of *Ginkgo biloba*.

The vast majority of recent clinical studies on herbal medicines are being carried out in Germany, France, Japan, and the People's Republic of China. In the latter two countries, most of these studies involve complex plant mixtures with a variety of names that are often duplicative. Thus, it is more difficult, but not impossible, to retrieve data from studies carried out with plant mixtures by means of on-line computer systems.

In summary, there are a variety of on-line databases that contain valuable information related to herbal medicine. Obtaining references to these studies by means of on-line access is thus a reality. However, many of the articles are not in the English language and many are difficult to acquire. Thus, an absolutely complete literature search on any herbal medicine is probably an unattainable goal at the present time.

REFERENCES

1. Farnsworth NR, Loub WC. Information gathering and data bases that are pertinent to the development of plant-derived drugs. *Workshop Proc Office Technol Assess* 178–195, 1982.
2. Loub WC, Farnsworth, NR, Soejarto DD, et al. NAPRALERT: Computer handling of natural product research data. *J Chem Inf Computer Sci* 25:99–103, 1985.
3. Melchart D, Linde K, Worku F, et al. Immunomodulation with Echinacea—A systematic review of controlled clinical trials. *Phytomedicine* 1(3):245–254, 1994.

Evaluation of Herbal Efficacy: Alternatives to the Randomized Controlled Trial

RICHARD L. KRAVITZ, M.D., M.S.P.H.

Despite tremendous progress during the last half-century, treatment of many chronic diseases using conventional medical therapy remains unsatisfactory. Corroborating this assessment, a recent report concluded that 34 percent of Americans regularly turn to unconventional therapies for common and uncommon medical ailments.[1] More specifically, a large proportion of these Americans reported that they had used herbs or botanicals. Given these trends, it is critical that rigorous studies be conducted to determine whether these agents are both safe and effective.

The controlled experiment or randomized clinical trial (RCT) has a long tradition and is widely accepted as the most rigorous approach to determining whether one thing (such as a drug or botanical) causes something else (such as an improvement or deterioration in health status). In this article, I will discuss briefly the advantages and disadvantages of RCTs in evaluating herbal efficacy. I will then evaluate some alternative approaches to the RCT in terms of validity, generalizability, and feasibility.

EXPERIMENTAL APPROACHES

The key features of the experimental approach to assessing herbal efficacy are randomization, blindedness, and measurement of predetermined outcomes. Of these, randomization is the most fundamental. The purpose of randomization is to maximize the likelihood that the groups being compared will differ only as to the treatment they receive. If two groups are comparable, differences in outcome can be ascribed to differences in treatment. With a large enough sample size, randomization produces treatment groups with approximately the same distribution of extraneous factors, including unmeasured risk factors for the outcomes in question. Unfortunately, "large enough" may be large indeed and it is still necessary to examine the data for differences between treatment groups in the analysis. For example, in a recent RCT of the use of feverfew for migraine,[2] patients assigned to the feverfew group had more headaches at baseline than patients assigned to placebo (mean 7.44 per month versus 3.94, respectively). This difference had to be accounted for in the data analysis.

The purpose of blindedness is to minimize bias by both patient and investigator. Patients who know which treatment they are receiving may develop and report benefits or side effects based on preconceived expectations. Unblinded investigators may unconsciously alter their interpretations of patients' symptoms or change their treatment strategies. Either response may distort the study results.

The measurement of predetermined outcomes is a property not just of RCTs but of good observational studies as well. Outcome assessment should be complete, appropriate, and accurate. Completeness refers to the measurement of all outcomes that are clinically relevant and important. For example, in the feverfew study, the investigators measured frequency of headache and severity of nausea and vomiting but not severity of headache or functional limitations imposed by the headaches. Analysis of these outcomes, which seem clinically relevant, might have either strengthened or weakened the researchers' conclusions that feverfew is effective therapy for migraine prophylaxis.

Associate Professor of Medicine, University of California, Davis, Sacramento, CA.

Appropriateness refers to measuring outcomes that are relevant to the questions being asked. For example, the evaluation of garlic as a cholesterol-reducing agent rests not only on its ability to lower serum low-density lipoprotein (LDL) levels, but ultimately to reduce cardiovascular and total mortality. Similarly, the real question in a study of acupuncture in HIV infection is not whether acupuncture raises CD4 counts but whether it prolongs survival or improves quality of life.

The accuracy of outcomes measurements is typically assessed in terms of reliability and validity. Reliability is the ability of a measure to obtain the same result over and over again (provided that the underlying condition of the patient does not change). Validity is the ability of a measure to gauge that which it purports to measure. It can be shown that reliability places an upper bound on validity; in other words, a measure can be no more valid than it is reliable.

The advantages of RCTs follow from their properties. Randomization minimizes the likelihood of both selection bias and confounding. Both of these forms of bias occur when individuals who choose or are assigned to different treatments differ on prognostic factors other than the treatment. For example, in a nonrandomized comparison of mortality among people who do and do not use herbs, herb users may be more likely to have lower mortality for other reasons, such as better baseline health or a genetic predisposition to a long lifespan. Blindedness minimizes information, or measurement, bias. In its most extreme form, this sort of bias leads to the misclassification of study subjects in terms of exposure, outcome, or both. For example, subjects who are true believers and know they are getting the active botanical may report fewer symptoms; and investigators may be more apt to pursue the diagnosis of adverse reactions among patients they believe are on the more toxic agent.

Despite their advantages for evaluating the efficacy of treatments, including botanicals, RCTs present some difficulties. The first issue is feasibility. Compared to some of the alternatives, RCTs are time-consuming and expensive to conduct. Getting patients and physicians to participate may be difficult because of firmly held beliefs that one form of treatment is preferable to another, even in the absence of scientific evidence supporting these views. Finally, RCTs, especially those with placebo arms, occasionally raise thorny ethical issues such as whether the relative worth of competing therapies is really a "toss-up," when to perform interim analyses, and when to stop a trial should one treatment appear to be much better than another.[3]

Aside from issues of feasibility, RCTs have some important scientific drawbacks, all of which relate to the generalizability of the results they produce. First, to enhance internal validity and to keep sample sizes reasonable, RCTs are often limited to a fairly narrow spectrum of patients. Women of childbearing age, persons with multiple medical conditions, patients with very mild or very severe disease, and the elderly are often excluded from RCTs. As a result, the conclusions derived from RCTs may not be applicable to large numbers of patients who suffer from the condition in actual practice. Second, RCTs are often conducted by experienced clinical investigators in academic centers. Especially when a technical procedure is involved, success rates may be lower in the real world. Even with drugs and botanicals, results may be better when the agent is administered by skilled practitioners with careful monitoring. Differences between efficacy (usefulness in the context of a clinical trial) and effectiveness (value in the real world) may be especially pronounced with over-the-counter drugs and botanicals, in situations when patients, not physicians, control the dose and frequency of administration. Finally, owing largely to resource limitations and resulting sample-size constraints, RCTs can only evaluate a few different doses and formulations at a time. Strictly speaking, the results are applicable only to the doses and formulations actually used in the trial. This may represent a major problem with trials involving botanicals, in which the active agent is sometimes not even known.

An important related issue is that practitioners who use botanicals claim that frequent regimen and dosage adjustments are often required, depending on the clinical response of the patient. These adjustments can be handled within the context of RCTs, but only if the entire treatment protocol or program is considered as the intervention. Such designs are infrequently applied to drug evaluation but are commonplace in health services research. One fairly recent example is a randomized trial of a clinical decision rule for triaging patients with chest pain.[4] Patients treated in conformity with the moderately complex algorithm being tested had equivalent outcomes at less cost than patients managed in standard fashion. This approach may require a philosophical and possibly legal sea change in the way drug therapies (including botanicals) are evaluated. The experimental question is no longer, "does Botanical A at dose B cause effect C?" but rather "does a treatment protocol in which patients are started on Botanical A at dose B but then switched to other specified doses or agents, depending on response, result in better outcomes than conventional therapy?"

ALTERNATIVE APPROACHES

In light of these limitations of the RCT, what are our alternatives? Essentially there are five: quasi-experiments, regression-discontinuity designs, cohort studies, case-control studies, and "N = 1" trials. In the remainder of this review, I describe and evaluate these approaches as they might be used to evaluate herbs.

Quasi-experiments

In quasi-experiments, patients are assigned to a treatment condition not as individuals but as members of a group. For example, a health maintenance organization may decide that all patients with uncomplicated, acute low-back pain at one facility will be referred to physical therapy, whereas those patients at another geographically distant facility will have the option of receiving an herbal poltice. Although quasi-experiments forego randomization and are almost always unblinded, they largely eliminate the selection bias that is the bane of purely observational studies. Baseline differences between groups must still be accounted for in the analysis, but assigning treatment rather than having patients choose their treatment reduces the possibility of unmeasured differences between groups. In addition, under many circumstances, quasiexperiments can be conducted so as to obviate the need for formal informed consent (e.g., when a new clinical policy that includes the *option* of herbal therapy is introduced at one facility but not another).

Regression-discontinuity

The regression-discontinuity design is a relatively recent methodologic innovation,[5] in which the design allows full experimental control without randomization. The design is based on the assumption that there are predictable relationships (linear or polynomial) between pretest and post-test scores for all subjects along some important outcome variable. For example, with all other things being equal, one would expect patients with severe pain at baseline to have more pain at follow-up than patients who started out with mild pain. These relationships can be exploited by choosing a *cutoff score*, above which everyone receives the experimental treatment and below which everyone receives the control treatment. For example, imagine a population of patients with chronic pain, whose visual analog pain scores at baseline range from 20 to 90 mm. Patients with scores of 60 or above are assigned to receive a new analgesic, whereas patients with scores of 59 or below receive placebo. After an appropriate interval, pain is reassessed, and pre- versus postintervention pain scores are plotted for the experimental and control groups. The control group scores fall along a regression line that describes the *expected* relationship for the experimental group. Any deviation from this line for the experimental group represents an effect of treatment.

The chief advantage of the regression-discontinuity design is that it obviates the psychologic and ethical problems of randomization. Patients are still assigned to treatment, but the assignment is based on severity of illness. The major drawback is that the technique requires approximately two to two-and-a-half times as many subjects as an RCT for equivalent statistical power. Also, the technique is relatively new and most researchers have no experience with it and, therefore, do not yet trust it.

Cohort studies

Cohort studies involve following a group of patients forward in time. Exposure status (for example, whether the patient used herbs) is noted at the beginning of the study, and disease status (e.g., whether the patient got better) is noted at the end of the follow-up period. Although all cohort studies have "forward directionality" (exposed and unexposed individuals are followed forward in time, looking for disease occurrence), they are of two types. Prospective cohort studies use data collection instruments designed expressly for the purposes of the study. A group of patients, some of whom were exposed and others not exposed to the agent of interest, is identified at the beginning of the study period and followed forward in time. Key outcomes are noted as they occur. A classic example is the

Framingham heart study, in which large numbers of residents of Framingham, MA, were systemically examined for decades.[6] Much of what we know of the risk factors for cardiovascular disease emerged from this study. Analogously, a prospective cohort study of botanical efficacy might follow a population forward for a period of time, looking at the relationship between the use of herbs and mortality, biomedical markers of severity of illness, and quality of life.

The other kind of cohort study might be called a retrospective or opportunistic cohort study. Here too, patients are followed forward in time but, in this case, the outcomes of interest have already occurred, and data on both exposure and outcomes has already been collected. Often, the data on both exposure and outcomes are found within large databases assembled for other purposes (e.g., a recent study used Medicaid data to calculate the risk of gastrointestinal bleeding among patients treated with corticosteroid).[7] In theory, there is no reason one could not use databases or registries to evaluate the efficacy of botanicals. However, it is obvious that, to be useful, such databases must contain information not only on exposure (what herbs were ingested, for what indication, when, and how much) but also on the major outcomes of interest.

Case-control studies

Another observational research design that has been widely applied in epidemiologic research is the case-control study. In this design, one identifies patients with and without the disease or outcome of interest at time $t = 0$. An attempt is made to select control patients that are as similar as possible to the case patients except on the outcome, optimally by selecting both cases and controls from the same population. One then assesses exposure status of both cases and controls at an earlier time ($t - 1$). Through some simple mathematics, the relationship between exposure and outcome can be quantified as an odds ratio. For example, a recent article used case-control methodology to show that there is no association between use of silicone breast implants and the development of scleroderma.[8] Case-control methods have also been applied to the analysis of acute illnesses, such as food poisoning.

An important issue permeating nonexperimental studies is the need for information on prognostic factors (besides exposure) that could influence patients' outcomes. In clinical studies, these issues are subsumed under the headings "case mix," "patient mix," and "severity of illness." For example, if people who ingest garlic for control of cholesterol also eat less fat in their diets and engage in more physical exercise than noneaters of garlic, then observing lower LDL and higher high-density lipoprotein cholesterol levels among the garlic eaters would not support the efficacy of garlic unless these confounding factors were controlled for. One can easily imagine that users of herbs in nonexperimental studies could easliy differ from nonusers across several parameters that might influence outcomes. Unfortunately, information on potentially confounding variables is rarely available from large administrative databases. Even if data collection is prospectively designed, it is all too easy to omit important variables, sometimes because all of the key prognostic factors for a particular condition are not known.

$N = 1$ trials

An alternative design that may be applicable to many of the conditions for which botanicals are considered is the "$N = 1$ clinical trial." This is a true experiment, but it is conducted with an individual patient. One first identifies a patient for whom there is doubt about treatment efficacy (e.g., "is that ginger my patient has been using for nausea really helping?"). Next, one establishes a set of measurable outcomes (e.g., a nausea frequency and severity scale). Finally, one sets up two to eight blinded treatment periods, in which the patient is given either active agent or placebo. The length of each treatment period, as well as any washout periods, is determined by the pharmacokinetics of the treatment and the nature of the underlying condition. Larson et al.[9] recently reported on his group's experience with an $N = 1$ clinical trial service at the University of Washington, Seattle. Definitive (statistically significant) judgments could be reached in a high percentage of cases. Among the agents evaluated were albuterol for chronic cough, lecithin for spasticity, and heparin for interstitial cystitis. In the experience of the University of Washington (Seattle) group, the average cost of an $N = 1$ trial was approximately $500.

THE IMPORTANCE OF OUTCOMES

No matter what the study design, the accurate measurement of appropriate outcomes is of prime importance in establishing the efficacy of botanicals. The most important legacy of the much-heralded outcomes research movement is the recognition that the outcomes that matter are the outcomes that are important to patients. Thus, clinical drug trials are beginning to incorporate measures of health-related quality of life in addition to more traditional biomedical parameters. For example, a comparison of an angiotensin-converting enzyme inhibitor, beta-blocker, and alpha-methyl-dopa showed equivalent blood pressure control but less impact on functioning for patients in the enalopril group.[10] Patient-centered outcomes can be either generic or disease-specific. Generic outcome measures include such scales as the RAND SF-36, the Quality of Well-Being Scale, and the Dartmouth COOP charts.[11] These measures assess various aspects of functional status and well-being, such as health perceptions, physical/mental/social functioning, bodily pain, the presence of other disabling symptoms, and global quality of life. Disease-specific scales, on the other hand, assess dimensions that are more pertinent to particular clinical states, such as angina, dyspnea, and arthritis.[12,13]

In the evaluation of botanicals, both types of measures have their places. Generic measures are valuable for gauging general changes in health status. The primary advantage of generic measures is demonstrated reliability and validity; such measures may be used directly "out of the box." More specific outcomes measures are needed to assess the efficacy of botanicals for ameliorating specific symptoms. General measures can complement specific ones by casting a broad net for unexpected benefits and hazards.

COMPARATIVE ADVANTAGES AND DISADVANTAGES

Each of the alternatives to RCTs addresses some of the problems of RCTs but also introduces new ones. From the standpoint of feasibility, prospective cohort studies are similar to RCTs in terms of time and effort, but patients and clinicians may be more willing to participate in nonrandomized studies, facilitating enrollment. Retrospective cohort and case-control studies are relatively inexpensive, and enrollment of patients and clinicians is not an issue. $N = 1$ trials are relatively cost effective, but patient withdrawal may be a problem.

From the standpoint of generalizability, observational studies offer the opportunity to study the entire range of patients who may wish to use herbs for medicinal purposes (including the very old, patients with multiple chronic conditions, pregnant women, etc). Observational studies also evaluate the use of herbs in actual practice—by practitioners who may not be expert in the administration of herbs and in doses and formulations that may not be evaluable in clinical trials of reasonable size. $N = 1$ trials, of course, skirt the issue of generalizability entirely, because their purpose is to assess efficacy in individual patients.

SUMMARY AND CONCLUSIONS

In summary, RCTs remain the best available method for assessing whether specific herbal formulations "work" for the average patient. Because of their limited sample size, however, RCTs are not usually the best way to evaluate toxicity. In addition, RCTs consume large numbers of resources and need to be conducted selectively. Furthermore, the information provided by RCTs is often not generalizable to the relevant target population. On the other hand, observational study designs are more vulnerable to various forms of bias. The best approach may be to combine RCTs with observational research methods, perhaps in an iterative fashion. Observations gleaned from nonexperimental studies can be used to select botanicals for rigorous evaluation in a RCT. In some cases the RCT can be designed as a test of a treatment program rather than of an individual agent. The generalizability of results from RCTs can then be tested out in a series of observational studies. The accumulated evidence from both experimental and nonexperimental studies can be woven into a judgment about the efficacy and effectiveness of the herb in question.

REFERENCES

1. Eisenberg DM, Kessler RC, Foster C, et al. Unconventional medicine in the United States: Prevalence, costs, and patterns of use. *N Engl J Med* 328(4):246–252, 1993.
2. Johnson ES, Kadam NP, Hylands DM, et al. Efficacy of feverfew as prophylactic treatment of migraine. *Br Med J* 291:569–573, 1985.

3. Rothman KJ, Michels KB. The continuing use of placebo controls. *N Engl J Med,* 331:394–397, 1994.
4. Selker HP, Griffith JL, D'Agostino RB. A tool for judging coronary care unit admission appropriateness, valid for both real-time and retrospective use: A time-insensitive predictive instrument (TIPI) for acute cardiac ischemia. A multicenter study. *Med Care* 29(12):1196–1211, 1991.
5. Trochim WMK. The regression discontinuity design. In: Sechrest L, Perrin E, Bunker J, eds. *AHCPR Conference Proceedings: Research Methodology. Strengthening Causal Interpretations of Nonexperimental Data.* Washington, DC: US DHHS, Agency for Health Care Policy and Research, 1990.
6. Bikkina M, Levy D, Evans JC, et al. Left ventricular mass and risk of stroke in an elderly cohort: The Framingham heart study. *JAMA* 272(1):33–36, 1994.
7. Carson JL, Strom BL, Schinnar R, et al. The low risk of upper gastrointestinal bleeding in patients dispensed corticosteroids. *Am J Med* 91(3):223–228, 1991.
8. Englert HJ, Brooks P. Scleroderma and augmentation mammoplasty—a causal relationship? *Austr New Zealand J Med* 24(1):74–80, 1994.
9. Larson EB, Ellsworth AJ, Oas J. Randomized clinical trials in single patients during a 2-year period. *JAMA* 270(22):2708–2712, 1993.
10. Hill JF, Bulpitt CJ, Fletcher AE. Angiotensin converting enzyme inhibitors and quality of life: The European trial. *J Hypertension* 3(2Suppl):S91–S94, 1985.
11. Stewart A, Ware JE (eds). *Measuring Functioning and Well-Being: The Medical Outcomes Study Approach.* Durham, NC: Duke University Press, 1992.
12. Feinstein AR, Fisher MB, Pigeon JG. Changes in dyspnea-fatigue ratings as indicators of quality of life in the treatment of congestive heart failure. *Am J Cardiol* 64(1):50–55, 1989.
13. Ramey DR, Raynauld JP, Fries JF. The health assessment questionnaire 1992: Status and review. *Arthritis Care Res* (3):119–129, 1992.

Synthesis of Evidence: Examples From the Agency for Health Care Policy and Research

VIC HASSELBLAD, Ph.D.

The Agency for Health Care Policy and Research (AHCPR) is responsible for facilitating the development, review, and updating of clinically relevant guidelines to assist health care practitioners in the prevention, diagnosis, treatment, and management of clinical conditions.[1] The foundation of AHCPR's methodologic approach to the development of guidelines is explicitness and available scientific knowledge. The intention is to rely on scientific and empirical evidence as much as possible, but professional judgment and group consensus also are used in many steps of the process. The logic used to reach conclusions must be described explicitly.

Guidelines are written to answer specific questions and the questions must be stated before the process of gathering evidence has begun. These questions should be stated in terms of meaningful health endpoints. A change in white blood cell counts is much less interesting than survival or the recovery from illness. An example of a question might be: "What is the reduction in mortality among patients with unstable angina resulting from treatment with beta blockers as compared to standard medical care?"

Once the question has been stated, then all relevant evidence should be obtained. There may be no studies, however, that answer the question directly. For example, the studies of beta-blockers have answered only the following question: "What is the reduction in mortality among patients with recent myocardial infarctions (MIs) resulting from treatment with beta blockers as compared to standard medical care?"

Finally, the evidence must be summarized in a manner that permits individuals to understand what information is available and, more importantly, what information is *not* available.

TYPES OF EVIDENCE

The guideline panels assembled by AHCPR have generally used three types of evidence: published evidence; information abstracted from databases specifically for the panel; and expert opinion. A brief description of each follows.

Published evidence

The guideline panels have used a wide variety of published literature. Most panels have not restricted the information to peer-reviewed journals and books. Access has been a primary concern and so information in drug submissions and other nonpublic sources have generally not been used. This has been a decision of each individual panel.

Databases

The use of well-documented databases has generally been accepted by the guideline panels. Certain cost estimates, which are required of each panel, are available only through standard databases. The Unstable Angina Guideline Panel specifically included information from several databases, one of which was the Duke Cardiovascular Database.

Expert opinion

AHCPR guideline panels have attempted to minimize their use of expert opinion. The following example, taken from David Eddy et al.,[2] illustrates the danger of using expert opinion to obtain quantitative estimates:

A medical specialty society that by request will remain anonymous convened a meeting to set a guideline about one of [its] most common

---

Associate Research Professor, Duke Clinical Research Institute, Durham, NC.

and important practices. The participants identified one particular outcome as being important; they agreed that a practitioner's belief about the magnitude of the outcome would largely determine his or her belief about proper use of the practice, and would determine their recommendations to patients. The practitioners, all specialists in the field, were then asked to write down their beliefs about the probability of the outcome.

It was found that the estimates are spread across the entire range of possible values and, in this case, little information was gained by eliciting the expert opinion. The problem with this example may be that the practitioners were asked to estimate a quantity that is not easily estimated from individual experience.

In general, the AHCPR guideline panels have not relied heavily on published expert opinion. The panel members are experts in their particular fields, and when expert opinion was necessary, it was taken from the panel itself. Although methods of resolving differences in expert opinions have been discussed in great detail at guideline panel meetings, it has been my experience that all differences were resolved without resorting to a vote or dissenting opinion statements. Perhaps the best use of expert opinion is to resolve comparability questions: An example from the Unstable Angina Guideline panel is discussed below.

Literature searches

The literature search is one of the most costly and time consuming parts of AHCPR's guideline panel process. The first guideline panels used staff at the National Library of Medicine to perform broad Medline searches. This process produced anywhere from 2000 to 100,000 titles and abstracts. The task of sifting through these references to find that subset of interest, and subsequently to retrieve the pertinent references, often took 8 months of what was scheduled to be a 15-month process. Since then, the AHCPR has attempted to use more focused searches and begin those searches prior to the first meeting of the entire panel.

The trade-off between finding a large percentage of the articles of interest and minimizing the number of articles that are not pertinent was discussed by Berstein.[3] In his attempt to find 99 percent of 499 candidate articles, some 134,181 were found by the search strategy. However, 80 percent of the articles could be found from a search strategy that produced 9643 candidate articles. Samsa* suggested a strategy of using a targeted Medline search followed by a check of the bibliographies of the retrieved articles. This process could be further augmented by including references from previous literature reviews or from expert panels. Samsa estimates conservatively that the procedure they described will find 95 percent of the relevant articles. Both of these articles restricted their attention to the problem of retrieving RCTs.

The problem of retrieving articles in fields in which the evidence is other than RCTs can be quite different. For example, the current AHCPR Panel on Recognition and Initial Assessment of Alzheimer's and Related Dementia found that approximately 25 percent of the articles of interest were not even in Medline. Obviously, a different strategy must be used for certain kinds of literature, but the general strategy of Samsa and colleagues is still appropriate.

Summarizing the evidence

The first step in summarizing the evidence is the creation of an evidence table. An evidence table, as defined by Eddy,[4] is a table that describes for each study the design, sample size(s), outcomes measured, types of subjects, interventions compared, potential biases, experimental conditions, and observed outcomes. Evidence tables have been used for many years: For example, Karl Pearson[5] presented evidence on the protective character of vaccination on mortality after incurring smallpox. An example of an evidence table for the effect of antibiotics on the cure of otitis media is shown in Table 1. This evidence was used in the creation of the Otitis Media Guideline.[6]

Any evidence table is valid only if it includes all available information. The published literature is particularly susceptible to the claim that it is unrepresentative of all studies that may have been conducted (the publication bias or file-drawer problem).[7] There is a strong tendency of the published literature to overrepresent statistically significant results. This problem makes the literature review

---

*Samsa, GP, personal communication, 1995.

TABLE 1. EFFECT OF ANTIBIOTICS ON THE CURE OF OTITIS MEDIA AS
MEASURED BY OTOSCOPY, TYMPANOMETRY, AND/OR ALGORITHM

Author	Antibiotic/control	Fraction cured	Outcome measure and time of measurement	Comments
Corwin et al. (1986)	Erythromycin 50 mg/kg/day and Sulfisoxazole 150 mg/kg/day	33/66	Otoscopy with tympanometry confirmation at 1 month	Not blinded, unusual drug
	Placebo	22/65		
Daly et al. (1988)	TMP 8 mg/kg/day, SMX 40 mg/kg/day	5/21	Pneumatic otoscopy and tympanometry at 2 weeks	Blinded, study of steroids in "high risk" patients
	Placebo	2/21		
Ernstonn et al. (1985)	Cefaclor 20 mg/kg/day for 10 days	24/46	Otoscopy and tympanometry (A and C1) and normal hearing = cured. Measured at 2–5 weeks	Not blinded, study of patients scheduled for surgery
	Placebo	5/45		
Healy (1984)	TMP 8 mg/kg/day + SMX 40 mg/kg/day	56/93	Positive otoscopy and type B or C tympanogram = not cured. Measured at 4 weeks	Not blinded, numbers do not add up
	No R_x	6/93		
Schloss et al. (1988)	Erythromycin 50 mg/kg/day + Sulfisoxazole	6/25	Pneumatic otoscopy, tympanometry, and audiometry measured at 2 weeks	Blinded, numbers calculated from percents
	Placebo	8/27		
Schwartz et al. (1982)	TMP-SMX 4 mg/kg/day	29/33	Pneumatic otoscopy and tympanometry measured at 42 days	Not blinded
	Placebo	32/36		
Sundberg (1984)	Erythromycin 40–60 mg/kg/day	21/47	Otoscopy with some tympanometry, audiometry, and myringotomy measured at 2–5 weeks	Assumed not to be blinded
	Placebo	11/72		

process an extremely important factor in the synthesis of evidence.

The use of an evidence table can be an end unto itself. The compilation of studies may produce a table so overwhelmingly positive or negative that further synthesis is not necessary. This is more likely to be the case when the object of the synthesis is the determination of statistical significance rather than the estimation of a health effect.

Once gathered, the evidence must be evaluated at two different levels. First, how well does a particular study (or piece of evidence) answer the questions that the study was designed to answer? Second, how well does the collection of studies or other evidence answer the question of interest? Because these are two separate questions, their evaluation must also be done separately.

EVALUATION OF AN INDIVIDUAL STUDY

The evaluation of an individual study has often been done using any one of a number of rating scales. One commonly used scale is that of Chalmers et al.[8] This scale, used primarily for RCTs, is a 30-item rating scale that is both time consuming and expensive. Thomas Chalmers estimates that the cost of such a rating is about $1,000 per article.[8] By its very nature, the evaluation of evidence using quality measures is controversial. Evidence supporting quality measures' usefulness is not definitive and may depend on the types of studies being scored.[9] There is some evidence on therapeutic trials that suggests that weak study designs—such as nonrandomized, unblinded, historically controlled trials—tend to overvalue the innovation. That is, the observed gain from the innovations is often larger than when the same treatment is evaluated in a tighter, randomized blinded investigation. Thus, there are grounds for believing that when a collection of studies have different designs there may be value in excluding or downweighting the studies with the weaker designs.[10]

On the other hand, when we restrict our consideration to double-blind RCTs, there is no evidence that the quality scores have a relation with the outcomes. Emerson et al. reported on 129 studies in seven meta-analyses that were quality scored.[11] No

TABLE 2. SUMMARY OF NUMBER OF REFERENCES AND NUMBERS OF RANDOMIZED CONTROL TRIALS FOR AHCPR'S PORTS

PORT review area	Number of references screened	Number of references included	Number of RCTs
AMI			
Therapy #1	2000	8	
Therapy #2	20,000	7	
Therapy #3	5000	200	
Diagnosis	25,000	ne[a]	
Biliary Tract			
Therapy	4000	200	0
Diagnosis	1614	30	0
Cataract			
Therapy #1	6113	90	4
Therapy #2	6113	90	4
Childbirth	15,268		
Therapy #1	3184	8	0
Therapy #2	1000	8	4
Therapy #3	5821	33	0
Diabetes			
Screening	ne	74	9
Natural History	ne	126	0
Hip	23,574		
Therapy	333	15	3
IHD			
Therapy #1	7700	250	5
Therapy #2	2600	200	8
Therapy #3	100	0	0
Diagnosis & Prognosis	47,800	400	0
Low Back Pain			
Therapy #1	625	74	0
Therapy #2	472	47	0
Diagnosis #1	81	28	0
Diagnosis #2	500	50	0
Diagnosis #3	750	70	0
Pneumonia			
Therapy	613	9	9
Prognosis	3878	108	0
Prostate			
Therapy #1	1600	144	1
Therapy #2	ne	ne	
Therapy #3	ne	ne	
Stroke	5642		
Therapy #1	143	33	33
Therapy #2	473	8	8
Diagnosis	643	68	0
Natural History	900	91	0
Risk Factor	112	0	0
Total Knee Replacement	1417		
Therapy #1	475	200	0
Therapy #2	475	ne	0
Therapy #3	475	ne	0
Therapy #4	475	ne	0
Therapy #5	475	ne	0
Therapy #6	475	ne	0

Courtesy of Claire Maklan, Center for Medical Effectiveness Research (CMER), Agency for Health Care Policy and Research (AHCPR).

[a]ne, no estimate available.

relationship between the quality scores and gains from treatment or variability of results was found. Naturally, this does not prove that there is no relation between gains and quality scores in RCTs. There may be specific areas of research in which these results will be related or it may be that a better scoring system will find the relationship.

In order to evaluate studies properly, one must understand the type of study being evaluated. There are at least five types of studies that have been used in AHCPR's Guideline Panels: efficacy or therapy studies; screening; diagnostic or prognostic test studies; studies of the incidence or prevalence in a population; and studies of risk factors reported as relative risks (or odds ratios). Although no survey of the types of evidence used has been made of the guideline panels, a comparable informal survey was made of AHCPR's Patient Outcome Research Teams (PORT) Literature Work Groups. The results of this survey are shown in Table 2. Note that although questions of therapy were common to most of the PORTs, questions on diagnosis, prognosis, screening, and natural history were also important. Also note that RCTs represented a small fraction of the studies included in the work of the PORTs.

Any method of evaluating evidence must reflect the diverse nature of these types of evidence. Given this diverse nature and the varied composition of the Guideline Panels, it is not surprising that each panel has chosen a slightly different method for evaluating evidence. Most panels have restricted their ratings to the evidence for a question rather than attempting to rate individual studies. One exception to this was AHCPR's Heart Failure Guideline Panel.[12] The basic assumption behind its rating scheme was that most sophisticated reviewers can recognize a well-done study. Furthermore, most reviewers can usually agree on flaws in a particular study. Starting with these assumptions, I constructed a series of rating schemes, shown in Tables 3 through 6. These scales have not been validated; they are presented to stimulate further discussion.

EVALUATION OF EVIDENCE FOR A QUESTION

Many of AHCPR's guideline panels have used a simple "A-B-C" grading scale to evaluate the evidence pertinent to a particular question. The "A" rat-

SYNTHESIS OF EVIDENCE

TABLE 3. QUALITY RATING SCALE FOR EFFICACY OR THERAPY STUDIES

Rating	Description
"A" rating: well-done study	RCTs with appropriate blinding, good follow-up, low crossover; reasonably consistent multiple studies
"B" rating: minor flaws or nonrandomized design	RCTs with lower follow-up rates or higher crossover; or RCTs with unblinded outcome assessment or well-executed nonrandomized controlled study (prospective); or carefully controlled database analysis
"C" rating: major flaws, including too many minor flaws	Unacceptable follow-up or crossover rates; or key covariates not measured; or no blinding where blinding was critical

TABLE 4. QUALITY RATING SCALE FOR SCREENING, DIAGNOSIS, OR PROGNOSTIC STUDIES

Rating	Description
"A" rating: well-done study	"Gold standard test" available, study done on consecutive samples in a well-defined population or on entire population
"B" rating: minor flaws or nonrandomized design	Random subsample of those testing "+" and "−" used, but fraction of each reported; or "gold standard" not completely definitive
"C" rating: major flaws, including too many minor flaws	Convenience sample taken; or study done retrospectively

TABLE 5. QUALITY RATING SCALE FOR STUDIES OF INCIDENCE OR PREVALENCE

Rating	Description
"A" rating: well-done study	Population-based sample from well-defined population
"B" rating: minor flaws or nonrandomized design	Population slightly different from that of interest; or endpoint measured not identical to the one of interest
"C" rating: major flaws, including too many minor flaws	Institution-based sample or convenience sample such as RCT; or endpoint quite different

TABLE 6. QUALITY RATING SCALE FOR STUDIES OF RELATIVE RISK (ODDS RATIO)

Rating	Description
"A" rating: well-done study	Population-based sample from well-defined population with all key covariates measured
"B" rating: minor flaws or nonrandomized design	Study population not well defined; or some minor covariates not measured; or endpoint defined slightly differently
"C" rating: major flaws, including too many minor flaws	Key covariates not measured; or institution-based sample; or endpoint quite different from one of interest

ing implies that there is good research-based evidence to support the recommendation. The "B" rating implies that there is fair research-based evidence to support the recommendation. The "C" rating implies that the recommendation is based on expert opinion and panel consensus. This rather nonspecific definition allows each panel some flexibility in its rating of evidence and yet is simple enough that individuals who are not familiar with synthesis of evidence can understand the system.

Perhaps the best-known scheme for rating evidence about a question, shown in Table 7, was given by the group at McMaster University, Hamilton, ON.[13] It is clear that this rating scheme is only ap-

TABLE 7. LEVELS OF EVIDENCE FOR THERAPY

If a high-quality overview is available	If no overview is available

When the lower limit of the confidence interval for the effect of treatment *exceeds* the clinically significant benefit and;
   individual study results are homogeneous: Level I+
   individual study results are heterogeneous: Level I−
 When the lower limit of the confidence interval for the effect of treatment *falls below* the clinically significant benefit (but the point estimate of its effect is at or above the clinically significant benefit) and:
   individual study results are homogeneous: Level II+
   individual study results are heterogeneous: Level II−
	Randomized trials with low false-positive (alpha) and low false-negative (beta) errors: Level I
	
	 Randomized trials with low false-positive (alpha) and high false-negative (beta) errors: Level II
	
	 Nonrandomized concurrent cohort studies: Level III
	 Nonrandomized historical cohort studies: Level IV
	 Case series: Level V

propriate for questions of efficacy or therapy. Unfortunately, it has also been used for questions other than those of therapy. Level I and II studies are RCTs with level II reserved for those studies of low power. Levels III, IV, and V were for concurrent cohort, historical cohort, and case series studies, respectively. Pluses and minuses were added to indicate the homogeneity of results.

One alternative to assigning a rating to the overall evidence is to rate the individual evidence and then describe explicitly the logic by which the overall conclusion was reached. This point is illustrated very well by the following discussion from the Unstable Angina Guideline[14] on the effect of beta-blockers in patients with unstable angina.

> No clear effect on mortality in unstable angina has been shown to date. However, randomized trials in acute MI, recent MI, and stable angina with silent ischemia have all shown a mortality benefit for beta-blockers. Thus, the overall rationale for the use of beta-blockers is compelling and sufficient to make them a routine part of care for patients with acute IHD [ischemic heart disease] in the absence of contraindications.

The question of using a rating scale versus an explicit description of logic was discussed extensively at a recent AHCPR meeting held specifically to resolve the problem of evaluating evidence. The opinion was so strong and divided that no consensus was reached.

COMBINING EVIDENCE

The methods of combining evidence, often known as meta-analysis or synthesis of evidence, have received a great deal of interest within the last 10 years. It is not possible to list all of the standard techniques, but the reader should consult any of the following sources: Rosenthal,[15] Hedges and Olkin,[7] Laird and Mosteller,[16] Hunter and Schmidt,[17] and Cooper and Hedges.[18] The justification for the use of formal meta-analysis as opposed to the global subjective judgment was given by Eddy.[19]

> The complexity of modern medicine exceeds the inherent limitations of the unaided human mind. It is unrealistic to think that individuals can synthesize in their heads scores of pieces of evidence and accurately estimate the outcomes of different options.

To illustrate some basic methods, consider the example from the Otitis Media guideline panel as shown in Table 1. Because there was some suspicion that a lack of blinding might bias the results, the data were split according to whether or not the study was blinded to the person who was evaluating the health outcomes. The primary outcome of interest was the difference in probability of cure at 4 months. The estimates and confidence intervals are shown in Figure 1. This kind of graph is common in meta-analysis, and has been used extensively by Lau et al.[20] Note that four of the five unblinded studies seem to suggest an effect of the antibiotic, whereas the two blinded studies do not. The two

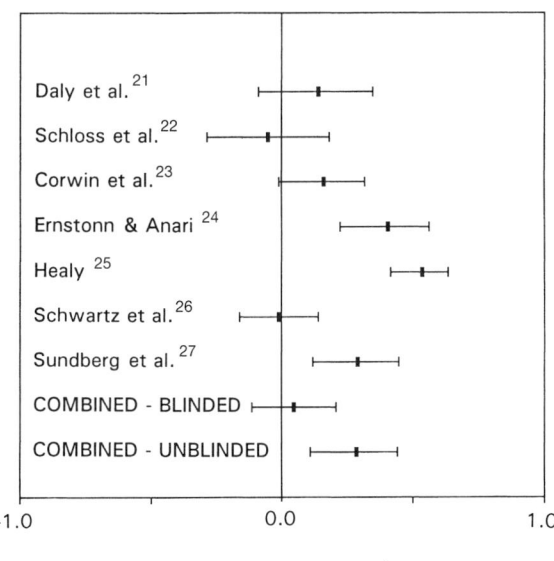

FIG. 1. Effect of antibiotics on otitis media with cure rates measured at 4 weeks using otoscopy and tympanometry.

groups of studies were combined, using a random effects model as described by Hedges and Olkin,[7] giving the combined results also shown in Figure 1.[21–27] These results confirm the fact that the combined five unblinded studies show a significant effect of treatment but the two blinded studies do not and, in fact, estimate an effect very near zero. This example serves to reinforce the well-known fact that researchers who measure health outcomes must be blinded to the treatment. AHCPR's Guideline on Otitis Media with Effusion in Young Children considered studies using several different measures of cure and its final conclusion was:

> When this small improvement in resolution of otitis media with effusion is weighed against the side effects and cost of antibiotic therapy, antibiotic therapy may not be preferable to observation in management of otitis media with effusion in the otherwise healthy young child with no craniofacial or neurologic abnormalities or sensory deficits.

Although there are several different methods for combining evidence in the literature, most of them yield similar results when applied to the same data.[28] The U.S. General Accounting Office (GAO)[29] recognized situations where neither RCTs nor database analyses separately could answer the question of interest. This problem resulted from the different populations used in the various kinds of studies. In general, RCTs will study very homogeneous groups and therefore may not be generalizable to other age groups, ethnic groups, or even another gender. The GAO's solution is a hybrid analysis that uses both kinds of studies. The GAO's method of combining the evidence can be summarized as follows.

1. Adjust each randomized study's treatment effect to subpopulations of interest.
2. Adjust each database analysis to the subpopulations of interest.
3. Match the various analyses by subpopulation.
4. Combine across subpopulations, adjusting for differences in quality.
5. Synthesize subpopulation estimates and project results to subpopulations when estimates are not available.

This method specifically recognizes the contribution of well-designed databases to the synthesis of evidence. Additional applications are needed to judge the effectiveness of the method. The method is completely consistent with the Confidence Profile Method.

The Confidence Profile Method

Some problems of combining evidence go beyond the standard methods; these problems usually can be analyzed using the Confidence Profile Method of Eddy et al.[2,19] The following example, taken from work done for AHCPR's Unstable Angina Guideline Panel,[14] was described by Hasselblad and McCrory,[28] using specialized software written specifically for the problem. If the assumptions are changed slightly, standard statistical software can be used to solve the problem.

Both heparin and aspirin have been shown to be effective in the reduction of MI in patients with unstable angina (see Wallentin[30] and Telford and Wilson[31] in Table 8). Heparin is significantly more costly to administer. The question is: "Does heparin offer decreased risk of MI when compared to aspirin in patients with unstable angina?" Problems of complications and side effects will be ignored. The only direct comparison of the two drugs was in the Theroux et al.[32] trial (Table 8) and this trial had very few cases of MI in either arm. All standard tests of significance fail to reject the null hypothesis (aspirin

TABLE 8. SUMMARY OF THE 5-DAY MI[a] RATES FOR TREATMENT WITH AND
WITHOUT ASPIRIN AND HEPARIN IN PATIENTS WITH UNSTABLE ANGINA

Study	MI rate in placebo group	MI rate in aspirin group	MI rate in heparin group
Theroux et al.[32]	14/118	4/121	1/121
Wallentin[30]	22/397	9/399	
Telford and Wilson[31]	17/114		3/100

[a]MI, myocardial infarction.

is just as good as heparin): The uncorrected chi-squared value is 1.76 ($P = 0.1843$) and Fisher's exact test gives a P value of 0.3699.

To combine the evidence from these studies assuming a fixed effects model, we can use any standard multiple logistic regression program. The parameters of the model are as follows:

q_p = Rate of MI in the placebo group (as defined by Theroux et al.[32])

q_{wp} = Rate of MI in the placebo group (as defined by Wallentin[30])

q_{tp} = Rate of MI in the placebo group (as defined by Telford and Wilson[31])

y_{ap} = Odds ratio for the risk of MI for the aspirin group versus the placebo group

y_{ha} = Odds ratio for the risk of MI for the heparin group versus the aspirin group. (This is the parameter of interest.)

Note that the odds ratios do not depend on the study, whereas the rates in the placebo group were specific to each study. This is the same assumption that would be made if we were combining several studies of just aspirin versus placebo using the Mantel-Haenszel method. The data set as entered into the multiple logistic regression program is shown in Table 9.

Using multiple logistic regression on the data in Table 9, the maximum likelihood estimate of the odds ratio of MI for heparin versus aspirin, y_{ha}, is 0.36 with 95 percent confidence limits of 0.11 and 1.26. The likelihood ratio test for the effect of heparin over aspirin gives a chi-squared value of 3.185 for 1 degree of freedom ($P = 0.0743$), which is much more suggestive of a beneficial effect of heparin versus aspirin than was suggested by the Theroux et al.[32] study alone. The results are similar to those found by Hasselblad and McCrory.[28] The slight differences can be explained by the difference in assuming common odds ratios instead of common relative risks.

DISCUSSION

The evaluation of evidence is difficult and, by its nature, subjective. It is clear that certain kinds of evidence are subject to bias. This bias potentially occurs whenever the individual (or group) responsible for the assessment of the health outcome is not blinded to the treatment. There are at least two solutions to the problem. The first is to use blinding such as is done in RCTs. The second method is to use databases that were collected for purposes other than evaluating the treatment of interest. The analysis of databases is difficult because many of the factors that were controlled for in the RCT must now be adjusted for in the analysis.

The synthesis of evidence is completely dependent on the completeness of the literature search and the accuracy of the evaluation of the evidence. There are a variety of methods used to combine evidence

TABLE 9. PARAMETER ESTIMATES EFFECT OF
ASPIRIN AND HEPARIN ON 5-DAY MI RATES
IN PATIENTS WITH UNSTABLE ANGINA

Parameter						
q_p	q_{wp}	q_{tp}	y_{ap}	y_{ha}	Dead	Alive
1	0	0	0	0	14	104
1	0	0	1	0	4	117
1	0	0	1	1	1	120
0	1	0	0	0	22	375
0	1	0	1	0	9	390
0	0	1	0	0	17	97
0	0	1	1	1	3	97

and fortunately most of these give similar answers. It must be remembered that the purpose of the synthesis is to answer a meaningful question involving a health outcome. If the evidence is not evaluated and combined in a manner that answers the question, then the evidence is of no value.

REFERENCES

1. Fiore MC, Bailey WC, Cohen SJ, et al. *Smoking Cessation, Clinical Practice Guideline* No. 18. Rockville, MD: U.S. Department of Health and Human Services, Public Health Service, Agency for Health Care Policy and Research. AHCPR Publication No. 96-0692. April 1996.
2. Eddy DM, Hasselblad V, Shachter R. A Bayesian method for synthesizing evidence: The Confidence Profile Method. *Int J Technol Assess Health Care* 6:31–56, 1990.
3. Berstein F. The retrieval of randomized clinical trials in liver diseases from the medical literature: A comparison of MEDLARS and manual methods. *Controlled Clin Trials* 9:23–31, 1988.
4. Eddy, DM. *Manual for Evaluating Health Practices & Designing Practice Policies.* Philadelphia: American College of Physicians, 1992, pp. 44–45.
5. Pearson K. Report on certain enteric fever inoculation statistics. *Br Med J* 2:1243–1246, 1904.
6. Stool S, Berg A, Berman S, et al. Otitis media with effusion in young children. *Clinical Practice Guideline*. No. 12. Rockville, MD.
7. Hedges LV, Olkin I. *Statistical Methods for a Meta-Analysis.* New York: Academic Press, 1985.
8. Chalmers TC, Smith H Jr, Blackburn B, et al. A method for assessing the quality of a randomized control trial. *Controlled Clin Trials* 2:31–49, 1981.
9. Hasselblad V, Mosteller F, Littenberg B, et al. A survey of current problems in meta-analysis: Discussion from the AHCPR Inter-PORT Work Group on Meta-Analysis. *Medical Care* 33(2):202–220, 1995.
10. Colditz GA, Miller JN, Mosteller F. How study design affects outcomes in comparisons of therapy. *Statistics Med* 8:441–454, 1989.
11. Emerson JD, Burdick E, Hoaglin DC, et al. An empirical study of the possible relation of treatment differences to quality scores in controlled randomized clinical trials. *Controlled Clin Trials* 11:339–352, 1990.
12. Konstam M, Dracup K, Baker D, et al. Heart failure: Evaluation and care of patients with left-ventricular systolic dysfunction. *Clinical Practice Guideline*, No. 11. Rockville, MD: Agency for Health Care Policy and Research, 1994 AHCPR Publication No. 94-0612.
13. Cook DJ, Guyatt GH, Laupacis A, et al. Rules of evidence and clinical recommendations on the use of antithrombotic agents. *Chest* 102(Suppl.):305S–311S, 1992.
14. Braunwald E, Mark D, Jones R, et al. Unstable angina: Diagnosis and management. *Clinical Practice Guideline.* No. 10. Rockville, MD: Agency for Health Care Policy and Research: National Heart, Lung, and Blood Institute; 1994; AHCPR Publication No. 94-0602.
15. Rosenthal R. *Meta-Analytic Procedures for Social Research.* Beverly Hills, CA: Sage Publications, 1984.
16. Laird NM, Mosteller F. Some statistical methods for combining experimental results. *Int J Technol Assess Health Care* 6:5–30, 1990.
17. Hunter JE, Schmidt FL. *Methods of Meta-Analysis.* Newbury Park, CA: Sage Publications, 1990.
18. Cooper HM, Hedges LV. *The Handbook of Research Synthesis.* New York: Russell Sage Foundation, 1994.
19. Eddy DM, Hasselblad V, Shachter RD. *Meta-Analysis by the Confidence Profile Method: The Statistical Synthesis of Evidence.* Boston: Academic Press, 1992.
20. Lau J, Antman EM, Jimenez-Silva J, et al. Cumulative meta-analyses of therapeutic trials for myocardial infarction. *N Engl J Med* 327:248–254, 1992.
21. Daly K, Giebink GS, Batalden PB, et al. Resolution of otitis media with effusion with the use of a stepped treatment regimen of trimethoprim-sulfamethoxazole and prednisone. *Pediatr Infect Dis J* 10(7):500–506, 1991.
22. Schloss MD, Dempsey EE, Rishikof E, et al. Double blind study comparing erythromycin-sulfisoxazole (Pediazole) TID to placebo in chronic otitis media with effusion. In: *Proceedings of the 4th International Symposium on Recent Advances in Otitis Media.* Burlington, Ontario: BC Decker, Inc; 1988, pp. 261–263.
23. Corwin MJ, Weiner LB, Daniels D. Efficacy of oral antibiotics for the treatment of persistent otitis media with effusion. *Int J Pediatr Otorhinolaryngol* 11(2):109–112, 1986.
24. Ernstomn S, Anari M. Cefaclor in the treatment of otitis media with effusion. *Acta Otolaryngol* [Stockh] (Suppl.) 424:17–21, 1985.
25. Healy GB. Antimicrobial therapy of chronic otitis media with effusion. *Int J Pediatr Otorhinolaryngol* 8(1):13–17, 1984.
26. Schwartz RH, Puglese J, Schwartz DM. Use of a short course of prednisone for treating middle ear effusion: A double-blind crossover study. *Ann Otol Rhinol Laryngol* 89:296–300, 1980.
27. Sundberg L, Eden T, Ernstson S, et al. Tissue penetration of erythromycin in Waldeyer's ring and bacteriology of secretory otitis media. *Acta Otolaryngol* 384(Suppl.), 1981.
28. Hasselblad V, McCrory D. Meta-analysis tools for medical decision making: A practical guide. *Med Decision Making* 15(1):81–96, 1995.
29. US General Accounting Office. *Cross Design Synthesis: A New Strategy for Medical Effectiveness Research* (GAO/PEMD-92-18). Washington, DC, 1992.
30. Wallentin LC. Aspirin (75 mg/day) after an episode of unstable coronary artery disease: Long-term effects on the risk for myocardial infarction, occurrence of severe angina and the need for revascularization. Research group on instability in coronary artery disease in southeast Sweden. *J Amer Coll Card* 18:1587–1593, 1991.
31. Telford AM, Wilson C. Trial of heparin versus atenolol in prevention of myocardial infarction in intermediate coronary syndrome. *Lancet* 2232:1225–1228, 1981.
32. Theroux P, Ouimet H, McCans J, et al. Aspirin, heparin, or both to treat acute unstable angina. *N Engl J Med* 319:1105–1111, 1988.

Establishing Consensus

JOHN H. FERGUSON, M.D.

The consensus development program at the National Institutes of Health (NIH) has generally revolved around the technical or scientific aspects of any set of issues. Consensus in the real world of health care—that is, establishing what works for people in treatment, diagnosis, prevention, or screening—often requires the use of information that is less stringent than so-called hard data. Thus, the question arises: "Do we realistically need scientifically derived data in order to provide the health care community with guidelines or recommendations for treatment, prevention, diagnosis, or screening?"

The need for consensus implies controversy, lack of agreement, a gap between knowledge and practice, or perhaps some aspect of the health care system that is missing or broken. One must define the problems or issues, there must be a desire to solve these problems, there must be ways to minimize bias, and, last but not least, there should be some data on which reasonable people could come together in agreement.

The requirements for consensus conferences at the NIH have primarily been: (1) An issue of public health importance affecting a fair number of people; (2) controversial or unresolved issues; and (3) data to resolve these issues. Other criteria have included wide practice variations, inappropriate use or distribution of certain technologies, lack of awareness by providers of nonuse of certain technologies, or a gap between research and practice. Occasionally, conferences have been carried out because of political concerns.[1]

Although the quantity and quality of data have varied from conference to conference, for many issues the randomized controlled trial (RCT) is still the gold standard. Obviously other types of experimental studies, such as controlled trials with quasi-randomization or crossover studies, can provide adequate data. In many areas, nonexperimental, observational, or even case studies are all that are available. The lowest quality of evidence, case reports, or opinions of experts, normally would not qualify as data.

The studies that qualify for producing viable data are done in sizeable populations and are experimental or observational. The results of these studies are, however, often meant to be applied to individuals. Herein lies a major disparity and an area of concern, disagreement, and controversy between physicians and other caregivers on the one side and epidemiologists, public health officials, and scientists on the other. These issues are of special concern for people involved with alternative or complementary medical therapies.

A consensus conference at the NIH is a three-part meeting:

1. It is open to the public, allowing for ample discussion time.
2. Scientific data are presented by experts on all sides of the issues.
3. There is a nongovernmental, nonbiased panel or jury. This panel hears the views of the public, listens carefully to the data presented by experts, and writes the summary statement by answering questions that have been performed by a planning committee. This statement is then read to the public and experts, critiqued by both, and then released for publication in medical journals for wide dissemination.

There is some variation from conference to conference in the quantity and quality of data. For the 1990 conference on adjuvant treatment for breast cancer, 17 large RCTs were presented. For the con-

---

Director, Office of Medical Applications of Research, National Institutes of Health, Bethesda, MD.

ference on laparoscopic cholecystectomy, no trials had been done and the data came mostly from large case series that were not controlled. For the conference on *Helicobacter pylori* and peptic ulcer disease, there were a few small RCTs. And for the conference on prenatal steroids in prevention of the problems of prematurity, there were many RCTs over many years, and several meta-analyses. All pointed in the same direction. The latter conference had one of the strongest databases of any consensus conference we have had at the NIH.

In order for a consensus conference to take place, there must be some data in human populations, preferably phase III or IV. The conference would be likely to occur somewhere before the technologies or treatments would be accepted as part of a guideline. At the NIH, medical science dictates when the topic is ripe for consensus-type synthesis. On the other hand, topics for medical guidelines are generally driven by the need for certain guidelines in medical practice. Obviously, on occasion there is overlap.[2]

For many of the issues in alternative medicine, actual double-blind RCTs seem to be rare or inadequately done. Part of the problem is that, with intimate practitioner–patient relationships and a lot of one-to-one interaction, it would be difficult, but not impossible, to carry out a trial. As intimated above, some practitioners in the alternative medicine community have thought randomizing not only difficult but perhaps unethical. It appears that the issue of botanicals, on the other hand, in that they represent a form of pharmacotherapy, would be very amenable to blinded RCTs.

Of the several studies that I have reviewed, the trials done with feverfew for migraine and ginger for hyperemesis gravidarum and sea sickness would appear to be reasonable examples. The trials using *Ginkgo biloba* for cerebral insufficiency leave something to be desired. In my view, the diagnosis of "cerebral vascular insufficiency" is sufficiently vague and subject to error that these studies are not of much use. With tighter definitions or endpoints they might be more acceptable.

Although the database that I have reviewed is quite small, and perhaps inadequate for what we have generally required for an NIH consensus conference, I would think that appropriate trials could indeed be done. I suspect that the lack of a large pharmaceutical company behind these products and, therefore, the lack of money to carry out the appropriate trials is a major stumbling point. Smaller and cheaper trials might be done in various medical settings, perhaps patterned after the so-called "metro health care firm" system, in which the patients are randomized as they enter one of three or four health sections in a health maintenance organization. Various treatments and procedures could be carried out in this way.

Furthermore, alternative therapies are being offered, in some cases, as a last resort, especially for pain, thereby diminishing the chances of efficacy. If some of these therapies had equal chances for use as the more conventional medical treatments and, therefore, got into the picture earlier, these alternative therapies might have a better chance of competing in the so-called mainstream health care system.

REFERENCES

1. Ferguson JH. The NIH consensus development program: The evolution of guidelines. *Int J Technol Assess Health Care* I12:460–474, 1996.
2. Ferguson JH. NIH consensus conferences: Dissemination and impact. *Ann NY Acad Sci* 703:180–199, 1993.

Controlled Clinical Trials for Botanicals: Available, Possible, Necessary?

DR. JOERG GRUENWALD

An analysis of the present situation regarding the proof of effectiveness of botanicals, using established methodology, such as placebo-controlled, double-blind studies, reveals great variation. Meta-analysis published in peer-reviewed journals exists for some of the best-studied botanicals; for example, garlic, in the *Annals of Internal Medicine* and the *Journal of Hypertension*, and *Ginkgo biloba* in the *British Journal of Clinical Pharmacology* and the *Lancet*. For a number of botanicals, such as St. John's Wort, hawthorn, valerian, ginger, and several more, some well-controlled studies are available; but, for the wide majority of botanicals, such studies are still missing. Is it more difficult to perform such studies with botanicals? And if so, what are the main reasons for this situation?

It is, in principle, possible to perform the same proof of efficacy for botanicals as required for new chemical entities, even though special problems, mainly with placebo control, have to be overcome in some cases. Garlic preparations, for example, exhibit a certain body odor, depending on the dosage. Therefore, stringent placebo-controlled, double-blind studies could not be performed with garlic, because the patients in the active group could be identified. The study protocols had to be adapted to this problem by eliminating the garlic-odor cases from the statistical analysis and comparing those results to the complete set of data. Additionally, the garlic placebos received a minor amount of garlic so as to be indistinguishable from active medication by taste or odor. Other problems with botanical preparations exist, especially for liquid forms. Because liquids often have specific tastes and aromas, it is time-consuming to produce matching placebos without the active compounds. Given that these problems can be overcome, why is the clinical documentation for most traditionally used botanicals in health care still missing?

This is mostly a regulatory and legal issue of the past. The largest market for phytomedicines has traditionally been in Europe, with 50 percent of the European market concentrated in Germany. The registration of these products has, so far, been based on plant monographs, developed by Commission E of the German health authorities, using safety and efficacy data. In the past, the producers of botanical products were not forced to perform clinical trials as long as a monograph existed for the plant to be marketed. Therefore, only very few manufacturers voluntarily invested in clinical research in botanicals not protectable by patents. Because of the harmonization of European Union laws, the registration situation in Europe now is changing. In the future there will be at least three categories for botanicals and their registration requirements in order to make claims. First, for a small group of phytomedicines, it will be possible to produce clinical documentation as good as that required for chemical drugs, along with quality and safety data, in order to make medical claims. A second group of botanicals with less efficacy data will be marketed as traditionally used products with mild, mostly prophylactic claims. A third group, the dietary supplements, will not be eligible for making health claims, but marketers will give certain functional explanations regarding their effects. (A fundamental difference exists between phytomedicines, which are an accepted part of mainstream drug treatment in Europe, and homeopathics, which conceptually are not based on

---

PhytoPharm Consulting, Institute for Phytopharmaceuticals, Berlin, Germany.

a scientific approach but on treatment experience. Therefore, often homeopathics have not been tested in placebo-controlled, double-blind studies and should be regarded separately.)

A major reason for the lack of clinical data for many phytomedicines is the lack of public funding for such research. Some first steps are the creation of University Chairs for "Natural Treatment" in Berlin and Ulm, Germany, and for "Contemporary Medicine" in Exeter, United Kingdom. This approach, with intensive public funding, is required for better differentiation among, and accepted use of, botanicals in health care internationally.

Summary and Conclusions

KA KIT HUI, M.D., F.A.C.P.

- From ancient times to the present, humans and animals on our planet have tested and used botanicals for relief of their suffering.
- A vast amount of information on therapeutic, efficacious natural products, including plants, has been accumulated and preserved, particularly in China and India, countries that have a long tradition of herbal use.
- Modern scientific investigations on plant-based medicine have been carried out in many parts of the world.
- In addition to empirical data, health care providers use knowledge generated from pharmacologic studies and therapeutic trials to guide their use of botanicals in patient care.
- There is a vast database on the scientific study and clinical application of natural products.
- It is feasible to conduct clinical trials of botanical combination products.
- Botanical products are often used in combination and are frequently adjusted to the changing pathophysiologic state of the patient. Clinical research methodologists should take these factors into consideration in designing trials.
- Randomized controlled trials (RCTs) have advantages and disadvantages in determining the efficacy of any therapeutic intervention, including botanicals.
- Subjecting botanicals to RCT-type studies to establish efficacy will take centuries, because of the vast number of botanical products. We should seek approaches other than conducting a clinical trial for each product to evaluate safety and efficacy.
- Alternatives to RCTs include quasi-experiments, cohort studies, case-control studies, and "$N = 1$" trials. These methods have their advantages and limitations but may be more suited to the evaluation of herbal efficacy.
- Accurate measures of patient-centered outcomes, either generic or disease-specific, are important regardless of the design of the study.
- The evaluation of evidence is difficult and by its nature, subjective. The synthesis of evidence is completely dependent on the *completeness* of the literature search, which is often not available in foreign studies, and the accuracy of the evaluation of the evidence.
- There are situations when neither RCTs nor database analyses separately can answer the question of interest because of different populations being used in the various kinds of studies.
- Consensus in the real world of health care often requires using information that is less stringent than so-called hard data.
- There is some variation on the quantity and quality of data in different NIH consensus conferences, ranging from multiple, large RCTs to single, large case series without any trials.

Director, UCLA Center for East-West Medicine, University of California, Los Angeles, School of Medicine, Department of Medicine, Los Angeles, California.

Part III

How Can We Know That These Products Are Safe?

Overview

Donald P. Waller, Ph.D., Professor in the Department of Pharmaceutics and Pharmacodynamics at the University of Illinois at Chicago, chaired the discussion on safety within the context of the widespread and essentially uncontrolled use of botanicals in the United States. As with other panels, the systems that are already up and running in other countries provided a useful point of comparison but also offered a challenge. Thus, a number of issues, arose around the political problems of communication in the bureaucratic and cultural context and how these factors interact. Some fairly specific questions were identified.

Most conference participants agreed that it will only be after these context/communication issues are handled that meaningful progress can be made on the more specific and scientific pharmacologic challenges of what has come to be called toxicovigilance; that is, surveillance of the adverse effects in the use of herbal products. As Virginia S.G. Murray, M.Sc., M.F.O.M. (Consultant, Occupational and Environmental Toxicologist at the National Poisons Unit, Guy's and St. Thomas' Hospital Trust, London, United Kingdom) phrased the challenge, the herb community really needs to begin to master the safety issues, lest these "potentially and incredibly valuable compounds" come to be seen by the public as being poisons rather than medicines.

COMMUNICATING ABOUT SAFETY IN THE UNITED STATES

The current system response to reports of adverse effects and safety: conclusions drawn by researchers and manufacturers

Even though the Food and Drug Administration (FDA) has established a unified point of contact for herbals in the office of Freddie Ann Hoffman, M.D., the FDA's liaison to the National Institutes of Health Office of Alternative Medicine, the FDA is not monitoring the safety of botanical use in America aggressively. This is neither the FDA's mandate (because of the dietary supplement classification) nor is it feasible, given how reports of problems develop. When the agency receives a report of an adverse reaction, it acts as only "the generation of a signal," said the FDA's Lori A. Love, M.D., Ph.D. (Office of Special Nutritionals, Center for Food Safety and Applied Nutrition of the FDA), which warns people that something may be amiss. The agency, however, is not responsible to formally follow-up, assess, or publicize the implications of the event. Consequently, the data that the FDA does get often remain too general to develop any conclusions about incidence or to establish any meaningful trends. Follow-up by the Agency is required to supplement the information in the original report but, unless the perceived threat is great (and it generally is not), aggressive investigation is unlikely.

In only some cases are manufacturers required to pass on to the FDA, the Centers for Disease Control and Prevention (CDC), or to other agencies possible safety problems they become aware of. And even when they do, it is not the government's role to issue scientific warnings without fairly elaborate and responsible inquiry. This rarely happens unless the event unequivocally poses a grave threat, a condition that is rarely met. The recent European experience with *Aristolochia* suggests that, when these conditions are present, they will probably be recognized. It seems fairly certain that few people are being acutely harmed in ways that are categorically related to botanicals. Unfortunately, less dramatic adverse effects, the impacts of long-term chronic use, and information assuring a product's safety remain vague and inconclusive because no coherent system exists to collect and publicize these data.

The industry is taking steps to overcome this. Beginning in 1995, the National Nutritional Foods Association (NNFA) is requiring all members to register labels in a central database. Many smaller manufacturers do not belong to the NNFA or even to the American Herbal Products Association (AHPA); it was hoped that some way to tighten this net could be found.

The FDA's general approach to safety is geared to carcinogenicity or hepatotoxicity; when these are suspected, the full rigor of proof is imposed. When they are not, chemistry and toxicology requirements have been loosened at the preliminary testing stages as an inducement to soliciting applications.

The United States' situation compared to other systems around the world

Barbara Steinhoff, Ph.D., German Nonprescription Drug Manufacturers Association, Bonn, Germany, reported that, according to the Commission E process in Germany, substances that have shown to cause no harm and are considered to be "well-known" comprise a class of phytomedicines that may only require bibliographic support to demonstrate safety. This contrasts with the United States' system, in which "all materials are considered equal," and any substance not fully registered must face new drug application (NDA) procedures. However, because botanicals are currently classified as dietary supplements, producers can avoid the responsibility to do testing, though they will thereby forego the chance to make specific proven health claims. If a problem does arise, the burden is on the agency to prove that the preparation is harmful or poisonous. In Germany, the Commission E monographs are inclusive, although the experts administrating the system have the discretion to require more proof if they believe that it is warranted. The Japanese medical system makes no distinction between chemical pharmaceuticals and their plant-based Kampo products. The same is true for Chinese patent medicines.

Factors hindering effective communication among systems, practitioners, and consumers

At the FDA, Dr. Hoffman's office, the working group, and the Center for Drug Evaluation and Research are all committed to establishing better communication with the pharmaceutical industry. Their cooperation with the December 1994 conference was seen as a possible prelude to collaborating with the AHPA and the NNFA in a search for ways to accomplish this. Roseann Philen, M.D., a Medical Epidemiologist at the CDC, also hoped that such a collaboration would include "hands across the sea," both to embrace data that has been collected abroad and to explore systematic ways to join forces. Alvin B. Segelman, Division of Corporate Health Sciences, Nature's Sunshine Products, recently attended a conference on so-called "designer foods" (that are mostly Japanese produced), and extolled the system, which he described as a high-level dialogue between two groups of credentialed scientists, one representing government, the other industry.

Whether such products and actual studies will arise in the American context, and where the funding might come from, remain important but unanswered questions. Simon Y. Mills, M.A., F.N.I.M.H., of the Center for Complementary Health Studies at the University of Exeter, United Kingdom, pointed out that a multinational group in Europe is working on a project to submit data generated in Italy, France, Germany, the Netherlands, and the United Kingdom for meta-analysis. The group hopes to make that and other data more accessible, to clarify and extricate the safety data, to develop uniform criteria for the quality of the data and the procedures used to obtain it, and to generally prescribe how research results and monographs should be reconciled to make them universally useful.

All agreed that nomenclature was a crucial hurdle. In the United States, the preference is for common names, which are required on labels. But a single plant may have dozens of common names and many plant names are so similar as to invite confusion. Only by cross referencing to the Latin binomials can this problem be addressed. In 1991, the AHPA published *Herbs of Commerce*, a compilation by botanists and herbalists of a list of approximately 600 substances found in the domestic market; The American Botanical Council, Austin, TX, offers this publication for sale. Dr. Murray pointed out that similar reference works exist in a number of countries and said that the project of compiling and reconciling them is essential for a truly functioning and cooperative international system of surveillance.

At the AHPA, the Standards Committee has begun an analogous study to evaluate toxicity data worldwide. The Committee would welcome the FDA's advice and help with this project, so that the results might be acceptable and utilized by the widest possible constituency.

PRIMARY CHALLENGES TO BUILDING A BETTER SYSTEM

Improving standards and definitions to pose the algorithms for scientific evaluations of safety

There are three basics. Nomenclature is one. Second is evaluating toxicity, a precondition of which is the chemical and microscopic analysis of plants for definitive identification. Third, once a substance is unequivocally identified, dosage and conditions of use must be specified in the context of safe practice recommendations for consumers. When problems arise, the best first guess is that the substance was taken inappropriately. People are determined, Dr. Murray's experience suggests, to not follow prescribed usage.

Useful information on safety comes from new trials and from the testing and evaluation that follows reported adverse events. But what is the value of "historical use"? In the absence of evidence to the contrary, a long history of safe use is suggestive, but not conclusive, it was agreed, to determine safety. Consider tobacco, which not too many decades ago, was even prescribed by some physicians. And acetaminophen, which has caused many patients to develop liver disease and more than a few to die, shows that long-term use of any substances, regardless of rigorous screening, may lead to biologic surprises. Judith K. Jones, M.D., Ph.D, The Degge Group, Arlington, Virginia, warned that a history of safe use can mislead us into overlooking the important exceptions.

In this context, several relevant observations were made about botanicals. Used in appropriate doses, their adverse impact on the national health is clearly negligible, in an era when tobacco, alcohol, and red meat have been implicated in most of our primary health problems. However, it is known that many natural products are consumed over long periods of time for chronic conditions. It is equally difficult to prove their efficacy as it is to prove their possible toxicity. This is especially true in the United States where, for all intents and purposes, botanical use is invisible to most allopathic providers.

Development of an effective and coordinated global toxicovigilance program

As of now, the primary net for catching adverse reactions to botanicals is the poison control centers. They were not, of course, designed specifically for natural products. Thus, while much valuable data are being accumulated, poison control centers remain a poor substitute for what should be a more comprehensive, traditional, and discerning adverse reporting reaction system for all therapeutics. Poisoning is often an euphemism for overdose; the majority of cases involve suicide attempts or accidental ingestion by children. These events distort the data and obscure any trends that might reveal the potential toxicity of botanicals in the more traditional sense. In addition, the reporting and follow-up system has very little accountability. Roseann Soloway, the director of the American Association of Poison Control Centers, nonetheless welcomes more information about botanicals, saying that the better information they had to begin with, the better the data they could deliver about possible problems with these substances.

The World Health Organization (WHO) in Uppsala, Sweden, maintains a Center for Drug Monitoring. WHO's agenda could serve as a guideline for preliminary efforts to address the problem in the United States. Dr. Murray's center in London has begun a project with the Royal Botanical Gardens at Kew to develop a uniform reference for the materials that could serve as the basic list of dangerous substances. This will mark an important first step, and she welcomes any collaboration from the United States for this effort.

Ultimately, observed Professor Waller, the United States must figure out its own solution to the dilemma of maintaining the public trust. Although most people at the conference believe that botanicals, by and large, are efficacious and, at the least, generally benign, panelists in this discussion focused on the issue of scientific responsibility. Safety probably should not be the area in which to try to erect the shield of "historical usage," because the methods and standards of scientific proof have changed so dramatically in recent times. With safety issues, the question is not simply what standard to impose, as was the case with efficacy. The government does not want to license a dangerous substance, to mislead the public, or, ultimately, to fail in its responsibility to monitor all products and substances in the marketplace for safety. What must be developed is a national and international commitment that will lay the foundation for a system of analyzing toxic episodes wherever they occur in the world. First, there must be uniform identification of materials, then the establishment of a system to catch all possible adverse reactions, and finally—the most difficult—there must be some figuring out how to find the resources and to develop the strategies to pursue the few cases that could uncover sources of danger that are currently unsuspected.

The Safety of Botanicals: A Historical Perspective

RYAN J. HUXTABLE, Ph.D.

SAFETY AS A RELATIVE RATHER THAN AN ABSOLUTE CONCEPT

It is a commonly held belief that certain herbs can be considered to be safe because of their long history of usage, dating back to classical times, or earlier in some cases. The virtues of *Teucrium* (germander) are described by Hesiod (eighth century BC), for example, while Hippocrates (fourth to fifth century BC) praised *Tussilago farfara* (coltsfoot) for its effects in respiratory diseases. However, safety to a pharmacologist is a relative concept, very different from the public's perception of safety as an absolute concept. For a pharmacologist, the question, "is this agent safe?" is without meaning unless the dose and frequency are included in the question. Toxicity, the opposite side of the coin to safety, is a function of dose and duration, among other factors. Toxicity can be shown for most substances, given certain conditions. What, for example, could be safer than water? Yet water intoxication has been frequently demonstrated. Water intoxication has been found in babies and children given large quantities of herbal teas[1–3] and in beer drinkers.[4] The two classical botanicals mentioned above are still used, and both have been recently implicated in human poisonings.[5,6]

Before examining the herbal literature, therefore, it is appropriate to consider some pharmacologic terms relevant to an understanding of safety.

PHARMACOLOGIC AND TOXICOLOGIC TERMINOLOGY RELATIVE TO CONCEPTS OF SAFETY

Drugs that affect body functions, such as blood pressure or diuresis, are called *pharmacodynamic* agents. Herbs are often used for their pharmacodynamic effects. Pharmacodynamics is the spectrum of biologic responses produced by an intervention at a given time. Production of diuresis or alteration in blood pressure are typical pharmacodynamic responses. The possession of a therapeutic pharmacodynamic activity implies a lack of safety at a high enough dose. Desired pharmacodynamic responses are always tempered in degree and duration. We want an anesthetic agent, for example, to reduce consciousness for a given period only. An aberrantly long duration of anesthesia is clearly an undesired effect. Curare, strychnine, digitalis, and morphine are all examples of useful pharmacodynamic agents that are unsafe when used inappropriately.

This analysis implies the impossibility of a herb having a pharmacologic but no toxicologic action. A completely safe agent would be without any activity whatsoever. A parameter that recognizes this dual aspect is the *therapeutic index*. This is the ratio of the dose required to exhibit toxicity to the dose required for therapeutic effectiveness. The higher the therapeutic index, the larger the margin of safety. It follows that consumers who exceed the therapeutic dose (in amount or frequency) increase the likelihood of developing toxicity regardless of how "safe" the preparation might be.

SAFETY IN RELATION TO LIFE EXPECTANCY AND MORTALITY CURVES

In considering the historical perspective, one must also consider that "safety" in traditional terms is very different from modern terms. Modern, industrialized populations exhibit mortality patterns that are unique to this century.

Professor, Department of Pharmacology, College of Medicine, University of Arizona Health Sciences Center, Tucson, AZ.

For prehistoric cultures, age of death can be determined by examination of skeletons.[7] From one 40,000-year-old paleolithic burial site in Morocco, examination shows that 50 percent of the population died before age 38, while only 5 percent lived to age 70. (For these and other calculations given here, deaths before the age of 5 are excluded: Including these would lower the numbers enormously.) By the Neolithic Age, 5000 years ago, 50 percent survival time had reached 42 years. This may be compared to an equivalent of 50 years for the modern !Kung, a tribe of hunter-gatherers living in the Kalahari desert. About 20 percent of !Kung live to see their seventieth birthdays. It is only in this century, and only in the industrialized nations, that 50 percent survival times rose much above 50 years. Indeed, mortality curves have remained surprisingly invariant over thousands of years and under a variety of cultural conditions, as illustrated in Table 1. The mortality curve for the paleolithic population approximates to a zero-order decay graph (Figure 1A). This means that in a population of a given initial age in a given year, the same number of people will die each year thereafter. The older a person is, the more likely he or she is to die that year, because a constant number of people die each year from a shrinking population. For the paleolithic population, for each 1000 people alive at age 10, 16 died each year thereafter. The curve for the modern !Kung is similar, with 13 per thousand of those attaining age 10 dying each year thereafter (Figure 1A).[8]

With the development of agriculture, higher population densities could be sustained, but mortality remained approximately the same. Then came civilization, in its literal sense of people congregating into cities. Among the undoubted benefits of city life, however, an increased life span was not to be found. Until very recently, mortality curves for cities were essentially unchanged from those for preagrarian societies. In Liverpool, United Kingdom, in 1860, for example, 20 percent of people born never saw their fifth birthdays. Those people who did had a life expectancy of 40 years. Despite a greater survival rate to age 10, the subsequent zero-order decay rate of 1.5 percent per year left the Victorian Merseysider only slightly better off than the paleolithic cave dweller (Figure 1A). In 1860, London was a distinctly better environment for attaining senescence, with a median age at death of 59 years. In the United States in 1900, life expectancy for people surviving infancy was 45 years.

In certain cities, probably as a result of epidemic diseases, mortality patterns followed a first-order decay curve. This is illustrated for imperial Rome (Figure 1B). For Rome between AD 0 and AD 400, of people surviving infancy to age 5, half died in every 14-year period thereafter. That is to say, the chance of dying in a given year was independent of age.

In the Western world, within this century, the median age of death has moved rapidly toward about 75 years. This has been achieved not by an increase in maximum life span but by an increase in the number of people attaining this life span. The median age of death for people surviving infancy in the societies under discussion are shown in Table 1. For the populations shown in Figure 1, "maximum" life expectancies calculated by extrapolation are 71, 80, and 88 years for paleolithic people, Victorian Liverpudlian, and modern !Kung, respectively (Table 1). For imperial Rome, it was 75 years. These numbers straddle the life expectancies for modern industrialized nations. The zero-order mortality curve, which ruled preagrarian, agrarian, and urban societies, has shifted in the modern United States to-

TABLE 1. MORTALITY PATTERNS OF VARIOUS SOCIETIES

	Max life span (years)	Median age of death[a] (years)	Kinetic order
California 1970	85	75	Rectangular
Rome AD 0–400	75	19[b]	First
Modern !Kung	88	50	Zero
Liverpool 1860[c]	80	43	Zero
Paleolithic	71	38	Zero

[a]For those alive at age 10.
[b]For those alive at age 5; half-life 14 yr.
[c]20 percent died before age 5. (See Fig. 1 for references.)

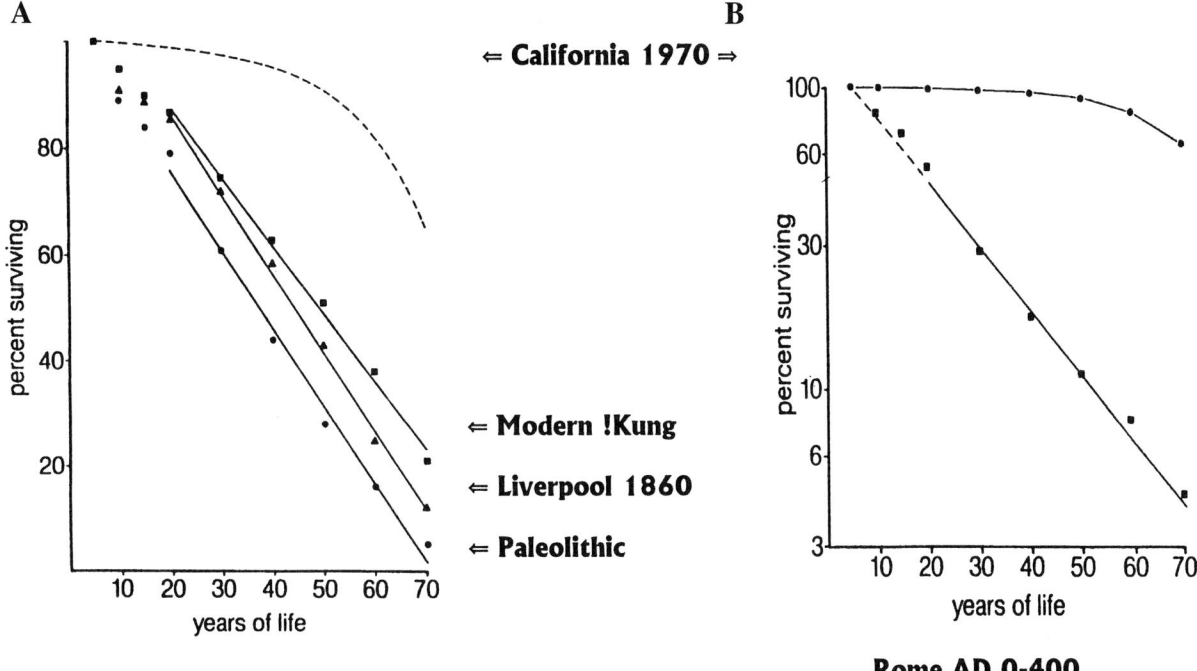

FIG. 1. (A). Mortality curves for various populations. The dotted line is for California (1970). In descending order, the other curves are for a modern hunter-gatherer society, the !Kung, the city of Liverpool in 1860, and a paleolithic population (40,000 years before the present). The curves show the percentage of people surviving to age 5 who live to the ages shown on the x-axis. For the three zero-order societies, correlation coefficients for 20–70 years are in excess of 0.99. **(B).** The top curve is for California (1970), and the lower curve for the city of Rome between AD 0 and AD 400. The curves show the logarithmic percentage of people surviving to age 5 who live to the ages shown on the x-axis. The data for California are from Chiang. Other data are from Cairns.

ward a rectangular curve (Figure 1A), in which an average citizen who avoids fights and wars, wears a seat belt, and does not smoke will have a reasonable expectation of living to 85 years of age, give or take a few years.[9] For the United States, it has been calculated that in 1900 the average citizen died 38 years prematurely.[9] Now it is a scant 12 years, three of these being due to violence.

The United States, however, is aberrant by the standards of much of the rest of the world (Figure 2). Life expectancy for the United States (256 million people) is 76 years. For 147 million people in Mesoamerica and the Caribbean nations, it is 68.3 years. For 300 million people in South America it is 66.8 years. For 1093 million people in central and south Asia, it is 58.3 years. For 490 million people in the black nations of Africa it is 50.7 years. For 252 million people in a subset of these nations, it is 47.3 years.[10] In all, more than 2 billion people have life expectancies 20 years less than what we in the "developed" nations take as being the norm.

In summary, mortality curves and life expectancies were very different in the societies that provide the historical database on herbal use, regardless of whether a classical Mediterranean culture is considered, or medieval Europe, or ancient India, or China. Much of the herbal use in the modern world also occurs in societies very different from the United States in mortality curves and life expectancies, and in the nature of "establishment" health care delivery. Thus, caution is needed in extrapolating data obtained from a nonmodern or nonwestern society to the United States.

VARIATION IN RISK–BENEFIT RATIO WITH VARYING EXPECTATIONS OF MORTALITY

A further consideration concerning the safety of a botanical preparation is the *risk–benefit ratio*. This is the ratio of the chance at a given dose that an untoward result will develop to the chance that a beneficial result will develop. Risk–benefit ratios, therefore, are applicable to population studies: If a given population takes a medicinal preparation, what pro-

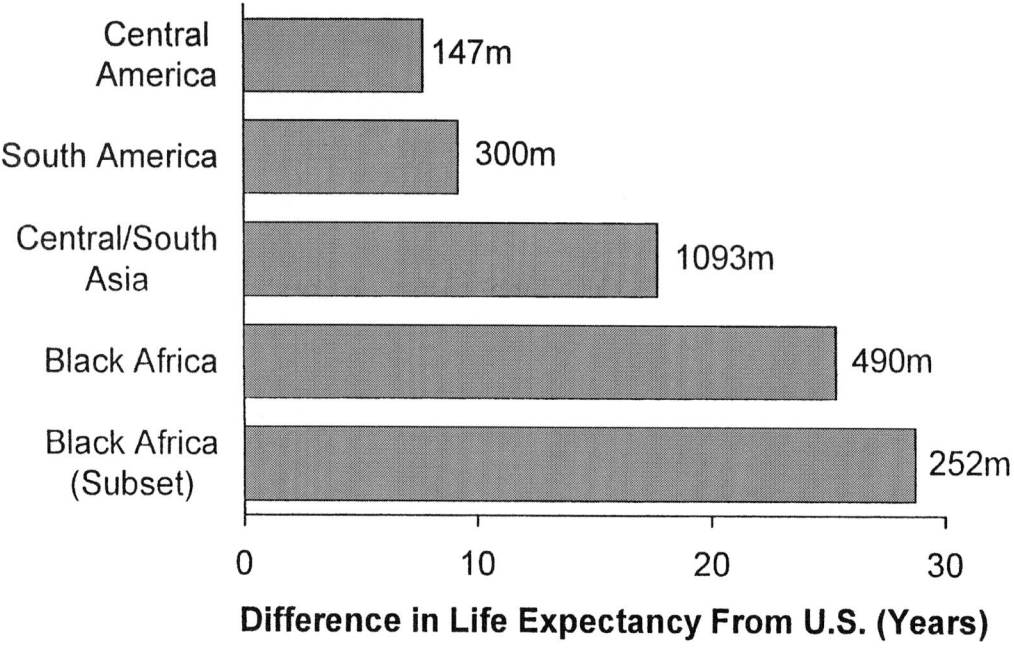

FIG. 2. Years lost to premature mortality compared with the United States. For the regions listed on the left, the populations are indicated on the bars. The differences in life expectancy from the United States are shown on the x-axis. (Data are taken from the National Geographic Society, *Atlas of the World.* Ref. 10.)

portion of the population will suffer harm? And what proportion will derive benefit? The lower the risk–benefit ratio, the more desirable the treatment. It is important to note that both risks and benefits affect the ratio. Thus, a preparation carrying low risk but no benefit could legitimately be considered as unacceptable, while a preparation carrying high risk but an even higher benefit could be considered to be acceptable. If comfrey causes liver disease in a small percentage of people who take this botanical preparation on a regular basis, but no corresponding beneficial effect can be identified, then the rational conclusion would be that the preparation should not be used. If a cancer chemotherapeutic agent causes several side effects in all people that use it, such as loss of hair, mouth ulceration, or gastrointestinal bleeding, but causes remission in an otherwise deadly cancer, the risk–benefit ratio would be considered to be unacceptable for those not suffering cancer, but highly acceptable for patients with the appropriate cancer.

An ideal agent would have a risk–benefit ratio of zero. In other words, a desired pharmacologic effect would be produced in 100 percent of the exposed population (i.e., a dose at the top of the dose-response curve, or ED_{100}, is being used) but would produce toxicity in none of the exposed population (i.e., the same dose used would be at the bottom of the dose-toxicity curve, or ED_0).

HISTORICAL USE OF BOTANICALS

Differences between traditional and modern usages of herbal materials

In considering the history of herbal use for insight into safety, one must consider how comparable the modern use is to the traditional use. In modern usage, typically, larger amounts may be taken, the material is used more frequently, it is used in the form of enriched extracts, and it may be used simultaneously with other synthetic drugs, such as anticonvulsants, that were not available earlier. An increasing number of drug–herb interactions are being reported.[11] Furthermore, whereas botanicals may have been traditionally taken as treatments for specific conditions, there is now increasing use of botanical preparations as prophylactic agents. That is, they are taken in the absence of any indicated conditions in order to prevent disturbances of health from occurring.

Many supposedly traditional herbs are now marketed in ways that are markedly different from their former use. The recent case of a Washington dentist who poisoned himself with ma huang (a preparation of *Ephedra sinica* containing the sympathomimetic ephedrine) provides an example of someone using a Traditional Chinese Medicine in a nontraditional manner.[12,13]

Because of the absence of mechanisms for gathering and collating long-term responses to botanicals, traditional use can give no insights as to the chronic toxicity of an agent. Thus, comfrey and similar preparations have been used since classical times, but it is only in the last 30 years that certain alkaloids in comfrey have been recognized as being severely hepatotoxic, at times causing liver cancers. Tobacco provides another example. This agent has been used for several hundred years in Western cultures and has, for a long time, been endorsed by the medical profession as being useful for a variety of conditions. It is only in the last 40 years that serious concerns have been raised about the health risks of tobacco. It has taken an intensive research and public health effort to derive sufficient data on this issue to convince the majority of the population.

Issues of chronic toxicity were of lower import in premodern societies, because of the shorter life spans and different kinetics of death, as discussed above. For most of the last several thousand years, the fact that a drug taken by a 30-year-old person carried a high risk of producing cancer within 20–30 years was simply irrelevant.

Herbs traditionally may have served as amelioratives or palliatives, because of nothing better being available to the care providers of the time. Valuable as these agents may have been in their historical context, in some cases, modern pharmaceutical agents may now provide better therapy. The general inefficacy of herbalism is suggested by the high morbidity and low life spans in societies employing herbalism as a major source of health care. Longevity and success in combating morbidity from such diseases as tuberculosis or syphilis correlate with the rise of modern pharmacology. Other problems with herbal preparations include the variability in pharmacologic constituents. This issue has been discussed at length.[14–22] It is probably safe to assume as a general rule that an herb widely used for a considerable period of time lacks acute toxicity when it is used in the traditional manner. Chronic toxicity from traditional, historical use of herbs, however, cannot typically be detected, and was of lower significance in premodern societies as a public health issue because of shorter life spans, differences in mortality curve, and the lack of other treatments.

Problems with collecting and evaluating historical information

The absence of a mechanism for recording and disseminating information on beneficial and adverse responses to herbs constitutes a major stumbling block in relying on traditional use as an indication of safety. The history of medicine is in part the history of dangerous interventions that persisted in some cases for centuries. One example is the universal use of bleeding for numerous conditions. This procedure probably hastened the deaths of tens of thousands of people, including Charles II of England and George Washington. In almost no case was bleeding beneficial to the patient by objective criteria (although it has been argued that phlebotomy can produce symptomatic or subjective improvement).[23] Substances we now accept to be frankly dangerous, such as tobacco and comfrey, were used for centuries before their risks were generally recognized.

Analysis of historical information available for selected herbs

Herbals quote from one another and their errors can be traced for centuries. Often, unverified claims are made for plants, the antiquity of the claims being indicated by the archaic medical terminology used. We can read in modern herbals that, among other actions, *Senecio aureus* stimulates the pelvic organs, relieves engorgement, is a completely safe aid in gynecologic disorders, is valuable in gravel, and strengthens flabby uterine ligaments. In addition, the plant can be used to treat coryza, dropsy, gleet, neurasthenia, phthisis, prostatitis, spermatic cord pain, renal colic, puerperal mania, spasmatic constipation, liver malfunction, and disturbances of the bloodstream caused by spasmodic character.[24,25] A similar list is given by Christopher.[26] *S. aureus* is, in addition, a pectoral, a tonic, and a vulnerary. Both sources agree that the plant is useful for leucorrhea.

Comfrey is also claimed to be useful for leucorrhea. This panacea is recommended for scrofula, ulceration of the kidneys, female debility, enlarged glands, psoas abscess, and the effects of sexual excess.[24] Comfrey is also said to be a vulnerary, an

TABLE 2. SOME CLASSICAL HERBALISTS OR WRITERS ON HERBS

Name	Period
Hesiod	8th C BC
Hippocrates	4th to 5th C BC
Theophrastus	3rd to 4th C BC
Dioscorides	1st C AD
Pliny the Elder	1st C AD
Galen	2nd C AD

alterative, and a blood purifier,[25] and highly suited for alleviating female debility.[26] Much more is claimed by these and other sources for these two herbs.

Three characteristics of such claims should be noted, which appear throughout the herbal literature:

1. The ancient medical terminology (e.g., phthisis, gravel, gleet)
2. The emphasis on treatment of symptoms rather than of causes (e.g., leucorrhea, enlarged glands)
3. The use of vague, all-encompassing descriptors (e.g., gynecologic disorders, liver malfunction, disturbances of the bloodstream)

These characteristics are indications both of the persistence of herbal lore and of its derivation from accepted medical practice in an era when etiologies were uncertain and diseases with similar symptoms could not be differentiated. In the past, the physician had little to aid him, apart from the patient's faith in him, laudanum, alcohol, and, in certain cases, the saw. Any ethnobotanic value held by such claims as those listed above are obviated by the lack of information as to the origin of the claims, the cultural groups that used the plants for the claimed purposes, and the extent and historic period of such uses. Names for herbs may be introduced without mention of other names used synonymously, separated by centuries or continents. Even books by academic writers are not exempt from these practices. Thus, one such book describes comfrey without mentioning its hepatotoxicity and carcinogenicity. Indeed, the book contains the statement, "toxicity is unlikely even after ingestion of moderately large quantities."[27]

Examples of available historical information

A partial list of writers and writings on herbs is given in Tables 2 through 4. These sources are all from the Judeo-Hellenic Western tradition. With non-Western systems, the difficulty of analysis is compounded by the absence of reliable, scholarly translations into English of the relevant historical literature. For example, Avicenna's *Cannon of Medicine*, translated from Arabic into Latin, was a standard textbook for 500 years in Europe, having an immeasurable influence on the development and practice of medicine. However, complete, modern translations of Avicenna's writings exist only in Russian, Uzbek, and Urdu. Where translations are available, they may be unreliable. Confidence in the accuracy of translations from Sanskrit texts in one book on Ayurvedic medicine, for example, is undermined when one finds misquotations of Western texts that can readily be checked.[28] Similarly, seven words are mangled in the title of Garcia de Orta's 1563 Spanish volume, *Colloquios dos Simples e Drogas e Cousas Medicinaes da India*, and the book is claimed to be in Latin. In general, the various sources listed in the tables are highly derivative and

TABLE 3. SOME MEDIEVAL TESTS ON HERBS

Author/editor	Title	Publisher/location
Anonymous	*Here Men May Se the Vertues off Herbes (Middle English Herbal)*	Brussels, Belgium: Scripta, 1981
Gosta, B	*Agnus Castus, a Middle English Herbal Reconstructed from Various Manuscripts*	Uppsala, Sweden: Nendeln/Liechtenstein, 1973
Rufinus	*The Herbal of Rufinus*	Chicago: University of Chicago, 1946
Apuleius Barbarus	*The Herbal of Apuleius Barbarus from the early 12th Century Manuscript Formerly in the Abbey of Bury St. Edmonds*	Oxford: Oxford University, 1925

TABLE 4. SOME LATER HERBALS

Author	Title	Publisher
Dioscorides	*The Greek Herbal of Dioscorides, Englished by John Goodyer, AD 1655*	Oxford: Oxford University, 1934
Green, T	*The Universal Herbal*	Liverpool: Caxton Press, 1816
Anonymous	*Livre des simples medicines, Codex Burxellensis IV 1024*	See Deluca EP, "Livre des simples medicines," Codex Bruxellensis IV 1024: A 15th-century french herbal. *Isis 1985,* 76 pp. 631–632.
Culpepper, N	*The English Physician Enlarged, with Three Hundred and Sixty Nine Medicines Made of English Herbs*	London: A. and J. Churchill, 1708 [original publication date 1653]
Pechey, J	*The Compleat Herbal of Physical Plants*	London: Henry Bonwicke, 1694
Chamberlayne, J	*A Family Herbal, or, The Treasure of Health*	London: W. Crooke, 1689
Archer, J	*Every Man his own Doctor, Compleated with an Herbal*	London, 1673
Lovell, R	*Panbotanologia, sive, Enchiridion Bontanicum, or A Compleat Herball*	Oxford, R. C. Davis, 1665
Coles, W	*Adam in Eden, or Natures Paradise: The History of Plants, Fruits, Herbs and Flowers*	London: C. J. Streater, 1657
Parkinson, J	*Paradisi in Sole, Paradisus Terrestris, or, A Choise Garden of All Sorts of Rarest Flowers*	London: Richard Thrale, 1656
Parkinson, J	*Theatrum Botanicum: The Theater of Plants, or An Herball of a Large Extent*	London: T. Cotes, 1640
Gerard, J	*The Herbal or Generall Historie of Plantes*	London: John Norton, 1597
Dodoens, DR	*A Niewe Herball or Historie of Plantes* [translated from French by Henry Lyte]	London: Gerard Dewes, 1578

metaphrastic. Little in the way of true, original observation is involved in many of them.

It is difficult to substantiate from an examination of the historical herbal literature that traditional use sanctifies safety. It is instructive to examine some case histories followed through the herbal literature from classical to modern times. A convenient beginning point is Nicholas Culpepper's *The English Physician Enlarged, or the Herbal.*[29] Culpepper (1616–1654) was a qualified physician and a graduate of Cambridge University. He made many contributions to medicine, the most important of which was his *Directory for Midwives*, a seminal text in the history of obstetrics. Culpepper's herbal was first published in 1653 and was enormously successful. The *Cambridge Biographical Dictionary* comments that this book formed the basis of subsequent herbalism in the English-speaking world. There have been over 100 editions of the work, and it was the first medical book published in the United States. It has never been out of print.

From Culpepper's herbal, we will consider some plants that are acutely toxic and some that are more likely to show subacute or chronic toxicity.

Hemlock—Conium maculatum. Hemlock is a frankly toxic plant. It contains the fast-acting and readily absorbed alkaloid coniine, which has a nicotine-like effect, causing drowsiness, nausea, labored respiration, paralysis, asphyxia, and death.

Culpepper was aware of the dangers of hemlock, but still considered it to be suitable for certain external uses (although coniine is probably readily absorbed through the skin and mucous membranes). He said:

I wonder why it may not be applied to the privities in a priapismus, or continual standing of the yard [penis], it being very beneficial to that disease... applied to the privities, it stops lustful thoughts. Hemlock is exceedingly cold, and very dangerous, especially to be taken inwardly.... If any shall through mistake eat the herb hemlock instead of parsley...whereby happeneth a kind of frenzy, or perturbation of the senses, as if they were stupid or drunk, the remedy is, as Pliny saith, to drink of the best and strongeth pure wine....

Culpepper's views on hemlock derive from the classical literature, Socrates having used the plant for his judicial suicide. Hemlock is the *koneion* of Dioscorides' herbal[30] of which he wrote: "This is of the venomous herbs killing by its coldness." When applied as an ointment, it "forbids the breasts to grow great in time of virginity."

In medieval Europe, hemlock was frequently to blame in intentional and accidental poisonings. The juice, under the name *succus conii*, was used in medicine for centuries as an antispasmodic, sedative, and anodyne.[31]

In general, herbalists have viewed this plant with suspicion, only reluctantly allowing its therapeutic use. As Gerard[32] put it, hemlock is "one of the most deadly poisons which killeth by his cold qualities, as Dioscorides writeth, saying, hemlocke is a very euill, dangerous, hurtfulle and poysonous herb insomuch that whosoever taketh of it into his body, dieth remedilesse, except the party drinks some wine . . . before the venom hath taken the heart . . . ." Gerard said that hemlock is "not to be applied outwardly, much lesse taken inwardly into the body," and concluded that "the great hemlocke doubtlesse is not possessed with any one good facultie, as appeareth by his loathsome smell, and other apparent signes, and therefore not to be used in phisicke."[32]

Dodoens[33] described hemlock as "this noughtie and dangerous herbe, groweth in places not toyled, under hedgerows and about pales [fences]."

He agreed with other herbalists that hemlock is an antigrowth substance and that it can be put on the stones (testicles) of boys or breasts of "maids" to prevent development. He warned, however, that "neverthelesse, it cause the such as do use it, to be sicke and weake all the dayes of their lives," and concluded that "Hemlocke is very cuyl, dangerous, hurtful, and venomous, in so much that whosoever taketh of it, dyethe, except he drinke good olde wine after it."[33]

Coles[34] referred to the Greeks believing that hemlock "did so intoxicate the brain of those that took the juyce thereof, that they presently fell a staggering, or else every thing seemed to them to turn round," a description more in accord with the actions of henbane. However, Coles said that he did not believe that English hemlock would do this. Along with Dodoens, he allowed the external use of hemlock, saying that the bruised leaves and tops could be applied to the genitals to prevent lust. "The same being applied to the Breasts of Maidens which are great and swagging, or hanging downe, causeth them to be contracted and to become round and lovely, without any danger, and repelleth the Milk of those that are oppressed therewith. . . . It may also be safely applyed to any Inflammations, Tumors, or Swellings in any part of the Body," and used externally for the gout, sore eyes, or for extraordinary pain. It works against pain because of "the narcoticall or benumming faculty that it hath."[34] In view of antigrowth activities attributed in herbals, it is not surprising to find that hemlock is recommended for the treatment of numerous kinds of cancer.[35]

Despite his restricting it to external use, Coles was unusual among the Elizabethan and Jacobean herbalists in discounting the dangers of taking hemlock inwardly. He knew, he said, that Socrates was condemned to death with hemlock, yet he quoted the learned Dr. Howe that the English hemlock is not so dangerous. Dr. Howe had tried it on beasts and then upon men without finding any pernicious action. However, Cole said that the plant was not to be used rashly and he quoted a story of some asses that fell into such a deep sleep by eating hemlock that the owner thought they were dead and skinned them. However, the asses eventually awoke and generally amused the onlookers by walking around without their skins.

Henbane—Hyocyamus niger, Black Henbane and H. albus, White Henbane. Henbane is another frankly toxic plant, because of its content of psychotomimetic tropane alkaloids. Culpepper[29] listed many uses for the plant, but warned: "Take notice, that this herb must never be taken inwardly." However, he did allow decoctions to be poured into the ears or to be used to treat toothache.

In this use, he was at one with the other herbalists. Gerard[36] wrote that "henbane causes drowsiness, and mitigates all kinds of pain . . . to wash the feet in the decoction of henbane causes sleep, or given in a clyster it does the same, and also the often smelling to the flowers. . . . The leaves, seed and juice taken inwardly cause an unquiet sleep like unto the sleep of drunkeness, which continues long and is deadly to the party."

Despite knowledge of its toxicity, henbane was well known and widely used in Elizabethan England. Henbane extract was widely used in the ears as a treatment for deafness and earache. Gerard commented that "the oile or juyce dropped into the eares is good against deafness."[36] Coles also reported the therapeutic use of henbane extract in the ears and mouth: "The oyl of the seed is helpful for the deafnesse, noise and worms in the ears, being dropped therein; and the juyce of the herb or root doth the same . . . the oyl of it, or the Juyce by itself, or the decoction of the root . . . being gargled warm in the mouth, is very effectuall in easing the pains of the teeth."[34]

Coles also reported that one treatment for toothache involved placing the henbane seeds on hot coals and breathing the smoke. But he said that he could not recommend this method, "as it may produce dangerous effects, intoxicating the head and troubling the sight."[34]

These authors presumably took their information from Dioscorides,[30] who claimed that the juice of henbane was useful not only for "ye ear paines" but also as a mouth wash and an enema (glister): "If any do glisterize him herewith that hath an ulcer in ye seat, that it works to the same effect. But ye root being sodden with Acetum is a collution for teeth pains. . . ." Henbane was also used for pain by the school of Salerno in the twelfth and thirteenth centuries. A narcotic preparation involved a sponge soaked in henbane, opium, hemlock, and belladonna, which was dried until used. The patient swallowed a moistened piece of the sponge prior to surgery. The seeds of henbane have also been found in the ruins of a Roman military hospital,[37] while the Roman writer Aulus Celsus described the use of a decoction of a mixture of poppy and henbane as a sedative.

Gerard recommended henbane for gout, swelling in the "stones," and tumors of women's breasts, and said that it "causes drowsinesse and mitigateth all kinde of pain." He said that it can be administered as a clyster (enema).[32] Other side effects include oliguria. "The root being eaten causeth great drought, stoppage of urine, and many other symptomes, as you gather from the story Mr. Parkinson relates concerning a friend of his, who eat the roots of henbane instead of parsnips."[34]

Dodoens recommended henbane for "heates, rheumes, and humours of the eyes, and the payne in the same, in the eares, and mother." He also said that the seeds are good for a cough and that the root, boiled in vinegar and held in the mouth, is good for toothache. According to him, all parts of the plant "coole inflammations, causeth sleepe, and swageth al payne."[33]

The most marked toxic actions of henbane are referable to the pyschotomimesis produced by the tropane alkaloids in the plant. Coles referred to these actions when he said that the Latins called henbane *apollinaris* perhaps because it made men mad like unto Apollo's creatures when they deliver his oracles. According to him, swine eating henbane become very disturbed and are in danger of their lives. Humans who eat it are apt to quarrel, while the Italians use it "to allay that enormity called priapismus."[34] Dodoens likewise was aware of the psychotomimetic action, and its potentially dangerous consequences: "Taken either alone or with wine, causeth raging, and longe sleepe, almost like onto drunkennesse, whiche remayneth a long space, and afterwarde killethe the partie."[33] Gerard similarly reported that, "the leaves, seed and juice taken inwardly cause an unquiet sleep like into the sleepe of drunkennesse, which continueth long, and is deadly to the partie."[36] It is for good reason that *insana* is given as a synonym for henbane in a fifteenth century listing of synonyma.[38]

The "Stockholm Medical Manuscript" of circa 1400 said that henbane produces nymphomania in women (*hem* having the sense of "them") (quoted in ref.[39]).

Amongis wommen if thou schuldist gon
And hennebanne hawe the up-on
This ilk cas schall be-falle,
It schall hem make to lowe the all.

Thus, despite the dangers of henbane, it was widely accepted practice to put extracts of henbane into body cavities, including the ears, mouth, vagina, and rectum.

Black Hellebore—Veratrum album. Veratrum are toxic plants because of their steroidal alkaloids; ingestion causes slowing of the heart, lowering of the blood pressure, respiratory difficulties, and hallucinations. Culpepper warned of potential problems, without giving specifics: "It is a herb of Saturn and therefore no marvel if it have some sullen conditions with it, and would be far safer, being purified by the art of the alchemist, than given raw. If you have taken any harm by taking it, the common cure is to take goat's milk: if you cannot get goat's milk; you must make a shift with such as you can get."[29] He then had a long list of conditions for which hellebore was recommended.

Hellebore is the elleboros of Dioscorides, who said: "It provokes sneezing, and kills mice being kneaded with honey and polenta."[30] There were no other warnings.

Of *Helleborus officinalis*, or *elleboros melas*, he said: "It purgeth the belly from above, drawing out phlegm and choler." The only warning was that "one must dig it with all celerity, because there is an headache by the exhalation."[30]

Some other markedly toxic plants. In general, herbalists can be relied upon to be aware of the acute toxicity of plants, at least in general terms, even if the specifics are inaccurate. A few examples follow.

Jimson weed—*Datura stramonium* is another tropane alkaloid-containing plant. Dioscorides said of it: "The root being drunk with wine the quantity of a dram has the power to effect not unpleasant fantasies. But two drams being drunk make one beside himself for three days and four being drunk kill him."[30] In 1694, John Pechey wrote that with the seed of *Datura* powdered and mixed in beer, "wenches give half a dram of it to their lovers.... Some are so well skilled in dosing of it, that they can make men mad for as many hours as they please."[40]

Aconitum (wolfsbane, or monkshood), contains highly toxic alkaloids. Gerard reported that, "All these plants are hot and dry in the fourth degree, and of a most venomous quality....The symptoms that follow these that do eat of these deadly herbs are these; their lips and tongue swell forthwith, their eyes hang out, their thighs are stiff, and their wits are taken from them."[32]

Ricinus communis, or castor bean, is highly toxic, because of the protein ricin. This has a minimum lethal dose (MLD) of 0.1 mg/kg, making it one of the most toxic compounds known. Dioscorides knew it as Krotone kiki. He wrote that oil from seeds "is not to be eaten, but is useful for candles and plasters," but went on to say that "30 grains of beaten seeds drank for belly phlegm and choler etc.... They do also more vomiting, but the purging after this way is harsh and extemely laboursome, mightly overturning the stomach."[30]

Foxglove—*Digitalis purpurea*. *Digitalis* contains cardiac glycosides that cause cardiac arrhythmias, disturbed vision, and intestinal problems. The plant is important herbally, and its principles are still widely used therapeutically. Culpepper gave no warnings, but said:

> The herb is familiarly and frequently used by the Italians, to heal any fresh or green wounds, the leaves being but bruised and bound thereon; and the juice thereof is also used in old sores to cleanse, dry and heal them. The decoction hereof made up with some sugar or honey is available to cleanse and purge the body both upwards and downwards, sometimes of rough phlegm and clammy humours; and to open obstructions of the liver and spleen. It hath been found by experience to be available for the King's Evil [tuberculosis of the lymph glands]...A decoction of two handfuls thereof with four ounces of polypody in ale hath been found by late experience to cure divers of the falling sickness [epilepsy], that hath been troubled with it above twenty years. Myself am confident that an ointment of it is one of the best remedies for a scabby head there is.

Gerard similarly gave no warnings. He listed as the complete "vertues": "Foxgloves boiled in water or wine and drunken, doth cut and consume the thick toughness of gross and slimy phlegm and naughty humors; It opens also the stopping of the liver, spleen and milt, and of other inward parts."[32]

Nerium oleander is a Mediterranean plant containing agents, the oleandrines, with properties similar to those of the cardiac glycosides. The plant is the Nerion of Dioscorides, who wrote, "The flower and the leaves have a power destructive of dogs and of asses and mules and of most four-footed living creatures, but a preserving one of men, being drank with wine against the bitings of venemous beasts, ... but the weak sort of living creature, as goat and sheep, die, if they drink the maceration of them."[30]

The Opium Poppy—Papaver somniferum. The opium poppy is another well-recognized and widely used therapeutic drug. The Mekon agrios of Dioscorides, the poppy had soporific properties well known to that writer: "The leaves and the heads being sodden in water, and fomented on, cause sleep. And the decoction is drank against want of sleep.... A little of it ... is a pain easer and a sleep causer, and a digester, helping coughs, and coeliacall affections. But being drank too much, it hurts, making men lethargical and it kills ... it is a duller of the sight ... except it were adulterated they would be blind which were anointed with it."[30]

One example from the later herbalists will suffice. Gerard also described the uses of poppy, although the species he intends is unclear.

> The knobs or heads, which do especially prevail to move sleep ... opium, or the condensed juice of poppy heads, is strongest of all... opium somewhat too plentifully taken, doth also bring death ... It mitigates all kinds of

pains, but it leaves behind oftimes a mischief worse than the disease itself, and that hard to be cured, as a dead palsy and such like.... Eye medicines made with opium have been hurtful to many, insomuch that they have weakened the eyes and dulled the sight of those that have used it.... The heads of poppies boiled in water with a little sugar and drunk cause sleep ... [and]... ease the cough.[32]

Comfrey—Symphytum officinale. *Symphytum* species contains pyrrolizidine alkaloids, that taken in high doses acutely or in low doses chronically, produce liver disease and cancers. The root is especially high in toxic alkaloids. The plant has been used since classical times and, despite its well-recognized dangers,[10,18,41–46] is still sold across the United States for internal consumption. Chronic toxicities of the kind exhibited by comfrey users are the type most likely to go unrecognized by traditional herb-using cultures.

Culpepper's entry is too long to quote in full. However, he praised the plant as having many uses, but gave no warnings of toxicity. He wrote,

> The great comfrey helpeth those that spit blood, or make a bloody urine. The root boiled in water or wine, and the decoction drunk, helpeth all inward hurts, bruises and wounds, and ulcers of the lungs, causing the phlegm that oppresseth them to be easily spit forth. It stayeth ... the fluxes of blood or humours by the belly, womens immoderate courses, as well the reds as the whites [leucorrhea], and the running of the reins [kidneys].... A decoction of the leaves hereof is available to all the purposes, though not so effectual as the roots.

He then listed a variety of topical uses, with no mention of toxicity.[29]

As is usual, much of what Culpepper wrote is a paraphrase of the classical herbalists. Thus, Dioscorides had a long description of "sumphuton" (*Symphytum*), saying that among other properties it "provokes spittle... conglutinates new wounds, and makes to join together pieces of flesh...." He had no warnings of toxicity.[30]

Pechey wrote: "Tis used in all fluxes, especially of the belly; and for a consumption. The flowers boiled in red wine, are very proper for those that make a bloody urine."[40] Gerard noted: "The slimy substance of the root made in a posset of ale, and given to drink against the pain in the back gotten by ... overmuch use of women...does in four or five days presently cure the same, although the involuntary flowering of the seed in man be gotten thereby."[32] Otherwise he gave no warnings. The other herbalists, likewise, give no warnings of toxicity.

One should not lose sight of the impact that statements such as these, although couched in archaic language, still have. These antiquated uses are still being quoted by modern herbalists. Ody, for example, paraphrases Gerard on the uses of comfrey to treat overindulgence in sexual activity.[47]

Other pyrrolizidine alkaloid-containing herbs. The herbal literature shows similar ignorance of the hazards of a large number of other pyrrolizidine alkaloid-containing herbs. Of turnsole (*Heliotropium*) Culpepper, basically quoting Dioscorides on his Eliotropion mega, wrote that, "a good handful of this, boiled in water and drunk, purgeth both choler and phlegm, and boiled with cumin and drunk, helpeth the stone in the reins, kidney or bladder, provoketh urine and women's courses, and causes an easy and speedy delivery in childbirth."[29] *Heliotropium* has caused numerous poisonings because of its content of pyrrolizidine alkaloids.[48–52]

Senecio is yet another genus containing hepatotoxic pyrrolizidine alkaloids.[53–56] Dioscorides said of one *Senecio* (erigeron) that "being drank new, they cause strangling."[30] The text, however, is unclear as to the exact preparation involved. Culpepper wrote that "this herb... is as gallant an universal medicine for all diseases coming of heat, whatsoever they be, or in what part of the body soever they lie, as the sun shines upon. 'Tis very safe and friendly to the body of man...." He went on to list the diseases for which it is effective.[29]

Gerard hinted at a problem with *Senecio*, in that "boiled in ale with a little honey and vinegar, it provokes vomit, especially if you add thereto a few roots of asarabacca."[32]

Of *S. cineraria*, the same author reported that "women troubled with hysteria are much eased by baths made of the leaves and flowers hereof."[32]

Tussilago farfara or coltsfoot is yet another pyrrolizidine alkaloid-containing herb.[6,57] Dioscorides listed the traditional uses of it, under the name bechion, but neither he nor subsequent herbalists gave information on toxicity.[30]

Terpene-containing herbs. Terpenes comprise a large group of natural products, many with toxic actions on the liver, central nervous system, or other organ systems. As one would anticipate, few of these toxic actions are recognized in the traditional herbal literature.

Mentha pulegium, or pennyroyal, is still being used for "women's troubles." In particular, it has a reputation as an emmenagogue and abortifacient. Unfortunately, it contains pulegone, a terpene, that can cause severe liver damage or neurotoxicity, particularly if taken with other potentially hepatotoxic agents, such as the over-the-counter medication acetaminophen. Its uses are ancient. Dioscorides said of *M. pulegium* (glechon) that "being drank it expells the menstrua and the embrya." He gave no warnings.[30] Pechey, likewise, advocated it for women: " 'Tis used to provoke the courses, and to help delivery. 'Tis good for the coughs, for the gripes, the stone, jaundice and dropsy...excellent remedy for whopping cough."[40] The other herbalists followed suit: Culpepper said that "being boiled and drunk, it provoketh women's courses, and expelleth the dead child and afterbirth, and stayeth the disposition to vomit.... Being given in wine, it helpeth the falling sickness.... It is very effectual for the cough, being boiled in milk, and drunk."[29] Gerard reported similarly about abortion and menses, again without indication of potential problems.[32]

Artemisia (wormwood) species, also contain terpenes. *A. absinthium* contains the convulsant and excitatory agents thujone, camphor, pinene, and menthol. This plant was one of the active ingredients in the drink absinthe, banned in Western European countries since the beginning of the century for its supposed role in causing absinthism.[58–61] Dioscorides knew *A. absinthium* as apsinthim: "We do not allow of it in potions, it being bad for the stomach, and causing headache."[30] Culpepper, alluding to the reason for its common English name, wrote in a rare critical vein that, "the seed of this wormwood is that which women usually give their children for the worms.... Of all wormwoods that grow here, this is the weakest; but doctors recommend it, and apothecaries sell it; the one must keep his credit, and the other get money, and that's the key of the work. The herb is good for something, because God made nothing in vain." He continued with a long entry for this and other wormwoods.[29] According to Pechey: "It strengthens the stomach and liver, excites appetite, opens obstruction, and curse diseases that are occasioned by them; as, the jaundice, dropsy, and the like. 'Tis good in long putrid fevers ... it expels worms from the bowels."[40] Added Dodoens: "if it be taken fasting in the morning it preserveth from drunkeness that day."[33]

Teucrium, or germander, contains the diterpenoid clerodanes, which serve to deter feeding on the plant. Germander was recently responsible for a series of poisonings reported from Europe.[5,62] This herb also escapes warnings in the herbal literature. Germander was listed in Dioscorides as polion, or skordion. He gave no information on safety.[30] Neither did Gerard[32] or the other metaphrastic herbalists.

Equisetum/Ephedra. Another problem with the herbal literature is that sometimes there is difficulty in establishing the identity (genus or species) of the plant under discussion. One example is the long-lived confusion between *Ephedra* and *Equisetum,* similarly appearing but quite different plants. Old-world *Ephedra* contain the sympathomimetic alkaloid ephedrine. *E. sinica* is the ma huang of Traditional Chinese Medicine. *Equisetum,* or horsetail, is a silicon-accumulating genus typically found growing along streams. These plants are also known as horsetail, horsegrass or shavegrass.

Dioscorides described a plant, Ippouris. Goodyear translates Dioscorides' Ippouris as *Equisetum*: "The juice of it does stop fluxes of blood which comes from the nostrils and being drank with wine, it helps dysentryes: it moves the urine also. But being beaten small and sprinkled on it closes bleeding wounds. Both the root and the herb do help the tussicall [coughing], and orthopnoicall [breathing]."[30] This description is similar to the one given by Pliny the Elder for the same plant, which "some call hippuris, others ephedron, others anabasis." He continued: "for cough, asthma and colic, it is given pounded in a dark-red, dry wine.... So wonderful is its nature, its mere touch stanches a patient's bleeding.... Its juice, kept in the nostrils, checks hemorrhage therefrom, and it also checks looseness of the bowels.... It promotes passage of urine, and cures cough and orthopnoea."[63]

These are perfect descriptions of the action of ephedrine. However, the properties are ascribed to *Equisetum*, and the illustrations given are clearly this plant and not an *Ephedra*.[30,63]

Gerard continues the confusion, writing that the plant is "of great and singular virtue in healing wounds.... The herb drunk either with water or wine is an excellent remedy against bleeding at the nose and other fluxes of blood. . . . Roots boiled in wine is very profitable for the ulcers of the kidneys and bladder, the cough and difficulties of breathing."[32] The drawings Gerard gives of *Equisetum* are readily recognizable as such. However, he lists *Ephedra* as a synonym for one horsegrass. The same confusion continues through the herbal literature, including the herbals of Dodoens[33] and Parkinson.[64]

CONCLUSIONS

In general, Culpepper had little to say about herbal toxicity or contraindications. He showed awareness of acute toxicity, but not of delayed actions such as alkaloid-induced liver damage. In these regards, his herbal was consistent with those of the other classical and medieval herbalists. It can be concluded that the herbal literature derives from societies that differed from modern Western societies in the following ways:

1. Mortality expectations and disease patterns differed. Life expectancies were much shorter; chronic conditions, such as parasitism, were endemic; and infectious diseases were much more significant.
2. Available medical treatments were much more limited than the ones available today. Common treatments, such as bleeding, were largely without efficacy; there were few ways of combating epidemic diseases such as the plague, which decimated the population of London in the 1660s; and conventional health care was economically beyond the means of much of the population.
3. The expectations of treatment were different. There was, for example, an emphasis on treating symptoms rather than causes. If the symptom, such as the lesion in gonorrhea, was cleared, the treatment was judged to be successful.
4. The acceptability of risk was higher. In a society in which life expectancy was approximately 45 years, it was immaterial if an agent being taken by a 40 year old carried a high risk of cancer in 20 years' time. Such a risk would be of considerable concern today. Severe side effects were an accepted part of therapy, as exemplified by the heavy metal treatments for venereal disease, which produced loss of teeth.

An examination of the herbal literature allows some conclusions to be drawn on the issue of safety.

1. These extracts should provide sufficient indication that herbalists copied extensively from each other over periods of thousands of years.
2. Information concerning acute toxicity is often accurate, even though the plants were still recommended for uses that today we would consider frankly dangerous.
3. Information that is accurate by modern standards is often mixed inextricably with nonsense, misconceptions, and other inaccuracies.
4. The identities of the plants are sometimes dubious, as regards both genus and species.
5. Information is missing on plants producing cumulative toxicity, or toxicity in which symptoms are delayed following plant ingestion.

A historical perspective yields only slight evidentiary value as to herbal safety. Much of the information recorded over the centuries is repetitive, deriving from authority rather than observation. Typically, the diseases and disease classifications around which herbal use is discussed differ from the diseases and disease classifications used by conventional medicine today. Furthermore, the expectations of earlier users for medicine and therapy differ from modern expectations.

REFERENCES

1. Anastassiades E, Wilson R, Stewart JS, et al. Fatal brain oedema due to accidental water intoxication. *Br Med J* 287:1181–1182, 1983.
2. Lipsitz DJ. Herbal teas and water intoxication in a young child. *J Fam Pract* 18:933–937, 1984.
3. Swanson AG, Iseri OA. Acute encephalopathy due to water intoxication. *N Engl J Med* 258:831–834, 1958.
4. Demanet JC, Bonnyns M, Bleiberg H, et al. Coma due to water intoxication in beer drinkers. *Lancet* ii:1115–1117, 1971.
5. Larrey D, Vial T, Pauwels A, et al. Hepatitis after germander (*Teucrium chamaedrys*) administration: Another instance of herbal medicine hepatotoxicity. *Ann Int Med* 117:129–132, 1992.
6. Roulet M, Laurin R, Rivier L, et al. Hepatic veno-occlusive disease in newborn infant of a woman drinking herbal tea. *J Pediatr* 112:433–436, 1988.
7. Cairns J. *Accomplishments in Cancer Research*, 1985, Fortner JG, and Rhoads JE, eds. Philadelphia: J.B. Lippincott, 1986, pp. 88–105.

8. Chiang CL. *Life Tables and Mortality Analysis.* Geneva: WHO, 1978.
9. Fries JF, Crapo LM. *Vitality and Aging: Implications of the Rectangular Curve.* San Francisco: W.H. Freeman, 1981.
10. National Geographic Society (U.S.). *Atlas of the World.* Washington, D.C.: National Geographic Society, 1992.
11. Datta DV, Khuroo MS, Mattocks AR, et al. Herbal medicines and veno-occlusive disease in India. *Postgrad Med J* 54:511–515, 1978.
12. Gorey JD, Wahlqvist ML, Boyce NW. Adverse reaction to a Chinese herbal remedy. *Med J Australia* 157:484–486, 1992.
13. Jones D, Egger T. Use of herbs containing natural source ephedrine alkaloids in weight loss programmes. *Int J Obesity* 17(Suppl. 1):S81, 1993.
14. Awang DVC, Dawson BA, Kindack DG. Parthenolide content of feverfew (*Tanacetum parthenium*) assessed by HPLC and 1H-NMR spectroscopy. *J Nat Prod* 54:1516–1521, 1991.
15. Heptinstall S, Awang DVC, Dawson BA, et al. Parthenolide content and bioactivity of feverfew (*Tanacetum parthenium* [L.] Schultz-Bip.): Estimation of commercial and authenticated feverfew products. *J Pharm Pharmacol* 44:391–395, 1992.
16. Huxtable RJ. Human health implications of pyrrolizidine alkaloids and herbs containing them. In: Cheeke PR, ed. *Toxicants of Plant Origin: Vol I. Alkaloids.* Boca Raton, FL: CRC Press, 1989, pp. 41–86.
17. Huxtable RJ. The harmful potential of herbal and other plant products. *Drug Safety* 5(Suppl. 1):126–136, 1990.
18. Huxtable RJ. The toxicology of alkaloids in foods and herbs. In: Tu AT, ed., *Handbook of Natural Toxins: Vol. 7. Food Poisoning.* New York: Marcel Dekker, 1992, pp. 237–262.
19. Huxtable RJ. The myth of beneficent nature: The risks of herbal preparations. *Ann Int Med* 117:165–166, 1992.
20. Huxtable RJ. Neurotoxins in herbs and plant foods. In: Isaacson RL, Jensen KF, eds. *The Vulnerable Brain and Environmental Risks: Vol. I. Malnutrition and Hazard Assessment.* New York: Plenum Publishing, 1992, pp. 77–108.
21. Huxtable RJ. Regulatory, legislative and other issues pertaining to dietary supplements. In: *Regulation of Dietary Supplements.* Washington, D.C.: U.S. Government Printing Office, 1994, pp. 167–173.
22. Huxtable RJ, Luthy J, Zweifel V. Toxicity of comfrey-pepsin preparations. *N Engl J Med* 315:1095, 1986.
23. Wiltshire J. *Samuel Johnson in the Medical World: The Doctor and the Patient.* Cambridge, U.K.: Cambridge University, 1991, pp. x–293.
24. Hutchens AR. *Indian Herbology of North America.* Windsor, Ontario: Merco, 1983.
25. Santillo H. *Natural Healing With Herbs.* Prescott Valley, AZ: Hohm Press, 1984.
26. Christopher JR. *School of Natural Healing.* Springsfield, UT: Christopher Publications, 1976.
27. Spoerke DG. *Herbal Medications.* Santa Barbara, CA: Woodbridge Press, 1980.
28. Dahanukar S, Thatte U. *Ayurveda Revisited.* Bombay: Popular Prakashan Pvt. 1989, pp. 1–159.
29. Culpepper N. *The English Physician Enlarged, With Three Hundred and Sixty Nine Medicines Made of English Herbs.* London: A. and J. Churchill, 1708.
30. Dioscorides. *The Greek Herbal of Dioscorides, Englished by John Goodyer, AD 1655.* Oxford: Oxford University, 1934.
31. *The Family Physician: A Manual of Domestic Medicine*, vol. III. London: Cassell and Co. 1884, pp. 577–880.
32. Gerard J. *The Herbal or Generall Historie of Plantes.* London: John Norton, 1597.
33. Dodoens DR. *A Niewe Herball or Historie of Plantes* (trans. from French by Henry Lyte). London: Gerard Dewes, 1578.
34. Coles W. *Adam in Eden, or Nature's Paradise: The History of Plants, Fruits, Herbs and Flowers.* London: C. J. Streater, 1657.
35. Duke JA. *CRC Handbook of Medicinal Herbs.* Boca Raton, FL: CRC Press, 1985, pp. 1–677.
36. Gerard J. *The Herball or Generall Historie of Plantes.* London: Norton and Whitakers, 1636.
37. Majno G. *The Healing Hand: Man and Wound in the Ancient World.* Boston, MA: Harvard University, 1977, pp. xxvi–571.
38. Hunt T. *Plant Names of Medieval England.* Cambridge: D. S. Brewer, 1989, pp. lvi–334.
39. Grigson G. *The Englishman's Flora.* London: Folio, 1987, pp. 1–478.
40. Pechey J. *The Compleat Herbal of Physical Plants.* London: Henry Bonwicke, 1694.
41. Bach N, Thung SN, Schaffner F. Comfrey herb tea-induced hepatic veno-occlusive disease. *Amer J Med* 87:97–99, 1989.
42. Huxtable RJ, Awang DVC. Pyrrolizidine poisoning. *Amer J Med* 89:547–548, 1990.
43. Mattocks AR. Toxic pyrrolizidine alkaloids in comfrey. *Lancet* ii:1136, 1980.
44. Ridker PM, Ohkuma S, McDermott WV, et al. Hepatic veno-occlusive disease associated with the consumption of pyrrolizidine-containing dietary supplements. *Gastroenterology* 88:1050–1054, 1985.
45. Weston CFM, Cooper BT, Davies JD, et al. Veno-occlusive disease of the liver secondary to ingestion of comfrey. *Br Med J* 295:183, 1987.
46. Yeong ML, Swinburn B, Kennedy M, et al. Hepatic veno-occlusive disease associated with comfrey ingestion. *J Gastroenterol Hepatol* 5:211–214, 1990.
47. Ody P. *The Complete Medicinal Herbal.* London: Dorling Kindersley, 1993: pp. 1–192.
48. Chauvin P, Dillon J-C, Moren A, et al. Heliotrope poisoning in Tadjikistan. *Lancet* 341:1663, 1993.
49. Culvenor CCJ, Edgar JA, Smith LW, et al. *Heliotropium lasiocarpum* Fisch and Mey identified as cause of veno-occlusive disease due to a herbal tea. *Lancet* i:978, 1986.
50. Mayer F, Lüthy J. Heliotrope poisoning in Tadjikistan. *Lancet* 342:246–247, 1993.
51. Tandon BN, Tandon RK, Tandon HD, et al. An epidemic of veno-occlusive disease of liver in central India. *Lancet* ii:271–272, 1976.

52. Tandon HD, Tandon BN, Mattocks AR. An epidemic of veno-occlusive disease of the liver in Afghanistan. *Am J Gastroenterol* 70:607–613, 1978.
53. Delaveau P, Ferry S, Barbagelatta M, et al. *Senecio vulgaris* L. (compositae) liver toxicity. *Ann Pharm Fr* 37(1-2):13–20, 1979.
54. Fox DW, Hart MC, Bergeson PS, et al. Pyrrolizidine (Senecio) intoxication mimicking Reye's syndrome. *J Pediatr* 93:980–982, 1978.
55. Margalith D, Heraief E, Schindler AM, et al. Veno-occlusive disease of the liver due to the use of tea made from Senecio plants: A report of two cases. *J Hepatol* 1(Suppl. 2):S280, 1985.
56. Willmot FC, Robertson GW. Senecio disease, or cirrhosis of the liver due to senecio poisoning. *Lancet* ii, October 23, 848–849, 1920.
57. Hirono I, Mori H, Culvenor CCJ. Carcinogenic activity of coltsfoot, *Tussilago farfara* L. *Gann Monograph Cancer Res* 67:125–129, 1976.
58. Arnold WN. Absinthe. *Sci Am* June 1989, pp. 112–117.
59. Max B. This and that: Cheap drinks and expensive drugs. *Trends Pharmacol Sci* 11:56–60, 1990.
60. Vogt DD. Absinthium: A nineteenth-century drug of abuse. *J Ethnopharmacol* 4:337–342, 1981.
61. Vogt DD, Montagne M. Absinthe: Behind the emerald mask. *Int J Addictions* 17:1015–1029, 1982.
62. Mostefa-Kara N, Pauwels A, Pines E, et al. Fatal hepatitis after herbal tea. *Lancet* 340:674, 1992.
63. Pliny the Elder. *Natural History*, vol. 8. Boston, MA: Harvard University, 1953.
64. Parkinson J. *Theatrum Botanicum: The Theater of Plants, or An Herball of a Large Extent.* London: T. Cotes, 1640.

The Information Base for Safety Assessment of Botanicals

DENNIS V.C. AWANG, Ph.D., F.C.I.C.

Data on safety/toxicity of botanicals may derive from a variety of sources in many guises and involve the practice of a range of scientific disciplines in addition to traditional reputation and anecdotal testimony. However, regardless of the character of safety/toxicity information, the element of paramount importance must be a confident determination of the botanical identity of the material in question.

As things stand today, to the best of my knowledge, no program of certification of botanical identity has yet been instituted, either nationally or internationally, such as was proposed in the World Health Organization (WHO) *Guidelines for the Assessment of Herbal Medicines.*[1]

Authoritative documentation of botanical identity at the grower/supplier end is unquestionably the most effective means of promoting accuracy and consistency of the botanical character of commercial plant products. In the absence of such authentication and certification frameworks, inordinate reliance must be placed on chemical identification, physical identification being well-nigh impossible from formulated products. In view of the fact that nature rarely provides plant species with uniquely characterizing chemical constituents, identification of plant source can usually only be had on the basis of markers and/or chromatographic/spectroscopic profiles. This can be daunting and dodgy work indeed. The challenge of confirming the presence of chaparral in recent cases of hepatotoxicity that implicated products purported to contain the plant are instructive in this regard; determination of any constituent(s) of the actual product responsible for the observed adverse effect elevates the scientific challenge up a notch. An unequivocal answer on either count, to my mind, has not yet been given.

A plethora of adverse reactions to purported plant products are subject to question on account of a lack of assurance of botanical identity. Indeed, many medical publications seem to be not at all concerned with establishing the botanical identity of such materials. Ryan J. Huxtable, Ph.D., Professor, Department of Pharmacology, College of Medicine, University of Arizona, Tucson, and I had occasion a few years ago to write to a medical journal[2] in opposition to the view expressed by some physicians that the symptoms of veno-occlusive disease (VOD)[3]* are now so clearly defined and recognizable that one need not know the identity of the offending unsaturated pyrrolizidine alkaloid (UPA)–containing species.

The fact is, however, that UPAs are generally recognized to vary significantly in toxic potential: Borage (*Borago officinalis*) herbage contains an extremely low level of PA (2–10 ppm), the leaves containing mainly the moderate- to low-toxic lycopsamine (a monoesterified dihydroxyretronecine) along with traces of amabiline (an ester of hydroxyretronecine); the only alkaloid so far detected in borage flowers is the *nontoxic* saturated PA, thesinine, which was also the only alkaloid found in immature seed: Mature seed contained thesinine and amabiline in a ratio of 10:1. No pyrrolizidine alkaloids have so far been detected in borage seed oil, which is widely available as a source of essential fatty acids. Only the leaves of borage ought to even be considered for assessment of toxic risk and a very low level of health hazard should be expected. However, the European com-

---

President, MediPlant, Ottawa, Ontario, Canada.
*VOD graphically exemplifies the type of delayed, cumulative cryptic damage that can result from chronic ingestion of even very low levels of certain poisonous substances. The condition was only recognized in 1957 by scientists at the University of the West Indies in Jamaica associated with consumption of a bush tea including *Senecio* and perhaps *Crotalaria* species as well.

munity (EC) included borage (herb and flowers) in a list of herbal remedies withdrawn for safety reasons. Yet many articles in respected journals and textbooks lump borage in with the highly toxic *Senecio*, *Crotalaria*, *Heliotropium*, and *Symphytum* species. And *Packera candidissima*[4] is being widely consumed in Mexico and the southwestern United States, while containing the most noxious type of hepatotoxic UPA, the macrocyclic diesterified alkaloids, which must surely be wreaking havoc, particularly among the juvenile populations of communities in those areas. This plant is as yet unregulated on both sides of the border!

In 1990, an infant's death in Switzerland was attributed to its mother consuming, during pregnancy, a herbal tea containing coltsfoot (*Tussilago farfara*). It was later claimed that the tea also contained butterbur (*Petasites officinalis*). Both plants are known to contain significant levels of toxic UPA.

The case of comfrey provides another good example of scientific miscarriage. Occasionally one encounters the charge that comfrey is carcinogenic. Comfrey, however, can be represented by different *Symphytum* species, most usually by *S. officinale* (common comfrey) and *S.* x *uplandicum* (Russian comfrey), a hybrid of *S. officinale* and *S. asperum* (prickly comfrey). In 1968, Furuya and Araki[5] published the results of a study indicating that comfrey was carcinogenic in rats. However, because of confusion of species designation, many readers and subsequent writers on the subject have propagated the idea that common comfrey (*S. officinale*) has been demonstrated to be carcinogenic in rats. Many people now share the conviction that the Japanese toxicologists were actually testing Russian comfrey (*S.* x *uplandicum*), which is widely recognized to be a more toxic species. In fact, because of its high content of echimidine, arguably the most toxic *Symphytum* PA, the UPA was deemed to be an adulterant in an amendment to the Canadian Food and Drug Act and Regulations. Later the general recognition of noxious potential of all *Symphytum* species led to a prohibition by Germany and other countries against ingestion of all types of comfrey, permitting only external use of comfrey products on unbroken skin.

The case involving germander, skullcap, and valerian illustrates the difficulty and attendant confusion that may result when one tries to adduce the botanical culprit(s) responsible for an observed adverse effect. There seems to be a pervasive tendency on the part of medical researchers to accept as gospel what the manufacturer declares to be the contents on the label of an herbal preparation. In 1989, a report appeared in the *British Medical Journal* concerning hepatotoxicity associated with consumption of herbal remedies.[6] Considering the listed plant components, the authors narrowed the list of possible culprits to skullcap (*Scuttelaria* spp.) and valerian (*Valeriana officinalis*). Noting that "there are no reports to date suggesting any toxic effects from oral ingestion of skullcap," the authors indicted valerian, because some of its chemical constituents (iridoid ester epoxides) had been shown to be "powerful alkylating agents capable of inhibiting incorporation of thymidine radio-labeled with carbon-14 into the DNA of certain carcinoma cells." The noted hepatotoxicity is more likely to have been due to germander (*Teucrium* spp.), substituted for skullcap. Germander, recognized as a common substitute for skullcap and implicated in a fatality and numerous cases of hepatotoxicity, is now widely prohibited from sale, and has been the subject of a WHO alert. A recent French study with mice has demonstrated the development of liver-cell necrosis after 24 hours following treatment of test animals with either a tea extract or a furano *neo*-clerodane terpenoid fraction.[7]

The sullying of the reputation of chamomile and the ginseng slur associated with the infamous "hairy baby" story are two glaring examples of the miscarriage of toxicity assessment of herbals by medical practitioners. The threat of anaphylactic shock attributed to chamomile was generated by an article in *The Medical Letter*, entitled "Toxic Reactions to Plant Products Sold in Health Food Stores,"[8] which warned consumers who are allergic to any member of the Compositae (Asteraceae) family to avoid teas made from chamomile and other such plants commonly used to make beverages. However, the paper cited therein, inflammatorily entitled "Anaphylactic Reaction to Chamomile Tea,"[9] cites neither genus nor species of the purported chamomile material implicated in the single case reported: a 35-year-old female who suffered from ragweed hayfever and developed anaphylaxis following ingestion of a single cup of the purported chamomile tea. Interestingly, the authors of this publication cited two cases of contact dermatitis caused by chamomile in support of their case; surprisingly, the first[10] deals with *An-*

themis cotula as a skin irritant, while the second[11] treats contact dermatitis caused by oil of clove—and oil of "chamomile tea (*Anthemis cotula*)"! Further, the former study explicitly reveals the results of a comparison between *Anthemis cotula* and *Matricaria chamomilla*. Of twelve normal people tested with these two plants "as purchased from the druggist," *all had marked 24-hour and delayed reactions to the first species and none reacted to the second.*

While there have been about 50 reports that refer to allergic reactions associated with "chamomile" contact, in only five cases does a formal botanical identification allow association of the most common commercial chamomile, *Matricaria recutita,* formerly *M. chamomilla, Chamomilla recutita* (German or Hungarian chamomile), with the observed reactions: Experimental studies in guinea pigs demonstrated only a low sensitizing capacity for this plant. The overwhelming majority of cases involved *Anthemis cotula* (stinking mayweed, Dog's chamomile, Dog fennel), which contains a much higher level of the highly toxic sesquiterpene lactone, anthecotulid, which proved to be responsible for commonly observed primary irritant contact dermatitis.[12] Finally, Hausen et al.[12] pointed out that the report of *M. chamomilla* containing anthecotulid in a concentration of up to 7.3 percent was erroneous because the investigated specimen of "*Matricaria*" had been wrongly identified: Examination of a voucher specimen lodged in the herbarium of the University of Texas at Austin revealed the plant to be *Anthemis cotula*!

A letter published in a 1990 issue of the *Journal of the American Medical Association (JAMA)*[13] described a case of neonatal/maternal androgenization (profuse growth of hair on the face, head, and pubic regions of mother and child) that was attributed to the mother's consumption of Siberian ginseng (*Eleutherococcus senticosus*), more properly termed eleuthero. The authors of the *JAMA* letter did not distinguish between Siberian ginseng and real ginseng (*Panax* spp.), and even cited information on the effects of *Panax*. However neither *Panax* spp. nor so-called Siberian ginseng appeared likely to have caused the observed androgenization. In fact, the product turned out to be *Periploca sepium* (Chinese silk vine), a common substitute for eleuthero on the U.S. market. A number of products distributed across Canada were made from Siberian ginseng obtained from the same supplier and all turned out to be *Periploca*. To add to the confusion, one of these products was found to have been sold not as Siberian ginseng (which it was supposed to be) nor as *Periploca* (which it actually was) but as "*Panax* ginseng."[14]

The presence of tropane alkaloid-containing plants is illustrative of poor quality control, producing symptoms distinctive enough not to be associated with the purported plants indicated on herbal packaging. Such adulteration has led to medical treatment for consumers of purported mallow (*Malva sylvestris*), burdock (*Arctium lappa*), comfrey (*Symphytum* spp.), and nettle (*Urtica dioica*),[15] all most likely deadly nightshade (*Atropa belladonna*). To the best of my knowledge, the hallucinations and other distinctive symptoms have never been attributed to the purported relatively innocuous plant materials. Symptoms of tropane-alkaloid poisoning could be due to the presence of other plants, such as *Hyoscyamus niger* (black henbane) and *Datura stramonium* (jimsonweed or thornapple), but these can usually be differentiated on the basis of *hyoscyamine* (atropine) content. Recently, northern Tanzanian farmers exhibited symptoms of tropane-alkaloid poisoning after consuming chapattis (flat bread) made of the wheat from their small local fields: *Datura stramonium*, a common weed in the area was implicated.[16]

A recent case involving feverfew provides an interesting example for conjecture regarding safety assessment of botanicals. A medical practitioner in British Columbia had a patient who had suffered frontal-lobe damage and was being maintained on Prozac® as well as being treated with Imitrex® for migraine headache. In view of the expense of Imitrex® medication and concern about possible cardiac side effects, the patient took the suggestion that she switch from Imitrex® to the natural migraine prophylactic feverfew (*Tanacetum parthenium*). The doctor and the pharmacist at the establishment from which the patient procured her supply of feverfew, believed that the severe suicidal episode that the patient suffered shortly after commencement of her feverfew treatment was a direct result of the natural medication. Consultation of the product package insert, which propounded the antiserotonin theory, reinforced that conviction, based on the established ability of feverfew extracts and the constituent sesquiterpene lactone, parthenolide, to inhibit the release of serotonin from blood platelets in vitro. While recognizing that such activity currently provides the most plausible and widely accepted theory of the effectiveness of feverfew leaf in migraine prevention, it must be acknowledged that no in vivo studies have yet demonstrated reduction of plasma levels of serotonin, or in any other way verified this mechanism of feverfew effectiveness in migraine prophylaxis. It would therefore seem premature to implicate the plant product as responsible for this apparent adverse reaction in so clearly a complex situation—and to make a judgement of health risk on the basis of a single such case.

Incidentally, the pharmacy promptly removed from its shelves all packages of the product Tanacet 125, the first in modern times to be granted a Drug Identification Number (DIN) in Canada for a specific therapeutic application. The distributor of the product has been issuing a warning against the use of the product by those suffering depression or afflicted with other serotonin-sensitive disorders. One can be reasonably confident of the identity of the plant constituting Tanacet 125; the plants originally supplied to the manufacturer were certified by a botanical authority; and a sample of raw material submitted to the Drugs Directorate of Canada's Health Protection Branch had been tested for content of parthenolide, the putative active principle, and found to exceed the prescribed minimum percentage content (0.2 percent) comfortably. Had the situation of *all* other herbal preparations obtained, one would have had much less assurance of botanical identity or chemical character. At least two other chemotypes of feverfew have been recognized, both of which contain no parthenolide.[17]

Both ends of the formulation spectrum need to be characterized—botanical and chemical—for one to be able to make confident and meaningful assessment of safety. Species confirmation is not entirely adequate, since the possibility of infraspecific variation requires that secondary metabolite profiles be assessed and distinguishing constituents identified.

Canada no longer performs analysis of material provided by applicants for DIN registration of herbal products and has no program for testing the identity, quality, and potency of commerical natural products. Manufacturers operate on a veritable honor system, largely dependent on in-house botanical-chemical knowledge, and an ability to discern their need for expert assistance, whether scientific or technologic. This ability would seem also to be a particularly desirable quality in the operatives of regulatory agencies.

REFERENCES

1. Akerele O. WHO guidelines for the assessment of herbal medicines. *HerbalGram* 28:3–20, 1993.
2. Huxtable RJ, Awang DVC. Pyrrolizidine poisoning. *Am J Med* 89:547, 1990.
3. Stuart KL, Bras G. Veno-occlusive disease of the liver. *Q J Med-New Series XXVI* 103:291–315, 1957.
4. Bah M, Bye R, Pereda-Miranda R. Hepatotoxic pyrrolizidine alkaloids in the Mexican medicinal plant *Packera candidissima* (Asteraceae: Senecioneae). *J Ethnopharm* 43:19–30, 1994.
5. Furuya S, Araki T, Araki K. Studies on constituents of new drugs: I. Alkaloids of *Symphytum officinale* LINN. *Chem Pharm Bull* 16:2512–2515, 1968.
6. MacGregor FB, Abernethy VE, Dahabra S, et al. Hepatotoxicity of herbal remedies. *Br Med J* 299:1156–1157, 1989.
7. Lowper J, Descatoriis V, Letteron P, et al. Hepatotoxicity of germander in mice. *Gastroenterology* 106:464–472, 1994.
8. Toxic reactions to plant products sold in health food stores. *The Medical Letter* 21:29–32, 1979.
9. Benner MH, Lee HJ. Anaphylactic reaction to chamomile tea. *J Allergy Clin Immunol* 52:307–308, 1973.
10. Rowe AH. Chamomile (*Anthemis cotula*) as a skin irritant. *J Allergy* 5:383–388, 1934.
11. Sternberg L. Contact dermatitis: Cases caused by oil of cloves and by oil of chamomile tea (*Anthemis cotula*). *J Allergy* 8:185–186, 1937.
12. Hausen BM, Busker E, Carle R. The sensitizing capacity of composite plants. *Planta Medica* 34:229–234, 1984.
13. Koren G, Randor S, Martin S, et al. Maternal ginseng use associated with neonatal androgenization. *JAMA* 264(22): 2866, 1990.
14. Awang DVC. Recalling the case of the hairy baby. *Natural Health Products Report* [Canada] 3:18–19, 1994.
15. Farnsworth NR. Relative safety of herbal medicines. *HerbalGram* 29:36A–36H, 1993.
16. Van Mears A, Cohen A, Edelbroek P. Atropine poisoning after eating chapattis contaminated with *Datura stramonium* (Thornapple) *Roy Soc Trop Med Hyg* 14:271, 1995.
17. Awang DVC. Feverfew fever. *HerbalGram* 29:34, 1993.

Safety Monitoring of Botanicals by Government Agencies

LORI A. LOVE, M.D., Ph.D.

This paper focuses on the scientific and regulatory aspects that are considered when evaluating the safety of botanical products. The safety evaluation of any regulated product is a composite of a number of assessments that depend in part upon the intended use of the botanical product. Products intended for use in the diagnosis, cure, mitigation, treatment, or prevention of a disease or condition are regulated as drugs; otherwise, botanical products may be categorized as foods or cosmetics, depending upon the use of the products.

The types of data used to evaluate safety for these different types of products are similar, but the degree of substantiation required may differ among these product categories (drugs, foods, cosmetics). These data may include the results of basic research (in vitro and animal studies), as well as human clinical trials that are specifically designed to assess the safety of a particular product under the intended conditions of use. Although human clinical trials are an important mechanism by which to evaluate the safety and effectiveness of a product, available clinical trials have recognized limitations: Most trials involve too few subjects, administration of a product for too short a duration, and inadequate long-term follow-up to address all safety issues fully. In addition, the population for which the product is intended may differ in demographics or other variables (including gender, age, race, ethnic origin, concurrent diseases, or usage of other medications) from the population in which the product was tested. Because of these limitations, rare or chronic adverse events that are associated with the use of a product will typically not be detected during premarket clinical trials.

An increasingly important mechanism by which we gain information about adverse reactions associated with the use of products, including botanicals, is via postmarketing surveillance. In most cases that concern botanical products, this surveillance is passive, meaning that it relies on voluntary reporting of adverse events. Passive systems have recognized limitations but can provide useful warnings of unusual or rare conditions.

These adverse events can be reported by a variety of mechanisms and to various groups with interests in public health, including the Food and Drug Administration (FDA), the Centers for Disease Control and Prevention (CDC), and state and local health agencies. Information about the events may be published as case reports in medical journals. In efforts to increase the usefulness of information reported on adverse reactions, the FDA has instituted the MedWatch program for health care provider reporting of adverse events or product problems associated with regulated products, including botanicals. MedWatch also receives and processes reports of adverse events or product problems from the manufacturers of regulated products. The goals of MedWatch are to increase health care providers' awareness of the occurrence of such problems, to facilitate the reporting of serious adverse events to the FDA, and to communicate to the health care community any subsequent actions taken related to such products. A number of mechanisms, including electronic submissions, are available to facilitate reporting of adverse events.

Office of Special Nutritionals, Center for Food Safety and Applied Nutrition, U.S. Food and Drug Administration, Washington, DC.

Safety Monitoring of Medicinal Plants in Europe (With Special Reference to Germany)

BARBARA STEINHOFF, Ph.D.

Herbal remedies are fully recognized as medicines under the German Drug Law, which is based on the European Directive 65/65/EEC. They are medicinal products containing as active ingredients only plants, parts of plants or plant materials, or combinations thereof, whether in the crude or processed state. For this reason, "phytomedicines" might be a better expression than "herbal remedies."

In accordance with the German Drug Law, the same regulations of pharmacovigilance and reporting mechanisms are applicable to botanicals as to chemical substances.

Each company that is marketing drugs is obliged to nominate a person with expert knowledge and the reliability necessary for exercising his or her function as the so-called "Commissioner of the Graduated Plan." He or she is responsible for the collection and evaluation of information on drug risks that become known and for coordination of necessary measures. He or she is also responsible for meeting the obligations to notify the authorities in case of drug risks. The proof of expert knowledge is given by university examination in either human medicine, veterinary medicine, or pharmaceutics. The competent authority is informed of this person's qualification.

Each company has established a system of collecting information on adverse reactions in order to guarantee that the Commissioner of the Graduated Plan is able to evaluate the reports to decide which measures have to be undertaken. Possible sources of reports are physicians, pharmacists, patients, and health authorities. The timeliness of response depends on the severity of the case. Possible response measures include additional information in the package leaflet (contraindications, side effects, special warnings), restriction in indication fields, restriction in package size, switch from over-the-counter to prescription status (by legal regulation), and withdrawal of a batch (e.g., in case of quality problems) or of the whole product. Furthermore, the Commissioner of the Graduated Plan is obliged to notify the health authorities and to provide all information available in case of a possible relationship between drug application and adverse event. Notification, either nationally or internationally, has to be submitted to the Bundesgesundheitsamt, the German health authority, or to the Council of International Organizations on Medical Science.

In case of risks, a follow-up procedure will be established by the Authority. This so-called Graduated Plan is also regulated by law. In this plan, the cooperation between the authorities and the companies is specified and the various measures and information means and channels are determined. There are two stages of a Graduated Plan Procedure. During stage I, exchange of information on risks of a substance or a product occurs between the Authority and the companies; in stage II, specified measures are announced by the Authority.

Current examples in the field of phytomedicines include:

1. The procedure concerning pyrrolizidine alkaloid plants, finalized in 1992, and
2. The current procedure concerning plant products containing anthraquinone laxatives

Phytomedicines containing 1,2-unsaturated pyrrolizidine alkaloids (PAs) are obliged to meet the re-

---

Bundesfachverband der Arzneimittel-Hersteller (Nonprescription Drug Manufacturers Association), Bonn, Germany.

quirements of PA limits published by the Health Authority. Because analytical procedures as well as elimination of alkaloids is very difficult, many products disappeared from the market.

Since 1992, a new benefit–risk assessment of anthraquinone laxatives has been undertaken by the authorities. Although single isolated substances such as emodin and aloe-emodin had shown mutagenic effects in vitro (e.g., by Ames test), a risk of carcinogenicity could not be proven in vivo, neither in animal experiments nor within a prospective case-control study performed recently. Although these products will remain on the market, the following restrictions are planned by the authorities: analytical data with respect to content of emodin and aloe-emodin; if necessary, in vitro and in vivo data; plus an adaptation of the package leaflets to Commission E monographs (revised 7/21/93).

In Europe, various draft guidelines on pharmacovigilance have been developed covering all kinds of medicines within the scope of EC Directive 65/66EEC. In each company, it must be ensured that a qualified person is available and responsible for meeting the requirements of pharmacovigilance and for reporting information on drug risks to the authorities, either solely to the authorities of the respective member states who granted registration, for products registered under the centralized procedure, or to the European Medicines Evaluation Agency (EMEA) in London.

All serious adverse drug reaction (ADR) reports within the EC must be filed within 15 days to the member state where it occurred; outside the EC, reporting must take place within 15 days to the member state where it occurred and to the EMEA. All unexpected ADRs that are not serious have to be reported within a periodic safety update to the member states and the EMEA.

Suspected serious ADR reports must be as complete as possible. They should contain patient details, company details (responsible person), original reporter's details, suspect product details (such as dose, indications, etc.), concomitant medication details, and suspected reaction details.

Safety of Herbal Remedies: Surveillance in the United Kingdom

VIRGINIA S.G. MURRAY, M.Sc., M.F.O.M., DEBBIE SHAW, and CHRISTINE LEON

Over the past 10 years there has been a considerable revival of interest in the use of herbal medicines in the United Kingdom. Apart from the use of the traditional European herbs, our multicultural society has introduced traditional medicines from countries such as China, India, Japan, and Africa. A particularly relevant example is Chinese herbal medicine, which has become increasingly popular for the treatment of chronic diseases such as psoriasis or eczema, for which there are no really effective long-term allopathic treatments.

In 1991, the report of a Working Party on Dietary Supplements and Health Foods recommended the establishment of a reporting scheme for adverse reactions associated with the use of herbal remedies and dietary supplements.[1] With the support of the Ministry of Agriculture, Fisheries and Foods, and the Department of Health, our project on traditional remedy surveillance was started at the National Poisons Unit in London to monitor the occurrence and severity of adverse reactions to these products in the United Kingdom.

NATIONAL POISONS UNIT

The National Poisons Unit, started in 1963, has three main functions: to provide information and advice to medical professionals and emergency services on a 24-hour basis; to provide a toxicologic analytical service for urgent analyses and a medical toxicology service to support the other services; and to manage cases of poisoning. The 24-hour information service received more than 150,000 calls in 1994. Case inquiries implicating the use of herbal remedies or food supplements were identified and passed on to the Traditional Remedies Surveillance Project.

TRADITIONAL REMEDY SURVEILLANCE

The project team has followed up inquiries on a wide range of products, including vitamins and minerals, herbals, royal jelly, fish oil, and practitioner prescribed medicines. The results of the pilot year (1991) have been published in *Drug Safety*.[2] In the period 1992–1993, of a total of 1245 inquiries, 427 were symptomatic at the time of the call. In 287 of these, there was a possibility of a relationship between product and effect. These figures include all ranges of severity—from nausea and vomiting to more serious effects such as hepatitis.

It is difficult to estimate the incidence of adverse reactions. It is well known that there is underreporting of adverse effects of pharmaceuticals, even though this is mandatory. The problems with reporting on herbal products and food supplements is far greater because it is still commonly believed that natural products are safe and, therefore, do not cause adverse effects. Many of these products are self-prescribed and not considered to be medicines, thereby further reducing the reporting rate. There is no single comprehensive source of side-effect or adverse-reaction data. In addition, it may not seem unreasonable to the public to consider that if a product is available for sale then it must be safe.

National Poisons Unit, Guy's and St. Thomas Hospital Trust, London, United Kingdom.

CASE REPORTS

The following case reports give an indication of the types of cases received and the problems that have been highlighted.

Copper toxicity

An adult male self-prescribed a daily intake of copper of 30 mg/day for 3 years and 60 mg/day for 1 year, which resulted in cirrhosis and liver failure requiring liver transplantation.[3] The maximum recommended daily dose of copper is 3 mg. Copper intoxication was confirmed analytically and histologically. This case illustrates the problems that may be associated with self-prescription, including chronic overdose of a single product or use of multiple products.

Consumers remain unaware of the potential hazards of using multiple products. Apart from possible interactions, there may be excessive intake where a single ingredient occurs in more than one product. In some cases, patients may be chronically using 10 different products. When there is no single ingredient overdose, it is difficult to relate symptoms to a single product or substance.

Herbal abortifacients

Pennyroyal (*Mentha pulegium*) and rue (*Ruta graveolens*) have been used in folk medicine as abortifacients. One of our female patients obtained both plants from the local herbalist with an intention to induce abortion. The preparation caused uterine contractions but not a proper abortion. The pregnancy was later terminated at a local hospital. Toxic effects as well as fatal outcomes were reported following the use of pennyroyal and rue for induction of abortion, and such practices ought to be discouraged.

Siberian ginseng

A 70-year-old female was taking one capsule daily of a food supplement containing 400 mg of Siberian ginseng (*Eleutherococcus senticosus*), vitamin B_6 (50 mg), and vitamin E (400 international units) for 16 years. She was otherwise healthy and was on no other medication. Hypertension (170/100) was detected. The food supplement was discontinued and her blood pressure dropped to 140/80. Reexposure to the same product on two occasions caused a rise in blood pressure, which returned to normal after the treatment was stopped. Positive dechallenge and rechallenge gives a highly probable link between exposure and effect in this case.[4] *Eleutherococcus* has been previously associated with elevated blood pressure[5] while vitamins B and E have not.

The project team has also had a number of reports involving traditional remedies from other countries. Ethnic communities may continue to seek medical advice from their traditional practitioners for cultural and linguistic reasons, even where there is free access to Western medicine. Often these treatments do not stay within the original community and there has been cross-cultural use of these remedies. These cases may be difficult to evaluate because of the lack of information on the constituents and differences in philosophy.

Lead poisoning

A number of cases have been identified in which lead or arsenic have been present in traditional remedies from the Indian subcontinent. A 19-year-old male using an Ayurvedic preparation for treatment of diabetes was found to have lead blood levels of 900 μg/L. The capsules were blister packed with a label that listed eight herbal ingredients, a "Vanga Bhasma" and a "Naga Bhasma" (see below). Analyses of the product revealed lead content of 600 ppm, which is sufficient to cause lead poisoning following chronic exposure. Manufacturers from India provided the following information on the ingredients: "Bhasmas are the end product in 'ash form' processed through systematic and scientific burning of metals like gold, silver, copper, iron, lead, tin etc. in particular temperature several times as laid down in Ayurvedic Method of manufacture. The Bhasmas, prepared through the established Ayurvedic Scientific Process will ensure desired therapeutic results without any toxicity. Bhasmas have been used in Ayurvedic treatment since ancient times. . . . Naga bhasma, the processed and purified lead in 'Ash or Bhasma form' is one of the active ingredients which is well known for its hypoglycaemic action."

The manufacturer's information also suggested that the capsules could not possibly cause any harm and that other explanations for this patient's ill health should be sought. The manufacturer did not seem to appreciate that lead poisoning was confirmed in this young man and that the source of intoxication was identified. The company's letter suggested that it was not aware of toxicologic hazards associated with exposure to heavy metals.

Chinese herbal medicine for eczema

Chinese herbal medicine presents a complex problem for surveillance because of the many ingredients contained in a single prescription or product. In addition, the ingredients are not consistent among patients treated for similar conditions. A number of reports of hepatitis following the use of Chinese herbal medicine for skin diseases, such as eczema or psoriasis, have been identified.

One case report was published in *Lancet* in 1992.[6] This is one of only two reports in which there has been a second exposure to Chinese herbs after recovery from the initial jaundice. A 28-year-old woman was admitted to the hospital with hepatitis, which resolved following treatment. About 8 months later she was again admitted to the hospital with jaundice, developed acute liver failure, and died following an unsuccessful liver transplant. It was only during her second episode of jaundice that it became known that she had been using Chinese herbs for her eczema. Prior to her first episode of hepatitis, she had used Chinese herbs for approximately 5–8 months. She had not taken any herbs again until about 3 weeks prior to her second hospital admission. Other causes of hepatitis were excluded and there was no history of exposure to hepatotoxic chemicals. She was not using any pharmaceuticals. No contamination with heavy metals, pharmaceuticals, pyrrollizidine alkaloids, or aflatoxins was found.

The project team has evaluated at least 11 cases and no single herb has occurred in all the prescriptions and no obviously hepatotoxic herbs have been prescribed. It, therefore, appears to be an idiosyncratic reaction. Idiosyncratic responses cannot be predicted and, therefore, susceptible patients cannot be excluded pretreatment. Monitoring of liver function is a method of identifying this group of patients during treatment.

"TOWARDS THE SAFER USE OF TRADITIONAL MEDICINES"

Following this work, and in order to stimulate rational dialogue between the groups, we organized a symposium, "Towards the Safer Use of Traditional Medicines," at the Royal Botanic Gardens, Kew, in early 1994.[7] The participants included Western allopathic doctors; European, Chinese, and Indian traditional practitioners; pharmacists; and representatives of the regulatory authorities. Recognizing the lack of a comprehensive structure for the use of these different medicines, there was considerable agreement on the potential problems and what needs to be done.

The key areas identified were training and maintenance of professional standards of practitioners and assurance of quality, safety, and efficacy of the herbal products used. In the United Kingdom, nonconventional therapies are not recognized by the regulatory authorities. Therefore, there is no way by which adequately and inadequately trained practitioners can be distinguished. The need for a single Register of Practitioners, setting educational and ethical standards, has been recognized both at the meeting at Kew and by the British Medical Association.[8]

Safety of medicinal plants requires accurate identification. In the absence of reliable standards or reference collection, authentication of plant material may be difficult. Reference standards are required for establishing quality control.

Some herbal and traditional remedies and food supplements have been associated with common and predictable side effects, which can generally be avoided. A number of preparations have been shown to contain hazardous ingredients, for example, aconitine or trace elements. Poisoning with these is preventable but requires some form of control over the availability of preparations or ingredients. Other remedies are associated with unpredictable effects that occur infrequently but may be serious. These adverse reactions cannot be prevented by regulations or controls over the products. Safety claims for many remedies are based on the lack of reports of adverse effects rather than on safety studies. Without a continuous, comprehensive, and mandatory reporting system it is not possible to be sure that there are no reports of adverse effects and, therefore, be sure that a given remedy is safe. Safe and effective treatment of the patient is the primary objective of all people involved.

CONCLUSION

Surveillance of traditional and herbal remedies is essential in order to identify toxic adverse health effects as rapidly as possible and to then act on this information to minimize further harm. It requires a multidisciplinary group of experts with medical toxicology, pharmacology, botany, analytical toxicology, phytochemistry, and epidemiology skills. Resources for such work is expensive, but to protect the public's health, such activity is essential, particularly as there appears to be increasing interest and demand for such remedies.

ACKNOWLEDGMENT

This project is supported by the Ministry of Agriculture, Fisheries and Food.

REFERENCES

1. Ministry of Agriculture, Fisheries and Food. *Dietary Supplements and Health Foods: Report of the Working Group.* London, MAFF, 1991.
2. Perharic L, Shaw D, Leon C, et al. Toxicological problems resulting from exposure to traditional remedies and food supplements. *Drug Safety* 11(4):284–294, 1994.
3. O'Donohue J, Reid M, Ramage J, et al. Micronodular cirrhosis and acute liver failure due to chronic copper self-intoxication. *European J Gastoenterol & Hepatol* 5:561–562, 1993.
4. Perharic L, Shaw D, Murray V. An appeal to pharmacists to report adverse effects of herbal and vitamin products. *Pharmaceutical J* 252:479, 1994.
5. Sonnenborn U, Haensel R. *Eleutherococcus senticosus.* In: de Smet PAGM, Keller K, Haensel R, Chandler RF, eds. *Adverse Effects of Herbal Drugs*, vol. 2. Stuttgart: Wissenshcafteilche Verlaggesellschafte, 1993, pp. 159-169.
6. Perharic-Walton L, Murray V. Toxicity of Chinese Medicines. *Lancet* 340:674, 1992.
7. Atherton DJ. Towards the safer use of traditional remedies. *Br Med J* 308:673, 1994.
8. British Medical Association. *Complementary Medicine—New Approaches to Good Practice.* Oxford, UK: Oxford University Press, 1993, pp. 57, 140, 148.

Part IV

How Can We Ensure That Botanical Preparations Will Be of Good Quality?

Overview

Jerome A. Halperin, Executive Director of the U.S. Pharmacopeia, chaired a discussion about the practical difficulties of turning the biodiverse raw material of the botanical world into a consistent product. Three elements appear to comprise that "equation": the industry practices and standards; the inherent difficulties of testing plants scientifically; and the living parts that comprise the system, the plants, and the people.

INDUSTRY PRODUCTS AND STANDARDS

Factors underlying botanical producers' good manufacturing practices (GMPs)

In the last two-plus decades, the American botanicals industry has been transformed from a noncoalition of independent small operations often "run out of kitchens" into an organized group of manufacturers that are beginning to appear more and more like large pharmaceutical firms. That evolution has raised the importance of quality higher on the manufacturers' lists of priorities. Testing for and ensuring quality, said Peggy Brevoort, Chief Executive Officer of East Earth Herb, has become economically worth supporting, as firms vie with one another in a growing marketplace.

Samuel W. Page, Ph.D., from the Natural Products Division of the Food and Drug Administration's (FDA's) Center for Food Safety and Applied Nutrition, acknowledged that, for the short term, that office has responsibility to oversee botanicals, which were classified as dietary supplements under the new legislation. And because most botanicals were already in the marketplace, there is small incentive for manufacturers to rush now to clinical trials to register their products with the FDA as drugs in order to be able to make claims. Thus, it is up to the industry to develop and maintain its own good practices, since the current oversight system is designed and funded only to deal with the problems and complaints resulting from adverse reports.

Dr. Page praised the work of Virginia S.G. Murray, M.Sc., M.F.O.M., National Poisons Unit, Guy and St. Thomas' Hospital Trust, London, United Kingdom, and her colleagues in Britain, where the Plato program is beginning to use modern computer graphic technology to aid in the identification and classification of plants and plant parts for a definitive database. He also stressed the value of pharmacognosists running spot tests, a much less technology-intensive way to identify a plant's active components.

As the primary industry trade association, the American Herbal Products Association (AHPA) imposes ethical standards on its members, which go beyond the Food GMPs conferred by law. The AHPA is currently devising a more refined set of GMPs tailored directly to herbals. The chapparal incident was cited as an example of industry joining the FDA to help remove a product from the marketplace to protect the public. Such self-policing can only help to solidify the image of responsibility that legitimate herbal producers aspire to as their industry becomes more seasoned and mature.

Development of standards that might serve as a future benchmark for product claims

At present, the primary standards used in the industry emerge from the U.S. Pharmacopeia (USP). Lee T. Grady, Ph.D., Vice President and Director of the Division of Standards Development there, explained that its system is continually incorporating the freshest data possible. The revision committee has continual turnover to incorporate fresh viewpoints, including those from the natural products realm. Advisory panels for food supplements are also continually being staffed with people who represent a wide range of viewpoints. And whenever a specific action is contemplated, the committee opens up the process as widely as possible with conferences and legal compulsion; most producers work to conform their natural products so that they can include the endorsement of the USP label on their products.

The conference also revealed a wealth of organized information about botanicals. Gordon M. Cragg, Ph.D., Chief of the Natural Products Branch at the National Cancer Institute, reported that the herbalists have provided his organization with much cooperation and expert counsel. He suggested that perhaps John H. Ferguson, M.D., who oversees the National Institutes of Health (NIH) consensus development conferences sponsored by the Office of Medical Applications of Research (of which he is Director), might consider such a conference on botanicals.

Dr. Ferguson stated that he was impressed with the amount of data available on botanicals. He described more than 200 newly retrotagged randomized controlled trials on botanicals recently moved into the Medline database that had satisfied working groups in Oxford, England, and Baltimore evaluating the validity of their methods. He acknowledged that it was a major distance from the forest or the cultivating field to a bottle of pills. He appraised the level of dialogue during the conference as being positive and well informed and thought it possible that the NIH could organize another conference, within the consensus development model, to look at the quality of the data or the scientific methods employed to gather it, or at developing an agenda for the near future.

Standards also need to be imposed at the practical level at the supplier/reseller interface. The American Herbal Products Association (AHPA) Standards Committee is developing a subcommittee to look at such issues as raw materials specifications. Many of the Chinese herbs are treated with sulfur dioxide, which is not permitted by United States regulators. Importers need to become aware of and learn to anticipate and deal with such situations. More testing in the country of origin is one obvious solution but, in the generally unregulated and fairly competitive indigenous environments, buyer/resellers can bring to bear only so much pressure. "Trust, but verify" was a watchword repeated throughout the conference and was particularly relevant with respect to products that resellers pass on to consumers. Especially important is the monitoring of a plant substance's concentration, which, at the retail level, translates into dose. As Robert Temple, M.D., Center for Drug Evaluation and Research, FDA, continued to emphasize: "Dose matters." James D. McChesney, Ph.D., Barnard Professor, School of Pharmacy, University of Mississippi, pointed out, with most herbals, the effects and possible toxicity are not as acute as with many pharmaceuticals; thus, the therapeutic index is greater. But he warned against accepting any sizable "margin of error." There exist pragmatic, economic, and staffing obstacles to a definitive, inclusive, FDA-type cataloging of all substances; nonetheless, the future of the industry will ultimately revolve around manufacturers' ability to deliver products with consistent quality.

SCIENTIFIC TESTING OF PLANTS

What methods work best and in what contexts?

Dr. McChesney described a "real world of testing" that often fell far short of reaching the limits of available technology. In the developing world, where much of the plant material originates, the sophisticated and expensive chemistry that might reveal a botanical's molecular detail definitively is not likely to be applied. A more reachable goal would be fingerprinting, which does not rely on a full range of tests with expensive chromatographic equipment. Looking at whole mass may be one approach. Another strategy to economize on the cost of testing is to find markers that are thought to reflect active biologic components. Thus, bioassays may be developed that fall short of revealing concentration but are still reliable to detect the presence of an ingredient.

Is the targeted bioassay a feasible alternative? Probably not, when the regulatory requirements are imposed, because the standard deviation in most such experiments runs as high as 40 percent, many times higher than most evaluators will accept. There is also the worldwide trend to reduce the number of animals used in testing. The FDA Center for Biologics has a lot of experience in trying to devise a context in which standards might be reasonably applied to the task of identifying an active ingredient for which biologic activity can vary over time in an unstable fashion. The presence (and amount) of cofactors, which in botanicals translates to the presence of other ingredients in the preparations, might have causal impact on the central biologic actors.

When trials are mounted, can satisfactory placebos be devised?

As the cannabis example demonstrates, in tests at the University of Mississippi sponsored by the National Institute on Drug Abuse, usually it is not the active ingredients that confer the properties that must be mimicked; for example, smell, texture, etc. Placebo "joints" have been successful and other researchers have reported no problem devising effective placebos in whatever form is required.

THE "TALENT POOL" AND BIODIVERSITY

Consider the following numbers:

- Perhaps 90 percent of the plants used by one European manufacturer are cultivated rather than collected in the wild; yet most of these find their way into the Western culture of the developed world.
- The USDA maintains a germ plasm collection to preserve the DNA of native American and other plants. It has thousands of samples of some fruit and vegetable species, but perhaps only one or two of echinacea, for example.
- An estimated 65–80 percent of the population in the developing world rely on medicinal plants as the "pharmaceuticals of choice" for their primary health care; of some 10,000 plants known to be sources of herbal remedies, less than 5 percent are cultivated, with the rest collected in the wild. It is estimated that unless sustainable production methods are imposed, those plants will disappear, perhaps in as little as 5 years, certainly in no more than 25 years.
- Approximately a dozen scientists work as fulltime ethnobotanists in the United States and even garden-variety professional botanists number probably fewer than a hundred. To begin to rectify this problem, training and staffing will be needed.

Clearly, the industry faces some major issues, most of which derive from the underlying biodiversity of the botanical world. Knowledge about growing, harvesting, and testing plant species is highly specific, and good botanical practices must be maintained throughout. It is common in traditional cultures to find only a few elders who are fully aware of the complexities of local flora, and younger people generally are not interested in developing the experience and awareness that will be necessary to succeed them effectively. Botanical businesses need to be aware of the grass-roots problems and help to solve them. The industry should encourage this as the first level of reciprocity.

Another level of involvement is the support of domestic herbaria and of the people who use and maintain them. Producers bringing raw materials into the United States can establish good working relationships with staff members and students in training, perhaps supplying grant money and collaborating on projects that, by enhancing the taxonomy, will eventually be of benefit to everyone. Identification and analysis cannot be "too correct." Both here and abroad, opportunities should be sought to train and support people who, in turn, can train others and, thus, spread the practical knowledge that is prerequisite to good practices.

A little-appreciated fact at the heart of the biodiversity crisis is that so few people are being trained to deal with and ameliorate it. The botanical community's plight is addressed in the recent publication "Systematics: Agenda 2000." Until recently, American academics were facing the same problem as the native herbalists referred to above. The older generation of botanists, pharmacognosists, and other professionals, each with a lifetime of invaluable experience, saw too few apprentices and aspiring scientists coming up after them. This was attributed to the popularity over the last several decades among students looking for science careers in molecular biology, a trend that has drawn potential candidates away from the botanical sciences. Now that trend seems to be slackening, at least to the point where academic support for the infrastructure of botanical science seems to be solid. But it is dangerously close to being too late, with the generation who possesses the wisdom and the technology leaving something of a knowledge and experience vacuum behind its retirement.

One answer to the problem is intensive training workshops, such as the international courses conducted for 2 weeks every other year at Purdue University's Center for New Crops and Plant Products, described by James E. Simon, Ph.D. Professor, Center for New Crops and Plant Products, Purdue University, West Lafayette, IN. Unfortunately, in the past years, industry has largely ignored this problem of training. More recently, industry leaders have demonstrated their awareness of the importance of quality and the price that will need to be paid for it, by investing in the plants and people to manage them.

Good Botanical Practices

MICHAEL J. BALICK, Ph.D.

The most significant contribution that a botanist can make to a discussion about furthering the incorporation of botanicals into the U.S. health care system concerns the importance of documenting the materials that are being studied or used in the clinical setting. As Norman R. Farnsworth, Ph.D., Research Professor of Pharmacognosy, College of Pharmacy, University of Illinois at Chicago,[1] has pointed out, at a minimum, 25 percent of the prescription drugs utilized in North America were derived from plant natural products. Globally, some three billion people receive their primary health care through traditional medical practices, heavily based on the use of plant products.[2] It is the botanist's responsibility to ensure that plants are identified with accurate and up-to-date nomenclature. This includes properly vouchering the material through the preparation of herbarium specimens. The foundation of this work is what I would refer to as "good botanical practices," the appropriate use of botanical skills in collecting, identifying, and documenting the plant species that are either part of a research program or directly used in clinical practices. Good botanical practices include the making of herbarium specimens that voucher each bulk collection, whatever its ultimate use.

PREPARATION OF HERBARIUM SPECIMENS

The proper collection of an herbarium specimen begins with the selection of a plant that is representative of its population. The collecting process involves making a complete collection, including leaf, fruit, flower, and other plant parts necessary for a proper determination. It is most often the case that plants that are in flower are not necessarily in fruit and vice versa. For a good portion of the year, many plants are found in a sterile condition, especially those in tropical locations where the growing season is year round, or those in dormancy in the temperate region. However, without flowers or fruits, the so-called "fertile" portion of the plant, it is difficult for a plant taxonomist to make a proper determination. Of course, there are taxonomists who work on specific groups of plants and are able to identify their plants even in a sterile condition. However, because there are so few taxonomists today, those who are practicing are overburdened with requests for determinations, and many taxonomists often decline to carry out work on incomplete specimens.

If the plant is small, such as an herb, then the entire organism can be collected and pressed for preservation. However, many of the botanicals come from trees and, thus, there must be selectivity in the collection. Sections of the stem that contain leaves, flowers and/or fruits are clipped off for pressing. Such specimens can also contain bark or root, especially if that part of the plant is used as a botanical medicine. Figure 1 is an example of a poor herbarium collection.

This particular taxon is described as coming from a two-meter-tall plant in the primary forest with a yellow flower. Unfortunately, the flower has not been collected, and only leaf fragments are present on the specimen. One specialist who examined it noted that it was definitely not a palm, while another one could not place it in the proper family. This particular species is used by local people in Ecuador to thatch roofs and tie bundles. As far as the botanist is concerned, it is an unidentifiable entity. Figure 2 is said to be a tree in the secondary forest, 25 feet tall with a white flower. Note that only a piece of this twig and a few leaves have been

---

Director and Philecology Curator of Economic Botany, Institute of Economic Botany, The New York Botanical Garden, Bronx, NY.

FIG. 1. Herbarium specimen comprised of leaf fragments only, without flowering or fruiting material provided to assist in the identification. Reproduced, courtesy of The New York Botanical Garden Herbarium.

FIG. 2. Herbarium specimen comprised of complete leaves and stem, but no flowering or fruiting material that could be used for identification. Reproduced, courtesy of The New York Botanical Garden Herbarium.

collected. It was felt to be in the family Euphorbiaceae, but the specialist who examined it pointed out that it was not in this family. The use of this particular plant is for firewood, and unfortunately because it is such a poor collection, it remains unidentified. Figure 3 is a medicinal plant used for skin burns. It is said to be a vine growing to two meters with purple tubular flowers and green fruits that turn red at maturity. Note that both fruits and flowers are present on the specimen, as well as a good section of the vine and numerous, representative leaves of various life stages. This one easily can be identified in the family Solanaceae, as *Lycianthes lenta*. Each of these specimens was made to document an ethnobotanical use by indigenous people. Unfortunately, only the plant in Figure 3 can be properly identified, and specimens shown in Figures 1 and 2 represent a waste of time involved in the collection, expenditure of research funds, and botanical expertise.

Unfortunately, botanists are the frequent recipients of such poor specimens. It is especially tragic when a great deal of funds have been invested in the collection and research of a species and care has been taken to make bulk samples, medicinal extracts, herbal tinctures, and the like. It is important to involve a botanist in the research and collection program from the very beginning, to avoid the possibility that the research project will be compromised by the lack of identification at a later date.

In addition to well-made specimens, it is important to take careful notes to accompany the specimens. These notes contain information on the collecting location, including the latitude and longitude, village, state or county, and country. The notes should also contain as complete a botanical description as possible, especially if the plants are large and cannot be completely preserved in the herbarium specimen. The latter case is common, for example, with palms, that might be 30 meters tall with 8-meter-long leaves. In this case, representative pieces of flower, fruit, leaves (pinnae), inflorescence, axis, and stem sections can be taken. In addition, copious photographs and notes are used to document the collection. As mentioned above, with herbaceous plants the situation is easier. But still, information is required on the size of the plant; general description; colors of flowers and fruits that might fade; any fragrance that might be present in flowers, fruits, leaves,

GOOD BOTANICAL PRACTICES

FIG. 3. Complete herbarium specimen containing leaves, stem, and fruiting material, making absolute identification possible. Good botanical practices should include making specimens of this quality to voucher any plant material, whether used for producing herbal products or conducting clinical studies. Only in this way can the studies be reproducible and of the highest quality. Reproduced, courtesy of The New York Botanical Garden Herbarium.

or stems; and information on the shape of fruits or stems that might be lost as part of the process of pressing the specimen. In addition, the date of collection, along with the names of all members of the collection team, should be provided in the lower portion of the label. Finally, credit given to collaborating institutions and foundations that have supported the research must appear on the label.

For the most part, plants are pressed in sheets of folded newspaper, and either preserved in an alcohol bath until they can be dried or plants are directly dried in the field. When preserved in an alcohol bath (usually less than 50 percent) the chemical integrity of the herbarium specimen is compromised, which can inhibit future research opportunities. Such preservation should be noted on the label. Drying plants in the field is difficult and involves taking, for example, a heater, plant press, cardboards, corrugates, ventilators, wooden presses, and straps into the area under study. If the area is remote, then this can be quite difficult, and short-term preservation (e.g., with alcohol) of the plant is the preferred method of collection.

Once the material returns to the institution where it is being studied and curated, the plants are sewn or glued to high-quality rag bond paper.

ETHNOBOTANICAL INQUIRY

The actual sourcing of ethnobotanical data, while appearing to be quite simple, is a complex series of activities that are successful only when the investigator is experienced and patient. The ethnobotanist must approach traditional healers with a great deal of sensitivity, respecting the cultural heritage and limitations of age, health, and time. It is very common for researchers to arrive unannounced at the home or clinic of the healer, bearing collection equipment, cameras, and notebooks poised for action, only to close the door they came to open. A better methodology is to seek an introduction, make several visits to sit and chat, and, within that exchange, explain the purpose of the research work and what role the traditional healer would play. Issues of intellectual property rights and compensation must be acknowledged and discussed. It must be made clear as to how the healer would receive fair recognition for his or her contribution. Some traditional healers do not wish to share their information and their decision should be respected and accepted gracefully, because there are usually valid reasons behind it.[3]

A frequent observation made by ethnobotanists is that people being interviewed often get the sense of what the interviewer wishes to hear and sometimes are happy to oblige that person, especially if he or she seems dissatisfied with the progress of the interview. Thus, herbaria as well as the scientific literature are filled with ethnobotanical collections and citations of questionable value.

To help address this, one recent development being implemented at The New York Botanical Garden (NYBG) Institute of Economic Botany is the establishment of a "credibility rating" for information that is collected on plant utilization, based on the idea of Elliott[4] as cited in Alexiades.[5] In the past, there has been little opportunity to evaluate the quality of data based on the way it has been collected during ethnobotanical studies. In reading through

TABLE 1. CREDIBILITY RATING FOR INFORMATION COLLECTED ON USE OF BOTANICALS

Category/example	Rating	Comment
Collector uses or directly observed use	1	Dr. Smith saw these *Orbignya cohune* leaves being used as thatch in Belize
Informant uses or directly observed use	2	Maya healer, D. Elijio, told Dr. Smith he uses these *Piper amalago* roots for snakebite
Informant heard/knew from a further source	3	Ethnographer on the Sioux reservation heard that the Sioux used the *Aster* for menstruation problems
Use reported from the literature	4	As for the Institute of Economic Botany's teaching collection, where uses will be gathered from the literature and summarized on the use label
Common knowledge	5	As, for example, a collection of a cultivar of coffee from a coffee plantation with a reported use as a stimulant beverage
Credibility of use information unknown	6	New field botanist neglected to write down any information about his informant

the ethnobotanical literature, it is rarely clear whether the investigator has actually observed or participated in the uses discussed or whether the plants have been collected during a casual walk through the forest pointing out plants or interviewing a younger person who remembers specific use by one of his forebearers. To address this, the credibility rating presented in Table 1 will be incorporated into the database utilized at the NYBG. Data with a rating of 1 have a reasonable certainty of being accurate, while those with a rating of 5 or 6 may be less authoritative. Although this rating is an experiment, and will certainly be revised over time, it is an attempt to begin to standardize the quality of data collected and evaluate its relative credibility.

THE CONCEPT OF THE MULTIPLE-USE CURVE

A key issue that needs to be addressed in ethnobotany involves sample size. When carrying out an ethnobotanical study of a particular group of plants, it is important to determine the number of collections that must be made and number of people contacted before one has a reasonable certainty

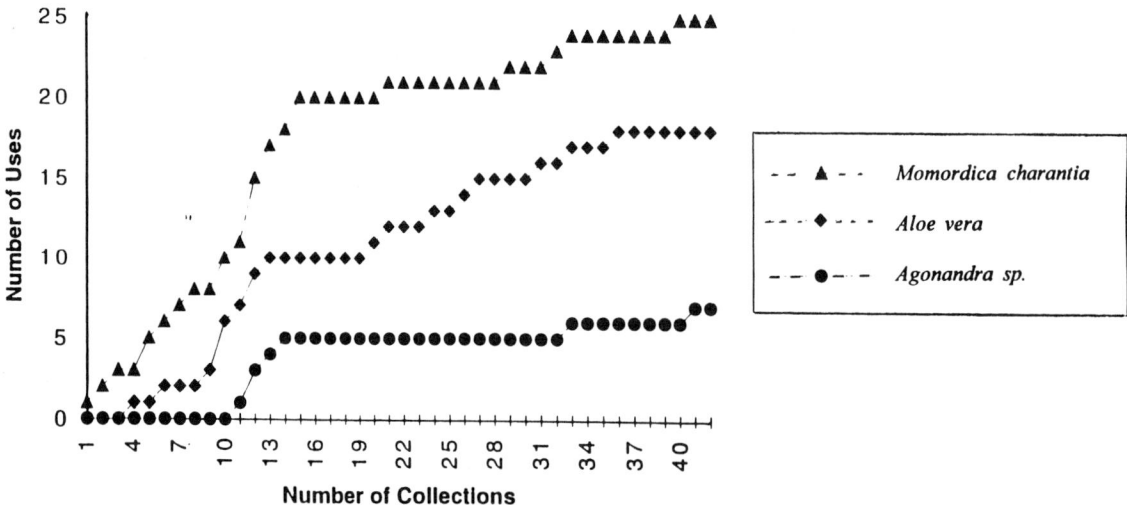

FIG. 4. Graph demonstrating the importance of multiple interviews in investigating local uses of economically important plants. The Number of Collections represents the number of people interviewed and the Number of Uses, the different ways in which each species is used. With each of the species represented in this graph, new uses are still being described after interviews with as many as 40 people.

that the compilation of information on a specific plant is relatively complete. Many ethnobotanical studies depend on one or several collections as the basis for their information and conclusions. In order to assess the adequacy of such numbers of collections or interviews, a mathematical relationship can be developed, based on the concept of the species-area curve.[6]

Figure 4 graphs the relationship between the number of different uses of three particular species (y-axis) versus the number of people interviewed (x-axis). In this example, a total of 42 interviews were undertaken in August and September 1994, in villages of Belize. Interviewees were, for the most part, not considered to be traditional healers but were primarily elderly people who were willing to discuss plant use. The group interviewed considered themselves to be Spanish, Creole, Maya, or Mestizo. Ten plants were discussed, and three were selected to illustrate the type of generalist knowledge obtained from people in these communities.

The upper curve in Figure 4 illustrates the uses of *Mormordica charantia*, a vining herb common to much of the Caribbean. The initial 13 interviews record 20 uses, but show that information on another five uses was obtained by the thirty-ninth interview. This curve illustrates a pattern for a "powerful plant,"[7] one that is widely known with multiple uses. The middle curve is for *Aloe vera*, a commonly known plant, but one that has a more focused series of uses, especially in the area of dermatology. The final species, *Agonandra* spp., is an example of a plant that is not commonly known throughout the community, and appears to have fewer uses, focused on "male" problems. It is also more limited in its habitat than the other two taxa, found primarily in the forest environment. An important point illustrated by the multiple-use curve for these three plants is the large number of interviews/collections necessary to obtain the maximum amount of data. Many ethnobotanical studies, including contemporary ones that utilize statistical methods, derive their information, and thus their conclusions, from a small number of interviews/collections per species. For some plants, such as those with specialist uses, a few collections from traditional healers may be sufficient. Others, such as the more widely used plants, may require several dozen interviews/collections before an idea of the totality of extant information can be obtained.

CONCLUSION

In a revitalization of the role of botanical medicines in the U.S. health care system, a proper understanding of the identification of the materials being collected, marketed, and utilized is essential. Some products currently on the market, which are improperly identified, pose a threat to consumers who have the feeling that all that is natural is safe. For example, an extract of *Pilocarpus* leaves, added to shampoo and hair products, could pose a danger of poisoning if it contains the alkaloid pilocarpine. To avoid potential problems such as this, the herbal industry should adopt strict "good botanical practices" that make vouchering all collections and bulk samples required, whether for research or product formulation, and have these vouchers properly identified and retained should questions arise in the future.

REFERENCES

1. Farnsworth NR. The role of medicinal plants in drug development. In: Krogsgaard-Larsen P, Christensen SB, Kofod H eds. *Natural Products and Drug Development*. London: Balliere, Tindall and Cox: 1984, pp. 8–98.
2. Farnsworth NR. The role of ethnopharmacology in drug development. In: Chadwick D, Marsh J eds. *Bioactive Compounds from Plants*. Chichester, England: John Wiley & Sons, 1990, pp. xi, 242.
3. Arvigo R, Balick MJ. *Rainforest Remedies: 100 Healing Herbs of Belize.* Twin Lakes, WI: Lotus Press, 1993.
4. Elliott ND. "Bioresources Database of Ethnobiology: Guidance for Contributors." Unpublished manuscript. London: Bioresources, Ltd., n.d.
5. Alexiades MN (Ed.) Selected Guidelines for Ethnobotanical Research: A Field Manual. *Advances in Economic Botany* 10:1–306, 1996.
6. Campbell DG, Daly DC, Prance GT, Maciel UN. Quantitative ecological inventory on terra firme and várzea tropical forest on the Rio Xingu, Brazilian Amazon. *Brittonia* 38:369–393, 1986.
7. Balick MJ. Ethnobotany and the identification of therapeutic agents from the rainforest. In Chadwick D, Marsh J eds. *Bioactive Compounds From Plants*. Chichester, England: John Wiley and Sons, 1990, pp. 22–31.

Quality of Botanical Preparations: Environmental Issues and Methodology for Detecting Environmental Contaminants

JAMES D. McCHESNEY, Ph.D.

In this paper I will address environmental factors and issues as they impact the quality and safety of botanicals. This is an area where we have very modest data. What data is available has been summarized and discussed by De Smet et al.[1] and Bernath[2] The following outline (Figure 1) will be the basis of this discussion.

A discussion such as this encompasses two points of view: (1) that of the botanical producer or grower who wishes to optimize yield from production; and (2) that of the processor-marketer who wishes to manufacture a product of uniform quality. Most data has been developed with enhanced production as the desired goal. In this chapter I seek a neutral position. Environmental factors can have dramatic effects on biomass yield and composition and, thus, quality assurance programs must be developed to ensure the consumer that the product is of consistent composition and quality. Figure 2 presents an outline of methodology available for detection of contaminants of environmental origin in botanical materials.

DRY MATTER AND ACTIVE PRINCIPLE PRODUCTION

As environmental factors change, thus causing a change in biomass production, this can have three general outcomes: The composition of the biomass may remain essentially unchanged; the concentration of active principle may rise; or the concentration of active principle may fall, either in direct proportion to changes in growth or by some complex relationship to changes in growth. Specific examples are presented below with regard to individual environmental factors.

ORGAN LOCALIZATION OF ACTIVE PRINCIPLE

Because many or most active principles are either biosynthesized or accumulated in a specific organ or tissue, any environmental factor that influences the ratios of those organs or tissues to the total biomass of the plant will have an effect on the quality of the biomass. However, very little data is available that takes into account possible effects on concentration in the specific organ as well as the ratio of organ production. From the point of view of the processor-marketer, the effect on the concentration of the active principle is paramount. Another important aspect is impact of stage of growth and development of the biomass on its composition. This derives from the changes in biosynthetic capability because of changes in the state of differentiation of the biomass and the tissues (organs) associated with active principle production/accumulation. Often, it is very difficult to separate effects of stage of development from environmental factors on composition of biomass. As before, specific examples are discussed under individual environmental factors.

Vice President, Natural Products Chemistry and Development, Napro BioTherapeutics, Inc., Boulder, CO.

> 1. Dry matter and active principal products
> 2. Organ localization of active principal
> 3. Factors affecting accumulation
>   A. Light
>   B. Temperature
>   C. Water availability
>   D. Nutrients
>   E. Macronutrients
> 4. Contaminants introduced during plant growth
>   A. Microorganisms
>   B. Heavy metals
>   C. The special case of pesticides
> 5. Postharvest issue
>   A. Drying
>   B. Composting
>   C. Molding
>   D. Long-term storage

FIG. 1. Environmental conditions and their effect on biomass quality.

FACTORS AFFECTING ACCUMULATION OF ACTIVE PRINCIPLE

Light

Numerous investigators have evaluated the influence of light on accumulation of active principles. Two characteristics of the light have been shown to have effect: light intensity and light quality (wavelength). Light intensity is of major concern from the commercial point of view. Increasing light intensity has usually been shown to stimulate active principle accumulation up to an optimum, and then, in many or most cases, a decline in active principle concentration is observed. These changes may follow simple or complex relationships. Importantly, season (day length) and latitude have been shown to have pronounced influence on biomass composition.

For example, *Atropa belladonna* has been shown to have an alkaloid content of 1.3 percent when grown in the Caucasus and only 0.3 percent when grown in Sweden. Light intensity may also modify the composition of the secondary metabolites of medicinal plants. For example, shade-grown *Mentha piperita* had not only a lower essential oil content, 1.09 percent versus 1.43 percent, but also showed diminished content of menthol in the oil, 57.5 percent versus 61.8 percent.

Temperature

Generally speaking, increases in temperature, up to a maximum wherein physiologic damage may result, favor increased secondary metabolite production. This has been noted both for alkaloid- and terpene-producing medicinal plants. As in the case of light, the relative composition of the secondary metabolite profile may also be altered. For example, increased proportions of morphine are found in resin of poppies grown under cool conditions, which also tend to decrease total alkaloid content. Similar observations have been made for various alkaloid-producing plants.

Water availability

The situation with regard to the influence of water availability on active principle accumulation is least well understood. This would perhaps appear to

> 1. Extraction methods
>   a. Water extraction
>   b. Solvent extraction
>   c. Supercritical fluid extraction
> 2. Chromatographic methods
>   a. Gas chromatography
>   b. High-performance fluid chromatography
>   c. Supercritical fluid extraction
> 3. Combined methods
>   a. Chromatography: mass spectrometry
>   b. Chromatography: infrared spectrophotometry
>   c. Chromatography: ultraviolet/visible spectrophotometry
> 4. Methods for metals
>   a. Atomic absorption spectrophotometry
>   b. Eductively coupled plasma: atomic emission spectrophotometry
>   c. Inductively coupled plasma: mass spectrometry
> 5. Radioactivity detection

FIG. 2. Methods of analysis for active principal concentration and environmental contaminants.

reflect differences in adaptation of the specific plant species to environmental water stress. Thus, for some plants, increased water availability suppresses secondary metabolite accumulation, for others it stimulates production, and for a third group no effect is seen. It must be noted that, under field conditions, it is difficult to sort out temperature, light intensity, and water availability effects.

Nutrients

Other than studies to verify that appropriate nutrient and soil pH were important to total secondary product formation, data accumulated thus far suggest that medium levels of nitrogen, phosphorous, and potassium (the usual nutrients that are supplemented in production of plants) were most nearly optimum for secondary metabolite production. It seems that, in some species, the effect of high nutrient availability parallels that of high light intensity. In others, there seems to be increased biomass production with no change in active principle accumulation while, in some, there is marked increase or decrease in active principle content. One must conclude at this point that no general situation prevails and each medicinal plant species must be considered individually. We have looked at nutrient availability effects upon production of two different medicinal plant species. In one species, biomass production is increased with no significant change in tissue composition of active principle. In the second, additional nitrogen had a very marked negative impact upon biomass production and active principle concentration.

Microorganisms

Almost no studies have been reported on the impact of various other organisms upon the production of active principle in medicinal plants. There does exist an extensive literature on phytoalexins, which are induced by microorganism infection of plant tissues. In most cases these phytoalexin compounds are produced in minute concentrations in the plant in absence of microorganism infection, thus, they would not ordinarily be considered to be importantly medicinally active substances. In very preliminary recent experiments in our laboratory, we have observed dramatic increases in active principle content of tissues exposed to soil microorganism preparations. Work is in progress to verify and extend these observations.

CONTAMINANTS INTRODUCED DURING PLANT GROWTH

Microorganisms

Microbial contamination of botanical materials may pose one of the following health risks: infection caused by pathogenic organisms, production of microbial toxins, or microbial transformation of normal constituents to toxic compounds.

The presence of microorganisms in botanical materials is ordinarily not so much the result of contamination during processing but the natural consequence of plant growth. From the point of view of potential health risk, it is important to know the extent of pathogenic microorganisms present rather than just the total number of organisms. It is unrealistic to develop regulations for botanicals that are more rigorous than those for foods for human consumption. Also, most microorganism contaminants are destroyed by preparation of the botanical materials with boiling water for tea.

Several studies have shown that crude botanical preparations can be infested with microorganisms capable of producing mycotoxins, the most notable being aflatoxin-producing *Aspergillus*. Some researchers have assayed botanical preparations directly for mycotoxins. As expected, the results show considerable variation in the prevalence and quantity of mycotoxin contamination. These studies do demonstrate the need to prevent aflatoxin contamination of medicinal plant material, especially in humid tropical and subtropical climates. Plant material must undergo rapid drying after the harvest and then be suitably stored to prevent fungal growth. However, one must remember that the exposure of individuals to aflatoxins is usually much greater via the food supply than from medicinal herbs.

The ability of microbial contaminants to transform normal botanical constituents into toxic substances has been most directly demonstrated by the formation of dicoumarol—a potent anticoagulant—from coumarin by fungi growing on sweet clover. Although poisoning from consumption of moldy sweet clover has been documented mostly in cattle, there have been instances of abnormal clotting time associated with herbal tea consumption. The presence of molded sweet clover and dicumarol however, were not documented.

Heavy metals

Two factors suggest that botanicals should be evaluated for heavy metal contamination: (1) the increasing prevalence of heavy metal contamination of our general environment due to such sources as industrial and traffic emissions and the use of agricultural agents, such as organic mercury fungicides and lead arsenic insecticides; and (2) the deliberate incorporation of heavy metals into medicinal formulations, especially those of Asian origin.

Crude medicinal herb samples available on the German market have been found to exceed the heavy metal concentrations allowable for foodstuffs. However, two points should be noted: (1) The allowable concentration for foodstuffs is based upon fresh weight whereas medicinal herbs were analyzed dry; and (2) the quantity of intake by individuals of foodstuffs and medicinal herbs should be very different. Thus, it is not clear that the observed higher heavy metal concentrations of medicinal herbs pose any real health risk. Also, follow-up studies on extraction of the heavy metals from the botanical materials during preparation of medicinal teas, for example, showed a low efficiency of extraction, usually less than 50 percent. Further extraction with less polar extraction fluids (e.g., ethanol) yielded even less efficiency of heavy metal extraction.

Also, it was observed that materials collected in the wild showed a wider range of heavy metal contamination than cultivated materials and that the levels of lead and cadmium in the same crude botanical varied considerably with plant part and habitat of growth. As in the case of microbial toxin exposures, the health risk of exposure to heavy metals is dependent upon total dose per day. Foodstuffs are most likely to be the predominent source because of their much greater quantity in the diet compared to botanicals.

Many reports have appeared in the medicinal and pharmaceutical literature documenting unacceptable levels of heavy metals in exotic remedies. Potential sources include brewing pots, grinding machines, and other preparation utensils. It is also possible that heavy metals are not an accidental contaminant. Many exotic Asian remedies contain heavy metal salts as intended ingredients. The deliberate incorporation of metal salts or oxides into the composition of traditional medicines and cosmetics is observed in various parts of the world. As these substances find their way into commerce, the incidence of heavy-metal poisoning is likely to increase.

Finally, I mention a special case; that of radioactive contamination of botanical products. This was brought to attention following the Chernobyl accident of April 26, 1986. Numerous isotopes were detected immediately following the incident; however, it was generally accepted that only long-lived isotopes were likely to pose a health threat to consumers. Using the standards established for foods, researchers were able to show that several herbal samples contained radioactive isotopes in excess of acceptable levels during the first year following the accident. The contamination varied according to plant part; with those materials consisting of leaves being more often in excess of acceptable levels than those materials consisting of flowers or fruits. Also, subsequent processing to produce teas yielded lower levels of radioactivity because there was a low level of efficiency of extraction.

The special case of pesticides

Although most countries have regulations restricting the use of pesticides, crude botanicals may still be contaminated by these substances. The reasons are several. Herbs may be imported from countries where restrictions are absent or disregarded. Also, the country of import may not be the country of origin. Botanicals may be gathered from natural stands where use of pesticides to protect the general vegetation can lead to unintentional contamination. Large-scale cultivation of medicinal plants is not economically feasible without the use of pesticides. Also, pesticides can persist for years in the environment and, thus, contamination may result even though the plants were not intentionally or accidentally treated.

Studies of pesticide contamination of botanicals have shown the presence of chlorinated hydrocarbons (several classes), organophosphates, carbamate insecticides and herbicides, fungicides, and triazine herbicides. Also, polychlorinated biphenyls have been reported as coming from raw botanical material as the result of general environmental pollution. As in the case of other contaminants, little regulation exists specifically for levels of pesticides in medicinal plant material. Most researchers have used the regulations applied to foodstuffs as the relevant standard. It should be noted that, even when botanicals exceed the levels acceptable for foods, this may not pose a health risk because of the low quantities of botanical material ingested per day. Consideration of potential increased susceptibility to pesticide poisoning caused by illness should be factored into any regulations developed for medicinal plant preparations. Finally, the efficiency of extraction of pesticide residues from the biomass during processing should also be taken into account. Because of the low solubility of many of the pesticides in water, it is not surprising that poor extraction efficiencies have been observed during the preparation of teas from the materials. Similarly, levels of extraction of pesticides from botanicals with ethanol have also been shown to be low.

On some occasions, the contamination of botanicals has not originated from exposure during growth but resulted from fumigation of stored material. However, consideration must be given to the relative health risks of contamination of stored material by molds producing strongly carcinogenic aflatoxins and toxicity resultant from any fumigation residues.

Postharvest issues

Harvest and postharvest handling and processing can have a very profound impact on the quality of botanical materials. The biomass must be rapidly stabilized by drying in order to protect quality. In addition, safeguard of the biomass from contamination from various sources of toxicants is very important. Processing equipment must not release heavy metals, fumigants should not alter biomass constituents or leave toxic residues, and molds or other microbes must be inhibited from growing, for example. Finally, the botanical must be sealed into proper containers to protect it from insect and rodent infestation during shipment and long-term storage. These are just some of the important issues that must be addressed after harvest of the botanicals.

METHODS FOR ANALYSIS OF BOTANICALS FOR ENVIRONMENTAL CONTAMINANTS

Several options for analysis of botanicals for environmental contaminants are listed in Figure 2. I would note especially that the following methods of extraction of contaminants must be standardized and appropriate internal standards developed, to allow confidence in the reproducibility of the methods from batch to batch. The suitability of the methods is also critically dependent upon the specific agent or agents being analyzed. For example, gas chromatography with electron capture detection is well suited for chlorinated hydrocarbon analyses but is probably not generally suitable for microbial toxin analysis.

Finally, development of appropriate microbiologic methods to assess microbial contamination of botanicals will utilize both microscopic observations for gross contamination (moldy biomass) and homogenization/extraction and subculturing approaches to identify the level of contamination (CFU/g) and the specific organism responsible for contamination.

REFERENCES

1. De Smet PAGM, Keller K, Hansel R, Chandler RF, eds. *Adverse Effects of Herbal Drugs.* New York: Springer-Verlag, 1992.
2. Bernath. In: Craker, Simon, eds. *Herbs, Spices and Medicinal Plants: Recent Advances in Botany, Horticulture and Pharmacology.* vol. 1. Phoenix: Oryx Press, 1986.

Domestication and Production Considerations in Quality Control of Botanicals

JAMES E. SIMON, Ph.D.

As an agricultural researcher, I have spent many years working toward the improvement of botanical quality from a domestication and production perspective. Whether the botanical product of interest is a single source or complex mixture of plants, many of the same considerations hold true. By looking toward the standards established for many other agricultural products, we have a starting point for a discussion of quality control (QC) in raw botanical products. Producing a consistently high quality raw material is essential if a high quality processed product is to result. In this brief chapter, I will highlight some of the keys to QC from a domestication and production perspective and point out the advantages of bringing into cultivation the plants used in botanical preparations. Domestication and production are important tools in the improvement of the raw materials that will then be processed and prepared.

PROPER IDENTIFICATION OF THE BOTANICAL

While an herb grown commercially may or may not be genetically uniform, it can be easily identified and the harvested product more easily kept pure and unadulterated. There are additional distinct ecologic advantages in the cultivation of botanicals besides improving the survival of wild stands of a botanical, many of which are becoming more endangered. The production of a crop normally leads to a more uniform product simply because only one species is being grown and harvested. Botanicals collected in the wild often include many nontarget plant species, whether intentional or not. And, plants that are distinctly different in shape, growth, form, or other parameters can be easily rogued or removed from a cultivated field. Production minimizes or can eliminate nontarget plant species from being sold. Herbarium vouchers and product samples for later tracking are also easily and inexpensively sampled and stored from cultivated crops compared to wildcrafted plants. In short, cultivating botanicals would minimize industry errors regarding the use of incorrect species, a problem well recognized in the industry today.

GENETIC UNIFORMITY OF THE BOTANICAL CROP

The domestication of herbs (brought into cultivation) will be more uniform in appearance (shape, color, vigor) and more consistent in the extractable yield of the natural plant chemical of interest. Whether the plants are high or low in secondary products—alkaloid, terpenes, aromatic propanoids, or others—is not really the only issue, though high levels are often desirable and required. Rather, it is the improved predictability of the genetic material that is being grown that permits more consistency in the quality of the raw product and the concentrations of the bioactive compounds and greater opportunity to meet future standards of quality for that raw product.

APPROPRIATE PRODUCTION MANAGEMENT

Improved uniformity of a crop and the use of developed varieties of a botanical will also lead to more uniform quality and purity. Physiochemical assessments of the raw botanical naturally can and

---

Professor, Center for New Crops and Plant Products, Purdue University, West Lafayette, IN.

should be done on all materials regardless of the source. An understanding of the plants' growth and development characteristics can often lead to higher agricultural yields and higher natural plant product yields. Proper site and soil selection, manipulation of fertility, and proper water management all appear to have significant impact on plant growth with their primary effects on the plants' rate of growth. Managing production appropriately can enhance yields of the raw material and again lead to improved consistency in product yield and delivery.

Producing botanicals under agricultural or agroforestry systems often mitigates against natural disasters facing wild populations. Also, as many studies have shown, the purposeful introduction of a stress, when correctly timed and of the appropriate duration and intensity, such as water stress, may, in some species, lead to an enhanced accumulation of secondary products.

If all botanicals were properly identified and if adulteration did not occur, then the American public and the medical community might have more confidence in the use of botanicals. I contend that these problems will continue to plague the industry until proper standards of raw product quality are developed. Standards such as the US Department of Agriculture (USDA) grades and standards of fruits and vegetables could be modified and used for raw materials, either from the field or from the wild. Such standards are used every day for our food supply and with most of the fruits and vegetables that one purchases daily. Why not have similar standards for botanicals? Standards of quality for the raw botanical are also important if we are to increase the use of botanicals in this country. First, though, we must define "quality" for both the raw and processed/finished product.

Freedom from pesticides, heavy metals, and microbiologic contamination

Raw crop quality. I would argue that quality can be defined in a multitude of ways, but if we would use USDA grades and standards as a guidepost, raw product standards and grades for botanicals should be as detailed, clear, concise, and reproducible as for any other product. Raw crop quality can be judged by visual appearance—color, shape, and form; freedom from bruises, damage, and extraneous materials; and freedom from any nonplant debris as appropriate for each commercially sold product. The identity of the product must be verified and the plant sampled in some manner, with a voucher specimen or by withdrawing a sample specimen.

The product could come with names of the packer; source, locale, region, and country of origin; genus, species, and variety; and a certification tag indicating the fact that quality assurance (QA) procedures have been followed; that is, good farming practices (GFP) would be followed just as good manufacturing practices (GMP) are now being discussed and implemented for botanicals.

Regarding the contents within the package, standards could address the minimum level of the natural product(s) (e.g., x% of parthenolides in feverfew, y% of essential oil in other plants) as well as moisture content, freedom from molds and contaminants (such as heavy metals, pesticides) and a listing of which other agricultural products are also within the package. It is the responsibility of the seller (possibly the farmer) to ensure that the raw product, fresh or dried (but unprocessed), meets such standards.

Genetic variation in natural product content and crop quality

Consistent high quality can best be achieved with the domestication and production of a plant. Exceptions to this are important to recognize, for example, in the case of ginseng, the highest quality as defined by the industry does not come from field-grown ginseng but from natural stands of ginseng in the woods.

Variation in secondary products, even within clones, will be influenced by the plant part harvested; the time of harvesting relative to stage of growth; management practices; growth rate; and environmental considerations. If we presume that the enhanced accumulation of secondary products is, in part, related to the availability of excess carbon skeletons after growth and repair, then it is easier to conceptualize the impact that growth rate has on levels of product accumulation.

Let us now look at some concrete examples:

Ancistrocladus korupensis. This is the only source of the promising anti-HIV agent, michellamine B, a dimeric alkaloid. This was discovered by the National Cancer Institute. The plant, a tropical liana, is found only in southwestern Cameroon, in a tropical rain forest area, and has probably survived only because of its geographic isolation from development.

We can collect the fallen leaves from the forest floor or collect different aged leaves and sample all the known populations comparatively. In the wild, individual plants contain a wide range—1.5–3.5 percent alkaloid—of michellamine B. Which would one rather process? By collecting other species that look almost identical, one will end up with a good-looking dried product with no michellamine B content. Genetics is the key, and recognizing and using genetic diversity to improve raw botanical is the first step taken in domestication. With that information, one can then clone the plants one wants and begin to bring into cultivation the best plants (i.e., most vigorous, highest yielding, highest level of bioactive compounds, disease resistance).

Artemisia annua. A member of the family Asteraceae, this plant is the source of artemisinin, a potent antimalarial. Genetically, wild lines of artemisia vary significantly in this sesquiterpene lactone. Considering that *Artemisia annua* is still collected in the wild, domesticated high-yielding lines would be of enormous benefit to the industry as this product becomes commercialized, because the processing costs are high and the purified natural product is one of the products of commerce. Collecting from the wild would, by comparison, generally result in varying levels of artemisinin, usually lower levels, and potentially more than one species would be collected and dried.

Ocimum. A less exotic herb, *Ocimum* (basil), is used in many countries as a medicinal, though we use it as a condiment, flavorant, and fragrance. In our studies, we find that distinct visual differences could be easily observed among several species, and unique chemotypes vary greatly in essential oil composition. For targeted natural products, domestication and production has permitted the introduction of new products to be consistently produced. Regardless of which species one would grow, the selection of a high vigor and high-yielding line would be most desirable for both the grower, buyer, and processor.

With raw botanical materials, the following points are important:

1. Significant variation in growth and bioactive compounds occurs naturally. Plants collected in the wild are bound to vary much more from year to year, from location to location, and even within lots than plants that are cultivated. For those of us in plant breeding and crop development, the natural variation is great; for those who are involved in the purchasing and processing of botanicals, working with unimproved plants can prove disastrous. This has been, in part, the basis for the lack of consistency in the raw product, a major stumbling block to quality control.
2. To enhance QC with respect to secondary products, domestication and commercial production offer unique opportunities to increase the consistency of the raw product. This is otherwise difficult to achieve given the genetic variability and probable inclusion of nontarget species in the sold material.

NONGENETIC VARIATIONS IN SOURCE MATERIALS

Localization of the compound

Most of the natural products that confer bioactivity to the botanical are actually compounds that are cytotoxic to the plant and thus compartmentalized in specialized structures of the plant. Knowledge of where the active compound is accumulated is paramount to ensure proper harvesting and collection of the botanical. Harvesting the leaves and flowering tops of a botanical may be convenient to us during shortage of root or rhizome availability but it does little for consumer confidence if the tops do not contain the same quality of the active compounds known to be in the roots.

Artemisia annua produces artemisinin: Within the vegetative period, the upper and middle leaves of the canopy contain the highest levels of artemisinin. This may only be important when this species is grown in the tropics and would remain vegetative for longer periods of time. In northern temperate zones, the plant was determined to be a short-day plant that is induced to flower when photoperiods reach approximately 13 hours. This is important to recognize because the greatest concentration of artemisinin appears to be at flowering because of the significant accumulation of this sesquiterpene in the flowers themselves. So, one may purchase pure Artemisia, but if there are no standards as to the minimum acceptable level of artemisinin, growers harvest a bountiful crop (more than 25 metric tons of dry material/hectare) of young vegetative leaves and containing little artemisinin, relative to harvesting the crop just prior to open bloom when the natural product would be significantly higher.

Environmental considerations

Any factor that influences growth can have an impact on secondary products. This might include water stress and water management. Peppermint, for example, grown under hydroponic conditions in which polyethylene glycol was put into the solution to induce a water stress—causes growth to decrease, concentration of essential oil in a leaf to increase, but overall total oil per area or relative to an agricultural yield to decrease. Consideration of per-plant response versus a whole-field response is quite critical. In general, we find that it is usually not productive to stress botanicals when high yields and high quality are sought, although a stress correctly timed and of the appropriate duration and intensity might be beneficial.

Let us examine the effect of water stress on development of true peppermint (*Mentha x piperita*). Constructing a crude economic analysis based on total essential oil yield from peppermint per area, we found that in Indiana (home to more than 25,000 acres of mint) over a four-year period, irrigation and proper water management was a key to successful farming. These results came during three years with above average rainfall. The effect of water stress is species dependent. Mint, for example, is a mesophytic species and thus a high water user.

Raw product quality is influenced by the plants' genetics, the environment, and postharvest handling and storage. While postharvest is a very important factor, I will focus these last comments on a controversial area that most would prefer to ignore; that is, the potential problem of pesticide contamination.

Pesticide contamination

A prior speaker addressed some of the environmental concerns that need to be included in the development of QA procedures for botanicals. My list would include the presence of radioactive materials, heavy metals, and air pollutants; water quality (water used in irrigation or to wash the harvested products); and the potential contamination from pesticides. Please note that for most herbs, spices, and medicinal and botanical plants there are few, if any, registered pesticides that are legally allowed to be used on those plants. That is, it is illegal to apply a pesticide (herbicide, insecticide, fungicide, etc.) to a botanical unless that pesticide has been registered for use on that crop, and then it must be applied according to the product label. While there are several mechanisms for pesticide registration in this country (national, state, or emergency, as well as a government program to facilitate registration of minor or specialty crops, under which botanicals would fall), the chance that many pesticides will be registered for botanicals looks rather bleak (with the exception of ginseng and mint). This is an important consideration, as weed control reflects one of the highest costs of production, and growers here and abroad may be tempted to use nonregistered herbicides.

We do keep a list of herbs and botanicals which have national pesticide approval. Several of the herbs listed do have certain insecticides registered to be used in accordance with the labels when needed. When one considers the wide range of botanicals and the laws governing pesticide use in this country, it becomes apparent that these plants generally need to be grown without the use of pesticides. This would include, for example, botanicals such as chamomile, feverfew, echinacea, blood root, black cohosh, and valerian, among many others. All botanicals, as is true with other agricultural products, must conform to U.S. pesticide laws regardless of whether the plants are grown here or abroad. This means that all botanicals imported into this country must be free from the same pesticides as would be required here. Few, if any, of the European, Asian, African, or South American botanicals that are imported into this country have pesticides registered for their use in the United States. Thus, if any chemical pesticides have been applied to them and these products contain pesticide residues, then the products should not be permitted to be used in the United States, and selling those products would be both improper and illegal. This is true regardless of whether the plants were cultivated, collected from the wild, or stored. The presence and contamination from pesticides is a real problem, particularly with imports and for products with which we are less familiar. This latter group is more challenging because it is difficult to identify the potential pesticides to screen in unfamiliar plants and plant mixtures. I would argue that the regular testing of botanicals for the presence of pesticides is needed, and that, in the future, there will be increased testing for these compounds.

CONCLUSION

In summary, the domestication and production of botanicals offers tremendous advantages in providing more uniform and consistent raw material; raw material that is identified and sampled easily and properly; and that minimizes adulteration caused by ignorance. The public must have confidence that the commercial products that they are purchasing are indeed the real product. I also would recommend that consideration be given to developing USDA types of standards for raw botanical products and that this would be separate from QA protocols for the finished or processed products. We should look at the success story of agricultural grades and standards used in other food products, such as the fresh fruit and vegetable industry or the processing industry, and try to consider its adaptation for botanicals. I suggest looking to the standards developed by the American Spice Trade Association and the European "Good Agricultural Practices Working Document," as well as the herbal industry gruidelines composed by the American Herbal Products Association.

Developing appropriate production systems and postharvest systems would go a long way toward improving the quality and consistency of raw material. Use of domesticated (through traditional selection and breeding) botanicals will also greatly improve the quality and quantity of the final harvested product: alkaloid-free comfrey, nonshattering borage, improved resistance to fungal diseases and insect pests, are among just a few traits that could be accomplished by plant breeding. Enhanced agricultural yields, and higher levels of bioactive compounds through improved varieties will improve the raw botanical product. Lastly, an improved understanding of the growth and development of the botanical and the development of appropriate production/collection systems of the botanical would ensure that a higher quality raw product consistently reach you the buyer, processor, and manufacturer.

Shipping, Handling, Receipt, and Short-Term Storage of Raw Plant Materials

TRISH FLASTER

Over the past 20 years I have worked in the botanicals industry as a horticulturist, teacher, chemist, botanist, purchasing agent, and ethnobotanist. For many of these years I worked in the Research and Development Analytical Laboratory for Celestial Seasonings, more recently for Shaman Pharmaceuticals, and currently as Chief Executive Officer of Botanical Liaisons, a consulting company. In all of these roles, I have worked with my peers to establish quality products. The botanicals industry has made adequate advances in research and quality assurance (QA) programs to meet and exceed the government standards to provide excellent products for maintaining one's personal health. My role is to present what guidelines are in place from the field to the manufacturing plant that ensure excellent quality and traceability to run a quality business and to fulfill regulatory agencies' requirements and consumers' needs. In this paper most of the examples I use are tropically based, wild harvested, and because techniques vary for individual species, generically based.

SPECIMEN IDENTIFICATION

The process begins in the field with the accurate identification of the plant that is supported by an international system of herbaria. Specimens are sent to the international herbaria, where there are resident specialists who verify the specimens' identities. Depending on where one is working, the vouchers need to be sent to the herbaria that concentrates on that geographical region of the world: for example, New York Botanical Garden—the New World; Missouri Botanical Garden—the New World, China, and Africa; Leiden—South East Asia; or Kew Royal Botanical Garden—Europe, China, and Africa. With this process in place, for well-known commodities, such as herbs in commerce, the growers and foresters know which plants they are to germinate, propagate, and manage. In the case of wild harvested plants or nonhorticultural varieties, field protocol is not relevant for plantations and is not appropriate to a natural setting. Primary to good quality control (QC) is sanitation or cleanliness in the field and forest, which will reduce contaminants. The gleaning of the unwanted fruits and other miscellaneous plant parts eliminates mold and decaying vegetation that could attract larger animals and other infestations. These extraneous plant parts can be easily removed from the fields and used as compost to fertilize the crops later. Because the majority of plants are grown in countries where field labor is plentiful, this process is completed periodically as needed and as contractually agreed upon.

During harvest and postharvest, this cleanliness is absolutely critical for maintaining the quality of the desirable plant parts. For example, during the harvest of the flowers, it is critical that they do not fall onto the ground; the ground must be kept clean from the rotting fruit of past harvests, and the flowers should fall on suspended nets or ground covers. This is also true for wild harvested flowers or dry dehiscing seeds. Plastic or cloth tarpaulins or nets can be placed upon the ground or suspended to catch the desired plant part. For seeds found within fleshy fruits, greater care must be given to prevent spoiling the seeds with rotting material. This is also true

---

Chief Executive Officer, Botanical Liaisons, Boulder, CO.

for root collections. The roots must be extracted carefully so as not to affect the next year's plant-growing ability. Then, when the roots are taken from the ground, all the soil must be removed prior to importation to the United States. Finally, bark collections require minimal harvesting so that individual trees do not die.

After it is harvested, the raw material is transported to a drying area. This area can be near the fields or forests, or at a centralized location in a building, depending on whether sun, shade, heat, or forced air is required. The exact drying specifications assure us of the maintenance of the desirable plant qualities, such as flavor, color, or chemical compounds.

In the case of pharmaceutical products, heat and sunlight are to be avoided. Drying is also critical because of the potential for mold. Therefore, freeze drying is preferable. Material must be dried to preserve its quality during transport to the manufacturing facilities. Drying prevents molds and their degradation products from infecting the crop. Dryness can be detected by simple organoleptic testing of the material and determining the crispness, the snap of the bark or stems, the ability of the leaves to crumble into powder but not into dust. Or more sophisticated systems can be used, such as analytical methods to determine moisture content or water levels within the plants that may increase the bioburden. Also, because purchase is by weight, water content is probably not in one's contract.

COLLECTION AND DRYING

In the case of wild plants or plants not found in commercial trade, accurate botanical identification is the most important QA one can provide with every collection. Because natural variation dominates the botanical world, a trained field collector is required: either a trained botanist or a person native to the area who is thoroughly knowledgeable about the local flora. A trained botanist can identify the plant by utilizing support literature, while the native person will know the plant by its location, appearance, color, taste, and smell. Both methods are adequate; voucher specimens can be collected by either party. Unlike the horticulturally acquired materials, wild crops are found in natural groupings and do not require fertilization or chemicals of any sort for growth and control. These plants may require greater time to collect, however, because of the distances between populations. Furthermore, only smaller quantities may be available because of environmental impact. With wild collections, greater care is given to the collection process because there is no centralized drying facility. For example, collections are made and then travel downriver or on pack animals until the material reaches a village where drying takes place.

PACKING AND STORAGE OF SPECIMENS

After materials are adequately dried, they may be placed into packaging for transport. Breathable natural-fiber containers are preferred to allow for the hygroscopic nature of plants, but the material must be woven tight enough to keep other plants or animals out. The type of storage containers used—barrels, bags, baskets, or boxes, for example—are determined by the textiles available in the country of origin. For the smaller collections used in the pharmaceutical industry—between 1 and 20 kilos—we provide muslin bags with labels. These are placed in warehouse locations until transport is arranged. As in the field, the storage must be clean and free of animals and loose materials that may attract infestations. At this point, costorage must be limited: Many materials can absorb or give off volatile oils and can contaminate each other easily. For example, orange peel can absorb flavors while peppermint's intense volatility may contaminate other plants. During storage, dried raw materials must be kept off the floor or ground to remain dry.

SPECIMEN TRACKING

When plants are cultivated, they can easily be labeled and tracked. Records are kept to monitor the date and quantity of fertilizer, mulch, and beneficial insects used, as well as weather conditions and harvest dates. In the case of wild harvested plants, if they are large specimens, such as trees, they can be numbered and routine growth parameters recorded; if they are small specimens, location details and subtle observations must be recorded for the contractor.

Two tracking forms, such as density and competing species, serve as examples. The first is used in the field by the physician and ethnobotanist when interviewing healers or shamans. On this form details are recorded describing symptoms of the disease(s) treated with the botanical by the healer, the vernacular name and the scientific name (if it is known by the botanist), preparation of the medication, the posology or administration of the medication, and the healer's background and position in the village. Second is the botanical form, noting the plant's location; the native collector and herbaria in which the specimens are kept; the plant's natural habitat; other plants associated with the plant being collected; the vernacular name; flowering and fruit time; and details of the flower's color, flavor, and fragrance. The latter are mostly for taxonomic purposes but are helpful when acquiring additional collections for which we desire the same bioactive molecule, and as environmental indicators.

The plants are dried and the containers in which they are placed are labeled with the plant name or with the number assigned to the botanical voucher that accompanies every collection. This verifies the plant's identity and allows the recipient to return to the place of origin either for reliable re-collections or to trace the source if clarification is needed. This is the most important point for pharmaceutical companies. Without being able to return to the same area of collection, bioactive molecules may not be found again and the discovery process for pharmaceutical products stops. During transportation, additional tracking systems should be in place.

SPECIMEN TRANSPORT

Permits for export and import must be acquired from the ministries of agriculture and the US Department of Agriculture. Commercial invoices for the shipping lines and specifications made by purchasing agents must all be verified and must accompany each shipment. Specimens shipped via sea or long overland transport require thoughtful packaging to be economical: Materials must be compressed so large quantities can be placed within small containers and care must be given to prevent condensation and seawater contamination. There are fewer concerns if small quantities are shipped via air transport. Airbill numbers thus become part of one's tracking system.

Fumigation of botanicals can be administered at the port, during transportation or upon arrival. Many countries require fumigation, but few methods are completely effective and most are not safe for the work environment. Some alternatives to the common use of methyl bromide and phostoxin are freezing, carbon dioxide, or the use of Integrated Pest Management (IPM) instead of fumigation. IPM is a system in which sticky traps with lures and feeders are placed in a 50,000-square-foot grid. It is strictly a monitoring system, not a control system. With the use of IPM, one can know at any given time the status of infestation of the raw materials. Fumigation, on the other hand, does not assure you that infestations are not present. Furthermore, insects have become resistant to phostoxin, and methyl bromide is not a preferred method. I believe IPM is a good alternative.

The following conditions are needed during transport: cleanliness should be maintained; like materials should be stored together (e.g., raw plant materials do not belong with poisons or chemicals); raw materials should be well sealed in containers and stored off the floor and away from the walls for inspection purposes; and an adequate IPM or carbon dioxide fumigation program should be in place. Of course, controlled temperatures and atmospheres are preferred, but it is not the norm nor is it required for most raw botanicals and it can be quite costly. Value-added products (products processed in the country of origin) may require greater storage controls.

RECEIPT OF SPECIMENS

Upon receipt of botanical materials, visual inspection should be performed in order to determine the most immediate needs pertaining to infestations, excess moisture, or other contaminations. Environmentally friendly fumigations should be the next step. When completed, all tracking systems should be verified and the accurate identification of the plant made. A small sample should be taken as a voucher for future chemical verification. Then the materials should be weighed and catalogued and their availability communicated to the inventory control department. The material is then stored until use. All botanical reference vouchers should be taken at this time and placed in long-term storage facilities. Herbarium cases are preferred because they deter insects and can give some protection from fire and smoke.

Frequently overlooked during this process is QC and the relationship with the supplier. It is the quality of the raw materials that makes a superior product and it is the person or community who provides one with the raw materials that will determine the extent of the quality. The provider must be knowledgeable in the techniques of farming or collecting and be able to provide one with quality voucher specimens and bulk materials. The provider can also give advice regarding methods to prevent infestations (e.g., intercropping with specific plants, natural plant pesticides, soil varieties, and which crops will perform well in the specific area).

These QC measures will save time and money. In order to sustain the relationships that guarantee our quality, one can provide supplies with support in the form of financial reimbursement herbarium supplies, and technology. For both phytopharmaceuticals and pharmaceuticals, this process should not be overlooked. With this type of reciprocity, one can rest assured that the material will arrive at one's doorstep in the best form possible. Without this relationship with growers or collectors, one may, instead, receive wet, soggy shipments of varying quality and contaminated and/or adulterated materials. Growers and collectors act as our arms and legs in the field and are therefore very valuable.

The foregoing is a summary of the steps required for the shipping, handling, and receiving of raw plant material. I indicated the QC steps that are already in place in the plant industry. Each company, however, has a unique system that has evolved over the years that is more or less elaborate, depending on the species of plants it is utilizing. I encourage everyone to continue to improve every step of the process in the future as the industry continues to expand.

The Processing of Botanicals

WERNER BUSSE, Ph.D.

This chapter addresses quality aspects of the raw botanical material and the manufacturing issues relevant to the active ingredient and finished product.

DEFINITION OF BOTANICALS

Botanicals have traditionally played a major role in European health care. Over the last several decades, interest and use have become even greater, due not only to a greater tendency toward natural products but also to a much higher quality of herbal products regarding galenical technologies and the scientific evidence of efficacy. Because of the "drug status" of most herbal remedies in Europe, several countries (e.g., Germany, France, Belgium, and Switzerland) have established national regulations concerning the quality, safety, and efficacy of such products.

According to a definition of the World Health Organization (WHO), "herbal medicines" contain as active ingredients plant parts or plant material in the crude or processed state and may contain excipients. Combinations with chemically defined active substances or isolated constituents are not considered to be herbal medicines. In addition to the WHO definition, it must be emphasized that homeopathic preparations are not classified as herbal remedies and herbal remedies are not automatically linked to an over-the-counter status. As a matter of fact, crude plants and the preparations made from them represent a complex mixture of substances. Nevertheless, by definition, the herbal drug or herbal drug preparation, in its entirety, is regarded as the active ingredient.

STARTING RAW MATERIAL

Usually the starting material consists of dried plants or plant parts. The use of fresh plant material is limited, for example, by availability during harvesting season, vulnerability to microbial growth, and deterioration during transport. Newly arrived containers of raw plant materials should be kept in separate areas (quarantine status) before sampling and analysis has taken place.

Control of the starting material involves several steps. The performance of an assay for herbal remedies depends on whether or not ingredients contributing to therapeutic efficacy of the herbal drug are known or not. In the case that the active ingredients are not yet known, a marker substance, which should be specific for the herbal drug, could be chosen for analytical purposes, although it can only serve for internal batch control. In the case that the crude plant material complies with all specifications (identity, purity, and content), the corresponding batch is transferred from the quarantine storage area to normal storage, where it may be used for further processing.

MANUFACTURE OF BOTANICALS

Extraction of herbal drugs

During the last several decades, the use of classical pharmacopoeial preparations (such as tinctures, fluid extracts, or combinations of both) has decreased in industrially prepared herbal products in Germany. Approximately 80 percent of the processed herbal remedies commercialized in Ger-

---

Head, Regulatory and Scientific Affairs, Dr. Willmar Schwabe GmbH and Co., Karlsruhe, Germany.

many contain mainly dry extracts. Because of the strict legal requirements for production, one can observe a trend toward mono- or oligo-preparations, which, as a rule, can be subjected to analysis more easily than multicombinations.

Parameters influencing the result of extraction. Extraction means selection. Extractable ingredients are those substances that may be removed by solvents under the corresponding extraction conditions. Drug components are not extractable from the residue.

The quality of extracts must be defined on the basis of the following parameters: the herbal matter used; the type and concentration of the solvent used for extraction; the extraction method; and the ratio of the amount of starting material to the final amount of native extract.

Solvents. As already pointed out, dry extracts represent the majority of extracts. Because they do not contain relevant amounts of residual solvents, a wider range of solvents can be used for their manufacture.

The withdrawal of a solvent from the material to be dried is frequently performed by applying subatmospheric pressure, which allows a lowering of the temperature. Excessive removal of solvents may result in the decomposition of ingredients.

Simple (total) and concentrated (purified) extract. Based on the composition, two extract types can be distinguished: total (simple) extracts containing effectors, coeffectors, and possibly ingredients with potential negative impact; and purified (concentrated) extracts consisting mainly of effectors and coeffectors.

It is the aim of every purification to remove the unwanted constituents quantitatively as far as possible without damaging the other extractive substances or producing changes having negative effects (e.g., reduced stability) as a result.

Standardization and normalization (adjustment). Simple plant preparations show great annual variations in pharmacologic efficacy. Therefore, herbal drug preparations should be standardized as far as possible.

Standardization is said to occur when the pharmaceutical quality of a botanical is ensured by its comparison with, for example, a pharmacopoeia standard. Standardization is achieved by defining the starting material and kind and concentration of the solvent and through a validated manufacturing process.

The adjustment of a drug to a previously defined standard value is called "normalization." Normalization is needed in order to allow for precise dosage. Unlike standardization, normalization always includes a manipulation. Normalization can be achieved either by blending the starting material or by the addition of inert material to the herbal drug preparation. More favorable is the prior technique in which the crude herbal drugs are mixed according to their content. This leads, via joint extraction of the material, to an extract with a constant content of effectors. It has to be emphasized that the addition of any isolated compounds to extracts for the purpose of adjustment does not make sense and is not allowed according to European guidelines.

MANUFACTURER OF THE FINISHED PRODUCT

Galenical formulations

Dry extracts can be incorporated in various formulations as active ingredients. The manufacturing of the finished product has to take into account some particularities of botanicals (e.g., the hygroscopicity of extracts) but is, in general, identical to the manufacturing of preparations containing chemical entities. Release specifications for a film-coated tablet, for example, include identity and potency determination as well as microbiologic tests. It has to be emphasized that the release specification for the content of extract is ± 5 percent (95–105 percent).

Another important test criterion for the finished product is the dissolution test. The incorporation of the same extract into two different galenical formulations may result in completely different release profiles of the active ingredients.

Stability testing/shelf life

The purpose of stability studies on the dosage form is to establish the product's expected shelf life under stated conditions of storage. Real-time stability studies are normally undertaken at 25°C (77°F) and 60 percent relative humidity. As a rule, it will not be sufficient to determine only the stability of the constituents that contribute to therapeutic activity, because plant materials or preparations thereof in their entirety are regarded as active ingredients. In addition, it has to be shown that other substances present are stable during the proposed shelf life and that their proportion remains constant. This can be achieved by fingerprint chromatography, for example.

Tracking of individual batches

A batch processing record is kept for each processed batch. The record is based on the approved manufacturing formula. This documentation must make it possible to trace the course of manufacture of each batch.

Package labeling

According to the European guidelines, the labeling of finishing botanicals, in principle, is not different from that of chemical entities. It includes special precautions for use, expiration date, and batch number.

CONCLUSION

The quantitative composition of the starting materials for a herbal-based drug is variable. Processing of herbal drugs may induce additional alterations of the ingredients. This implies that a constant quality can only be produced by standardization and control of the starting materials, inprocess controls during manufacture, and standardization and control of the active ingredient as well as of the finished product. The quality requirements and controls during the processing of botanicals must ensure that reproducible therapeutic results can be achieved.

Worldwide Harmonization of Botanical Standards: A Pharmacopeial View

LEE T. GRADY, Ph.D.

The recent resurgence of botanicals in American health care brings with it the necessity for reconsideration of the status of pharmacopeial standards for these products, which, in the past, had been abundant among pharmacopeial monographs. Here we proceed on the presumptions that some additional monographs are to be added to the U.S. Pharmacopeia (USP), with the highest priorities going to those botanicals in use in more than one geographic region of the country.

To facilitate international commerce, one concludes immediately that some harmonization of pharmacopeial standards would be to the advantage of all. This would be consistent with the General Agreement on Tariffs and Trade (GATT). I do not go into the differences in legal recognition of pharmacopeias other than to note that pharmacopeial labeling requirements must also be consistent with the regulations of each country. The status of dietary supplements was recently resolved in the United States, establishing a difference with respect to the legal treatment of these diverse materials. In contrast to dietary supplements, for which manufacturers cannot make specific claims with regard to disease states, it is to be understood that the topic under consideration here is botanical materials (and their preparations) that are used for medical purposes. And if past is prologue, we can look to present and former pharmacopeial monographs as guideposts in any effort for future harmonization.

PROSPECTS FOR HARMONIZATION

The task of global pharmacopeial harmonization is hopeless unless we set out a minimal condition: recognition in at least two or more *regional* pharmacopeias worldwide. Professor Parak of Czechoslovakia reported to the International Federation of Pharmacy that there are about 35 pharmacopeias worldwide. Multibody harmonization obviously is an impossible administrative task. But, in 1989, the USP, along with the European and Japanese pharmacopoeias, formed the Pharmacopeial Discussion Group (PDG). The vast majority of the worldwide market, in the allopathic sense, is represented by these three pharmacopeias. In the future, we must cope with the Chinese and Indian situations, and, specifically for the United States, we must look initially to Canada and Mexico because of the North American Free Trade Agreement (NAFTA). (The Appendix to this chapter is a partial printout from a database constructed at USP headquarters that represents today's point-in-time list of monographs that show commonalities among the pharmacopeias of the PDG. It is a composite of 10 shorter lists, which are identified by the footnote to the chapter appendix.)

Europe alone presents a clear illustration of the challenge to harmonization. Keller[1] reported at an international meeting on pharmacopeias in Rome that the European economic community uses some 1200 vegetable drugs. Countries were asked to re-

---

Vice President and Director, Division of Standards Development, U.S. Pharmacopeia, Rockville, MD.

port usage: With the restriction that one-half of the reportees (that is, 5 out of 10 countries) had to have the same drug for it to make the select list, a list was prepared of 140 vegetable drugs used widely in Europe. But half of these are not in any pharmacopeia! Only 26 of these are in the European pharmacopoeia; although there are 43 others that are in some national pharmacopeias but not in the European pharmacopoeia. In contrast, USP 23-NF-18 recognizes 27 botanicals, exclusive of oils. These appear in the chapter appendix either as USP 23 or as NF 18.

So Europe itself, currently the major user of botanicals in health care, is in a truly sorry state of harmony when botanicals are viewed broadly. The clue to the solution for international harmonization is parallel usage. Select only those botanicals that have found use in a variety of areas and possibly through a long period of time.

This represents a conundrum for the USP. Although international harmonization of botanical standards could receive a priority designation, one must recognize that we are precommitted both to the United States market and to NAFTA. So there is a clash of priorities experienced by the USP, just as there will be a clash of priorities experienced by the European pharmacopoeia, considering that there is a long way to go just to harmonize the situation within Europe. One can conclude at the outset, then, that it will be impossible to make everyone happy, and that only a well-constructed set of mutual priorities holds out hope for progress without despair. The relative priorities of the revision program for the USP will be established at the USP Convention, where resolutions will be considered and this topic will be part of those discussions.

There are definite trends to be addressed here. Since the USP was first published in 1820, 320 botanicals have been recognized, exclusive of isolated compounds: More than 600 monographs can be included when first preparations also are counted. But for the last 100 or more years, it has been a race between adoption of new monographs and the deletion of previous monographs. At the turn of the century, there were 169 botanicals remaining, and there have been few additions since. The last additions were Ipomea root (*Ipomea orizabensis*) and chaulmoogra oil from *Taraktogenos kurzii* and *Hydnocarpus* seeds, added in 1920. Then, in 1942, rosin from *Pinus* species and rice polishings were included in the USP. Fewer still remain in USP 23-NF-18.

But this is not a situation peculiar to the USP. The Italian pharmacopoeia[2] reported that, whereas botanicals were 40 percent of its monographs (20 percent were substances) in 1940, that dropped to 15 percent in 1965, and down to 4 percent in 1985. But the Italian pharmacopoeia is seeing now some resurgence so that, in 1991, 12 percent of its monographs are botanical products. Thus, there is a precedent for a turnaround in the fortunes, so to speak, of botanical products within pharmacopoeias. And one may reasonably look forward to an increase in the number of botanical products in the USP in the near future.

Clearly, both pharmacopoeias responded to the century-old pressure to have purified active principles, in defined dose forms. Ever since Pelletier and Caventou isolated strychnine in 1818, and quinine in 1820, there has been an attempt to find the active principles of vegetable drugs. It is reported by Galeffi[3] that, industrially, 119 substances are isolated today from 90 plants. We must expect, then, that the botanicals that we discuss this year could yet succumb to this separate culture (other than as prevented by the high cost of marketing of a new chemical entity).

The Japanese pharmacopoeia has many natural products, but lists only 47 as being Occidental, of which 20 are in the European pharmacopoeia. But many of the monographs in the Japanese pharmacopoeia would fail the test of being recognized in at least two regional pharmacopoeias.

However, we have the information necessary to establish relative priorities for botanical monographs, which, by and large, could be acceptable both to the European and Japanese pharmacopoeias, based on our accumulated experience in the PDG. What may be more difficult to harmonize is the general priority assigned to botanical medicinals in the overall work programs of these three regional pharmacopoeias. I already stated the role of the USP convention in establishing overall priorities for the USP. Similarly, each regional pharmacopoeia has different general priorities, based on what is expected regionally and their relative roles in drug quality and in the drug registration process.

Modes of harmonization

Harmonization as a word covers many individual realities. The pharmacopeias have found that *prospective* harmonization of yet-to-be-adopted monographs or reference standards is easier to achieve than *retrospect* harmonization of existing monographs that differ. Differences in existing monographs arose out of different laboratory practices and environments and different decades of adoption.

Forward harmonization[4] is a concept agreed upon by the members of the forerunner of the PDG, the British, European, Japanese, and U.S. pharmacopeias. It means selection of methods that would be acceptable well into the future, that any pharmacopeia can retain any meaningful standard even if not adopted by the others, and that harmonization does not inhibit unilateral progress on the part of any pharmacopeia. Although agreed to, this has been difficult to achieve.

Progressions in quality challenges

With a list of priorities in hand, we can then proceed to the individual plant species, with various challenges arising according to the history and presentation of the medicament in question. We can divide the botanical articles into three general categories, for example, based on the *article of commerce*. One cateogry could be plant parts or powdered botanicals; a second may be articles derived by minimal processing of the botanical so as to end up with, say, a simple extract or infusion; the third would be preparations that require extensive chemistry in extraction or processing, such as the characteristic mixture of components. An example of the last is the current USP monograph for Sennosides, which is the result of a specific process. Wholly different standards-setting strategies can be applied to these three types of botanical articles. Consistent with the scope of this book, we do not consider further those articles that are the result of extensive processing but will limit ourselves to those things that are plant parts, powders, or simple extracts or infusions.

Standardization strategies also can be affected by the intended mode of use of the botanical preparation by the public. Frank[5] recommended three classes: first, those that are prepared by consumers using boiling water, such as teas; second, those that are taken either with cold water or as dry tablets or capsules; and third, relatively processed items, such as extractions or tinctures. What is the common element for this way of classifying botanicals? In this case, obviously it is the microbial content, so that processing, which decreases bioburden, as does boiling with water, therefore would allow more permissive standards for the original botanical materials. But those botanical materials carrying through without a reduction in bioburden to the consumers should be subjected to significant limits on the microbial content.

SCIENTIFIC ISSUES IN STANDARDIZATION

Underlying standardization strategies for botanicals is the general definition of the plant as the active material,[1] whether or not the active constituents are known. This concept has substantial implications, for example, when we assign an expiration date before which reliable performance can be expected. Identity and purity tests must support this definition. Pharmacopeial monographs intrinsically are shelf-life standards, so one can expect that the pharmacopeial monographs will select technology that will exclude definitively decomposed botanical materials.

We also can see herbs simply as diluted drugs[6] and, therefore, we must standardize them with respect to strength. The USP introduced assays in the year 1900 for 20 botanical products, so the precedent is clear.

We must then ask what was appropriate technology at the turn of the last century, and what is appropriate technology at the turn of this century. What constitutes a modern standard of *identification*? Which botanical materials would require an *assay* for strength? Which can be standardized based on general strategy exclusive of demonstration of strength?

Identification

The first challenge is pharmacognostic. Here, past is prologue. The sine qua non for botanicals is identification. Refer to the USP monograph for Belladonna Leaf for a complete botanical description by the language of pharmacognosy in full flower. But for the pharmacopeias to harmonize on pharmacognostics, they face a significant challenge. The standard is unenforceable if industry and regulators cannot obtain analysts with the correct training to interpret a botanical description accurately.

Histology is a rich and critical resource but even

this is not in all cases completely sufficient for the monograph identification. Here again, the training of the analyst is of the highest significance because it is so specialized and is not a characteristic to be found widely in analytical laboratories. Fortunately, in the United States, there is an established pattern of using specialized laboratories by contract and for specialization among Food and Drug Administration regional laboratories, so this is not an insurmountable problem. Also, pharmacy colleges can be called upon to reintroduce some of this training.

Reference materials are most certain to be a critical aspect of identification, for both general botanical and histologic parameters and for specifications. For the pharmacopeias, the harmonization challenge here is in the sharing or issuance of compatible reference materials so that comparison against two different reference materials does not confuse the issue in any one examining laboratory. The pharmacopeias have made some progress with regard to harmonization of reference standards but much is left to be desired here. The patterns of usage of reference standards in the three different regions has been significantly different; and, therefore, it makes administrative coordination of harmonized reference standards over a period of a decade or so a source of some irritation. But this also is not insurmountable.

We have so far discussed standardization that was appropriate at the turn of the last century. At the turn of this century, botany will not be enough, except in a few circumstances. It is very clear that the marketplace will expect a higher degree of identification. Recall the earlier statements about shelf life, and recognize the commonalities of procedures.

In this regard, *thin-layer chromatography* has the greatest promise because it is available worldwide for use in a wide variety of circumstances. It is a reasonable global expectation to be placed on sources of supply as well as at ports of import.

But, we ask, chromatography of what? For example, are the active constituents of the botanical preparation known? Or would we look instead at what are called *markers*, that is, those characteristic, quantifiable plant constituents to be used in quality control when actives are uncertain or not found? We can only verify markers as characteristic, or that a pattern of active ingredients is characteristic, by examination of a fairly large number of batches of the authentic botanical product, perhaps from more than one source or process. Authentic specimens (i.e., reference standards) will probably be inescapable for comparison because of the known variation in chromatographic supplies. Even in the simple, synthetic, organic medicinal world, chromatography against a reference material has been inescapable. This requirement applies to plant parts and to powders as well as to simple extracts or infusions.

Where the botanical is used because of its volatile constituents, then gas chromatography (GC) is the obvious means of identification. We reasonably may expect GC to be workable anywhere in the world today since the advent of solid-state instrumentation. Research-grade gas chromatographs are not necessary to accomplish this purpose and, indeed, the botanical industry was an early user of GC in identification, assay, and other general quality control considerations. And that was in the days when thermal conductivity detectors were all that was available.

So, the most important standardization issue, by way of abundance, is *identification*, requiring very little by way of conceptual development. Appropriate technology is available worldwide, and no large differences would be expected among pharmacopeias in the rationalization of tests and specifications to identify botanicals.

Assays

Quantitative determination of active ingredients or characteristic markers may be inescapable for certain preparations and plant materials. The label of the consumer article may well state a strength, and the general recommendations by the Committee for Proprietary Medical Products (CPMP) in Europe and by the World Health Organization (WHO) is for this to be the case. It is not necessary that assays per se be stability-indicating, even though stability assurance is a critical outcome of a pharmacopeial monograph. The assay need only be quantitative, and it may be that the identification test, chromatographic purity test, or colorimetric test within the monograph will be sufficient to exclude decomposed botanicals.

It is the area of assays where harmonization becomes much more difficult among the pharmacopeias. The USP tends to use instrumental methods to solve standardization problems because, in the United States, electronics are cheap and people's time is expensive when compared to the situation in some other places in the world. It is also important that literature reports of the efficacy of botanical preparations use well-characterized materials and reliable assays. This would in no small part lend a degree of assurance to the interpretation of literature reports.

Chromatography (liquid chromatography and GC) finds extensive application in assays. It best fulfills the nineteenth-century and analytical object of making measurements on purified specimens because there is simultaneous purification (separation) and measurement (detection). The pharmacopeias have been able to harmonize adequately here, even though commercial chromatographic packings vary.

Special purity limits

Individual botanical preparations may require tests and specifications that are peculiar to specific items, especially when safety is the issue. For example, there is currently a discussion in Europe for a limit of estragole in fennel oil. Thus, one may set limits on things that may be considered to be "negative markers," or negative botanical characteristics, or histologic parameters. Another example is a limit of anthrone in the bark of *Rhamnus* spp. in the European pharmacopoeia. Glycosides are regarded generally as being less toxic than the aglyca; for example, rhein is less toxic than emodin. For USP sennosides, the aglycon is aloe-emodin and there are current questions as to the carcinogenicity of the preparation. One would not expect much difficulty in harmonizing such requirements among regional pharmacopeias because the safety issue would be recognizable to all.

Special limits that would not be successful in harmonization are exemplified by radionuclides, for example, in reactor accidents. This would not need to be harmonized because this would be a national or regional requirement.

Another example of where harmonization will not be possible is in the use of ethylene oxide (ETO) or perhaps the postharvest treatments. Indeed, it has been reported that the Europeans face a confusing situation with respect to ETO and microbial limits, so that published standards in force today can be met by only a minority of products in the marketplace.

General purity limits

There appears to be general agreement among the pharamacopeias and such groups as the CPMP and the WHO that certain general quality parameters would be expected to apply to most if not all botanical items (e.g., a determination of ash—total ash, or acid-insoluble or water-soluble ash—because sand or other mineral contents of botanicals are a predictable occurrence).

The USP already unilaterally recognized *residue on ignition* and *sulphated ash* for the synthetic organic medicinals in harmonizing with the other pharmacopeias. Our faster process allows us to do this, although the other pharmacopeias have yet to reciprocate because their decision-making and publication processes are not on the same time schedule. But eventual harmonization of these general quality characteristics is a reasonable expectation.

Metals

Tests for *heavy metals* also have been harmonized by the PDG, and the botanical monographs would take advantage of this. What is difficult to harmonize is application of specific tests for elements, such as cadmium or lead, when instruments such as inductively coupled plasma or atomic absorption were to be used. This became an issue in worldwide commerce because of the expense of the methods. We currently are working on such an example, specifically for cadmium and nickel, in international harmonization of the excipient magnesium stearate.[7] This exercise is predictive of the situation that would be found for botanicals when appreciable quantities could be expected to be ingested. Although all may agree that toxicity-based limits is the proper way to establish specifications, toxicologists have a habit of coming up with different numbers.

Other requirements

Limits on water and volatiles are obvious monograph elements, and pharmacopeias have the general tests necessary to support this. It is reasonable to expect harmonization here. Water-extractable matter also is a characteristic that would be harmonized easily when that was an issue for a specific botanical. Other specific botanicals may require tests for bitterness or tannins; hemolytic activity tests for saponins; or some functionality testing, such as for swelling and foaming. There may be, at least for tannins and hemolytic activity, modern chromatographic methods that could be substituted. There may be little difficulty in harmonization on these less frequently standardized parameters.

Pesticides

Botanicals are products of nature and in the world of cultivation, pesticides are ubiquitous. The USP has already been through this exercise with the Modified Lanolin monograph in which 34 pesticides are tested for because sheep are part of the various agriculture environments. For botanicals, postharvest treatment also comes to mind. So testing for toxic residues when a botanical is to be ingested is an issue in standardization.

Earlier I mentioned Frank's triaging of botanicals based on processing or usage in such a way as to reduce bioburden. The pattern of use of any botanical product will seldom be obscure, so one can expect the pharmacopeias to reach reasonable agreement by analogy on those monographs on botanicals for which a limit on pesticides would be appropriate. Then the situation becomes very complex.

There is enormous variety to the pesticides in use in the world, and regions and nations differ in this respect. As reflected in the WHO guidelines, it is now expected in worldwide commerce that imported articles specify the country of origin. One could theoretically prepare different lists of pesticides in legal use in various countries and establish a series of tests that would encompass all possibilities based on labeled origin. The Italian pharmacopoeia specifies 26 pesticides for just that market.

A similar procedure has been recommended recently by the WHO,[8] which has a list of about 42 pesticides to be minimally tested in botanicals. WHO now suggests that there be: (1) a list of pesticides not to be used in the cultivation of botanicals for medicinal use; and (2) a list of those pesticides to be favored in this regard. This would greatly reduce the combinations to be coped with in the analytical laboratories worldwide in determining the absence of unwanted quantities of pesticide residues.

Pesticide limits will be an expensive part of laboratory testing of botanical quality. One would be testing for organochlorines, for organophosphorus, and for perhaps some postharvest treatments. Typically, these methods tie chromatographs up (although these devices are often automatable) for a significant period of time. The pharmacopeias have been successful in harmonizing on methodology. The capital investment in the laboratory is appreciable, and supplies of reference materials may sometimes be unreliable or obscure. An impractical situation is presented when a pesticide not legally available in one country is a pesticide used in the country from which the botanical is sourced and, thus, must be obtained as a reference. One would have to rely on a certificate upon purchase, but this is not an easy thing to do with in international commerce.

Microbial limits

Everyone agrees on the need for the absence of pathogens, such as *Salmonella*. And everyone agrees to some limits on *Enterobacteriaceae* and *E. coli* for botanicals that are to be ingested. But different expert groups will come up with limits that may differ by one order of magnitude or more. Little disagreement is expected on the fact that modest limits are appropriate for botanicals that are crude and are expected to be used for further (bioburden-reducing) processing. On the other hand, relaxed *E. coli* and mold limits would be all that would be necessary other than absence of *Salmonella*. Those botanicals for topical use, or with some sort of a pretreatment such as boiling, could require a lower level of enteral forms and perhaps a limit on total aerobes. But total aerobic count is an area of significant disagreement among groups of experts, because this is essentially a concomitant of the moisture. It is difficult enough to get agreement within the scope of one pharmacopeia on total aerobic counts, much less international agreement.[9]

The application of limits for molds also is an area in which there will be differences of opinion. Some people would test strictly by chemical means for aflatoxins, and others would take the more general microbiologic approach. One possibility for testing for molds would be a screening test based on serologic response to *Aspergillus* antigen, which could be done by contract laboratories, and then, only if this were positive, one could look for aflatoxins.

Although *Lactobacillus* and *Leuconostoc* are common organisms in botanicals, specific tests for these usually are not done. There may be some basis for testing for pseudomonads, depending on the use of the botanical. Although the pharmacopeias would be unlikely to make specific tests, one would presume that under the USP General Notice on Foreign Substances such contaminating organisms as mycotoxin-producing molds, *Clostridia* or *Bacillus aureus* spore formers, would be viewed in the same sense as *Salmonella*, as unacceptable organisms.

Processing

Pharmacopeias may need to specify the process by which extracts or infusions are made, as indeed this was the case decades ago. An official reference material is inescapable. For the plant parts, powders, and simple extracts and infusions included in the scope of this chapter, this is not a particular issue and can easily be handled in the monograph: rubric definition. What becomes a problem are the different results from different manufacturers when more extensive processing is involved. We must be careful in the pharmacopeias not to establish monographs that place one manufacturer at a disadvantage relative to another because of processing peculiarities that are not supported by safety or efficacy considerations. Internationally, this is a GATT issue. This is entirely consistent with previous discussion of toxicity-based limits for unwanted materials.

Labeling

There seems to be a convergence of opinion on what elements need to appear in labeling. Clearly, all of the pharmacopoeias expect the genus and species of a plant, the part of the plant that is used, as well as the source of that material to be identified, when it is a matter of importance. This already was typical of the pharmacopeias at the turn of the century. One, then, can expect the pharmacopeias to be entirely harmonious on these items. Also, labeling may require some statement as to moisture or the content of actives or markers, either as the intermediate material in international commerce prior to additional processing or as the consumer article.

Pharmacopeias may not differ, even though responding to different laws or customs as, for example, in the labeling of inactive ingredients when the botanical is a simple admixture with unobjectionable materials. This is an expectation in the USP and, indeed, is a requirement for the CPMP and an aspect of the WHO guidelines.

A very large difference, however, may be experienced once the labeling moves away from content to the expected use of the article. As many people have said, the statement of claims is the dividing line between drug and nondrug use in the United States. But, beyond that, is the issue of advice to the consumer or patient, such as is incorporated in the USP's information databases and ancillary publications. Simultaneous use of any botanical with prescribed or over-the-counter pharmacologic agents of various classes may need warnings of interactions along with typical side effects, and so forth. This is a topic to be explored, I hope, at some conference concurrent with pharmacopeial monograph emergence. Standards must be set with pattern of use in mind, and pattern of use must underlie conclusions as to what constitutes labeling. For the USP, there is the additional decision to make as to how to include the botanical preparations in its treatment of drugs in general in its information database.

REFERENCES

1. Keller K. Pharmacopoeias and the quality control of drugs. *Proceedings of the Third International Conference*, Nov 1992, Rome: Fondaz. Rhone-Poulenc Rorer Sci. Medich., Editrice Compositori-Bologna; 243–250, 291–293, 1993.
2. Cingolani G. Op. cit.:277–281.
3. Galeffi C. Op. cit.: 251–256.
4. Grady L. Conference on the International Harmonization of Pharmaceutical Quality—Vision of Pharmacopoeia in the 21st Century. Sept. 1989. Tokyo: Pharm. Manuf. Assoc; Tokyo and Osaka Pharma. Manuf. Assoc. 25–31, 1990.
5. Frank B. Botanical specifications. *Deutsche Apotheker Zeitung* 129:617–623, 1989.
6. Tyler V. *The New Honest Herbal*. Philadelphia: Geo. F. Stickley, 1987.
7. Subcommittee on Excipients, Magnesium stearate. *Pharmacopeial Forum* 21(1):86–90, 1995.
8. World Health Organization *Quality Control Methods for Medicinal Plant Materials*. Geneva: World Health Organization, Geneva WHO/Pharm/92.559; document for disscussion, 1992.
9. Opalchenova G. Ibid. 20(4):7872–7877, 1994.

CHAPTER APPENDIX: BOTANICALS OF INTEREST TO USP

Plant name	Listing	Part(s) used	Pharmacopeial name
Abies balsamea canadensis	USP-TOC[a]	oleoresin	Terebinthinia
Abies excelsa	USP-OLD	resin exudate	Pix burgundica
Acacia catechu	USP-TOC	wood	Catechu
Acacia senegal	NF 18	exudate	Acacia
Acacia senegal	JAPAN PH.		
Acaciae gummi	PH.EUR		
Achillea	USP-OLD	leaves, tops	Achillea
Achillea millefolium	US TOP 50		
Achillea millefolium	EURO-140	herba	
Achillea millefolium	CAN.FOOD		
Achyranthes fauriei, bidentata	JAPAN PH.	root	
Aconitum napellus	USP-TOC	tuber-root, leaves	Aconite
Acorus calamus	USP-TOC	rhizome	Calamus
Acorus calamus	EURO-140	rhizoma	
Acorus gramineus	J-CRUDE	rhizome	
Adenophora	J-CRUDE	root	
Agathotes chirayta	USP-OLD		Chiretta
Agrimonia eupatoria	EURO-140	herba	
Agrimonia procera	EURO-140	herba	
Agropyron repens	USP-TOC	rhizome	Triticum
Agropyron repens	EURO-140	rhizoma	
Agropyron repens	CAN.FOOD	rhizome	
Akebia quinata	JAPAN PH.	stem	
Alchemilla vulgaris	EURO-140	herba	
Aletris farinosa	USP-OLD	root	Aletris
Alisma orientale	JAPAN PH.	rhizome	
Allii sativi	PH.EUR/DE	bulb	
Allium cepa	EURO-140	bulbus	
Allium ratium	USP-TOC	bulb	Allium
Allium sativum	US TOP 50		
Allium sativum	USP-OLD	bulbus	Allium
Allium sativum	EURO-140	bulbus	Allium
Aloes barbadensis	USP 23		Aloe
Aloe barbadensis	PH.EUR		
Aloe capensis	PH.EUR		
Aloe extractum siccum normatum	PH.EUR		
Aloe ferox, spp.	JAPAN PH.	juice of leaves	
Aloe species (barbadensis, capensis, ferox)	EURO-140	succus (sicc.)	
Aloe (vera) barbadensis, ferox	USP 23	leaf latex	Aloe
Aloe (vera) barbadensis, ferox	US TOP 50	leaf latex	Aloe
Aloe vera, perryi, spicata, chinensis, socotrina	USP-TOC	juice of leaves	Aloe
Alpinia officinarum	EURO-140	rhizoma	
Alpinia officinarum	J-CRUDE	rhizome	
Alpinia oxyphylla	JAPAN PH.	fruit	

[a]Definitions of listings as follows:

USP-OLD, (>100 years ago): recognized at any time 1820–1899

USP-TOC, (<100 years ago): adopted at turn of century, published 1907

USP-WW2, (50 years ago): remaining official—published 1947

USP 23, NF 18, (Now): remaining official, 1995–2000

EURO-140, Survey by European Union (see reference 1)

US TOP 50, Survey in *Medical Herbalism*, P. Bergner, ed. Portland, OR, Spring 1994; and P. Brevoort, "Economics of U.S. Botanical Market," East-Earth Herb, Inc., 1994

CAN. FOOD, Second Report, Expert Advisory Committee on Herbs and Botanical Preparations, Ministry of Health Canada, October 1993

PH.EUR. (DEV.), European Pharmacopoeia (Dev.—in progress)

JAPAN PH., Japanese Pharmacopoeia

J-CRUDE, "Japanese Crude Drugs," Japan International Corporate Welfare Services, Tokyo, 1989.

Note: A different treatment of individual botanicals including by length of time in USP, is available by Boyle W. *Botanical Substances in U.S. Pharmacopeia*. East Palestine, OH: Buckeye Naturopathic Press, 1991.

WORLDWIDE HARMONIZATION OF BOTANICAL STANDARDS

CHAPTER APPENDIX: BOTANICALS OF INTEREST TO USP (Cont'd)

Plant name	Listing	Part(s) used	Pharmacopeial name
Althaea officinalis	USP-TOC	root	Althaea
Althaea officinalis	CAN.FOOD		
Althaea officinalis	EURO-140	flores	
Althaea officinalis	EURO-140	folium	
Althaea officinalis	EURO-140	radix	
Althaea radix	PH.EUR/DE		
Amomum xanthioides	JAPAN PH.	seed	
Amygdalis communis	USP-OLD		Almond oil
Amygdalis communis	USP-OLD	kernel	A. Amara, Dulcis
Amylum pregelatinicum	PH.EUR/DE		
Amylum solubile	PH.EUR/DE		
Anacyclus pyrethrum	USP-OLD	root	Pyrethrum
Anamirta cocculus	USP-WW2	seed	Picrotoxin
Andira araroba	USP-WW2	wood	Chrysarobin
Anemarrhena asphodeloides	JAPAN PH.	rhizome	
Anemone pulsatilla	USP-OLD	herb	Pulsatilla
Anethum graveolens	EURO-140	fructus	
Angelica acutiloba	JAPAN PH.	root	
Angelica archangelica	USP-OLD		Angelica
Angelica archangelica	EURO-140	radix	
Angelica atropurpurea archangelica	USP-OLD		
Angelica dahurica	JAPAN PH.	root	
Angelica pubescens	J-CRUDE	root	
Angelica sinensis	US TOP 50		
Anisi aetheroleum	PH.EUR		
Anisi fructus	PH.EUR		
Anisi stellati fructus	PH.EUR/DE		
Anthemis nobilis	USP-TOC	flower-heads	Anthemis
Apocynum cannabinum	USP-TOC	rhizome	Apocynum
Arachis hypogaea	NF 18	seed kernel oil	Peanut oil
Aralia cordata	J-CRUDE	rhizome, bark	
Aralia spinosa	USP-OLD	bark	Aralia
Arctium lappa	USP-TOC	root	Lappa
Arctium lappa	EURO-140	radix	
Arctium lappa	J-CRUDE		
Arctostaphylos uva-ursi	USP-TOC	leaves	Uva Ursi
Arctostaphylos uva-ursi	EURO-140	folium	
Arctostaphylos uva-ursi	JAPAN PH.	leaf	
Areca catechu	JAPAN PH.	seed	
Areca pericarp	J-CRUDE	seed	
Arisaema	J-CRUDE	tuber	
Aristolochia reticulata	USP-TOC	roots	Serpentaria
Aristolochia serpentaria	USP-TOC	rhizomes	Serpentaria
Armoracia	USP-OLD	horseradish	
Armoracia rusticana	EURO-140	radix	
Arnicae montana	USP-OLD	root	Arnicae radix
Arnica montana	EURO-140	flores	
Artanthe elongata	USP-OLD	leaves	Matico
Artemisia absinthium	USP-OLD	leaves and tops	Absinthium
Artemisia absinthium	CAN.FOOD		
Artemisia absinthium	EURO-140	herba	
Artemisia capillaris	J-CRUDE	flower	
Artemisia cina	CAN.FOOD		
Artemisia maritima	CAN.FOOD		
Artemisia pauciflora	USP-TOC	flower-heads	Santonica
Artemisia vulgaris	CAN.FOOD		
Arctium lappa	US TOP 50		
Arum triphyllum	USP-OLD	corm	Arum
Asarum canadense	USP-OLD	root	Asarum
Asclepias tuberosa	USP-TOC	root	Asclepias
Asiasarum sieboldi, heterotropoides	JAPAN PH.	root	

CHAPTER APPENDIX: BOTANICALS OF INTEREST TO USP *(Cont'd)*

Plant name	Listing	Part(s) used	Pharmacopeial name
Asparagus	J-CRUDE	tuber	
Aspidium felix-mas	USP-OLD	rhizome	Filix-mas
Aspidosperma quebracho blanco	USP-OLD	bark	Aspidosperma
Aster	J-CRUDE	root	
Astragalus gummifer	NF 18	exudate	Tragacanth
Astragalus gummifer	USP-TOC	exudate	Tragacantha
Astragalus gummifer	JAPAN PH.	exudate	
Astragalus gummifer	CAN.FOOD	exudate	
Astragalus membranaceus	US TOP 50		
Astragalus membranaceus, spp.	JAPAN PH.	root	
Atractylodes japonica, ovata	JAPAN PH.	rhizome	
Atractylodes lancea, chinensis	JAPAN PH.	rhizome	
Atropa belladonna	USP-TOC	leaves and roots	Belladonna
Atropa belladonna	EURO-140	folium	
Atropa belladonna	JAPAN PH.	root	
Aurantii flos aetheroleum	PH.EUR/DE		
Avena sativa	USP-OLD	seed-meal	Avenae farina
Avena sativa	US TOP 50		
Balsamodendron	USP-OLD	juice	Myrrha
Balsamum	USP-TOC		
Balsamum peruvianum	PH.EUR		
Bamboo caulis	J-CRUDE		
Bardenia	JAPAN PH.	fruit	
Barosma betulina	USP-TOC	leaves	Buchu
Barosma betulina	EURO-140	folium	
Belladonnae folium	PH.EUR		
Belladonnae pulvis normatus	PH.EUR		
Benincasa	J-CRUDE	seed	
Berberis aquifolium (Oregon grape)	USP-TOC	rhizome and root	Berberis
Berberis aquifolium	US TOP 50		
Berberis vulgaris	USP-OLD	root bark	Berberis
Betula lenta	USP-WW2	distilled oil/bark	*Oleum betulae*
Betula pendula	EURO-140	folium	
Boldo	PH.EUR/DE		
Borago officinalis	CAN.FOOD	leaves and tops	
Brassica campestris	JAPAN PH.	fixed oil	
Brassica nigra, juncea	USP-WW2	seed	Black Mustard
Breyera anthelmintica	USP-OLD	flowers, fruit	Brayers
Bryonia alba	USP-OLD	root	Bryonia
Bryonia dioica	USP-OLD	root	Bryonia
Bupleurum falcatum	JAPAN PH.	root	
Calendula officinalis	USP-TOC	flores	Calendula
Calendula officinalis	EURO-140	flores	
Calendula officinalis	US TOP 50		Calendula
Camphea officinale	USP 23		Camphor
Canella alfa	USP-OLD		Canella
Cannabis sativa	USP-TOC	flower tops	Cannabis Indica
Capsella bursa-pastoris	EURO-140	herba	
Capsicum annuum, frutescens	USP 23	oleoresin	Capsicum Oleoresin
Capsicum annuum, frutescens	CAN.FOOD	fruit	
Capsicum annuum	US TOP 50		
Capsicum annuum	EURO-140	fructus	
Capsicum annuum	JAPAN PH.	fruit	
Capsicum frutescens	USP-TOC	fruit	Capsicum
Cardui mariae fructus	PH.EUR/DE		
Carica papaya	CAN.FOOD	dried latex, leaves	
Carthamus tinctorius	NF 18	seed oil	Safflower oil
Carthamus tinctorius	JAPAN PH.	flower	
Carum carvi	USP-WW2	distilled oil	*Oleum cari*
Carum carvi	EURO-140	fructus	
Carvi fructus	PH.EUR/DE		

WORLDWIDE HARMONIZATION OF BOTANICAL STANDARDS

CHAPTER APPENDIX: BOTANICALS OF INTEREST TO USP (Cont'd)

Plant name	Listing	Part(s) used	Pharmacopeial name
Caryophyllus aromaticus	USP-TOC	distilled oil	*Oleum caryophylli*
Caryphylli flos	PH.EUR		
Cassava (spp.)	USP-OLD		Tapioca
Cassia acutifolia	USP 23	leaflets	Senna
Cassia acutifolia	JAPAN PH.	leaflets	
Cassia angustifolia	USP 23	leaflets	Senna
Cassia angustifolia	USRO-140	folium	
Cassia fistula	USP-TOC	fruit	Cassia Fistula
Cassia marilandica	USP-OLD	leaflets	
Cassia obtusifolia	JAPAN PH.	seed	
Cassia senna	EURO-140	folium, fructus	
Castanea dentata, pumile	USP-TOC	leaves	Castanea
Catalpa ovata	JAPAN PH.	fruit	
Caulophyllum thalictroides	USP-TOC	rhizomes and roots	Caulophyllum
Centaurium erythraea	EURO-140	herba	
Centilla asiatica	US TOP 50		
Cephaelis acuminata	USP 23	root and rhizome	Ipecacuanhua, Ipecac
Cephaelis ipecacuanha	USP 23	root and rhizome	Ipecacuanhua, Ipecac
Cephaelis ipecacuanha	JAPAN PH.	root	
Cephaelis ipecacuanha	EURO-140	radix	
Cetraria islandica	USP-TOC		Cetraria
Cetraria islandica	CAN.FOOD		Cetraria
Chaenomeles	J-CRUDE	fruit	
Chamomilla recutita	EURO-140	flores	
Chamomilla recutica	US TOP 50		
Chamomillae romanae flos	PH.EUR		
Chelidonium majus	USP-TOC	plant	Chelidonium
Chenopodium ambrosioides var. anthelminticum	USP-TOC	volatile oil	Oleum Chenopodium
Cherry	J-CRUDE	bark	
Chimaphila umbellata	USP-TOC	plant	Chimaphila
Chinese bayberry	J-CRUDE	bark	
Chondrodendron tomentosum	USP-TOC	root	Pareira
Chondrus crispus	USP-TOC	plant	Chondrus
Chondrus crispus	USP-TOC	thallus	
Chondrus crispus	EURO-140	thallus	
Chondrus crispus	CAN.FOOD	thallus	
Chrysanthemum	J-CRUDE	flower	
Chrysanthemum parthenium	US TOP 50		
Chrysanthemum parthenium	CAN.FOOD		
Cichorium intybus	CAN.FOOD	root	
Cimicifuga racemosa	USP-TOC	rhizome/root	Cimicifuga
Cimicifuga racemosa	EURO-140	rhizoma	
Cimicifuga racemosa	US TOP 50		
Cimicifuga simplex	JAPAN PH.	rhizome	
Cinchona calisaya	USP-TOC	bark	Cinchona
Cinchona ledgeriana	USP-TOC	bark	Cinchona
Cinchona officinalis	USP-TOC	bark	Cinchona
Cinchona succirubra	USP-TOC	bark	*Cinchona rubra*
Cinchonae cortex	PH.EUR		
Cinnamomi cortex	PH.EUR		
Cinnamomum	USP-TOC	oleoresin	Cinnamomum Saigonicum
Cinnamomum aromaticum	EURO-140	cortex	
Cinnamomum laureirii	USP-WW2	bark	Cinnamon bark
Cinnamomum zeylanicum	USP-TOC	bark	Zeylonicum
Cinnamonum cassia	USP-WW2	oil	Cinnamon oil
Cinnamonum cassia	JAPAN PH.	bark	
Cissampelos pareira	USP-OLD	root	Pareira
Citrullus colocynthis	USP-TOC	fruit	Colocynth
Citrus aurantium	USP-WW2	distilled oil of fruit	Bitter orange oil
Citrus aurantium	CAN.FOOD	petals, fruit	
Citrus aurantium	JAPAN PH.	peel	

Chapter Appendix: Botanicals of Interest to USP *(Cont'd)*

Plant name	Listing	Part(s) used	Pharmacopeial name
Citrus aurantium	JAPAN PH.	oil	
Citrus bergamia	USP-TOC	volatile oil	Oleum bergamottae
Citrus limon	EURO-140	aetheroleum	
Citrus limonium	USP-WW2	peel oil	Lemon oil
Citrus limonium	CAN.FOOD	peel	
Citrus tachibana	J-CRUDE	peel	
Citrus unshiu	JAPAN PH.	peel	
Claviceps purpurea	USP-TOC	sclerotium on secale cereale (rye)	Ergota
Clematis	J-CRUDE	root	
Cnicus benedictus	EURO-140	herba	
Cnidium officinale	JAPAN PH.	rhizome	
Cocculus palmatus	USP-OLD	root	Calumba
Cocos nucifera	JAPAN PH.	oil	
Coffea arabica	USP-OLD		
Coix lachryma-jobi	JAPAN PH.	fruit	
Cola nitida	EURO-140	semen	
Colchicum autumnale	USP-TOC	seed and corm (and root in 1890)	Colchici Cormus, Semen
Commiphora molmol	EURO-140	gum-resin	
Commiphora myrrha	USP-WW2	gum-resin	Myrrha
Conium maculatum	USP-TOC	fruit	Conium
Contrayervia	USP-OLD		
Convallaria majalis	USP-TOC	rhizome/root	Convallaria
Convolvulus scammonium	USP-TOC	gum-resin	Scammonium
Copaiba spp. (*Copiafera*)	USP-TOC	oleoresin	Copaiba
Copernicia cerifera	NF 18		Carnauba wax
Coptis japonica	JAPAN PH.	rhizoma	
Coptis trifolia	USP-OLD	root	
Coriander sativum	USP-TOC	fruit	Coriander
Coriandrum sativum	USP-WW2	distilled oil	Oleum Coriandri
Coriandrum sativum	EURO-140	fructus	
Cornus officinalis	JAPAN PH.	sarcocarp	
Cornus spp.	USP-OLD		Cornus
Corydalis turtschaninovii	JAPAN PH.	tuber	
Crataegus	J-CRUDE	fruit	
Crataegus laevigata	EURO-140	folium	
Crataegus oxycantha	US TOP 50		
Crocus sativus	USP-TOC	stigmas	Crocus
Crocus sativus	JAPAN PH.	stigma	
Crocus sativus	EURO-140	stigma	
Crocus sativus	CAN.FOOD	stigma	
Croton eluteria	USP-OLD	bark	Cascarilla
Croton tiglium	USP-TOC	expressed seeds	Oleum Tiglii
Cubeba officinalis	USP-OLD	fruit	Cubeba
Cucurbita pepo	USP-TOC	seed	Pepo
Curcuma longa	EURO-140	rhizoma	
Curcuma zedoaria	JAPAN PH.	rhizome	
Curcurbita spp.	CAN.FOOD	seeds	
Cusperia felcifuga	USP-OLD		
Cyamopsis tetragonolobus	NF 18	gum	Guar gum
Cydonia vulgaris	USP-OLD		Cydonium
Cynara scolymus	EURO-140	folium	
Cyperus rotundus	JAPAN PH.	rhizome	
Cypripedium hirsutum parvi florum	USP-TOC	rhizome/root	Cypripedium
Cytisus scoparius	CAN.FOOD	flowering tops	
Cytisus scoparius	USP-TOC	tops	Scoparius
Daphne mezereum and spp.	USP-TOC	bark	Mezereum
Datura stramonium	USP-WW2	leaves	Stramonium
Daucus carota	USP-OLD	fruit	Carota
Delphinium	USP-OLD		Delphinium
Delphinium	CAN.FOOD		Delphinium

WORLDWIDE HARMONIZATION OF BOTANICAL STANDARDS

CHAPTER APPENDIX: BOTANICALS OF INTEREST TO USP *(Cont'd)*

Plant name	Listing	Part(s) used	Pharmacopeial name
Delphinium staphisagria	USP-TOC	seed	Staphisagria
Digenea simplex	JAPAN PH.	whole algae	
Digitalis purpurea	USP 23	leaves	Digitalis
Digitalis purpurea	JAPAN PH.	leaf	
Digitalis purpurea folium	PH.EUR		
Dioscorea japonica	JAPAN PH.	rhizome	
Dioscorea villosa	US TOP 50		
Diospyros virginiana	USP-OLD	fruit	Diospyros
Dolichos	J-CRUDE	bean	
Dracontium foetidum	USP-OLD	root	Dracontium
Drimia maritima	—		
Drosera rotundifolia	EURO-140	herba	
Dryopteris filix-mas	USP-WW2	dried rhizome	Aspidium
Dryopteris marginalis	USP-TOC		
Echinacea angustifolia	US TOP 50	rhizome and root	
Echinacea radix	PH.EUR/DE		
Elettaria cardamomum	USP-WW2	seed	Elaterium, Cardamom
Elettaria cardamomum	JAPAN PH.	fruit	
Eleutherococcus senticosus	US TOP 50		
Ephedra sinensis	US TOP 50		
Ephedra sinica	JAPAN PH.	stem	
Equiseti herba	PH.EUR/DE		
Equisetum arvense	EURO-140	herba	
Erigerontis canadensis	USP-TOC	oil/herb, flower	Erigeron
Eriodictyon californicum	USP-OLD	leaves	Eriodictyon
Eryngium	USP-OLD		
Erythronium	USP-OLD		
Erythroxylon coca, Tuxillense	USP-TOC	leaves	Coca
Eucalypti aetheroleum	PH.EUR		
Eucalyptus globulus	USP-WW2	vol. oil-leaves	Eucalyptus oil
Eucalyptus globulus	JAPAN PH.	oil	
Eucalyptus spp.	EURO-140	aetheroleum	
Eugenia caryophyllata	USP 21/NF	distilled oil	Clove oil
Eugenia pimenta	USP-OLD	leaves	Pimenta
Euonymus atropurpureus	USP-TOC	root bark	Euonymus
Eupatorium perfoliatum	USP-TOC	tops and leaves	Eupatorium
Eupatorium purpureum	USP-OLD		
Eupatorium purpureum	USP-OLD		
Eupatorium teuciifolium			
Euphorbia ipecacuanna, corollata	USP-OLD		
Evodia rutaecarpa	JAPAN PH.	fruit	
Exogonium purga	USP-TOC	tuber-root	Jalapa
Fagara clavae-herculis	USP-TOC	bark	Xanthoxylem
Ferula	USP-TOC	root and rhizome	Sumbul
Ferula asa-foetida	EURO-140	gum-resin	
Ferula foetida	USP-TOC	root's gum-resin	Asafoetida
Ficus carica	USP-TOC	fig fruit	Ficus
Ficus carica	EURO-140	fructus	
Filipendula ulmaria	EURO-140	flores, herba	
Filix-mas	USP-TOC		
Foeniculi fructus	PH.EUR		
Foeniculum vulgare	USP-WW2	distilled oil	Fennel oil
Foeniculum vulgare	USP-TOC	fruit	Foeniculum
Foeniculum vulgare	JAPAN PH.	fruit	
Foeniculum vulgare var. *vulgare*	EURO-140	aetheroleum	
Foeniculum vulgare var. *vulgare*	EURO-140	fructus	
Forsythia suspensa	JAPAN PH.	fruit	
Frangulae cortex	PH.EUR		
Frasera walteri	USP-OLD	root	Frasera
Fraxinus excelsior	EURO-140	cortex	
Fraxinus excelsior	EURO-140	folium	
Fraxinus ornus	USP-TOC	exudate	Manna

CHAPTER APPENDIX: BOTANICALS OF INTEREST TO USP (Continued)

Plant name	Listing	Part(s) used	Pharmacopeial name
Fritillaria	J-CRUDE	bulb	
Fucus vesiculosus	EURO-140	thallus	
Fumaria officinalis	EURO-140	herba	
Galbanum berula	USP-OLD	root	Galbanum
Galipea officinalis	USP-OLD	bark	Angustrura
Gallium aparine	US TOP 50		
Garcinia hanburii	USP-TOC	gum-resin	Cambogia
Gardenia jasminoides	JAPAN PH.	fruit	
Gastrodia	J-CRUDE	tuber	
Gaultheria procumbens	USP-TOC	distilled oil/leaves	Oleum Gaultheria
Gelidium amansii	JAPAN PH.		
Gelidium cartilagineum	NF 18	extract	Agar
Gelsemium sempervirens	USP-TOC	rhizomes and roots	Gelsemium
Gentiana lutea	USP-WW2	rhizomes and roots	Gentiana
Gentiana lutea	JAPAN PH.	root	
Gentiana scabra	JAPAN PH.	root	
Gentianae radix	PH.EUR		
Geranium maculatum	USP-TOC	rhizomes	Geranium
Geranium robertianum	EURO-140	herba	
Geranium thundergii	JAPAN PH.	herb	
German chamomile	J-CRUDE		
Gillenia stipulacea, trifoliata	USP-OLD	root	Gillenia
Gingko bilobae folium	PH.EUR/DE		
Gingko biloba	US TOP 50		
Gingko biloba	CAN.FOOD	leaf extract	
Ginseng radix	PH.EUR/DE		
Glehnia littoralis	JAPAN PH.	root	
Glycine max	JAPAN PH.	oil	
Glycine soya	NF 18	soybean oil	
Glycyrrhiza glabra	EURO-140	radix	
Glycyrrhiza glabra	CAN.FOOD	rhizome and roots	
Glycyrrhiza glabra glandulifera	USP-WW2	rhizomes and roots	Glycyrrhiza
Glycyrrhiza glabra typica	USP-TOC	rhizomes and roots	Glycyrrhiza
Glycyrrhiza spp.	US TOP 50		
Glycyrrhiza uralensis, glabra	JAPAN PH.	root and stolon	
Gossypii herbaceum	USP 23		
Gossypii herbaceum	NF 18	seed hair, oil	Cottonseed oil
Gossypii herbaceum	USP-TOC	root bark	Gossypii cortex
Gracilaria confervoides	NF 18	extract	Agar
Gracilaria confervoides	PH.EUR	extract	Agar
Grindelia robusta, squarrosa	USP-TOC	leaves and tops	Grindelia
Guaiacum officinalis	USP-TOC	resin	Guaiacum
Guaiacum sanctum	USP-TOC		Sanctum
Guar galactomannanum	PH.EUR/DE		
Guarea rusbyi	—	bark	
Haematoxylon campechianum	USP-TOC	heart-wood	Haematoxylon
Hagenia abyssinica	USP-TOC	panicles	Cusso
Hamamelidis folium	PH.EUR/DE		
Hamamelis virginiana	USP 23	twig distillate	Witch hazel
Hamamelis virginiana	US TOP 50		
Hamamelis virginiana	EURO-140	folium	
Harpagophyti radix	PH.EUR/DE		
Harpagophytum procumbens	CAN.FOOD	roots	
Harpagophytum procumbens	EURO-140	radix	
Hedeoma pulegioides	USP-TOC	leaves and tops	Hedeoma
Hedeoma pulegioides, Mentha pulegium	CAN.FOOD	leaves	
Hedera helix	EURO-140	folium	
Helianthemum canadense	USP-OLD	herb	Helianthemum
Helleborus niger	USP-OLD		Hellebore
Hemp	J-CRUDE	fruit	
Hepatica americana	USP-OLD	leaves	Hepatica
Heraclium gummiferumrium	USP-OLD		

WORLDWIDE HARMONIZATION OF BOTANICAL STANDARDS

Chapter Appendix: Botanicals of Interest to USP *(Cont'd)*

Plant name	Listing	Part(s) used	Pharmacopeial name
Heuchera americana	USP-OLD	rhizome	Heuchera
Hevea spp.	USP-TOC	milk-juice	Elastica (Rubber)
Hibiscus sabdariffa	CAN.FOOD	flowers	
Hordeum distichon	USP-TOC	partially germinated grain of barley	Maltum
Houttuynia cordata	JAPAN PH.	herb	
Humuli lupuli strobuli	PH.EUR/DE		
Humulus lupulus	USP-TOC	fruit trichomes	Lupulinum
Humulus lupulus	USP-TOC	strobiles	Humulus
Humulus lupulus	US TOP 50		
Humulus lupulus	EURO-140	glandula	
Humulus lupulus	EURO-140	strobuli	
Humulus lupulus	CAN.FOOD	fruits	
Hydnocarpus anthelmitica	USP-OLD	seeds	Oleum Chaulmoogra
Hydrangea macrophylla	JAPAN PH.	leaf and twig	
Hydrastis canadensis	USP-TOC	rhizome and root	Hydrastis
Hydrastis canadensis	US TOP 50		
Hydrastis canadensis	EURO-140	rhizoma	
Hydrastis canadensis	US TOP 50		
Hydrastis canadensis	CAN.FOOD	root, extract	
Hyoscyami folium	PH.EUR		
Hyoscyami pulvis normatus	PH.EUR		
Hyoscyamus niger	USP-WW2	leaves and tops	Hyoscyamus
Hypericum perforatum	US TOP 50		
Hypericum perforatum	EURO-140	herba	
Hypericum perforatum	CAN.FOOD		
Hyssopus officinalis	EURO-140	herba	
Ichthammolum	PH.EUR/DE		
Ilex paraguariensis	—		
Illicium verum	USP-TOC	distilled oil of fruit	Oleum Anisi
Illicium verum	EURO-140	fructus	
Imperata cylindrica	JAPAN PH.	rhizome	
Inula helenium	USP-TOC	root	Inula
Inula helenium	CAN.FOOD	root	Inula
Inula helenium	EURO-140	rhizoma	
Ipecacuanhae pulvis normatus	PH.EUR		
Ipecacuanhae radix	PH.EUR		
Ipomea orizabensis	USP-OLD	root	Ipomea
Iris versicolor	USP-TOC	rhizomes and roots	Iris
Isonandra gutta	USP-OLD	juice	Gutta-percha
Janipha manihot	USP-OLD	root starch	Tapioca
Japanese apricot	J-CRUDE	fruit	
Japanese oak	J-CRUDE	bark	
Jateorhiza calumba	JAPAN PH.	root	
Jateorhiza palmata	USP-TOC	root	Calumba
Juglans cinerea	USP-TOC	root bark	Juglans
Juniperi communis	USP-TOC	distilled oil/fruit	Oleum Juniperi
Juniperus communis	EURO-140	fructus	
Juniperus oxycedrus	USP 23	wood oil	Juniper tar
Juniperus sabina	USP-TOC	tops	Sabina
Juniperus virginica	USP-OLD	tops	Juniperus virginiana
Krameria argentea	USP-TOC	root	Krameria
Krameria triandra	USP-TOC	root	Krameria
Krameria triandra	EURO-140	radix	
Lacca	PH.EUR/DE		
Lactia elongata	USP-OLD		
Lactuca virosa	USP-TOC	milk-juice	Lactucarium
Laminaria, Macrocystis, *Nereocystis,* and *Fucus* spp.	CAN.FOOD	plant	
Lamium album	EURO-140	flores	
Lappa minor	USP-OLD	root	Lappa
Laurus nobilis	EURO-140	folium	
Lavandula angustifolia	EURO-140	flores	

Chapter Appendix: Botanicals of Interest to USP (Cont'd)

Plant name	Listing	Part(s) used	Pharmacopeial name
Lavandula angustifolia	CAN.FOOD		
Lavandula officinalis	USP-WW2	oil/tops	Lavender oil
Lavandulae aetheroleum	PH.EUR/DE		
Leonurus	J-CRUDE	herb	
Leonurus cardiaca	US TOP 50		
Leptandra virginica	USP-OLD	rhizoma and root	Leptandra
Levisticum officinale	EURO-140	radix	
Ligusticum porteri	US TOP 50		
Ligusticum sinense	J-CRUDE	rhizome	
Lily	J-CRUDE	bulb	
Limonis aetheroleum	PH.EUR		
Lindera	J-CRUDE	root	
Lini semen	PH.EUR		
Linum usitatissimum	USP-TOC	seed	Linum
Linum usitatissimum	EURO-140	semen	
Liquidambar orientalis	USP-WW2	balsam wood and inner bark	Styrax, Storax
Liquiritiae radix	PH.EUR		
Liriodendron tulipfera	USP-OLD	bark	
Lithospermum erythrorhizon	JAPAN PH.	root	
Lobelia inflata	USP-TOC	leaves and tops	Lobelia
Lobelia inflata	US TOP 50		
Lobelia inflata	EURO-140	herba	
Lomatium dissectum	US TOP 50		
Longan	J-DRUDE	pulp	
Lonicera	J-CRUDE	leaf and stem	
Lonicera	J-CRUDE	flower, leaf, and stem	
Loquat	J-CRUDE	leaf	
Lotus	J-CRUDE	seed	
Lycium	J-CRUDE	root bark	
Lycium	J-CRUDE	fruit, leaf	
Lycopodium clavatum	USP-TOC	spores	Lycopodium
Lycopus virginicus	USP-OLD	herb	Lycopus
Magnolia	J-CRUDE	flower	
Magnolia obovata	JAPAN PH.	bark	
Magnolia spp.	USP-OLD	bean	
Mahonia aquifolium	CAN.FOOD	root or its extracts	
Mallotus	J-CRUDE	bark	
Mallotus phillippinensis	USP-TOC	hairs of capsules	Kamala
Malva sylvestris	EURO-140	flores	
Malva sylvestris	EURO-140	folium	
Manihot utilissima	USP 23	granules from tuber	Starch
Maranta arundinacea	USP-OLD		Maranta
Maranta arundinacea	CAN.FOOD		
Mardenia cundurango	JAPAN PH.	bark	
Marrubium vulgare	USP-TOC	leaves and tops	Marrubium
Marrubium vulgare	USP-TOC	flower, leaves	Marrubium
Marrubium vulgare	EURO-140	flores	
Marrubium vulgare	EURO-140	herba	
Matricaria chamomilla	USP-TOC	flower-heads	Matricaria
Matricariae flos	PH.EUR		
Maydis amylum	PH.EUR		
Medicago sativa	CAN.FOOD	leaves and tops	
Melaleuca leucadendron	USP-TOC	oil/leaves, twigs	Oleum cajuputi
Melaleuca spp.	EURO-140	aetheroleum	
Melia azederach	USP-OLD	bark and root	Azedarach
Melissa officinalis	USP-TOC	leaves and tops	Melissa
Melissa officinalis	USP-OLD		
Melissa officinalis	US TOP 50		
Melissa officinalis	EURO-140	folium	
Menispermum canadense	USP-TOC	rhizomes and roots	Menispermum
Mentha arvensis	JAPAN PH.	herb, oil	
Mentha x piperita	CAN.FOOD	leaves	

WORLDWIDE HARMONIZATION OF BOTANICAL STANDARDS

CHAPTER APPENDIX: BOTANICALS OF INTEREST TO USP *(Cont'd)*

Plant name	Listing	Part(s) used	Pharmacopeial name
Mentha piperita	USP 23	leaves and tops, oil	Peppermint
Mentha piperita	US TOP 50		
Mentha piperita	EURO-140	folium	
Mentha piperita	EURO-140		Aetheroleum
Mentha spicata	USP-WW2	leaves and tops	Spearmint
Mentha viridis	USP-TOC	leaves and tops	M. Viridis (Spearmint)
Mentha viridis	CAN. FOOD	leaves	M. Viridis (Spearmint)
Menthae piperitae aetheroleum	PH.EUR		
Menthae piperitae folium	PH.EUR		
Menyanthes	USP-OLD		
Menyanthes trifoliata	EURO-140	folium	
Monarda punctata	USP-OLD	leaves, tops	Monarda
Monordica elaterium	USP-OLD	fruit juice	Elaterium
Morus alba	JAPAN PH.	root bark	
Moutan paeonia suffruticosa	JAPAN PH.	bark	
Mucuna pruriens	USP-OLD	pod hairs	Mucuna
Mugwort	J-CRUDE	leaf	
Myrcia acris	USP-TOC	volatile oil	Oleum myrciae
Myrcia spp.	—	bark, leaves	Oleum myrciae
Myristica fragrans	USP-WW2	seed kernel	Myristica
Myristica fragrans	EURO-140	semen, arilus	
Myrobalan	J-CRUDE	fruit	
Myrospermum	USP-TOC		
Myroxylon balsamum	USP-WW2	gum-resin	Tolu balsam
Myroxylon balsamum var. pereirae	EURO-140	balsamum	
Myroxylon pereirae	USP-WW2	gum-resin	Peruvian balsam
Narthex assafoetida	USP-OLD	gum-resin	Assafoetida
Nectandra rodiei	USP-OLD	bark	Nectandra
Nepata cataria	CAN.FOOD	leaves and tops	
Nepata cataria	USP-OLD	leaves, tops	Cataria
Nicotiana tabacum	USP-OLD	leaves	Tabacum
Notopterygium	J-CRUDE	rhizome	
Nuphar japonicum	JAPAN PH.	rhizome	
Nutmeg	J-CRUDE		
Ocimum basilicum	—		
Olea europaea	USP 23	expressed oil-fruit	Olive oil
Olea europaea	EURO-140	folium	
Olea europaea	EURO-140	oleum	
Olea europaea	JAPAN PH.	oil	
Ophiopogon aponicus	JAPAN PH.	tuber	
Opium	PH.EUR		
Oplopanax horridum	US TOP 50		
Origanum vulgare	USP-OLD		Origanum
Origanum vulgare	EURO-140	herba	
Oryza sativa	USP-OLD	rice bran	Perpolitiones oryzae
Oryza sativa	CAN.FOOD	rice bran	
Oryza sativa	JAPAN PH.	seed	
Oryzae amylum	PH.EUR		
Osmorhiza	J-CRUDE	rhizome	
Ourouparia gambir	USP-TOC	ext. of leaves, leaves and twigs	Gambir
Paeonia lactiflora	JAPAN PH.	root	
Palaquium gutta	USP 23		Gutta Percha
Panax ginseng	USP-OLD	radix	Panax
Panax ginseng	EURO-140	radix	
Ginseng (unspecified) *(Panax spp., Eleutherococcus senticosus, etc.)*	US TOP 50		
Panax ginseng	JAPAN PH.	root	
Panax japonicus	JAPAN PH.	rhizome	
Papaver rhoeas	EURO-140	flores	
Papaver somniferum	USP 23	exudate	Opium

CHAPTER APPENDIX: BOTANICALS OF INTEREST TO USP (Cont'd)

Plant name	Listing	Part(s) used	Pharmacopeial name
Papaver somniferum	JAPAN PH.	latex	
Passiflora incarnata	US TOP 50		
Passiflora incarnata	EURO-140	planta tota	
Passiflorae herba	PH.EUR/DE		
Patchouly	J-CRUDE		
Paullinia cupana, sorbilis	USP-TOC	seed paste	Guarana
Pausinystalia yohimba	—	bark	
Pereirae	USP-TOC		Pervianum
Perilla frutescens	JAPAN PH.	leaf and twig	
Persimmon	J-CRUDE	calyx	
Petroselinum crispum	CA.FOOD	leaves	
Petroselinum sativum	USP-OLD	fruit	Petroselinum
Peucedanum	J-CRUDE	root	
Peumus boldus	EURO-140	folium	
Pharbitis nil	JAPAN PH.	seed	
Phellodendron amurense	JAPAN PH.	bark	
Physostigma venenosum	USP-TOC	seed	Physostigma
Phytolacca decandra	USP-TOC	root	Phytolacca
Picrasma excelsa	USP-TOC	wood	Quassia
Picrasma quassioides	JAPAN PH.	wood	
Pilocarpus jaborandi	USP-TOC	leaflets	Pilocarpus
Pilocarpus microphyllus	USP-TOC		Pilocarpus
Pimenta officinalis	USP-TOC	fruit	Pimenta
Pimpinella anisum	USP-WW2	fructus, oil	Anisum
Pimpinella anisum	EURO-140	fructus aetheroleum	
Pinellia ternata	JAPAN PH.	tuber	
Pinus montana (mugo)	USP-OLD	distilled oil	Oleum pini pumilionis
Pinus palustris	USP-WW2	oleoresin	Pine tar (Terebinthina)
Pinus palustris	USP-OLD	oleoresin	Resina
Pinus spp.	JAPAN PH.	oil	
Pinus spp.	JAPAN PH.	exudate	
Piper angustifolium	USP-TOC	leaves	Matico
Piper cubeba	USP-TOC	fruit	Cubeba
Piper nigrum	USP-TOC	fruit	Piper
Pistacia lentiscus	USP-TOC	resin exudate	Mastiche
Plantago asiatica	JAPAN PH.	herb, seed	
Plantago ovata	EURO-140	semen	
Plantago psyllium, indica	USP 23	seed coat	Plantago seed
Plantago psyllium, indica	US TOP 50		
Platycodon grandiflorum	JAPAN PH.	root	
Plectranthus	J-CRUDE	herb	
Podophyllum peltatum	USP 23	rhizome; resin	Podophyllum
Podophyllum peltatum	EURO-140	rhizoma, resina	
Polygala senega	USP-TOC	root	Senega
Polygala senega	JAPAN PH.	root, leaves	
Polygala tenuifolia	JAPAN PH.	root	
Polygalae radix	PH.EUR		
Polygonatum	J-CRUDE	rhizome	
Polygonum aviculare	EURO-140	herba	
Polygonum multiflorum	J-CRUDE	root	
Polyporus umbellatus	JAPAN PH.	sclerotium	
Populi candicans, tacamahaca	—	bud	
Poria cocos	JAPAN PH.	sclerotium	
Potentilla erecta	EURO-140	rhizoma	
Potentilla tormentilla	USP-OLD	rhizoma	Tormentilla
Primula veris	EURO-140	radix	
Prinos verticillatus	USP-OLD	bark	Prinos
Prunella vulgaris	JAPAN PH.	spike	
Prunus amygdalus	NF 18	kernel oil	Almond oil
Prunus amygdalus var. *amara*	USP-TOC	seed	Amygdala amara
Prunus armeniaca	USP-WW2	oil	Persic oil
Prunus armeniaca, spp.	JAPAN PH.	kernel	
Prunus cerasus spp. *acida*	EURO-140	stipites	

WORLDWIDE HARMONIZATION OF BOTANICAL STANDARDS

CHAPTER APPENDIX: BOTANICALS OF INTEREST TO USP *(Cont'd)*

Plant name	Listing	Part(s) used	Pharmacopeial name
Prunus domestica	USP-TOC	fruit	Prunum
Prunus persica	JAPAN PH.	seed	
Prunus serotina	USP-WW2	bark	Prunus virginiana
Prunus serotina	CAN.FOOD	bark	
Prunus spinosa	EURO-140	flores	
Psylli semen	PH.EUR		
Pterocarpus marsupium	USP-TOC	inspissated juice	Kino
Pterocarpus santalinus	USP-WW2	heart-wood	Santalum rubrum (Red saunders)
Pueraria lobata	JAPAN PH.	root	
Punica granatum	USP-TOC	root bark	Granatum
Quercus alba	USP-TOC	bark	Quercus
Quercus alba	CAN.FOOD	bark	Quercus
Quercus infectoria	USP-WW2	excrescence	Tannic acid (Nutgall)
Quercus robur	EURO-140	cortex	
Quillaja saponaria	USP-TOC	bark	Quillaja
Quillaja saponaria	EURO-140	cortex	
Ranunculus bulbosus	USP-OLD	corm, herb	Ranunculus
Ratanhiae radix	PH.EUR		
Rauwolfia serpentina	USP 23	root	Rauwolfia serpentina
Rehmannia glutinosa	JAPAN PH.	root	
Rhamni purshianae cortex	PH.EUR		
Rhamnus frangula	USP-TOC	bark	Frangula
Rhamnus frangula	EURO-140	cortex	
Rhamnus purshiana, frangula	USP 23	bark	Cascara sagrada
Rhamnus purshiana	US TOP 50		
Rhamnus purshianus	EURO-140	cortex	Rhamnus
Rhei radix	PH.EUR		
Rheum officinale	EURO-140	radix	
Rheum officinalis	USP-WW2	rhizome	Rheum
Rheum palmatum	USP-TOC		
Rheum palmatum, spp.	JAPAN PH.	rhizome	
Rheum officinalis	CAN.FOOD	rhizome	Rheum
Rhodophyceae genera	NF 18	extract	Carrageenan
Rhus glabra	USP-TOC	fruit	Rhus glabra
Rhus radicans	USP-OLD	leaves	Rhus Toxicodendron
Rhus vinifera	—	exudate	
Ricinus communis	USP 23	fixed oil	Castor oil (Oleum Ricinii)
Rocella spp.	—	powder-lichen	
Rosa canina	EURO-140	fructus	
Rosa centifolia	EURO-140	flores	
Rosa damascena	USP-TOC	flower	Oleum Rosae
Rosa gallica	USP 23	flower oil	Rose oil
Rosa gallica	USP-TOC	petals	Rosa Gallica
Rosa gallica	CAN.FOOD	buds	
Rosa multiflora	JAPAN PH.	fruit	
Rosemarinus officinalis	US TOP 50		
Rosmarinus officinalis	USP-WW2	tops	Oleum Rosmarini
Rosmarinus officinalis	EURO-140	folium	
Rottlera tinctoria	USP-OLD	capsules	Rottlera
Rubia tinctorum	USP-OLD	root	Rubia
Rubus idaeus and *R. strigosus*	CAN.FOOD	leaves	
Rubus fruticosus	EURO-140	folium	
Rubus ideaus	USP-OLD	fruit	
Rubus ideaus	US TOP 50		
Rubus ideaus	EURO-140	folium	
Rubus villosus	USP-TOC	rhizome	Rubus
Rumex crispus	USP-OLD	root	Rumex
Ruta graveolens	USP-OLD	leaves	Rue
Sabbatia angularis	USP-OLD	herb	Sabbatia
Sagus rumphii	USP-OLD	pith	Sago
Salicis cortex	PH.EUR/DE		
Salivae folium	PH.EUR/DE		

CHAPTER APPENDIX: BOTANICALS OF INTEREST TO USP *(Cont'd)*

Plant name	Listing	Part(s) used	Pharmacopeial name
Salix alba	USP-OLD	bark	
Salix alba	US TOP 50		
Salvia officinalis	USP-TOC	leaves	Salvia
Salvia officinalis	EURO-140	folium	
Sambuci flos	PH.EUR/DE		
Sambucus canadensis	USP-OLD	flower	Sambucus
Sambucus nigra	US TOP 50		
Sambucus canadensis	CAN.FOOD	flower	Sambucus
Sambucus nigra	EURO-140	flores	
Sambucus canadensis	USP-TOC	rhizome	Sanguinaria
Santalum album	USP-TOC	distilled oil/wood	Oleum Santali
Saposhnikovia divaricata	JAPAN PH.	root	
Sappan	J-CRUDE	wood	
Sargrasso aletin	USP-OLD		
Sarothamnus scoparius	USP-OLD	tops	Scoparius
Sassafras albidium	USP-WW2	oil	Sassafras oil
Sassafras variifolium	USP-TOC	root bark	Sassafras
Saussurea lappa	JAPAN PH.	root	
Schisandra chinensis	JAPAN PH.	fruit	
Schizonepeta tenuifolia	JAPAN PH.	spike	
Scilla maritima	USP-OLD		Squill
Scopola carniolica	USP-TOC	rhizome	Scopola
Scopolia japonica	JAPAN PH.	rhizome and root	
Scrophularia	J-CRUDE	root	
Scutellaria baicalensis	JAPAN PH.	root	
Scutellaria lateriflora	CAN.FOOD	overground plant	
Scutellaria lateriflora	USP-TOC	plant	Scutellaria
Scutellaria lateriflora	US TOP 50		
Secale cornutum	USP-OLD		
Sennae folium	PH.EUR		
Sennae fructus acutifoliae	PH.EUR		
Sennae fructus angustifoliae	PH.EUR		
Serenoa repens	US TOP 50	fruit	Sabal
Serenoa serrulata	US TOP 50	fruit	Sabal
Sesamum indicum	USP 23	seed oil	Sesame oil
Sesamum indicum	USP-OLD	seeds	Sesami
Sesamum indicum	USP-OLD	expressed oil	Oleum sesami
Sesamum indicum	JAPAN PH.	oil	
Silybum marianum	US TOP 50		
Silybum marianum	EURO-140	fructus	
Silybum marianum	EURO-140	herba	
Simaruba officinalis	USP-OLD	bark	Simaruba
Simmondsia chinensis	—	oil	
Sinapis alba	USP-TOC	seed	Sinapis Alba
Sinapis nigra	USP-TOC	seed	Sinapis Nigra
Sinomenium acutum	JAPAN PH.	stem	
Smilax glabra	JAPAN PH.	rhizome	
Smilax officinalis	US TOP 50		
Smilax spp.	CAN.FOOD	roots	
Smilax spp.	USP-WW2	root	Sarsaparilla
Solani amylum	PH.EUR		
Solanum dulcamara	USP-TOC	branches	Dulcamara
Solanum tuberosum	USP 23	tuber	Starch
Solanum tuberosum	JAPAN PH.	tuber	
Solidago odora	USP-OLD		
Solidago virgaurea	EURO-140	herba	
Sophora flavescens	JAPAN PH.	root	
Spigelia marilandica	USP-TOC	rhizomes and roots	Spigelia
Spiraea tomentosa	USP-OLD	root	Spiraea
Statice limonium	USP-OLD	root	Statice
Stellaria media	CAN.FOOD	leaves and stems	
Stellaria media	US TOP 50		
Sterculia spp.	—	gum	

WORLDWIDE HARMONIZATION OF BOTANICAL STANDARDS

CHAPTER APPENDIX: BOTANICALS OF INTEREST TO USP *(Cont'd)*

Plant name	Listing	Part(s) used	Pharmacopeial name
Stillingia sylvatica	USP-TOC	root	Stillingia
Stillingia sylvatica	CAN.FOOD	root	
Stramonii folium	PH.EUR		
Stramonii pulvis normatus	PH.EUR		
Strophanthus kombe, gratus	USP-TOC	seed	Strophanthus
Strychnos ignatia	USP-OLD		Ignatia
Strychnos nux vomica	USP-TOC	seed	*Nux vomica*
Strychnos nux vomica	JAPAN PH.	seed	
Styrax benzoin	USP 23	resin	Benzoinum
Styrax benzoin	USP-TOC	resin	Benzoinum
Styrax benzoin	JAPAN PH.	resin	
Swertia chirayita	USP-TOC	plant	Chirata
Swertia japonica	JAPAN PH.	herb	
Symphytum officinalis	US TOP 50		
Syriaca incarnata	USP-OLD	root	Asclepias
Syzgium aromaticum	JAPAN PH.	bud	
Tabebuia impetiginosa	US TOP 50		
Tamarindus indica	USP-TOC	fruit pulp	Tamarindus
Tamarindus indica	EURO-140	fructus	
Tanacetum parthenium	USP-TOC	leaves	
Tanacetum parthenium	US TOP 50		
Tanacetum vulgare	USP-TOC	leaves and tops	Tanacetum
Taraktogenos kurzi	USP-OLD	seeds	Oleum chaulmoograe
Taraxacum officinalis (Densleonis)	USP-OLD	root	Taraxacum
Taraxacum officinalis	USP TOP 50		
Taraxacum officinale	EURO-140	radix	
Theobroma cacao	USP-WW2	roasted seeds	Oleum Theobromatis
Thuja occidentalis	USP-WW2	oil	Cedar leaf oil
Thymi aetheroleum	PH.EUR/DE		
Thymi herba	PH.EUR		
Thymus serphyllum	EURO-140	herba	
Thymus vulgaris	USP-TOC	leaves and tops	Oleum Thymi
Thymus vulgaris	EURO-140	herba	
Tilia spp.	CAN.FOOD	flowers	
Tilia cordata	EURO-140	flores	
Tilia flos	PH.EUR/DE		Tiliae flos
Toluifera	USP-TOC		Balsamum toluifera
Toluifera balsamum	USP-TOC	balsam	Balsamum tolutanum
Toluifera pereirae	USP-TOC	balsamum	Balsamum peruvianum
Toluifera peruvianum	USP-TOC		Balsamum tolutanum
Tragantha	PH.EUR		
Tribulus	J-CRUDE	fruit	
Trichosanthes kirilowii	JAPAN PH.	root	
Trifolium pratense	CAN.FOOD	flowers	
Trifolium pratanse	US TOP 50		
Trigonella foenum-graecum	EURO-140	semen	
Triostium perfoliatum	USP-OLD		
Tritici amylum	PH.EUR		
Triticum aestivum	NF 18	granules from grain	Starch (wheat)
Triticum aestivum	JAPAN PH.	starch	
Turmeric	J-CRUDE		
Turnera diffusa	—	leaves and stem	
Turnera diffusa var. *aphrodisiaca*	CAN.FOOD	leaves	
Ulmus fulva	USP 23	bark	Ulmus
Ulmus fulva	USP-TOC	bark	Ulmus
Ulmus fulva	US TOP 50		
Umbelliferae spp.	USP-TOC	rhizomes and roots	Sumbul
Uncaria	J-CRUDE	thorn	
Uncaria gambir	JAPAN PH.	leaves and twigs	
Urginea maritima	USP-TOC	bulb	Scilla
Urtica dioica	CAN.FOOD	overground plant	
Urtica dioica	US TOP 50		
Urtica dioica	EURO-140	radix	

CHAPTER APPENDIX: BOTANICALS OF INTEREST TO USP (Cont'd)

Plant name	Listing	Part(s) used	Pharmacopeial name
Usnea barbata	US TOP 50		
Ustilago chimoidinum	USP-OLD		
Uvae ursi folium	PH.EUR/DE		
Vaccinium macrocarpon	—	fruit	
Vaccinium myrtillus	EURO-140	folium	
Valeriana fauriei	JAPAN PH.	root and rhizome	
Valeriana officinalis	CAN.FOOD	roots	
Valeriana officinalis	USP-TOC	rhizomes and roots	Valeriana
Valeriana officinalis	EURO-140	radix	
Valeriana officinalis	US TOP 50		
Valerianae radix	PH.EUR		
Vanilla planifolia	USP-TOC	fruit	Vanilla
Veratrum sabadilla	USP-OLD	seed	
Veratrum viride	USP-TOC	rhizomes and roots	veratrum
Verbascum phlomoides	EURO-140	flores	
Verbascum thapsus	CAN.FOOD	leaves, flowers	
Verbascum thapsus	EURO-140	flores	
Verbascum thapsus	US TOP 50		
Verbena officinalis	EURO-140	herba	
Veronica virginica	USP-TOC	rhizomes and roots	Leptandra
Viburnum opulus	USP-TOC	bark	Viburnum opulus
Viburnum prunifolium, lentago	USP-TOC	root bark	Viburnum prunifolium
Viburnum prunifolium	UEOR-140	cortex	
Viola odorata	EURO-140	flores	
Viola pedata	USP-OLD	flower	Viola
Viola tricolor	USP-OLD	flower	Viola tricolor
Viola tricolor	EURO-140	flores	
Viola tricolor	EURO-140	herba	
Viola tricolor comus	USP-OLD		
Vitex agnus-castus	US TOP 50		
Vitex fruit	J-CRUDE		
Vitis vinifera	USP-OLD	dried fruit	Uva passa
Vitis vinifera	EURO-140	folium	
Water chestnut	J-CRUDE		
Wintera aromatica	USP-OLD		
Xanthan gummi	PH.EUR/DE		
Xanthorrhiza apiifolia	USP-OLD	root	Xanthorrhiza
Xanthoxylum americanum	USP-TOC	bark	Xanthoxylum
Zanthoxylum piperitum	JAPAN PH.	fruit	
Zea mays	USP 23	granules from grain	Starch
Zea mays	USP 23	oil (seed)	Corn oil
Zea mays	USP-TOC	styles and stigmas	Zea
Zea mays	CAN.FOOD	styles and stigmas	
Zea mays	EURO-140	stipites	
Zea mays	JAPAN PH.	granules from seeds	
Zingiber officinalis	USP-WW2		Ginger
Zingiber officinalis	US TOP 50		
Zingiber officinalis	EURO-140	rhizoma	
Zingiber officinalis	JAPAN PH.		
Ziziphus jujuba	JAPAN PH.	fruit	

Part V

How Do Regulations Affect the Marketplace and Impact the Cost of Health Care?

Overview

Loren D. Israelsen, Executive Director of the Utah Natural Products Alliance, Salt Lake City, chaired the closing session, during which representatives from the Food and Drug Administration (FDA) responded to many of the questions and concerns that arose throughout the conference. The discussion was conducted in pragmatic terms, centering around economic incentives and regulatory burdens. On the panel, in addition to Robert Temple, M.D., Center for Drug Evaluation and Research, FDA, were Mitchell Zeller, J.D., from the FDA's Office of Policy, Peter Rheinstein, M.D., J.D., from the Office of Health Affairs, and Michael Kennedy of the Center for Drug Evaluation and Research, Office of Over the Counter Drug Products. Together they demonstrated that the future of botanicals in the United States can include candid and constructive dialogue with the government.

In response to an offhand suggestion, Alan Trachtenberg, M.D., Acting Director of the Office of Alternative Medicine, National Institutes of Health (NIH), was unequivocal that the NIH did not have a regulatory role in the process. The Institutes are, however, well situated to continue to serve as the point of contact for the discussion. A number of organizations, such as the National Institute on Aging and the National Institute for Nursing Research, address issues related to the whole person, not just to disease or organ specific problems. And many of the NIH's basic scientists are interested in the scientific and medicinal aspects of botanicals.

THE DILEMMA OF PROPRIETARY ASSETS: WHY SHOULD A COMPANY, NOW LEGITIMATELY MARKETING A PRODUCT AS A DIETARY SUPPLEMENT, FACE THE BURDEN AND RISKS OF APPLYING IT FOR STATUS AS A DRUG?

If a company could gain a competitive marketing advantage, the cost of a New Drug Application (NDA) (with consequent testing and clinical trials) might be offset by near-term profits. The dilemma comes from the fact that, while the successful applicant might be entitled to 5 years' exclusivity under the Waxman–Hatch legislation, the botanical from which the product was derived would most likely be used, legally, by other producers. In providing a similar product, their only real disadvantage would be the inability to make claims of efficacy and safety that the successful applicant could make. Is the difference significant enough to warrant the costs of application? The case of L-carnitine suggests that it probably is not.

But would not a manufacturer want to undertake whatever testing seems warranted, irrespective of market advantage, to ensure that the product is safe? This rhetorical question will nearly always be answered affirmatively in abstract discussions. But when facing the competitive pressures of the marketplace, what testing to fund may be less clear cut. The majority of manufacturers, and indeed most conferees, expressed their belief that most botanicals, when used properly, are safe. And most of the regulators concurred with this generalization. The problem is not safety per se, but rather claims of safety (and efficacy), ratified by the authority and prestige of the government. Without the full system of checks and balances to ensure product quality, consistency, and concentration, any generalization about a botanical is just that—a generalization.

Where, then, is the incentive to do the research? The answer seems to depend on the scale of the enterprise. Those people who are satisfied with the market size and share they have enjoyed under the dietary supplement era have probably seen their companies' positions solidified by the new legislation; in general, these are the small- and medium-sized firms. But the larger phytopharmaceutical manufacturers, many of which belong to EAPC (European–American Phytomedicine Coalition), may be more interested in aggressively marketing a product that could be protected. They are encouraged by the German system, with its Commission E monographs, and by Europe in general: The development of a usable set of standards for well-established herbals based on monographs and literature analysis seems only a matter of time.

Based on this example, could something similar happen in the United States? For now, the FDA remains firm in holding its policy line, while being supportive of people willing to engage the agency in serious discussion; although it is possible that Congress could eventually change the FDA's mandate. Congress is to consider a Presidential Commission recommendation for regulating the industry, and this conference may mark the start of a campaign to devise a different system of analysis for a certain class of traditional and popular botanicals—a class roughly equivalent to the more successful Kampo drugs in Japan and phytomedicines in Europe.

In the new environment, forceful arguments are being mounted by the industry—based on examples in Europe, in the Orient, and at the World Health Organization (WHO)—that studies exist that should be used to validate a cumulative "dossier" of monographs, although they may fall short of the standards the FDA applies to NDAs. Some skepticism was expressed about whether a number of the over-the-counter (OTC) botanicals that have been approved on the basis of monographs are really founded on better data than is being collected and adduced on behalf of these botanicals.

THE IMPACT OF THE NEW LEGISLATION

The agency is still in the initial stages of sorting out what new responsibilities and mechanisms it may have inherited on October 15, 1994, when the new legislation on dietary supplements was passed by Congress. Nutritional Labeling and Education Act of 1990 (NLEA) permits certain science-based claims to be made about nutrients in foods, rather than products per se. This approach may not draw lines as clearly as many manufacturers would like. Recently, an FDA warning letter defined an herbal tea as a food additive (to water), and disputed any claims about a "daytime sedative effect." The agency took the position that the tea had not been tested and approved for such a claim.

Will more studies outside of the NDA framework—OTC monograph petitions, for example—have much impact? Dr. Temple and his colleagues continue to urge more and better studies (ideally randomized controlled trials); they reiterated their intention to make the testing system as user-friendly as possible, to encourage more formal applications. They do not believe that their standards are onerous and contend that the enormous costs cited by critics are neither a fair nor an accurate measure of going forward with an inquiry. The agency has an office set up to facilitate this process, and believes that the solid research methods established in the last decades for new research should be the ones applied to this new class of materials. By mandate, that is Dr. Temple et al.'s present position, until some change in law or regulation is effected—clearly a process that may take years—they urge herbalists to join the FDA in a collaborative inquiry to test and validate the efficacy and safety of the products in question. Under the new law, studies funded by industry may be more acceptable. Formerly, ipso facto, most were disqualified. Similarly, brand names of a product being tested may begin to appear in such studies.

Valerian is at the moment under consideration, by way of an OTC monograph petition. The file is open to the public, and anyone is free to examine, comment on, or supplement it. Presumably, the motive is to be able to take the herb to market as a sleep aid. Robert Pinco, J.D., Akin, Gump, Strauss, Hauer, and Feld, Washington, DC, suggests that, in such a claim, the FDA category of "structure–function" may apply; if this proves to be correct, then the "either/or" (dietary supplement or NDA) may prove to be inadequate, and a new alternative might emerge. By the time the Presidential Commission reports to Congress, the conversation begun at this conference may have advanced to the point that a coherent new class of materials is described and an appropriate way to regulate them is devised.

DIFFERENCES BETWEEN EUROPE AND THE UNITED STATES

It was observed that there seems to be much more inherent tension between regulators and industry here than in Europe. However, Hubertus Cranz, Ph.D., Pharmacist and Executive Director, European Proprietary Medicines Manufacturers' Association (AESGP), Brussels, Belgium, believed that both systems could be fairly characterized as encouraging open dialogue among industry, regula-

OVERVIEW

tors, and scientists. Roy Upton, President of the American Herbalists Guild, Soquel, CA, made the distinction that in the United States, the oversight process has come about in the context of "big-money" pharmaceuticals, and, thus, a very expensive regulatory system has evolved, focused on arguments about how to devise a marketable product. Ideally, and to some extent realized in the model developed by WHO, Mr. Upton hoped that this market-pressure-driven system would eventually give way to one in which the main perspective was "what is best for the people and their health."

The central point was made repeatedly: In other cultures, herbal medicines are mainstream; thus, conventional practitioners prescribe them. In the United States, there is no way to enter practice as a licensed herbalist; in order to prescribe herbs legally, one must graduate from one of the three recognized schools of naturopathic medicine or become licensed by a state as an acupuncturist.

The Economics of Botanicals: The European Experience

MELVILLE K. EAVES

In Western Europe, botanicals, or plant-based medicines, represent a significant part of usual drug therapy. Most notably, in Germany, France, Italy, Austria, and Switzerland, plant drugs and phytomedicines are an integral part of conventional medicine. In addition to their extensive over-the-counter (OTC) use, they are also widely prescribed by M.D.s and are varyingly reimbursable under the different national health insurance schemes, both public and private.

Even in the sophisticated European environment, with generally good market data including excellent Institute of Medical Statistics (IMS) health care audit reports, however, it has historically been extremely difficult to obtain meaningful and reliable comparative data on the overall market size for phytomedicines, herbal remedies, and supplements. Difficulties have included the significant problems of definition and data sorting: Botanical products are almost invariably classified according to their therapeutic class rather than by their natural or synthetic heritage. Lack of appropriate audit coverage of nonpharmacy outlets, especially in smaller and medium-sized markets, has also been a factor.

Notwithstanding the broad impact of economic pressures caused by health care reform packages in several European countries, this chapter shows that the European phytomedicines market is, in fact, considerably larger than indicated by previously available figures. The French market, in particular, has been substantially underestimated. In addition, figures for Germany have, so far, taken no account of the market development in former East Germany since reunification.

Before getting into market figures, there is one thing that I would like to clarify: In Europe phytomedicines fall almost entirely into the category of *nonprescription medicines*. I have been told that there is a fairly common misconception in the United States that because many phytomedicines are prescribed, they are, therefore, perceived as prescription-only medicines. This is most definitely not the case. Dependent partially on the country or to a somewhat lesser extent on the therapeutic class, phytomedicines, in common with the majority of synthetic OTC drugs in Europe, are largely "pharmacy-only" (a regulatory categorization that does not exist in the United States). Alternatively, phytomedicines fall into the "general sale" category. The most noteworthy exceptions are Austria and Italy, which historically have had the most stringent prescription-only restrictions in Europe, but where changes are either imminent or already underway. On the other hand, belladonna and digitalis extract, for example, are prescription-only medicines in Germany, but they have no economic relevance and in no way feature in any of the comments or figures that I present here.

Let us move on to facts and figures. Germany is the largest phytomedicine market in Europe by a large margin. This year, for the first time, IMS publicly presented outline data on the market for nonprescription phytomedicines through pharmacy outlets in West Germany.

NONPRESCRIPTION DRUGS IN WEST GERMAN PHARMACIES, 1993

Total sales of nonprescription drugs in Germany in 1993 were $7 billion, approximately half of which were prescribed, with the other half purchased by

---

Dr. Willmar Schwabe GmbH and Co., Karlsruhe, Germany.

TABLE 1. NONPRESCRIPTION DRUGS IN WEST GERMAN PHARMACIES, 1993: RETAIL DOLLARS: BILLIONS[a]

	Prescribed	Self-medication	Total
Total all nonprescription drugs	3.5	3.5	7.0
Exclusively plant-based[b]	1.0	0.9	1.9
	30%	24%	27%

Source: M.K. Eaves based on IMS/BAH data.
[a]Minor discrepancies due to $ conversion and roundings.
[b]*Excluding*: combinations with chemically defined substances, chemically defined substances of natural origin, and homeopathics.

consumers for self-medication. Twenty-seven percent of the $7 billion, or $1.9 billion, was accounted for by *exclusively* plant-based *allopathic* medicines. This does not include any chemically defined substances, even if of natural origin, or any combinations with chemically defined substances. It also excludes any homeopathic products. Note that, as a group, just over half (54 percent) of these exclusively plant-based medicines were prescribed, accounting for 30 percent of all prescribing of nonprescription drugs (see Table 1).

NONPRESCRIPTION PHYTOMEDICINES IN WEST GERMAN PHARMACIES
(Major Categories, 1993)

What kind of products are these, and what are they used for? In Table 2, the total $1.9 billion is expressed more precisely as $1,860 million, which is split into five main categories, plus an "Other" category. The largest category overall is Heart and Circulation, accounting for $433 million, followed by Cough and Cold/Respiratory Tract and Gastrointestinal (GI) Tract, with 15 percent and 14 percent respectively. The largest subcategory under GI tract is laxatives, including bulking agents. Other significant subcategories include cholagogues and liver protectants.

When we look at self-medication within the total, then the single largest category, at just over $200 million, is products under the umbrella heading of Tonics, Geriatrics, Immunostimulants.

The most significant subcategory under Other is Central Nervous System, covering such areas as sleep disorders, nervous tension, and mood disturbance. I think that we can say safely that this is the largest subgroup here, both overall and for self-medication. It includes valerian, *Hypericum* (St. Johns wort), and kava kava, for example.

PHYTOMEDICINES/HERBALS THROUGHOUT ALL GERMAN RETAIL OUTLETS, 1993

The above is an analysis of exclusively plant-based medicines in West German pharmacies only. Let us look quickly at how we get from there to a global figure for the total German market. In Table 3, I draw attention to the virtual nonexistence of an herbal supplement market in Germany: Ninety-eight percent of the products are regulated as medicines! The new federal states of former East Germany added more than $0.5 billion, to produce a total German market in 1993 of $3 billion.

TABLE 2. NONPRESCRIPTION PHYTOMEDICINES IN WEST GERMAN PHARMACIES MAJOR CATEGORIES 1993 (RETAIL DOLLARS—MILLIONS)

Category	$ millions			
	Total	%	Self-medication	%
Heart/Circulation	433	23	82	10
Cough and cold/Respiratory tract	280	15	136	16
Gastrointestinal tract	258	14	131	15
Tonics, geriatrics, immunostimulants	240	13	204	24
Urology/Gynecology (Menopause, Menstrual disorders)	225	12	57	7
Other[a]	424	23	240	28
	1,860	100	850	100

[a]Major subcategory: Central nervous system (sleep disorders, nervous tension, mood disturbance).
Source: M.K. Eaves based on IMS data.

TABLE 3. PHYTOMEDICINES/HERBALS THROUGHOUT ALL GERMAN RETAIL OUTLETS, 1993

	Retail dollars: Billions
Pharmacies	
Exclusively plant based	1.86
Combinations with chemically defined	0.19
Total pharmacy phytomedicines	2.05
Nonpharmacy outlets	
Plant-based medicines	0.36
Plant-based supplements	0.04
Total nonpharmacy herbals	0.40
Total phytomedicines/herbals	
West Germany	2.45
East Germany	0.55
Total Germany	$3.00 BN

Source: M.K. Eaves based on IMS/BAH data and industry estimates.

Three billion dollars, in fact, represents fully one half of the total European Union (EU, formerly European Economic Community [EEC]) sales of plant-based medicines equal to $6 billion. The estimated individual market sizes are shown in Table 4.

PHYTOMEDICINES/HERBAL SALES IN EU STATES, 1993

The only market that I would like to comment upon a little more deeply here is France, which, at $1.6 billion, is the second largest European phyto/herbal market, accounting for 27 percent of the total EU. Anyone who has an acquaintance with earlier European market estimates will recognize that $1.6 billion is vastly larger than the figure of $210 million incorporated into the previous best-available analysis that related to the year 1990. This huge difference is not due to any explosion of the French market over the past three years, but rather reflects a failure to identify and incorporate virtually every major phytomedicine on the French market. For those who still doubt that the French market can be $1.6 billion, in Table 5, I have listed a selection of 10 out of the top 20 phytomedicines in France.

First, these ten selected products alone have sales of $.75 billion. In other words, all but one-half of the total market and these ten alone equal three-and-a-half times the previously quoted figure. Next, notice the plant preparations involved. Apart from the fact that there are some interesting plants and plant parts listed, note that these are all extracts. In fact, they are virtually all *standardized* extracts.

Now, let us return briefly to the table of European markets. With Austria and Switzerland added (Table 4), this makes a total Western European market (excluding Scandinavia) of $6.3 billion. What we also see in this table is the per capita expenditure or consumption by country ranging from $37 per person, per year in Germany down to $5 per person, per year in the United Kingdom and Belgium. The average for the 14 countries and 360 million people concerned is $17.40 per head per year. If this European average were to be reflected in the United States, then, based on a population of 258 million, the U.S. herbal medicine/supplement market, through retail outlets only, would equate to $4.5 billion.

TABLE 4. PER CAPITA PHYTOMEDICINE/HERBAL SALES IN EUROPE, 1993 (PLUS AUSTRIA AND SWITZERLAND)

Country	Sales ($ millions)	Population[a] (millions)	$/head/yr
Germany	3000	81.2	37
France	1600	57.7	28
Switzerland	190	7.0	27
Austria	110	7.9	14
Italy	600	57.9	10.5
Netherlands	100	15.3	6.5
Spain	230	39.1	6
United Kingdom	300	58.1	5
Belgium	40	10.1	4
Remaining EU	130	29.2	4.5
Total above countries	6300	362.8	17.4

[a]*Encyclopedia Britannica:* Population mid-1993.
Source: M.K. Eaves based on IMS data.

TABLE 5. LEADING PHYTOMEDICINES IN FRANCE, 1993 (RETAIL DOLLARS): TEN EXAMPLES SELECTED FROM THE TOP 20 PHYTOMEDICINES

Extract/product	$ millions RSP[a]
Ginkgo biloba standardized extract	170
Bitter-orange peel standardized extract	140
Grape seed standardized extract	80
Saw palmetto standardized extract	80
Pygeum africanum standardized extract	70
Melitot standardized extract	60
Butcher's broom standardized extract	60
Avocado oil + Soy extract	40
Bilberry standardized extract	20
Valerian extract (combined with hawthorn + passiflora)	20
Total above products	740

[a]Extrapolated from MSP (Manufacturers' Selling Price) and rounded for presentation.
Source: M.K. Eaves based on IMS data.

TABLE 6. PROFILE SUMMARY OF EAPC EUROPEAN MEMBER COMPANIES (1993)

	Year founded	Years in operation	Total staff	R&D staff	Total sales	Phyto Sales	Countries marketed	Published papers
Schwabe	1866	128	1850	150	$375 M	95%	>40	>500
Madaus	1919	75	1500	100	$280 M	85%	>70	>500
Indena	1921	73	580	80	$110 M	100%	>20	170
Beaufour	1929	65	3000	500	$555 M	50%	>40	1,500
Pharmaton	1942	51	175	20	$160 M	100%	>70	>80
Botanicare	1948	46	600	10	$100 M	15%	>20	na[a]
Bioforce	1963	31	600	12	$ 75 M	95%	>30	na
Lichtwer	1981	13	220	16	$ 60 M	100%	25	>300

Source: EAPC members.
[a]na, not applicable.

What kind of companies are engaged in the European phytomedicines market? There is a rather wide spectrum, which is not surprising when one considers that there are approximately 180 companies marketing plant-based medicines in Germany alone. There are, however, scarcely more than a handful of companies actively involved in every facet, namely, from cultivation, followed by extraction, through true research and development, to clinical research and international marketing. The European American Phytomedicines Coalition (EAPC) is an association of European and American companies that have joined together to petition the Food and Drug Administration (FDA) to permit filing of data on phytomedicines marketed in Europe that the EAPC believes should be acceptable to meet the FDAs "old" drug requirements of marketing as applied under the OTC Drug Review.

A summary of information on the European member companies is presented in Table 6.

These companies and their major associates are based in France, Germany, Israel, Italy, the Netherlands, and Switzerland. On average, the companies have been in operation for 60 years and, although in the main virtually entirely dedicated to phytomedicines, are part of the mainstream pharmaceutical industry.

ACQUISITION OR ESTABLISHMENT OF HERBAL/PHYTOMEDICINE COMPANIES BY MULTINATIONAL AND MAJOR PHARMACEUTICAL GROUPS

There are some 180 companies in Germany that market plant-based medicines. In recent years, major international companies and groups have started to move into the botanicals area, principally via acquisitions.

In Tables 7, 8 and 9, note the wide international backgrounds of the acquiring corporations. Yet, the companies acquired are almost all based in Germany, France, or Switzerland. Note also the extent to which U.S. corporations are featured. It seems that the American pharmaceutical industry at least recognizes the economic value of botanicals in Eu-

TABLE 7. ACQUISITION OR ESTABLISHMENT OF HERBAL/PHYTOMEDICINE COMPANIES BY GERMAN, SWISS, BRITISH, AND DUTCH MULTINATIONALS AND MAJOR PHARMACEUTICAL GROUPS

AKZO	Ardeval (F)[a]
Boehringer Ingelheim	Pharmaton (CH)
Boots	Dacour (F)
	Kanoldt (D)
Ciba-Geigy	Zyma (CH)
	Valverde (CH)
Degussa	Asta (D)
Roche	Priorin (CH)
Sandoz	Monal (F)

[a]Abbreviations within the parentheses represent the nationality (international symbol) of the company acquired.

TABLE 8. ACQUISITION OR ESTABLISHMENT OF HERBAL/PHYTOMEDICINE COMPANIES BY FRENCH, BELGIAN, AND JAPANESE MULTINATIONALS AND MAJOR PHARMACEUTICAL GROUPS

Beaufour	Natura Medica (F)[a]
P. Fabre	Plantes et Medicines (F)
Fournier	Debat (F)
Fujisawa	Klinge (D)
Sanofi	Plantorgan (D)
Solvay	Kali (D)
Synthelabo	Inverni (I)

[a]Abbreviations within the parentheses represent the nationality (international symbol) of the company acquired.

TABLE 9. ACQUISITION OR ESTABLISHMENT OF HERBAL/PHYTOMEDICINE COMPANIES BY U.S. MULTINATIONALS AND MAJOR PHARMACEUTICAL GROUPS

American Home Products	Dr. Much (D)
	Kytta (D)
	Brenner/Efeka (D)
J&J/Merck	Woelm (D)
Pfizer	Mack (D)
Rhone Poulenc Rorer	Nattermann (D)
Searle	Heumann (D)
SmithKline Beecham	Fink (D)
Warner Lambert	Phygiene (F)

Abbreviations within the parentheses represent the nationality (international symbol) of the company acquired.

rope, even if the regulatory environment in the United States has, up until now, inhibited venturing into this segment at home.

In 1991, a survey of herbal drugs in the EU was undertaken by the Committee for Proprietary Medical Products (CPMP), the European coordinating committee for drug regulatory affairs. After consulting member states, the CPMP came up with a list of 145 herbal drugs used in half of the member states (5 out of the then 10 countries; see Table 10).

These 145 herbal drugs are presented in Table 11.

The surprising fact is that quite a large number of major herbal drugs in Europe are not, in fact, included in this list!

These specifically include *Ginkgo biloba* and saw palmetto, despite the fact that, quite clearly, extracts from these plants had marketing authorizations in more than 5 out of the 10 member states! See Table 12 regarding saw palmetto, for example.

My own hypothesis is that, when the CPMP asked member states for a list of phytomedicinal drugs in each country, some products were simply not identified as such. There may have been two reasons for this, which I believe could have pertained to France, for example. First, some plant extracts are such an integral part of orthodox medicine in some European countries that people, whether doctors or regulators, fail to recognize them as "plant-based" products. Second, the term "Médicament de Phytothérapie" in France actually has a different slant than in most non-Francophone countries. In France, this term is used to cover simple herbal preparations, such as milled or powdered dried leaf or root, and not more sophisticated and scientifically tested plant extracts, which would, therefore, simply not be included if administrators asked for a list of plants used in phytotherapy.

MAJOR PHYTOMEDICINES IN EUROPE 1993—A BROAD OVERVIEW

I would now like to offer my own list of the 20 most relevant phytomedicines in Europe, based on estimates of their retail sales value in the current 12 EU countries plus Austria and Switzerland. This is a somewhat simplified overview, which ideally should be accompanied by multiple footnotes because of the vagaries of data collection and definition. Some of the data can be regarded as being fairly hard, with an equal portion of somewhat soft data, with some falling in between. I, nevertheless, consider this list to be broadly reflective of the European phytomedicine market. I would be more than happy for any qualified person to correct or improve on any of the individual estimates.

Table 13 shows the top 20 medicinal plants across Europe, and where appropriate, they are listed in the dominant form in which they present. Although implicit in the estimates on the right-hand side of the table, I have not actually listed rankings on the left for the reasons already mentioned. Nevertheless, the chart clearly indicated *Ginkgo biloba* extract to be the number one phytomedicine in Europe, which will probably not surprise most people.

Valerian is the next biggest phytomedicine, which may or may not be surprising. Certainly, this figure requires some explanation, as it comprises probably three-quarters or more combination products that are very popular for valerian in Europe. Most often, although not always, valerian is the dominant component (which is why the sales value is then attributed to valerian). Popular combination candidates include hops, passiflora, melissa (or lemon balm) and, particularly in France, hawthorn.

Similar considerations apply in the case of ginseng where, for the purpose of this analysis, I have added together ginseng extract single preparations and ginseng-based tonics, which mostly contain ginseng plus vitamins and minerals and where the ginseng contribution can be of varying significance.

TABLE 10. THE TEN EU MEMBER STATES IN 1991

Belgium	Ireland
Denmark	Italy
France	Luxemburg
Germany	Netherlands
Greece	United Kingdom

TABLE 11. CPMP Herbal Drugs Survey 1991: 145 Most Relevant Herbal Drugs

Plant name	Plant part	Plant name	Plant part
Achillea millefolium	herba	Glycyrrhiza glabra	radix
Acorus calamus	rhizoma	Hamamelis virginiana	folium
Aesculus hippocastanum	semen	Harpagophytum procumbens	radix
Agar		Hedera helix	folium
Agrimonia eupatoria	herba	Humulus lupulus	glandula
Agrimonia procera	herba	Humulus lupulus	rhizoma
Agropyron repens	rhizoma	Hypericum perforatum	herba
Alchemilla vulgaris	herba	Hyssopus officinalis	herba
Allium cepa	bulbus	Illicium verum	fructus
Allium sativum	bulbus	Inula helenium	rhizoma
Aloe spp. (barbadensis, capensis, ferox)	succus (sicc.)	Juniperus communis	fructus
		Krameria triandra	radix
Alpinia officinarum	rhizoma	Lamium album	flores
Althea officinalis	flores	Laurus nobilis	folium
Althea officinalis	folium	Lavandula angustifolia	flores
Althea officinalis	radix	Levisticum officinale	radix
Anethum graveolens	fructus	Linum usitatissimum	semen
Angelica archangelica	radix	Lobelia inflata	herba
Arctium lappa	radix	Malva sylvestris	flores
Arctostaphylos uva-ursi	folium	Malva sylvestris	folium
Amoracia rusticana	radix	Marrubium vulgare	flores
Arnica montana	flores	Marrubium vulgare	herba
Artemisia absinthium	herba	Melaleuca species	atheroleum
Atropa bella-donna	folium	Melissa officinalis	folium
Barosma betulina	folium	Mentha piperita	aetheroleum
Betula pendula	folium	Mentha piperita	folium
Calendula officinalis	flores	Menyanthes trifoliata	folium
Capsella bursa-pastoris	herba	Myristica fragrans	semen, arillus
Capsicum annum	fructus	Myroxylon balsamum var. pereirae	balsamum
Carum carvi	fructus		
Cassia angustifolia	folium	Olea europaea	folium
Cassia senna	folium, fructus	Olea europaea	oleum
Centaurium erythraea	herba	Origanum vulgare	herba
Cephaelis ipecacuanha	radix	Panax ginseng	radix
Chamomilla recutica	flores	Papaver rhoeas	flores
Chondrus crispus	thallus	Passiflora incarnata	planta tota
Cimicifuga racemosa	rhizoma	Peumus boldus	folium
Cinnamomum aromaticum	cortex	Pimpinella anisum	fructus
Citrus limon	aetheroleum	Pimpinella anisum	fructus, aetheroleum
Cnicus benedictus	herba	Pinus spp. (Terpentin)	aetheroleum
Cola nitida	semen	Plantago ovata	semen
Commiphora molmol	gum-resin	Podophyllum peltatum	rhizoma, resina
Coriandrum sativum	fructus	Polygonum aviculare	herba
Crataegus laevigata	folium	Potentilla erecta	rhizoma
Crocus sativus	stigma	Primula veris	radix
Curcuma longa	rhizoma	Prunus cerasus spp. acida	stipites
Cynara scolymus	folium	Prunus spinosa	flores
Drosera rotundifolia	herba	Quercus robur	cortex
Equisetum arvense	herba	Quillaja saponaria	cortex
Eucalyptus species	aetheroleum	Rhamnus frangula	cortex
Ferula asa-foetida	gum-resin	Rhamnus purshianus	cortex
Ficus carica	fructus	Rheum officinale	radix
Filipendula ulmaria	flores, herba	Rosa canina	fructus
Foeniculum vulgare var. vulgare	aetherroleum	Rosa centifolia	flores
		Rosmarinus officinalis	folium
Foeniculum vulgare var. vulgare	fructus	Rubus fruticosus	folium
		Rubus idaeus	folium
Fraxinus excelsior	cortex	Salvia officinalis	folium
Fraxinus excelsior	folium	Sambucus nigra	flores
Fucus vesiculosus	thallus	Silybum marianum	fructus
Fumaria officinalis	herba	Silybum marianum	herba
Geranium robertianum	herba	Solidago virgaurea	herba

TABLE 11. CPMP HERBAL DRUGS SURVEY 1991: 145 MOST RELEVANT HERBAL DRUGS *(Continued)*

Plant name	Plant part
Tamarindus indica	fructus
Taraxacum officinale	radix
Thymus serpyllum	herba
Thymus vulgaris	herba
Tilia cordata	flores
Trigonella foenum-graecum	semen
Urtica dioica	radix
Vaccinium myrtillus	folium
Valeriana officinalis	radix
Verbascum phlomoides	flores
Verbascum thapsus	flores
Verbena officinalis	herba
Viburnum prunifolium	cortex
Viola odorata	flores
Viola tricolor	flores
Viola tricolor	herba
Vitis vinifera	folium
Zea mays	stipites
Zingiber officinale	rhizoma

Valerian and ginseng are then two examples of how these sales figures require interpretation and multiple footnoting. Finally, purists may ask: Why include combinations? Why not simply give estimates for plain valerian or plain ginseng? In my mind, that would have vastly understated the true economic significance of these two plants or plant extracts and provided a lopsided picture of the European market. On the other hand, in the case of ginseng, one can argue that, in real terms, it does not have the significance indicated here because the content in many tonics is rather low, as I am told.

Evening primrose oil, with retail sales of more than $100 million, is an interesting item for several reasons. The original product from Efamol/Scotia of Canada is possibly the second-best studied botanical worldwide after EGb 761, the original standardized *Ginkgo* extract developed by Schwabe, Karlsruhe, Germany. It is this level of scientific and clinical study that allowed the Efamol company to accomplish the transition from the herbal supplement sector to an ethical medicine with a full product license in the United Kingdom, Canada, Germany, and many other countries. This is the one figure in this table that reflects such a strong element of dual status, supplement, and semiethical medicine, estimated at roughly 50:50 in 1993.

CONCLUSION

To conclude, let me just mention a couple of other points with economic relevance. Evening primrose is one of the many plants that are specially cultivated with great care and expertise specifically for the production of phytomedicines. Others include milk thistle, echinacea, chamomile, and last, but certainly not least, *Ginkgo biloba*. My own company, Schwabe, and our partner in this project, Beaufour of Paris, France, have established *Ginkgo* plantations at specially selected sites in Europe and in South Carolina, with approximately 20 million trees. These plantations are maintained with a lot of

TABLE 12. SAW PALMETTO[a] IN EU STATES AS PER 1991

Year of First Marketing Authorization Respectively First Introduction

EU Member State	Year
Germany	1936[b]
Belgium	1958
Spain	1963
France	1982
Italy	1985
Greece	1987

Source: M.K. Eaves based on IMS data.
[a]Saw palmetto botanical synonyms: *Sabal serrulata/Serenoa repens.*
[b]Also, e.g., 1956, 1968, 1987, and 1990.

TABLE 13. MAJOR PHYTOMEDICINES IN EUROPE 1993: A BROAD OVERVIEW

Estimated Sales (Retail Dollars, Millions)

Plant/extract	$ millions RSP
Ginkgo biloba extract	600
Valerian extract	300
Horse chestnut extract	250
Saw palmetto extract	230
Bitter-orange peel extract	220
Garlic	200
Hawthorn extract	140
Ginseng extract + ginseng based tonics	140
Psyllium	125
Echinacea	120
Butcher's broom extract	120
Evening primrose oil	110
Pygeum africanum extract	105
Melilot extract	100
Grape seed extract	90
Milk thistle extract	80
Melissa (lemon balm) extract	65
Urtica (nettle) extract	60
Bilberry extract	60
Chamomile	45

Source: M.K. Eaves based on IMS data and industry estimates.

effort, care, and quality control. Special cultivation and the use of renewable source materials also help to avoid negative environmental impacts. I am not aware of any environmental problems regarding any of the plant sources listed here with the single exception of *Pygeum africanum*, when the extraction is made from the bark stripped from the trees. I understand that some environmental botanists see this as a gradually developing issue.

The mention of extraction prompts me to draw attention to the fact that, in almost every botanical in Table 13, we are dealing with extracts, more specifically, standardized extracts. This is the form that is therefore shown preference by doctors and consumers alike. The twenty phytomedicines, as listed in Table 13, are estimated to have total sales approaching $3.2 billion, equivalent to more than 50 percent of the total phytomedicine/herbal market in the 14 countries discussed. I can say, however, that there are also many interesting and valuable phytomedicines in the remaining 50 percent of the market. I hope that I have been able to demonstrate the economic significance of botanicals or plant-based medicines in the European experience and to show that there is nothing "fringe" or "alternative" about their role in European health care. Many surveys in Germany, France, and other European countries show that this is what consumers, and for that matter doctors, want. Unfortunately, it was beyond the scope of this chapter to discuss some of the findings of these surveys. Popular support on this side of the Atlantic for recent dietary supplement initiatives indicates to me that a significant portion of the U.S. population also has a clear desire to see the four Rs for plant-based medicine in the United States, namely Recognition, Respectability, and Reasonable Regulation.

The Economics of Botanicals: The U.S. Experience

PEGGY BREVOORT

I have been involved in the American herb industry since 1971, both as a co-owner and chief executive officer of an herbal manufacturing and sales company in Eugene, Oregon, and also as the immediate past president of the American Herbal Products Association (AHPA). In that time, I have watched the industry grow from a few mail-order suppliers of crude bulk herbs to an industry estimated at $1.5 billion at retail today. It is remarkable that during all that time the industry was regulated entirely as "foods" and by law could give no information about the efficacy of its products. That does not mean that the industry did not label and disseminate information creatively, but frankly it grew in spite of a limiting regulatory environment (from a marketing point of view). The previous chapter by Melville K. Eaves, Dr. Willmar Schwabe GmbH and Co., Karlsruhe, Germany, on the European phytopharmaceutical market, points out the difference between the two regulatory systems and the resulting increased retail sales at $6.5 billion (Europe) when health information accompanies products. It also indicates to me that the U.S. market for medicinal botanicals still represents a significant economic entity, considering that health claims could not accompany products and that the industry itself is barely 25 years old.

The information I present in this chapter is by no means all inclusive. There is a lack of good economic data on the American herbal market. This is for several reasons:

1. A quickly growing and changing market in which it is very hard to get a handle on the change
2. A market made up of a few large and many small, closely held companies that consider their financial information highly proprietary and are not willing to share it
3. A lack of a good differentiating tracking mechanism at the purchase point for the herbal category in natural-food stores
4. The herbal industry as a whole not being a large enough marketplace for a national market data research company to invest in in-depth analysis.

I am not attempting here to do statistical analysis. What I have done is compile some secondary data from a wide spectrum of industry sources, including marketing reports, trade magazine reports, individuals, trade associations, individual companies, scientific articles, and supplier catalogs. I am only presenting what I consider to be a few "snapshots" of the industry, not a complete picture. This report focuses on the "medicinal" botanical category and does not include spices, herbs used for flavoring, potpourri, beverage teas, herbs used in cosmetics, or aromatherapy. It does include topical salves as well as bulk herbs, extracts, tinctures, tablets, capsules, and medicinal teas.

U.S. MEDICINAL HERB INDUSTRY

Table 1 shows a comparison of several surveys done on the medicinal herb industry. Different surveys break out results by different categories.

HERB SALES IN NATURAL-FOOD RETAIL STORES

Table 2 shows the results of surveys by the three industry trade magazines. The dollar amounts are at retail. There are approximately 8000 natural

---

Chief Executive Officer, East Earth Herb, Inc., Eugene, OR.

Table 1. U.S. Medicinal Herb Industry

	Millions US$ at Retail			
	1991	1992	1993	1994
AHPA Report	1,160			1,500[a]
(Includes herbal teas)				
Natural foods	176			
Mail order	45			
Multilevel	180			
Mass market with psyllium	423			
Health care practitioners	27			
Asian herb shops	55			
Beverage herb tea	180			
Homeopathic remedy	40			
Green Food sales	34			
McAlpine, Thorpe and Warrier		970		
(does not include herbal teas)				
Nicholas Hall	567	635	730	840
(includes herbal teas, excludes garlic)				
Packaged Facts	455	541	667	720
(includes herbal teas)				
Health and natural food stores			406	
Multilevel marketing			159	
Drug stores			42	
Mail order			28	
Food stores			23	
Discount stores			9	
Business Genetics Co.				1,783
Natural foods				470
Mail order				200
Multilevel				300
Health care practitioners				43
Asian herb shops				80
Beverage herb tea				165
Mass market				525

[a]Informal conversations with major herb suppliers indicate individual company growth between 20 percent and 35 percent for 1994.

food stores in the United States. As the industry continues to expand into more mass-market chains, the number of outlets will increase dramatically and the industry sales should rise proportionately.

Table 2. Herb Sales in Natural Food Retail Stores[a]

	In Millions of US $			
	1991	1992	1993	1994
Health Foods Business Magazine	653	633	679	
"Medicinal" sales broken out		354	353	
Whole Foods Magazine				
"Medicinal" sales not broken out	621	702		
Natural Foods Merchandiser	176	288	467	553
Broken out by "medicinal" category: herbs in bulk, capsules, extracts, tinctures, tablets, tea for medicinal use				

[a]Total number of natural foods stores in U.S. is about ±8,000.

TOP-SELLING HERBS IN U.S. COMMERCE

Table 3 reflects the fall 1994 commercial price per pound for some of the top-selling herbs in the United States; seen here are the wholesale prices that a store would pay and does not reflect consumer cost. There are several lists available of the "top 25 herbs in commerce." This does not purport to be the definitive list. I also include, at the bottom, five herbs used that have official OTC regulatory status. Because they are sold as OTC products, I did not list their individual price per pound. They are also sold in the natural foods industry in their crude form.

U.S. IMPORT/EXPORT STATISTICS FOR GINSENG AND OTHER MEDICINAL PLANTS, 1992

Table 4 compares the import and export poundage and value for ginseng in 1992. Most cultivated

TABLE 3. TOP SELLING HERBS IN US COMMERCE

Name	Botanical name	Commercial price per lb. ($US)[a]
Aloe	*Aloe vera*	10.50
Astragalus	*Astragalus membranaceus*	10.50
Cayenne	*Capiscum annuum*	3.20
Chamomile	*Matricaria chamomilla*	4.70
Dong Quai	*Angelica sinensis*	8.00
Echinacea	*Echinacea angustifolia*	27.50
Ephedra	*Ephedra sinica*	4.50
Feverfew	*Tanacetum parthenium*	9.75
Garlic	*Allium sativum*	2.60
Ginger	*Zingiber officinale*	3.75
Ginkgo	*Ginkgo biloba*	7.50
Ginseng	*Panax ginseng*	25.00
Goldenseal	*Hydrastis canadensis*	40.00
Gotu Kola	*Centella asiatica*	2.70
Hawthorn Berries	*Crataegus oxycantha*	2.90
Hops	*Humulus lupulus*	6.00
Licorice	*Glycyrrhiza glabra*	5.25
Milk Thistle	*Silybum marianum*	8.00
Pau d'arco	*Tabebuia impetiginosa*	4.25
Peppermint	*Mentha piperita*	5.25
Red Clover	*Trifolium pratense*	8.50
Saw Palmetto	*Serenoa repens*	4.95
Siberian Ginseng	*Eleutherococcus senticosus*	5.25
Valerian	*Valeriana officinalis*	6.00
White Willow	*Salix alba*	2.70
As ingredients in OTC[b] preparations:		
Cascara	*Cascara sagrada*	na[c]
Senna	*Senna alexandrina*	na
Psyllium	*Plantago* spp.	na
Slippery Elm	*Ulmus fulva*	na
Witch Hazel	*Hamamelis virginiana*	na

[a]na, not applicable.
[b]OTC, over-the-counter.
[c]Fall 1994.

TABLE 4. UNITED STATES IMPORT/EXPORT STATISTICS FOR GINSENG AND OTHER MEDICINAL PLANTS, 1992

	Export		Import	
	Pounds	Value in US$	Pounds	Value in US$
Ginseng[a]				
Cultivated	1,661,231	80,102,300	942,858	10,391,100
Ginseng[a]				
Wild	220,598	24,452,400	31,911	420,600[b]
Total	1,881,829	104,554,700	974,769	10,811,700
All medicinal plants, plant parts, extracts[c]				127,300,000
All medicinal plants, plant parts, and extracts excluding ginseng				116,488,300
Estimate of source of plants used in US medical botanical industry:[d]				
Imported: 75%				
Domestic: 25%				

[a]U.S. Dept. of Commerce/Horticulture and tropical products division.
[b]This figure is not reflective of current price for Chinese wild ginseng: Semi-wild ginseng sells for approximately US$300 per ounce. Cultivated wild ginseng sells for US$500 per pound. Therefore, dollar value should probably be $500 × 31,911 pounds totalling an estimated US$15,955,500.
[c]*Prescription for Extinction*, Gaski and Johnson, World Wildlife Federation.
[d]*Medicine from the Wild*, Fuller, World Wildlife Federation.

American ginseng comes from Wisconsin and is exported to the Orient. Wild ginseng is harvested from the Appalachian mountain region. Imported Chinese ginseng comes from the Orient. Based on my personal knowledge of ginseng prices, the figure for value of imported wild ginseng is not correct. It is probably closer to $16 million (see footnote for Table 4). I can only surmise that the figures were misrepresented for customs value. Three other herbs of economic importance that are exported primarily to Europe for manufacture of European phytopharmaceutical products are *Gingko biloba*, saw palmetto, and echinacea. I do not have any figures on poundage or value of export for these.

NATIVE NORTH AMERICAN MEDICINAL HERBS IN COMMERCIAL DEMAND

Table 5 is a compilation of native American herbs used medicinally. It was compiled because many of these are endangered species. The chart is from *Medicine in the Wild*, Fuller, World Wildlife Federation, reproduced with permission.

COST: PHARMACEUTICALS VERSUS BOTANICALS

Table 6 compares a per-day dosage cost (to the patient) for some common pharmaceutical drugs

TABLE 5. NATIVE NORTH AMERICAN MEDICINAL HERBS IN COMMERCIAL DEMAND (PRIMARILY WILD-HARVESTED)

Scientific name	Common name	Part used	Scientific name	Common name	Part used
Acorus calamus	calamus	rhizome	J. virginiana	red ceder	fruit
Adiantum pedatum	maidenhair fern	leaf	Larrea tridentata	chapparal	leaf
Agastache foeniculum	anise hyssop	leaf	Lactuca spp.	wild lettuce	fruit
Aletris farinosa	colic root	root	Lobelia inflata	lobelia	herb
Aralia nudicaulis	sarasparilla	root	Ligusticum porteri	osha root	root
A. racemosa	spikenard	root	Mahonia aquifolium	Oregon grape	root
Aristolochia serpentaria	Virginia snakeroot	root	Myrica cerifera	wax myrtle	leaf
Asarum canadense	Canada snakeroot	root	M. gale	sweet gale	fruit
Asclepias tuberosa	pleurisy root	root	M. pensylvanica	bayberry	leaf
Caulophyllum thalictroides	blue cohosh	root	Panax quinquefolius	ginseng	root
Ceanothus americanus	New Jersey tea	root	Parthenium integrifolium	wild quinine	root
Chimaphila umbellata	pipsissewa	leaf	Passiflora incarnata	passionflower	fruit, flower
Chionanthus virginica	fringetree	bark	Pinus strobus	white pine	bark
Cimicifuga racemosa	black cohosh	root	Podophyllum peltatum	mayapple	rhizome
Collinsonia canadensis	stoneroot	root, leaf	Polygonatum biforum	Solomons seal	root
Crataegus oxyacantha	hawthorn	berries	Populus balsamifera	quaking aspen	leaf buds
Cypripedium acaule	pink lady slipper	root	Prunus serotina	black cherry	bark
C. calceolus	yellow ladyslipper	root	Quercus alba	white oak	bark
Dioscorea villosa	wild yam	fruit, root	Rhamnus purshiana	cascara sagrada	bark
Echinacea angustifolia	purple coneflower	root, whole	Rhus glabra	sumac	berries
E. pallida	purple coneflower	root, whole	Salix spp.	willow	bark
E. purpurea	purple coneflower	root, whole	Sambucus canadensis	elderberry	flowers
Equisetum hyemale	shavegrass	whole	Sanguinaria canadensis	bloodroot	root
Eupatorium perfoliatum	boneset	flowers	Sassafras albidum	sassafras	root, bark
E. purpureum	joe-pye weed	leaf, root	Scutellaria lateriflora	scullcap	leaf
Gaultheria procumbens	wintergreen	leaf	Serenoa repens	saw palmetto	berries
Geranium maculatum	wild cranesbill	root	Spigelia marilandica	pink root	root
Hamamelis virginiana	witch hazel	bark	Taxus brevifolia	Pacific yew	bark
Hedeoma pulegioides	pennyroyal	fruit	Teucrium canadense	germander	whole
Hydrangea arborescens	hydrangea	root, leaf	Trilisa odoratissima	deer's tongue	leaf
Hydrastis canadensis	goldenseal	root, whole	Trillium spp.	trillium	root
Juglans nigra	black walnut	fruit	Veronicastrum virginicum	culver's root	root
Juniperus communis	common juniper	fruit	Zanthoxylum americanum	prickly ash	bark, berries
			Z. clava-herculis	prickly ash	bark, berries

Sources: Foster 1990a; Foster and Duke 1990; Stuart 1982; Gleason and Cronquiest 1963; USDI 1985; additional species from catalog survey and personal communications. In some species many parts are used, but only the main parts are listed above.

TABLE 6. COST: PHARMACEUTICALS VS. BOTANICALS[a]

Cholesterol	Patient cost per day
Mevacor®	$1.92
Garlic	0.56

Sleep aid	Patient cost per day
Halcion®	$0.89
Chamomile	0.14

Prostate medication	Patient cost per day
Proscar	$2.17
Saw Palmetto	0.86

Topical ointment	Patient cost per day
Zostrix®	$15.50
Cayenne and Lanolin	0.05
Herbal extract daily dosage as prescribed by an acupuncturist	$1.00/day

Source: Peggy Brevoort/East Earth Herb/Economics of American Botanical Market, Dec. 16, 1994.

[a]As of March 8, 1994.

against their crude herbal counterparts as well as quoting the approximate cost per day for a dosage of a traditional Chinese herbal extract as prescribed by a licensed acupuncturist.

COMPARATIVE COST OF HERBAL MEDICINES: UNITED STATES

Table 7 compares some costs in three symptomatic categories: cold and flu, headache, and sleep aid for five different delivery systems of herbal products. All are per dosage in tablet or capsule form. The first is a standardized European phytopharmaceutical; the second is the crude form of the same herb; the third, a homeopathic delivery; the fourth, an OTC product with an herbal base; and the fifth, a standard chemical OTC product for the same symptomatic condition.

TOP 50 HERBS USED IN U.S. HEALTH CARE PRACTICES

The list in Table 8 was based on a survey conducted by Paul Bergner for readers of his newsletter, *Medical Herbalism, A Clinical Newsletter for Health Practitioners*. He asked them to report on the herbs they most commonly prescribed over a 12-month period. The first column shows the number of prescriptions in one year's time.

UNCONVENTIONAL MEDICINE IN THE UNITED STATES

Table 9 is the chart from David Eisenberg's report in *The New England Journal of Medicine* on usage of unconventional medicine in the United States. Herbal medicine is highlighted, showing that

TABLE 7. COMPARATIVE COST OF HERBAL MEDICINES: UNITED STATES

	Cold and flu	Headache	Sleep aid
European Source Phytopharmaceuticals			
	Echinaguard—100s	Mygrafew—90s	Valerian nighttime—100s
Bottle	$19.99	$17.99	$19.95
Per dose	$ 0.20	$ 0.20	$ 0.20
American Dried Herb			
	Echinacea herb—180s	Feverfew leaf—100s	Valerian root—100s
Bottle	$14.95	$10.49	$7.49
Per dose	$ 0.08	$ 0.10	$ 0.07
Homeopathic			
	B&T Echinacea—100s	B&T Migrade—100s	Boiron Quietude—60s
Bottle	$4.75	$6.95	$7.00
Per dose	$0.05	$0.07	$0.12
Herbal-base OTC[a]			
	Cold Care—20s	Sinus stop—20s	
Bottle	$7.00	$6.49	
Per dose	$0.35	$0.32	
Standard OTC			
	Contac—20s	Advil—100s	Unisom—32s
Bottle	$4.98	$6.75	$6.99
Per dose	$0.24	$0.07	$0.21

[a]OTC, over-the-counter.

TABLE 8. TOP 50 HERBS USED IN U.S. HEALTH CARE PRACTICES

No. of prescriptions during 1 yr.	Botanical name	Prescribed for
74	*Echinacea* spp.	Immune stimulant/tonic
34	*Hydrastis canadensis* (Goldenseal)	Antibiotic, astringent
33	*Taraxacum officinale* (Dandelion)	Alterative
26	*Urtica dioica* (Nettles)	Alterative, astringent
23	Ginseng (unspecified) (*Panax* spp., *Eleutherococcus senticosus*, etc.)	Energy tonic
21	*Crataegus oxyacantha* (Hawthorn)	Cardiac tonic
20	*Allium sativa* (Garlic)	Cardiovascular tonic, antibiotic
19	*Valeriana officinalis* (Valerian)	Sedative, analgesic
18	*Silybum marianum* (Milk thistle)	Liver tonic
18	*Glycyrrhiza* spp. (Licorice)	Energy tonic, respiratory, digestive, female system
17	*Capsicum annuum* (Cayenne)	Circulatory stimulant, heating synergist
17	*Articum lappa* (Burdock)	Alterative
17	*Mentha piperita* (Peppermint)	Digestive
16	*Astragalus membranaceus*	Immune tonic
16	*Ginkgo biloba* (Ginkgo leaf)	Cardiovascular tonic
16	*Zingiber officinalis* (Ginger)	Digestive, antinauseant, heating synergist
15	*Vitex agnus-castus* (Chaste Berry)	Female system
14	*Chamomilla recutita* (Chamomile)	Sedative, digestive
14	*Dioscorea villosa* (Wild Yam)	Antispasmodic, female system
13	*Scutellaria lateriflora* (Scullcap)	Sedative
13	*Hypericum perforatum* (St. John's Wort)	Nervine, topical
11	*Centella asiatica* (Gotu Kola)	Cerebral stimulant
10	*Avena sativa* (Oat)	Nervine, tonic
8	*Achillea millefolium* (Yarrow)	Diaphoretic
8	*Angelica sinensis* (Dong quai)	Female system
8	*Verbascum thapsus* (Mullein)	Respiratory
7	*Berberis aquifolium* (Oregon grape)	Alterative
7	*Tanacetum parthenium* (Feverfew)	Headache
7	*Rubus ideaus* (Raspberry)	Female tonic
7	*Symphytum off.* (Comfrey)	Demulcent
7	*Trifolium pratense* (Red Clover)	Alterative, expectorant
7	*Ulmus fulva* (Slippery elm)	Demulcent
6	*Cimicifuga racemosa* (Black cohosh)	Female system, antispasmodic
6	*Ligusticum porteri* (Osha root)	Respiratory, antiviral
6	*Lobelia inflata* (Lobelia)	Respiratory
6	*Serenoa repens* (Saw palmetto)	Male urogenital
5	*Leonurus cardiaca* (Motherwort)	Female system, sedative
5	*Passiflora incarnata* (Passion flower)	Sedative
4	*Calendula officinalis* (Calendula)	Antibiotic, wound healing
4	*Ephedra sinica* (Ma huang)	Antiallergy, stimulant
4	*Lomatium dissectum* (Lomatium)	Antiviral
4	*Tabebuia impetiginosa* (Pau D'Arco)	Antifungal
4	*Rosmarinus officinalis* (Rosemary)	Nerve tonic, circulatory and disgestive, stimulant
4	*Stellaria media* (Chickweed)	Used in ointments, alterative
4	*Usnea barbata* (Usnea)	Antibiotic
3	*Oplopanax horridum* (Devils Club)	Hypoglycemic, alterative
3	*Sambucus nigra* (Elder flowers)	Diaphoretic
3	*Galium aparine* (Cleavers)	Urinary tract
3	*Melissa officinalis* (Lemon Balm)	Sedative
3	*Smilax officinalis* (Sarsaparilla)	Alterative

Source: *Medical Herbalism, A Clinical Newsletter for Health Practitioners*, Paul Bergner (ed.); Portland, OR; Spring 1994.

3 percent of the respondents reported using herbal medicine in the last 12 months and 10 percent saw a provider who used herbal medicine in his practice. Eisenberg notes that, in 1990, Americans made an estimated 425 million visits to providers of unconventional therapy. That is, excluding exercise and prayer, one in three respondents used at least one unconventional therapy in 1990. Expenditures associated with use of unconventional therapy amounted to approximately $13.7 billion, of which

TABLE 9. UNCONVENTIONAL MEDICINE IN THE US: PREVALENCE AND FREQUENCY OF USE OF UNCONVENTIONAL THERAPY AMONG 1539 ADULT RESPONDENTS IN 1990

Type of therapy	Used in past 12 months (%)	Saw a provider (%)
Relaxation techniques	13	9
Chiropractic	10	70
Massage	7	41
Imagery	4	15
Spiritual healing	4	9
Commercial weight-loss programs	4	24
Lifestyle diets (e.g., macrobiotics)	4	13
Herbal medicine	3	10
Megavitamin therapy	2	12
Self-help groups	2	38
Energy healing	1	32
Biofeedback	1	21
Hypnosis	1	52
Homeopathy	1	32
Acupuncture	<1	91
Folk remedies	<1	0
Exercise[a]	26	—
Prayer[a]	25	—
Unconventional therapy[b]	34	36

Source: Eisenberg DM, et al. *N Engl J Med* 1993.
[a]Respondents who used exercise or prayer were not asked for details about this use.
[b]Excluding exercise and prayer.

approximately three quarters ($10.3 billion) was paid out-of-pocket. This figure is comparable to the $12.8 billion spent out-of-pocket annually for all hospitalizations in the United States.

OVERVIEW OF CURRENT PROJECTS ON BOTANICAL MEDICINES IN THE UNITED STATES

The following is a list of some current projects being undertaken within the botanical community in response to the need for more safety data and research.

1. The Herb Research Foundation performed a high-quality peer-reviewed literature search on the safety of a single herb.
2. The American Herbal Products Association (AHPA) is undertaking a project to review the herbs listed in its Herbs of Commerce publication by cross-referencing them through 30 pharmacopoeias and other herbal texts in order to ascertain if any warnings, restrictions for usage, or

TABLE 10. OVERVIEW OF CURRENT PROJECTS ON BOTANICAL MEDICINES IN THE U.S.

Peer-reviewed safety study of individual herb	
Herb Research Foundation	$7,500 Each herb
Labeling and Use Guidelines for herbs in U.S. Commerce	
AHPA (trade association) project	$20,000 Projected budget
Development of American Herbal Pharmacopoeia	
Herbal industry project	$170,000 Yearly budget
Clinical study of herbal efficacy	
Harvard University	$400,000 One study
Clinical trial of herbal formula	
Office of Alternative Medicine to	$30,000 Grant amount
Columbia University	$150,000 Projected budget
Translation and publication of 410 Commission E herb Monographs	
American Botanical Council	$75,000 Projected cost
Grant: develop and operate Alternative Medicine Center for research in HIV/AIDS (% for investigation of botanical therapy)	
Bastyr University	$840,000 3-year grant

other safety messages should be included on the labeling of these herbs. This project includes volunteer time, which accounts for its low cost of approximately $20,000.
3. The development of an American Herbal Pharmacopoeia estimates an annual ongoing yearly budget of $170,000, which includes salary and administrative overhead.
4. Harvard University, Boston, MA, will do a clinical study of one herb for $400,000.
5. The Office of Alternative Medicine, National Institutes of Health, has awarded three grants to conduct clinical trials on Chinese herbal products. One of the recipients, Columbia University, estimates that direct costs for this small trial will be $150,000.
6. Several speakers mentioned the German Commission E monographs, which have been translated and published in the United States by the American Botanical Council (ABC), Austin, TX. ABC estimates its budget to be $75,000 for this project.
7. Bastyr University, Bothell, WA, was given an $840,000 three-year grant to investigate research in HIV/AIDS, an unknown percentage of which will be for investigation of botanical therapies.

CONCLUSION

With passage awhile back of the new Dietary Supplement Health and Education Act, it is anticipated that the herbal marketplace will undergo some significant changes. Certainly the ability to include structure and function label claims is going to increase sales of herbal products. And, certainly, consumers will benefit from the increased information available to them. There will be some costs associated with these changes. They may include the cost of relabeling, which could add up to 5% of the total gross sales for a year for an individual company; the cost of new literature to accompany labels, adding an additional $500 to $50,000 per company; and the costs associated with the need for compliance to new Good Manufacturing Practice (GMP) dietary supplement standards.

For the first time, however, there will be an economic incentive for companies to fund research and scientific validation for their herbal products because validation will allow a company to include more information on its labels and in its literature.

Although the herb industry may have to pass some of these costs on to consumers, the benefits from this increased information should outweigh the costs. Sales should increase because of a company's legal ability to tell more about its products. This, of course, includes an increased responsibility by herbal companies to conduct safety studies, implement GMPs, conduct more research, and label products truthfully.

It is hard to predict how market economics will change with these labeling laws. In conclusion, I would say that the first 25 years of this industry saw enormous changes and growth. I think we are all looking forward to the beginning of the next 25 years in a new regulatory and economic environment.

ACKNOWLEDGMENTS

Barbara Almeter, Threshold Enterprises, Scotts Valley, CA
American Association of Naturopathic Physicians, Seattle, WA
American Herbal Products Association, Austin, TX
Paul Bergner, Portland, OR
Mark Blumenthal, American Botanical Council, Austin, TX
Cheryl Bottger, Nature's Fresh! Northwest, Portland, OR
Lyn Ciocca, Business Genetics, Cliffside Park, NJ
Milt Cutler, Bastyr University, Bothell, WA
Bill Egloff, Crane Enterprises, Plymouth, MA
Dr. David Eisenberg, Harvard University, Boston, MA
Monica Erhlich, Natural Foods Merchandiser, Boulder, CO
Steven Foster, Fayetteville, AR
Health Food Business Magazine, Hackensack, NJ
Jack Klein, Monera Associates, San Rafael, CA
Dr. Fredi Kronenberg, Columbia University, New York, NY
McAlpine, Thorpe and Warrier, London, England
Rob McCaleb, Herb Research Foundation, Boulder, CO
Michael McGuffin, McZand Herbal, Santa Monica, CA
Dr. Barbara Mitchell, National Commission for Certification of Acupuncturists, Seattle, WA
Martha Oelman, U.S. Center for Homeopathy, Alexandria, VA
Packaged Facts, New York, NY

Filomena Pead, Nicholas Hall Ltd., London, England
Charles Slotkin, Nature's Equity, New York, NY
Starwest Herb Co., Fall 1994 Catalog, Rancho Cordova, CA
Tree of Life Northwest, Fall 1994 catalog, Kent, WA
Roy Upton, Planetary Formulas, Soquel, CA
U.S. Dept of Commerce, Washington, DC
Whole Foods Magazine, South Plainfield, NJ
Whole Herb Co., Fall 1994 Catalog, Mill Valley, CA
World Wildlife Federation, Washington, DC

The Botanical Agenda, Science, and Incentives for Research

TED J. KAPTCHUK, O.M.D., C.A.

The utilization of botanicals for health care is supported by two distinct communities: a provider-dependent community and a self-prescribing community of consumers. The practitioner sector of the herbal delivery system is composed of a wide variety of health care providers, some of whom are licensed, who prescribe herbs for health maintenance, disease prevention, and the treatment of illness. This category of providers includes naturopaths (licensed in nine states)[1]; acupuncturists (licensed in 27 states, many of which allow or do not prohibit the use of herbs)[2]; Ayurvedic practitioners (not licensed in any state)[3]; chiropractors (licensed in all states, most of which allow the use of herbs)[4]; lay herbalists (not licensed in any state); medical practitioners[5]; and practitioners of various culture-bound healing systems including African-American "rootwork,"[6] Puerto Rican *spiritism*,[7] and Mexican-American *curanderismo*.[8] The self-prescribing community is primarily composed of individual consumers who use herbs to treat common health complaints (e.g., colds and menstrual problems);[9] individuals who use herbs to supplement their conventional medical treatments (e.g., taking astragalus to "improve the immune system" while undergoing chemotherapy or treatment with AZT);[10] or as part of a personal regime for health maintenance and disease prevention.[11] Incorporating herbs into a person's life can be the result of many factors, including a belief in the benevolent power of nature, seeking a therapeutic edge in a medical situation, a folk tradition, or, in some cases, desperation.

Although the use of herbs for health is widespread, the sources of herbal knowledge in both the professional and lay communities are diverse and, at times, even contradictory.[12] The utilization of herbs is generally not dependent upon any type of scientific program or agenda. Growers, manufacturers, distributors, prescribers, and consumers of botanical medicine have not traditionally used scientific evidence as a source of knowledge regarding the utility and efficacy of botanicals. History of utilization and tradition have been considered to be sufficient evidence for herbal efficacy. Western herbal reform movements of the nineteenth century, such as the Thomsonian, the Physio-Medical, and the Eclectic Medical movements believed in the concept of vis medicatrix naturae rather than the progressive revelation of science.[13] Proponents of these movements claimed that plant and natural-product-derived medicines were superior to chemically produced drugs. And these proponents were generally opposed to the orthodox scientific agenda. Indeed, throughout history, the Western tradition of herbalism has been more antagonistic toward conventional science than supportive of it.

In the last 5 years, however, alternative medicines and medical practices have attempted to redefine themselves as "complementary" rather than "alternative" to conventional Western medicine. Herbalism is no exception. This redefinition has altered the position of botanical medicine in the United States as well as its relationship to science. Along with a greater acceptance of science by the herbal community, there has been a recognition that deeply held beliefs in the efficacy of herbs can and should be proven by dispassionate scientific investigation. As the medicinal plant industry continues to grow rapidly, herb companies and providers realize that rigorous scientific research supporting the safety and efficacy of herbal therapies would boost economic prospects as well. The industry senses and acknowledges the need to accept new responsibilities and that conducting scientific research must be at the foreground. Developing better market surveillance with attention to side effects and toxicity

---

Associate Director, Center for Alternative Medicine Research, Beth Israel Deaconness Medical Center, Boston, MA.

must also become a priority. Consumers are demanding scientific research, information, synthesis, and reliable information. The times have changed—and it is probably a good time for the herbal industry to make a commitment to work within the realm of science and to establish a scientific agenda.

REFERENCES

1. Baer HA. The potential rejuvenation of American naturopathy as a consequence of the holistic health movement. *Med Anthropol* 13:369–383, 1992.
2. National Acupuncture Foundation. *State Acupuncture Laws*. Washington, DC, 1993.
3. Goldman B. The selling of Ayurvedic medicine. *Can Med Assn J* 144(1):53–55, 1991.
4. National Board of Chiropractic Examiners. *Job Analysis of Chiropractic*. Greeley, CO, 1993.
5. Goldstein MS, et al., Holistic physicians and family practitioners: Similarities, differences, and implications for health policy. *Soc Sci Med* 26(8):853–961, 1988.
6. Mathews HF, Rootwork: Description of an ethnomedical system in the American South. *Southern Med J* 80(7):885–891, 1987.
7. Fisch S. Botanicas and spiritualism in a metropolis. *Milbank Memorial Fund Q* 46(3):377–388, 1968.
8. Martinez C, Martin HW. Folk diseases among urban Mexican-Americans. *JAMA* 196(2):161–164, 1966.
9. Cook C, Baisden D. Ancillary use of folk medicine by patients in primary care clinics in southwestern West Virginia. *Southern Med J* 79:1098–1101, 1986.
10. Kassler WJ, et al. The use of medicinal herbs by human immunodeficiency virus-infected patients. *Arch Int Med* 151:2281–2288, 1991.
11. Dubick MA. Historical perspectives on the use of herbal preparations to promote health. *J Nutr* 16:1348–1354, 1986.
12. Kaptchuk TJ. Herbal and magical medicine: Traditional healing today [book rev.]. *Soc Sci Med* 38:199–200, 1994.
13. Haller JS. *Medical Protestants: The Eclectics in American Medicine, 1825–1939*. Carbondale, IL: Southern Illinois University Press, 1994.

Industry Views on Plant Monographs

HUBERTUS CRANZ, M.D.

CURRENT SITUATION CONCERNING PHYTOMEDICINES

On the worldwide level, the situation for herbal medicines is characterized by a certain dilemma. On the one hand, there is a growing public awareness of the value of herbal medicines; on the other hand, there are regulatory and legal uncertainties that result in varying regulations of herbal medicines around the world. The most important issues in this respect are the differing classifications of plants used for therapeutic purposes. In some countries these botanicals are mainly classified as foods, while in other countries botanicals are mainly classified as medicines. In those countries where plant-based products are recognized as medicines, they are sometimes reimbursed by social security systems.

Efforts have been made to reach some kind of consensus with regard to the assessment of phytomedicines. However, because of the traditional use and philosophies behind the use of these medicines, consensus is often difficult to achieve. Given the worldwide trend to facilitate the free movement of all goods, including medicines, the question is now becoming increasingly urgent as to how this international transfer may also be achieved for this sector. Manufacturers of herbal medicines obviously have a particular interest in these developments.

In this context, monographs of widely used medicinal plants might be useful, as they affect the scientific assessment of quality, safety, and efficacy. This holds particularly true in the European Union (EU), where the free circulation of goods, including medicines, is an important objective.

DEVELOPMENTS IN EUROPE

The process of reaching more unification and harmonization in the European Community (EC) has been specifically pursued over the last 40 years. The goal to achieve a common market by December 31, 1992, within the then 12 Member States of the European Union stimulated many discussions about the harmonization of regulatory and legal requirements regarding medicinal products. Since 1965, a sophisticated regulatory system has been established for the marketing authorization of medicinal products reaching a high level of standardization in registration of medicinal products around Europe. In principle, this also includes all kinds of phytomedicines that have to be proved, as does any other medicine, for their safety, quality, and efficacy. The European Union Directives lay down two principal ways of proving a product's safety and efficacy. The first way is through scientific evidence, including clinical trials. The second way, which is highly relevant for phytomedicines, is to cite published bibliographic references as evidence of well-established use of the products. This also takes into account the traditional use of phytomedicines. Besides this, there is an EC guideline on abridged applications giving some additional explanations.

While most phytomedicines in the EU fall under the category of medicinal products, the EC nevertheless saw the need to develop some specific requirements, without deviating from the general criteria of safety, efficacy, and quality. A guideline covering the issue of quality, for example, was adopted in 1988 and complemented in 1991 with a specific guideline on Good Manufacturing Practice

---

Director General, European Proprietary Medicines Manufacturers' Association (AESGP), Brussels, Belgium.

for Herbal Medicines, which includes a precise definition of requirements concerning manufacturing premises and documentation.

MARKETING AUTHORIZATION OF PHYTOMEDICINES

It is worth noting that the whole review process of the so-called old medicines in the EC also referred to phytomedicines. This meant that through Article 39 of the EC Directive 75/319/EEC, manufacturers of all medicinal products, including phytomedicines, had to provide proof of their safety, efficacy, and quality up to May 20, 1990. However, this process, because of its complexity, has not yet been completely finalized. In addition, there were considerable differences between the medicinal products after they had been assessed according to the various means in effect in the respective European Union Member States. These differences arise because of different interpretations, different decision-making processes at the national level, and also a different history and culture concerning medicinal products. It is also important to note that in this review process, particularly for phytomedicines, some countries follow very pragmatic approaches, (e.g., France and the United Kingdom), while others choose more scientific ways of collecting material and developing assessment monographs (e.g., Germany). As a result, a key question in the EU is therefore not solved: How can herbal medicinal products be circulated freely throughout Europe? Although the new marketing authorization system established the principle of "mutual recognition" for phytomedicines as well, many countries are still not prepared to accept certain products from the outside.

THE NEW SYSTEM

To facilitate the free circulation of medicinal products in the EC, the new marketing authorization system installed two mechanisms in the EU in addition to existing legislation:

1. The "Centralized Procedure," which provides the opportunity to obtain a European marketing authorization directly for biotechnologic products, for which it is mandatory, and for high-tech products as well as for new chemical entities. For the latter, the system is an option, as they may also go through the "decentralized procedure." In the center of this system is the European Medicine Evaluation Agency (EMEA), which coordinates the national expertise in assessing an application. The EMEA became operational on January 1, 1995, and was officially inaugurated on January 26, 1995. It is located at Canary Wharf in the east of London.
2. The "Decentralized System," which shall allow an easy access to other markets based on a national marketing authorization through a system of mutual recognition.

It remains possible to apply for a purely "national marketing authorization" for a company that would like to see its products only marketed in one Member State.

For phytomedicines, normally the "Decentralized System" would offer the opportunity to gain access to other markets. However, it is obvious that because of different assessments up to now, this system is not problem free. In fact, there are still doubts whether or not the mutual recognition system can be fully used for phytomedicines. The point of that issue is to know to what extent the existing dossiers for nonprescription medicines (and so phytomedicines) would need to be updated. Such an update is not necessarily foreseen in the European legislation but may be demanded by national authorities.

Another major problem for the free circulation of phytomedicines comes from the fact that there is currently no uniform European legal classification of medicinal plants. The consequence is that the classification of medicinal plants, either as medicinal products or food supplements, is independently decided by each Member State for its national market. Many of the plant-based products fall into the category of medicinal products. Phytomedicines should, however, fall completely under medicinal legislation. In other words, they have to fulfill, as any other medicines, the three criteria of safety, efficacy, and quality.

FUTURE PERSPECTIVES

There is growing public support to study the existing situation regarding medicinal plant preparations. In particular, there are frequent requests to study if European Community rules relating to these preparations present any difficulties and what clarification may be required regarding the legal status of medicinal plant preparations, with reference to the European Community provisions on proprietary medicinal products. There are also important developments that should be taken into consideration on the level of the World Health Organization (WHO). The *WHO Guidelines for the Assessment of Herbal Medicines*[1,2] were agreed on by the International Conference on Drug Regulatory Authorities (ICDRA) in Ottawa in 1991 and were developed in cooperation with the World Federation of Proprietary Medicines Manufacturers with particular input from the European Proprietary Medicines Manufacturers' Association. In addition, these guidelines may serve as a basis for an international policy on phytomedicines, which recognizes their growing acceptance in Europe and worldwide and ensures their free circulation. This policy should address two main areas:

1. Development of guidelines for the assessment of phytomedicines, particularly requirements for the assessment of the safety and efficacy of phytomedicines: As for the proof of quality and Good Manufacturing Practice, some peculiarities justify the definition of certain requirements for phytomedicines. In this respect, the WHO Guidelines on the assessment of herbal medicines are a good basis for these considerations.

2. Development of plant monographs: This forms an important basis for the harmonization of key phytomedicines. Certain plants, broadly recognized for their therapeutic value, may indeed be standardized by reference to these monographs. Based on such a standardized scientific assessment, access to other countries of all products that have respected the criteria laid down in these monographs should be facilitated.

Based on the *WHO Guidelines for the Assessment of Herbal Medicines* and the priorities defined during the ICDRA in 1994 in the Netherlands, intensive work has taken place to develop approximately 30 model monographs on plants that are widely used in medicinal products. In summary, developing these proposals could lead to a high-quality product and increased worldwide harmonization. This would promote worldwide transfer of phytomedicines as far as possible, which would be beneficial for all people around the world.

REFERENCES

1. Akerele O. Summary of WHO guidelines for the assessment of herbal medicines. *Fitoterapia* 63(2), 1992. [Reprinted in *HerbalGram*. 13–16, 1993.]
2. World Health Organization Programme on Traditional Medicines, 1991. *Guideline for the Assessment of Herbal Medicines*. Geneva: WHO. [Reprinted in *HerbalGram*. 28:17–20, 1993.]

Dietary Supplement Legislation

STEPHEN H. McNAMARA, ESQ.

This paper provides a review of the federal legislation that will govern the regulation of herbs and other botanical substances in products that are intended for use as dietary supplements. After passing the House of Representatives by unanimous consent at approximately 3:00 A.M. on Friday morning, October 7, 1994, the dietary supplement legislation then passed the Senate, also by unanimous consent, at approximately 12:30 A.M. on Saturday morning, October 8, 1994. The President signed the new law on October 25.

Like most legislation, the law is a compromise. It does not include all of the provisions that the dietary supplement industry originally wanted and, in order to obtain sufficient support for passage, the legislation includes some new restraints on dietary supplement products. Nevertheless, viewed as a whole, the legislation should prove to be very helpful to those who want to sell herbs and other botanical substances as dietary supplement (i.e., *food*) products.

The following is a summary of the key provisions of the legislation.

MAJOR PROVISIONS OF THE LEGISLATION

The legislation is officially named the "Dietary Supplement Health and Education Act of 1994." Its provisions are incorporated as amendments into the Federal Food, Drug, and Cosmetic Act (FDC Act), which is enforced by the U.S. Food and Drug Administration (FDA).

Definition of "dietary supplement"

The legislation provides an extended definition of "dietary supplement," to be clear about the products that are covered by the new provisions.

A dietary supplement is defined as a "product (other than tobacco) intended to supplement the diet that bears or contains one or more of certain specified dietary ingredients." The specified dietary ingredients are "a vitamin," "a mineral," "an herb or other botanical," "an amino acid," "a dietary substance for use by [people] to supplement the diet by increasing the total dietary intake," and "a concentrate, metabolite, constituent, extract, or combination" of any of the foregoing ingredients.

Note that under this definition, insofar as a substance is not a vitamin/mineral/herb/botanical/amino acid, and not a concentrate/metabolite/constituent/extract/combination of such an ingredient, the FDA may continue to try to argue (as it has for certain substances in the past) that such a substance is not eligible for dietary ingredient status or for dietary supplement status if it is not truly a "dietary" substance. The FDA might try to make this sort of argument about a purported "dietary supplement" of melatonin or of chemically derived ephedrine, for example. ("Dietary" is not defined in the legislation.) However, "an herb or other botanical" would appear presumptively to qualify as a "dietary ingredient." A dietary supplement must either be in the form of a tablet, capsule, powder, softgel, gelcap, or liquid droplet, or, be in some other form that is not represented as "a conventional food."

Note that the legislation deletes a former provision of the FDC Act that had provided that products that "simulate...conventional food" (e.g., a cookie or wafer that resembles a conventional food, or a tonic or protein shake that resembles a conventional beverage) were not eligible for protection under the Proxmire Amendments of 1976. Now, such products that simulate conventional foods are eligible for dietary supplement status if they are not represented as being conventional foods. (How-

Hyman, Phelps and McNamara, Washington, DC.

ever, under the legislation it remains true that a dietary supplement may not be represented for use as a "sole item of a meal or the diet." Thus, a product represented as a "meal replacement," for example, would not be eligible for dietary supplement status.)

The definition of dietary supplement includes some highly technical provisions about the situation in which an ingredient in a supplement is also approved by the FDA for use as a drug. In general, if an article has been marketed as a dietary supplement or as a food before the FDA approves it as a new drug, certifies it as an antibiotic, or licenses it as a biologic, it may continue to be marketed as a dietary supplement unless the FDA publishes a prohibitory regulation (which would be subject to judicial review).

On the other hand if, before an article is marketed as a dietary supplement or as a food, (1) the FDA has approved the article as a new drug, certified the article as an antibiotic, or licensed the article as a biologic; or (2) the FDA has authorized the article for investigation as a new drug, antibiotic, or biologic; "substantial clinical investigations have been instituted"; and "the existence of such investigations has been made public," the article may not be marketed as a dietary supplement unless the FDA first issues an approving regulation.

Dietary supplements deemed to be foods

The legislation provides that, "[e]xcept for purposes of section 201(g), a dietary supplement shall be deemed to be a food." This provision will prevent the FDA from arguing, as it has sometimes tried to do in the past, that a product that otherwise meets the requirements of law as a dietary supplement is nevertheless not a food. The FDA had tried to argue, for example, that some herb and amino acid dietary supplement products were not "used primarily for taste, aroma, or nutritional value" and therefore were not eligible for food status.

Note, however, that the phrase "[e]xcept for purposes of section 201(g)" leaves the FDA free to argue that a dietary supplement product is also subject to regulation as a drug if the FDA can show that the supplement is "intended" for a use that triggers the drug definition (e.g., intended to prevent disease, per 21 U.S.C. § 321(g)(1)(B)).

Exemption from "food additive" status

The FDC Act is amended by the legislation to provide that the definition of a "food additive" does not include a dietary ingredient that is "in, or intended for use in, a dietary supplement." This provision should put an end to numerous previous FDA allegations that various dietary ingredients used in dietary supplements were illegal because they were unapproved food additives. This should mean that dietary ingredients including herbs or other botanicals—such as lobelia, St. John's wort, chinaberry, evening primrose oil, black currant oil, borage oil, or linseed/flaxseed oil and also including other dietary substances, such as calcium acetate, coenzyme Q10, chlorella, magnesium orotate, or other orotate compounds—can no longer be objected to by the FDA on the asserted premise that they are "unapproved food additives."

New safety requirements

To replace the precious, more burdensome food additive provisions,* the legislation creates new, less burdensome, but nevertheless significant safety-related requirements for dietary ingredients in dietary supplements.

In general, the legislation provides that a dietary supplement shall be deemed to be "adulterated" (and therefore subject to regulatory action) if it "presents a significant or unreasonable risk of illness or injury" under "conditions of use recommended or suggested in labeling" or, if no conditions of use are suggested in labeling, "under ordinary conditions of use."

Before the FDA may report a violation of the new provision to a U.S. attorney for a civil proceeding in court, the FDA must provide the "person against whom such proceeding would be initiated" an "appropriate notice and the opportunity to present views, orally and in writing." The legislation also provides that a dietary supplement shall be deemed to be adulterated if it contains a "new dietary ingredient" for which "there is inadequate information to provide reasonable assurance that such in-

---

*In essence, based on the food additive provisions of the FDC Act, the FDA argued in the past that, if it did not agree that a substance was "generally recognized as safe" by experts, the substance could be deemed to be a food additive and thus illegal for use unless and until the FDA published an approving food additive regulation. [21 U.S.C. §§ 321(s), 342(a)(2)(C), 348]

gredient does not present a significant or unreasonable risk of illness or injury."

In addition, the legislation authorizes the Secretary of Health and Human Resources to declare that a dietary supplement or ingredient presents an "imminent hazard to public health or safety," in which case it immediately would become illegal to market the supplement or ingredient. However, the legislation provides that this authority may be exercised only by the Secretary and may not be delegated to the FDA. Furthermore, if such authority is exercised, the legislation provided that "promptly after such a declaration," there must be a formal rulemaking proceeding of the type that would allow the dietary supplement industry to cross-examine FDA witnesses (not just notice-and-comment rulemaking). The legislation also retains the existing section of the FDC Act that allows the FDA to take action against a dietary supplement if it "bears or contains any poisonous or deleterious substance which may render it injurious to health." [21 U.S.C. § 342(a)(1)]

Additional requirements for new dietary ingredients

The new legislation also provides that a dietary supplement that contains a "new dietary ingredient" shall be deemed to be adulterated (and subject to regulatory action) unless it meets one of the following requirements:

1. The dietary supplement contains "only dietary ingredients which have been present in the food supply as an article used for food in a form in which the food has not been chemically altered."
2. There is a "history of use or other evidence of safety establishing that the dietary ingredient when used under the conditions recommended or suggested in the labeling of the dietary supplement will reasonably be expected to be safe." In addition, a least 75 days before such a new dietary ingredient is introduced or delivered for introduction into interstate commerce, the manufacturer or distributor of the dietary ingredient or dietary supplement containing the ingredient must provide the FDA with "information, including any citation to published articles, which is the basis on which the manufacturer or distributor has concluded that a dietary supplement containing such dietary ingredient will reasonably be expected to be safe."

A "new dietary ingredient" is defined to mean "a dietary ingredient that was not marketed in the United States before October 15, 1994."

The legislation provides that any person may file with the FDA a petition proposing the issuance of an order prescribing conditions under which the use of a new dietary ingredient will reasonably be expected to be safe. The FDA is required to make a decision on such a petition within 180 days. (Note, however, that the FDA is also required by law to act on food additive petitions within 180 days; and yet typical food additive rulemaking proceedings in fact often take 5 years or more under current FDA practice and procedure. It remains to be seen how quickly the FDA will act on a petition for a new dietary ingredient.)

Use of publications to promote products

In a significant new provision, the legislation provides that a "publication," including "an article, a chapter in a book, or an official abstract of a peer-reviewed scientific publication that appears in an article and was prepared by the author or the editors of the publication," "shall not be defined as labeling" and may be "used in connection with the sale of a dietary supplement to consumers" if the publication is "reprinted in its entirety" and meets certain specific criteria. Among the criteria that must be met: (1) the publication must not be "false or misleading"; (2) it must not "promote a particular manufacturer or brand of a dietary supplement"; (3) it must be "displayed...so as to present a balanced view of the available scientific information"; (4) if "displayed in an establishment," it must be "physically separate from the dietary supplements" and; (5) the publication must not "have appended to it any information by sticker or any other method."

These provisions would appear to authorize a salesperson (so long as the restrictive criteria are met) to call to the attention of a potential customer published nutritional or other scientific literature describing the health benefits of nutrients.

Furthermore, there is an affirmative provision that the legislation shall not "restrict a retailer or wholesaler of dietary supplements in any way whatsoever in the sale of books or other publications as a part of the business of such retailer or wholesaler." This is the first affirmative provision in the FDC Act that protects the right of sellers of dietary supplements also to sell books or other publications—publications that would, of course, be anticipated to describe the health-related benefits of nutrients.

A note of caution here: If the FDA could show that a particular book or other publication used in connection with the sale of a product was in fact written or otherwise created by the manufacturer or distributor of that same product, the FDA might still try to argue that such a book or other publication is not truly an independent publication within the meaning of this new law, but instead, "labeling" for the product. For the present, at least, in connection with the sale of any product, it would appear to be prudent to use only publications by independent third parties.

"Statements of nutritional support"

The new legislation identifies four types of "statements of nutritional support":

1. A "statement [that] claims a benefit related to a classical nutrient deficiency disease and discloses the prevalence of such disease in the United States."
2. A statement that "describes the role of a nutrient or dietary ingredient intended to affect the structure or function in humans."
3. A statement that "characterizes the documented mechanism by which a nutrient or dietary ingredient acts to maintain such structure or function."
4. A statement that "describes general well-being from consumption of a nutrient or dietary ingredient."

The legislation provides that such a statement may be made in labeling if:

1. The manufacturer "has substantiation that such statement is truthful and not misleading."
2. The labeling contains, prominently displayed, the following additional text: "This statement has not been evaluated by the Food and Drug Administration. This product is not intended to diagnose, treat, cure, or prevent any disease."
3. The manufacturer notifies the FDA "no later than 30 days after the first marketing of the dietary supplement with such statement that such a statement is being made."

Additional new labeling requirements

The legislation requires that the label of a dietary supplement identify the product as a "dietary supplement" (the term may be modified with the name of a dietary ingredient). Furthermore, the label or labeling must list the name and quantity of each dietary ingredient (or, with respect to a "proprietary blend" of dietary ingredients, the total quantity of all such ingredients in the blend). If a supplement contains an herb or other botanical, the label or labeling must also identify "any part of the plant from which the ingredient is derived."

New format for nutrition labeling on dietary supplements

The FDA is required to issue regulations to provide that the nutrition information on dietary supplement labels "shall first list those dietary ingredients that are present in the product in a significant amount and for which a recommendation for daily consumption has been established" by FDA and then "list any other dietary ingredient present and identified as having no such recommendation." The listing of dietary ingredients "shall include the quantity" of each ingredient (or of a proprietary blend) per serving. The listing "may include" the source of a dietary ingredient. After the listing of the dietary ingredients, any other ingredient information required shall follow immediately, except that no ingredient shall be required to be identified a second time.

"Percentage level claims"

Under the already existing FDA regulations on "nutrient content claims," which have gone into effect for dietary supplements in July 1995, no "nutrient content claim" (e.g., "high in vitamin C," or "a great source of allicin) may be made on the label or other labeling for a dietary supplement unless the FDA has first published a regulation authorizing the use of the claim.[†]

The legislation creates a limited exemption from this requirement, for certain "percentage level claims" in labeling for dietary supplements. The legislation provides that the requirement for an FDA regulation approving a nutrient content claim "does not apply to a statement in the labeling of a dietary supplement that characterizes the percentage level

---

[†]However, no such authorizing regulations have been published by the FDA except for the vitamins, minerals, and other nutrients for which the agency has published RDIs or DRVs.

of a dietary ingredient for which [the FDA] has not established a reference daily intake [RDI], daily recommended value [DRV], or other recommendation for daily consumption." This would, for example, appear to permit claims such as "one tablet provides 100 percent of the allicin found in an ordinary clove of garlic," or contains twice the omega-3 fatty acids as [named competing product]."

Note, however, that this exemption from nutrient content claim status for certain claims that "characterize the percentage level of a dietary ingredient" does not appear to cover all nutrient content claims for dietary supplement products for which the FDA has not established a recommendation for daily consumption. For example, if claims were made for a dietary supplement of coenzyme Q10 to the effect that it was a "great source of coenzyme Q10," or "high in coenzyme Q10," the FDA probably would deem such claims to be "nutrient content claims." Unless these claims could be said to characterize the percentage level of coenzyme Q10, such claims would not appear to qualify for the limited exemption from nutrient content claim status, and instead would appear to require the approval of an FDA nutrient-content claim regulation before they could be used. There probably will be a "gray area" of uncertainty for some time with respect to the FDA's interpretation and enforcement concerning these types of claims.

Effective date

The regulations provide that dietary supplements that are labeled after the date of enactment (i.e., after October 25, 1994) may be labeled in accordance with the amendments made by the legislation and that all dietary supplements shall be labeled after December 31, 1996, in accordance with the new legislation.

Compendial or other specifications

The legislation provides that if a supplement is "covered by" and "represented as conforming to" the specifications of an "official compendium," it shall be deemed to be misbranded (and therefore illegal) if it "fails to so conform." If a supplement is not covered by the specifications of an official compendium, the legislation specifies that it will be deemed to be misbranded (illegal) if it "fails to have the identity and strength that the supplement is represented to have," or if it "fails to meet the quality (including tablet or capsule disintegration), purity, or compositional specifications, based on validated assay or other appropriate methods, that the supplement is represented to meet."

Good manufacturing practices

The legislation authorizes the FDA to issue "current good manufacturing practice regulations:" to describe mandatory conditions under which dietary supplements must be "prepared, packed or held," including "regulations requiring, when necessary, expiration date labeling." The legislation provides that such regulations "shall be modeled after current good manufacturing practice regulations for food and may not impose standards for which there is no current and generally available analytical methodology." Once such regulations are issued and in effect, a dietary supplement that is manufactured in violation of the requirements would be deemed to be adulterated and subject to regulatory action.

Directions, conditions of use, or warnings

The legislation provides that a dietary supplement shall not be deemed misbranded (and thus illegal) "solely because its label or labeling contains directions or conditions of use or warnings."

ANPR voided

The legislation declares that the advance notice of proposed rulemaking (ANPR) about dietary supplements that the FDA published in the *Federal Register* of June 18, 1993 (58 Fed. Reg. 33690-33700) is "null and void and of no force or effect." This ANPR had threatened to initiate rulemaking or regulatory actions against dietary supplements of herbs, amino acids, and other substances, and had asserted that dietary ingredients in dietary supplements were subject to regulation as food additives. Pursuant to the legislation, the FDA announced the withdrawal of the ANPR in the *Federal Register* of December 6, 1994 (59 Fed. Reg. 62644).

Commission on dietary supplement labels

The legislation created an independent agency to be known as the Commission on Dietary Supplement Labels, which is directed to conduct a study on and to provide recommendations for the regulation of label claims and statements for dietary supplements. A final report is required not later than 24 months after the date of enactment. Within 90 days thereafter, the FDA is required to publish in the *Federal Register* a notice of any recommendation of the Commission for changes in FDA's dietary supplement regulations and a notice of proposed rulemaking on any such changes. Such rulemaking is required to be completed not later than two years after the date of issuance of the report. If such rulemaking is not completed on time, the FDA's final regulations on health claims for dietary supplements (which now prohibit the use in labeling for dietary supplements of any "health claim" that has not been approved by a final FDA regulation) "shall not be in effect."

Office of dietary supplements

The legislation also created the Office of Dietary Supplements within the National Institutes of Health (NIH). The purpose of the Office is to "explore more fully the potential role of dietary supplements...to improve health care," and "to promote scientific study of the benefits of dietary supplements in maintaining health and preventing chronic disease and other health-related conditions."

STATEMENT OF AGREEMENT/STIPULATED LEGISLATIVE HISTORY

The chief sponsors of the legislation also issued a document entitled "Statement of Agreement." This five-paragraph statement is stipulated to comprise "the entire legislative history" for the new legislation. "It is the intent of the chief sponsors of the bill (Senators Orrin Hatch, Tom Harkin and Ted Kennedy, and Congresspeople Richardson, Bliley, Moorhead, Gallegly, Dingell, Waxman) that no other reports or statements be considered as legislative history for the bill."

Perhaps the two most important provisions of the statement are paragraphs 4 and 5. Paragraph 4 states that the provision in the legislation for "statements of nutritional support," with respect to which a manufacturer is required to notify the FDA "no later than 30 days after the first marketing of the dietary supplement with such statement that such a statement is being made," *"does not permit premarket approval or require premarket review by the FDA of any statement permitted under that provision"* [emphasis added].

Paragraph 5 of the Statement of Agreement relates to the provision of the legislation that a "new dietary ingredient" may be marketed without sending any notice or information to the FDA if the ingredient has been "present in the food supply as an article used for food in a form in which the food has not been chemically altered." This paragraph states that the term "chemically altered" does not include the following "physical modifications": "minor loss of volatile components; dehydration; lyophilization; milling; tincture or solution in water; slurry; powder; or solid in suspension."

CONCLUSION

The legislation should result in some substantial changes in the way the FDA regulates dietary supplement products, including herbs and other botanical substances. For the most part, these changes will help to secure a defensible regulatory status for ingredients in existing products; will facilitate the introduction of new products, and will enable promotion of products with truthful information. The FDA has, however, been given additional powers; and, for a while, at least, there will probably be some uncertainty and confusion about how some of these provisions will be interpreted and applied by the FDA or the courts. On balance this legislation appeared to be remarkably good news for the dietary supplement industry.

Regulatory Models for Approval of Botanicals as Traditional Medicines

MARK BLUMENTHAL

This chapter briefly reviews the World Health Organization (WHO) policy on traditional medicines and then gives a skeletal overview of systems of regulation that approve botanicals as traditional and/or over-the-counter medicines in four industrialized nations, Australia, Canada, France, and Germany. In this author's opinion, the regulatory systems in the four nations discussed below and the framework provided by the WHO encompass most of the essential elements that should be necessary to consider the development of appropriate regulatory criteria and mechanisms for the evaluation of the quality, safety, and efficacy of herbs and phytomedicines here in the United States.

WHO GUIDELINES

In 1991 the WHO published its *Guidelines for the Assessment of Herbal Medicines*.[1] This document was created over a period of 5 years at several International Conferences of Drug Regulatory Authorities (Tokyo 1986, Paris 1989, and Ottawa 1991) based on WHO's recognition that 80 percent of the world's population in developing countries rely on traditional medicine; "a major part of the traditional therapies involves the use of plant extracts or their active constituents"; and "considerable growth has occurred in popular, official and commercial interest in the use of natural products," among other factors. In addition, WHO was acting on a World Health Assembly resolution called the Declaration of Alma-Ata (1978), which recommended "the accommodation of proven, traditional remedies in national policies and regulatory measures."[1]

The WHO Guidelines define "herbal medicines" as

Finished, labelled medicinal products that contain as active ingredients aerial or underground parts of plants, or other plant material, or combinations thereof, whether in crude state or as plant preparations. Plant material incudes juices, gums, fatty oils, essential oils, and any other substances of this nature. Herbal medicines may contain excipients in addition to the active ingredients. Medicine containing plant material combined with chemically defined active substances, including chemically defined, isolated constituents of plants, are not considered to be herbal medicines. Exceptionally, in some countries herbal medicines may also contain, by tradition, natural organic or inorganic active ingredients which are not of plant origin.[2]

Furthermore, in recognition of the widespread use of herbal medicines, the WHO guidelines declare that "in both developed and developing countries, consumers and health care providers need to be supplied with up-to-date and authoritative information on the beneficial properties, and possible harmful effects, of all herbal medicines."[2]

The objective of the guidelines "is to define basic criteria for the evaluation of quality, safety, and efficacy of herbal medicines and thereby to assist national regulatory authorities, scientific organizations, and manufacturers to undertake an assessment of the documentation/submission/dossiers in respect of such products. As a general rule in this assessment, traditional experience means that long-term use as well as the medical, historical and ethnolog-

---

Founder and Executive Director, American Botanical Council, Austin, TX.

ical background of those products shall be taken into account."[2]

Depending on each country's situation:

> the definition of long-term use may vary, but would be at least several decades....Prolonged and apparently uneventful use of a substance usually offers testimony of its safety. In a few instances investigations of the potential toxicity of naturally occurring substances widely used as ingredients in these preparations have revealed previously unsuspected potential for systemic toxicity, carcinogenicity and teratogenicity. Regulatory authorities need to be quickly and reliably informed of these findings. They should also have the authority to respond promptly to such alerts, either by withdrawing or varying the licences of registered products containing the suspect substance, or by rescheduling the substance in order to limit its use to medical prescription.[2]

According to O. Akerele, M.D., former Director of the Programme for Traditional Medicine at WHO, "safety should be the overriding criterion in the selection of herbal medicines for use in health service systems."[1] However, he and WHO believe that "a less stringent selection procedure could be applied to the first two groups [herbal medicines comprised of either whole or parts of plants, or crude extracts] (especially in cases of long-standing usage)," while the procedure for isolated pure phytochemicals "should be identical to that for synthetic drugs."[1]

The WHO guidelines also call for various assessments of quality, safety, efficacy, and intended use of herbal medicines. The guidelines call for reference to pharmacopeia monographs, if they exist. If none exist, a manufacturer applying for marketing licenses or registration should supply a monograph with the same components as an official pharmacopeia. All procedures should correspond to Good Manufacturing Practices (GMPs) and there needs to be stability testing of the product in its final packaging form.

With regard to safety, "a guiding principle should be that if the product has been traditionally used without demonstrated harm, no specific restrictive regulatory action should be undertaken unless new evidence demands a revised risk–benefit assesment."[2]

The WHO guidelines make provision for herbal products that may not indicate short-term toxicity but may create cryptic toxic conditions over the long term, such as the case of ingestion of pyrrolizidine alkaloids in comfrey (*Symphytum* spp.) The guidelines state that "although experience of long-term use without any evidence of risks may indicate harmlessness of a medicine, it is not certain in some cases to what extent reliance can be placed solely upon long-term usage to provide assurance of innocuousness in the light of concern generated in recent years over long-term hazards of some herbal medicines....If long-term traditional use cannot be documented, or doubts on safety exist, toxicity data should be submitted."[2]

Regarding the assessment for efficacy and intended use, the WHO guidelines allow for a variation in proof of efficacy depending on the type of indication:

> For treatment of minor disorders and for nonspecific indications, some relaxation is justified in the requirements for proof of efficacy, taking into account the extent of traditional use; the same considerations may apply to prophylactic use. Experience with individual cases recorded in reports from physicians, traditional health practitioners, or treated patients should be taken into account. Where traditional use has not been established, appropriate clinical evidence should be required.[2]

WHO has provided for the assessment of efficacy for traditional herbal formulas. "In the case of traditionally used combination products, the documentation of traditional use (classical texts such as Ayurveda, Traditional Chinese Medicine, Unani, Sida) and experience may serve for documentation of efficacy." The assessment should make a distinction between old and new combination products. "An explanation of a new combination of well-known substances including effective dose ranges and compatibility should be required in addition to the documentation of traditional knowledge of each single ingredient. Each active ingredient must contribute to the efficacy of the medicine."[2]

Finally, consumer product information is recommended, including a quantitative list of active ingredients, dosage, dosage form, indications, mode of administration, duration of use, any major adverse effects, overdose information, contraindications, warnings, precautions and major drug interactions, pregnancy and lactation warnings, expiration date, and lot number. WHO suggests that active ingredients be listed by Latin name as well as common name.

AUSTRALIA

The use of herbal products in Australia has been widespread over many years, as evidenced by the presence of an active organization of herbalists formed in 1920. In 1985, the Australian Parliament established the Working Party on Natural and Nutritional Supplements to review the quality, safety, efficacy, and labeling of herbs and related products for appropriate regulation under the Therapeutic Goods Act (TGA) of 1990.

The Working Party's report deals with approximately 1144 herbs as "therapeutic substances," dividing them into three groups, each having a recommended level of control and labeling "appropriate to their level of toxicity."[3]

Group 1 includes substances presenting *minimal risk* to the consumer. The controls that are deemed to be necessary are mandatory adherence to the Code of Good Manufacturing Practice for therapeutic goods; mandatory adherence to an advertising code based on the principles encompassed in the Therapeutic Advertising Code; labeling statements based on the Commonwealth Therapeutic Goods Order No. 22, which indicates directions for use, proportion, and name of active ingredients, when appropriate; when appropriate products will bear the phrase "for External Use Only"; and when the active ingredient is of a strength greater than 0.1 percent, the label will include the identification of the plant part used.

Group 2 deals with substances presenting *low risk* to the consumer. The controls that are required include the same as Group 1 above, except with regard to label statements. The following statements must appear on the label: "Keep out of reach of children"; "Use strictly as directed"; in instances where internal use is intended; "Warning—Do not exceed the stated dose"; and, when appropriate; "For external use only."

Group 3 represents substances presenting *moderate risk* to the consumer. The necessary controls include those in Group 1 with the following additions: Specific label statements are required for some of the herbs in this group; certain homeopathics are exempted from requirements of Group 2 and 3; traditional claims for herbal remedies and homeopathic preparations will be allowed, providing that general advertising requirements are compiled with and such claims can be justified by literature references; essential oils must be labeled either "natural" or "synthetic" to specify their origins; a Standing Subcommittee reporting to the Controlled Substances Advisory Council will be established to continue the long-term review of control of specific preparations; that the Subcommittee's finding and recommendations with respect to preparations detailed in Appendix 6 of the report (i.e., control of poisons and prohibited substances) will be referred to the National Health and Medical Research Council for consideration.[3,4]

When an herbal product is sold with detailed information on dosage and intended use, a product manufacturer must declare a "statement of purpose" and is required to possess an appropriate claim. "Such a product must be registered on the Australian Register of Therapeutic Goods before it is allowed to be sold, and must also disclose the formula according to the quantity or proportion of ingredients in a combination."[5]

The Act provides "that traditional claims for herbal remedies be allowed, providing general advertising requirements are complied with and providing such claims are justified by literature references."

The Therapeutic Goods Act (TGA) also exempts compounding of herbal products by practitioners: "Compounding by practitioners of preparations intended for dispensing to individual patients as part of the normal practitioner/patient process be exempted from this requirement (providing the 'manufacture' occurs on the premises at which treatment/consultation occurs."[5]

The implementation of the TGA has had an adverse impact on a number of small herbal products manufacturers in Australia. The TGA established GMPs and product registration fees for each herbal product, similar to GMPs and fees required of pharmaceutical manufacturers. Many small firms who were not able to pay this fee simply ceased operation or limited their variety of products offered. This has had a "trickle down" effect on raw material suppliers and others who now have less market for their products, with the result that consumer prices for products have increased.[5]

As a parenthetical note, it might be constructive to add that the American Herbal Products Association (AHPA) is currently reviewing about 1000 herbs commonly traded in U.S. commerce and categorizing them according to safety as noted in numerous authoritative pharmacognosy and botany texts. The resultant document will be called Label and Use Guidelines (LUG) and somewhat parallels the Australian system noted above. The LUG will include recommended safety precautions for each herb listed in three safety categories. This process has been initiated for over the past year but the final publication date is yet uncertain.[6,7*] [See Reference No. 8.]

CANADA

Like the U.S. FDA, Canada's Health Protection Branch (HPB) is divided into several branches, depending on the type of products being regulated. The HPB is composed in part of a Food Directorate and a Drugs Directorate. Ironically, in 1985, the Director General of the *Foods* Directorate convened a special Expert Advisory Committee on Herbs and Botanical Preparations (EACHBP) to consider how herbs should be regulated. This committee consisted of three pharmacists, two herbalists, one nutritionist, and a physician.

The committee issued a report in 1986 suggesting the implementation of a new class of drugs for herbs—Folklore Medicines. It also made a distinction among the following types of herbs: those unacceptable for use in or as foods; those generally acceptable as foods; those acceptable as foods under specific conditions; and those generally used for medicinal purposes. The panel was reconvened in 1993 to consider some safety concerns.

The panel's 1986 recommendation that the HPB establish a separate new category for herbs as traditional herbal medicines was not initially adopted by the HPB in any formal document. Rather than establish a new category, the HPB incorporated the EACHBP's recommendation to establish Traditional Herbal Medicine (THM) status into the already existing DIN (drug identification number) system for over-the-counter (OTC) drugs. Therefore, since around 1986 herb manufacturers have been able to petition HPB for a therapeutic claim for herbs based on traditional uses as long as the claim is validated by authoritative pharmacognosy, pharmacy, botany, ethnobotany, and related texts. It bears mentioning that the Canadian regulatory environment is characterized by a greater spirit of cooperation between the government and industry, consistent with regulatory systems in Europe. This is contrasted to the more adversarial attitude that so often pervades regulatory dynamics here in the United States.

In January of 1990 the HPB issued Information Letter (IL) No. 771 in which it clarified its policy that herbs could be sold as THMs under the existing DIN system instead of creating a new class of drugs as "Folklore Medicines." This document clarified some aspects of an earlier publication (IL 705, March 11, 1989), which listed 64 herbs that were considered unsafe adulterants as *foods* but, in many cases, could still be sold legally as *drugs*. IL 771 stated, "since a claim must be made for drugs in order to guide the consumer in their [sic] selection and use, a claim will result and appear on the label of every product which receives a DIN. In essence, if the herbal ingredient and/or formulation has *significant real or reputed pharmacological action* [italics added], it will be considered to be a drug and may not be sold without a DIN."

In addition IL 771 recognizes two categories of herbs: First are "herbs listed in pharmacopoeias and major pharmacological reference works. These generally have their properties, dosage, indications, and contraindications for use well established." Second are "herbs which have received relatively little attention in the world scientific literature and therefore may not be well-known in Canada. Nonetheless, there is a large body of literature describing the traditional use of these ingredients for medicinal purposes although this may be on an empirical or anecdotal basis."

The Canadian regulations limit herbal claims that are not well documented in pharmacopeias to minor ailments. "In accepting herbal medicines in this second group it is expected that they will be used for minor self-limiting conditions. Existing prohibitions continue to apply for claims respecting the prevention or treatment of serious diseases," which are listed elsewhere in the Food and Drug Act, "or diseases which are otherwise inappropriate for self-diagnosis and treatment."

Of particular interest is the fact that the Canadian regulations acknowledge that consumers are not generally familiar with the uses of herbal remedies. IL 771 stated: "The labelling of medicinal products containing ingredients that are not generally familiar to the public requires particular attention. Con-

---

*McGuffin M, personal communication, December 9, 1994.

sequently, those herbal medicinal products which are based on traditional or folkloric use should be designated as Traditional Medicines. In addition, *the consumer should be able to judge the purpose of the product from the information provided by the label, and the instructions for use should enable the consumer to use the product wisely.*" [italics added]

In 1992 the HPB submitted to the Canadian Parliament a regulatory proposal that was published in the *Canada Gazette*, Part I (comparable to the U.S. *Federal Register*), based on a revision of IL 705, originally published in 1989. Listed were 64 herbs that were considered to be "adulterants" to foods and could no longer be marketed in herbal products sold as foods. However, IL 705 did not preclude these herbs from being sold as drugs with DINs under the provisions of IL 771 discussed above.

Plants on this list include betel nut (*Areca catechu*), calabar bean (*Physostigma venenosum*), comfrey (*Symphytum* spp.), deadly nightshade (*Atropa belladonna*), European mandrake (*Mandragora officinarum*), goldenseal root (*Hydrastis canadensis*), the poison hemlock (*Conium maculatum*), and even feverfew (*Tanacetum parthenium*) and St. John's wort (*Hypericum perforatum*). Also included is a section on herbs that can be used in flavoring alcoholic beverages as long as certain potentially toxic components have been removed (e.g., sassafras oil with safrole removed). In addition, IL 705 contains a schedule of seven herbs that are contraindicated in pregnancy (e.g., black cohosh [*Cimicifuga racemosa*], blue cohosh [*Caulophyllum thalictroides*], dong quai [*Angelica sinensis*], parsley oil [*Petroselinum crispum*], rue [*Ruta graveolens*], sage oil [*Salvia officinalis*], and uva ursi [*Arctostaphylos uva ursi*]).

The HPB invited public comment on the list. Unfortunately, much confusion reigned among the Canadian populace and health foods industry as to the intent of IL 705. Believing that the government was attempting to remove these herbs from the market, consumers wrote several thousand letters to HPB demanding that they be allowed to maintain access to these herbs. In addition, a number of expert botanists, phytochemists, herbalists, and pharmacognosists pointed out the inconsistencies and inaccuracies in the evaluation of some familiar medicinal plants. The government responded by trying to clarify the matter and in 1992 reconvened the original Expert Advisory Committee, which issued its report in October 1993.

The *Second Report of the Expert Advisory Committee on Herbs and Botanical Preparations* is a document that could serve as part of the much-needed reform of the U.S. regulatory system (or lack thereof) for herbs. The second report builds on the recommendations of the first report in 1986 and deals primarily with safety concerns. One important recommendation is the removal of ginkgo (*Ginkgo biloba*) from the list of adulterants to food in IL 705. The committee "agreed that its (ginkgo) consumption as a food does not produce known harmful effects and therefore, recommended that this plant not be included in Schedule No. 705." Otherwise, the committee agreed that herbs that were potentially unsafe should remain on 705, including comfrey (*Symphytum* spp.) because of the presence of pyrrolizidine alkaloids. This does not mean, however, that comfrey could not be used in drug products under specified restrictions.

The EACHBP:

agreed that toxicity should remain the main concern in regulating herbs and recognized that long-term toxicity, as opposed to acute toxicity, is usually the main concern. In assessing the safety of herbs and botanical preparations, potency and levels of consumption were viewed as important parameters to consider. . . . The committee agreed that herbs sold for medicinal purposes should *not* be regulated as foods and that easy-to-use criteria are needed to classify herbs as either foods or drugs. However, the committee recognized that the parallel sale of herbs as foods *and* as drugs may be appropriate depending on factors such as: label claims; traditional uses (e.g., as food or flavouring/colouring agent); modalities of use (e.g., regular or infrequent use); pharmacological/toxicological activity at level of intake, and product presentation (e.g., raw herb or concentrated form).[8]

The committee also presented a list of 76 herbs that it reviewed for general safety and that it considered safe when consumed as foods.

One criticism, sometimes leveled at the Canadian model, is that the original requirements in IL 771 make no provision for ensuring the correct botanical species of the herbal ingredients in commercial products. However, the regulations attempt to deal with this by proposing the establishment of "Standardized Drug Monographs (herbal)" or "SDM herbal" for short. The HPB has contacted several nongovernment experts in pharmacognosy to develop monographs on goldenseal, echinacea, and other herbs. This list was updated and prioritized in the second report from the EACHBP and now encompasses chaparral (*Larrea tridentata*), coltsfoot (*Tussilago farfara*), comfrey (*Symphytum* spp.), feverfew (*Tanacetum parthenium*), germander (*Teucrium chamaedrys*), *Ginkgo biloba*, goldenseal (*Hydrastis canadensis*), hawthorn (*Crataegus* spp.), Oregon grape root (*Mahonia* spp.), St. John's wort (*Hypericum perforatum*), and wormwood (*Artemisia absinthium*). Some of these herbs are included for safety concerns (e.g., chaparral, coltsfoot, comfrey, germander, and wormwood); the others because of widespread use.

The drug monograph system that was originally envisioned in previous documents was also recommended to facilitate registration of traditional herbal medicines as nonprescription (OTC) drugs. The committee recommended the *British Herbal Pharmacopoeia* as a useful reference.

The Canadian system of allowing herbs to be sold as OTC drugs with label claims for their traditional uses allows consumers in Canada the option of choosing these products with at least some rational basis for their uses and potential health benefits. The Canadian system is consistent with the WHO's *Guidelines for the Assessment of Herbal Medicines* and with international trends in regulating herbs for their well-documented historical uses.

FRANCE

The French system of regulation of herbal products offers some interesting components for possible consideration in the United States. Approximately 200 herbs are approved as OTC medicines with varying claims. Licensing approval for phytomedicines is subject to the regulations generally required of all drugs. This includes evaluation according to quality, safety, and efficacy. However, according to A. Artiges, Minister of Solidarity of Health and Protection, Directorate of Pharmacy and Medicine, "for some vegetable drugs and preparations of traditional use, the demonstration of efficacy, according to current scientific protocols, is particularly difficult, or even impossible. In the same way, carrying out toxicologic studies complying with the European requirements would cost too much compared to the potential valuable information obtained on safety of the drug of traditional national use."[9]

Since 1981, the drug licensing committee has set up an evaluation process for phytomedicines that was suitable for their particular situation, which included an abbreviated or abridged application. Artiges is quick to point out, however, "that there are not two levels for a marketing authorisation; there is no abridged license, there is only one type of license; but for some vegetable drugs and preparations, this license is granted on the basis of an adapted documentation and an abridged application."[9]

Thirty-five therapeutic categories are allowed as long as they correspond to a validated traditional use. "If the applicant claims these indications, agreed by the scientific community, a total exemption of the clinical documentation is granted. If the applicant claims other therapeutical indications, he has to provide relevant toxicological, pharmacological and clinical documentation.... On the other hand, all the uses related to major pathologies, for which it could be dangerous not to use therapeutics of demonstrated efficacy, have been excluded."[9]

The French system accepts three levels of therapeutic indications relative to the level of known demonstrated efficacy: "traditionally used"; "used in..."; or therapeutic indications without the word "used."

In 1990, 115 herbal medicine plus 31 laxatives were involved in this approval procedure of various galenic forms. In a later notice review, 205 herbal drugs were listed. The notice is intended as a guide of the most common traditional vegetable drugs used in France and "represents a compendium of medical and pharmaceutical information, which, on the one hand, insures the quality of the medicine, and on the other hand avoids a waste and a duplication of work in the toxicological and clinical fields."[9] So the granting of an application for either a traditional, classical phytopharmaceutical preparation or a new phytotherapy preparation is available to anybody provided that person can make a product of good quality and give adequate information in connection with therapeutic indications claimed."[9]

THE GERMAN COMMISSION E

In reviewing the various systems of regulations for herbs and phytomedicines in industrialized nations, one particular model stands out: the German

Commission E. The Commission E is an independent division of the German Federal Health Agency (*Bundesgesundheitsamt*) that *actively* collects information on herbal medicines and evaluates them in relation to their safety and efficacy. These evaluations are published in the form of brief monographs that either approve or disapprove the particular herbal drug for OTC use.

This method of approval is quite interesting. Commission E reviews information about each herb's history of use, chemistry, pharmacologic and experimental studies on animals, human clinical studies when available, epidemiologic studies, and even subjective evaluations by patients and physicians from clinical experience. Emphasis is placed on safety when efficacy judgments are made.

According to Varro E. Tyler, Ph.D., Sc.D., Distinguished Professor Emeritus of Pharmacognosy at Purdue University, West Lafayette, IN, and senior author of the textbook *Pharmacognosy*: "Commission E evaluates efficacy based on a doctrine of *reasonable certainty*," as contrasted with our Food and Drug Administration's (FDA's) insistence on a "doctrine of absolute proof," based on information that is *passively* submitted to the FDA from drug manufacturers.[10]

The Commission E was established in 1978 and has since published about 400 monographs covering over 300 herbs and herb combinations sold in Germany. The Commission includes people with expertise in various aspects of medicinal plant research and use, including physicians, pharmacists, pharmacologists, and toxicologists, as well as representatives of the pharmaceutical industry and laypersons. Of these monographs, about 200 are positive; that is, they approve the use of an herb for particular use or uses. About 100 are negative assessments, usually based on either lack of sufficient data to approve actions and/or significant toxicity concerns.

Herbs and medicinal plant products have always been popular and widely respected in Germany. In his introduction to the American Botanical Council's English translations of these monographs, Professor Tyler wrote, "The therapeutic use of herbs and phytomedicines has always been very popular in Germany. About 600–700 different plant drugs are currently sold there, singly and in combination, in *Apotheken* (pharmacies), *Drogerien* (drugstores), *Reformhäuser* (health food stores), and *Märkte* (markets)."[10]

In addition to the self-selection of herbal products by consumers, approximately 70 percent of the physicians in general practice prescribe the thousands of registered herbal remedies, and a significant portion of the $1.7 billion annual sales (a conservative estimate) is paid for by government health insurance. In 1988, 5.4 million prescriptions were written for a single phytomedicine, *Ginkgo biloba* extract, a figure that does not include the substantial OTC sales of the product.

"In view of this significant role which phytomedicines play in Germany, it is only natural that the government there would develop a mechanism to assure users of their safety and efficacy. The process is unique. For various reasons, even other advanced nations have not yet chosen to emulate it. But it is worthy of imitation, and it is probably only a matter of time before consumers in other countries are able to benefit from the German experience."[10]

In a review of the first 285 monographs, most have a positive assessment, while 66 percent mention various risks, and 58 had no plausible evidence of efficacy resulting in a negative assessment. The monographs list known contraindications for the various herbs. Some of the more frequently mentioned contraindications include allergy to active constituent (63 monographs), restricted use during pregnancy and/or lactation (24 monographs), gallstones (15 monographs), and inflammatory kidney disease (seven monographs). Thirty-five monographs limit the period of use to reduce side effects. Types of side effects include gastrointestinal disorders (35 monographs), allergic reactions—mostly skin reactions with some more severe generalized reactions—(30 monographs), and photosensitivity (five monographs). In addition, seven monographs mention that the herb may influence the absorption of other drugs taken simultaneously.[11,12]

The American Botanical Council (ABC), a not-for-profit research and educational organization, has undertaken the translation and publication in English of the German Commission E Monographs. All monographs published in Germany through 1995 have been translated and published in 1998 (American Botanical Council). Multiple cross-references and indices have been created to increase the usefulness and ease of use of the monographs. Professor Tyler has some glowing words for the Commission E Monographs: "They represent the most accurate information available in the entire world on the safety and efficacy of herbs and phytomedicines. As such, they are worthy of careful study by anyone interested in any type of drug therapy. Ignorance of the Commission E monographs is ignorance of a substantial segment of modern medicine."[10]

CONCLUSION

It would be most constructive and beneficial to the overall health of the American public if scientists, health professionals, industry, and regulators begin to review and consider the most reasonable and compelling elements of the various systems briefly outlined above as part of a comprehensive reform of the manner in which herbs are evaluated for their quality, safety, and efficacy when sold in the United States. The time has come for serious deliberations and cooperation from all parties to create a rational, meaningful system for herbal regulation—one that is consistent with the goals and objectives of the WHO Guidelines and that supports the general health of the American people.

REFERENCES

1. Akerele O. Summary of WHO Guidelines for the Assessment of Herbal Medicines. *Fitoterapia*. 1992; LXIII, No. 2. [Reprinted in *HerbalGram*. 13–16, 1993.]
2. World Health Organization Programme on Traditional Medicines, 1991. *Guideline for the Assessment of Herbal Medicines*. Geneva: WHO. [Reprinted in *HerbalGram*. 28:17–20, 1993.]
3. Report of the South Australian Working Party on Natural and Nutritional Supplements. South Australian Health Commission, Public & Environmental Health Division, 1990.
4. Bayne H, Israelsen LD, Blumenthal M. *Review of Regulations of Herbs and Phytomedicines in Industrialized Nations*. Austin, TX: American Botanical Council, 1995.
5. Upton R. *Regulation of Herbal Medicine & Herbal Products Abroad With an Overview of Dietary Supplement Regulation in America*. Soquel, CA: American Herbalists Guild, 1993.
6. McGuffin M. Personal communication, December 9, 1994.
7. Hobbs, C, Upton R, Goldberg A. *American Herbal Product Association's Botanical Safety Handbook*. Boca Raton, FL: CRC Press, 1997.
8. Blumenthal M. Canadian expert advisory committee on herbs and botanical preparations, second report. *HerbalGram* 32:23–24, 58, 1994.
9. Artiges A. What are the legal requirements for the use of phytopharmaceuticals drugs in France? *J Ethnopharmacol*. 32:231–234, 1991.
10. Tyler VE. Foreword. In: Blumenthal M, Busse WR, Goldberg A, Gruenwald J, Hall T, Riggins CW, Rister RS (Eds.); Klein S and Rister RS (trans.) *The Complete German Commission E Monographs—Therapeutic Guide to Herbal Medicines*. Austin, TX: American Botanical Council; Boston: Integrative Medicine Communications, 1998.
11. Bergner P. German evaluation of herbal medicines. *HerbalGram*. 30:17, 64, 1994.
12. Keller K. Results of the revision of herbal drugs in the Federal Republic of Germany with a special focus on risk aspects. *Zeitschrift für Phytoterapie*. 13:116–120, 1992.

Summary of Principal Findings and Policy Initiatives

1. We have learned a great deal about the size and scope of the botanical marketplace, and it is larger than we thought.
2. Botanicals are widely used in many forms by diverse populations for varying reasons.
3. Botanicals are not widely used by conventional medical doctors and other orthodox health professionals in the United States. This is in contrast to the European experience, in which botanicals are widely recommended and prescribed by physicians and dispensed by pharmacists.
4. To assess the efficacy of botanicals, we must continue to gather and analyze the available data and, through appropriate forums, identify a spectrum of opinions to acknowledge their utility and benefits. Continued research is important; and research methodologies must be flexible and pragmatic in approaching these issues.
5. There is a need to monitor the safety of botanicals when used as dietary supplements or traditional medicines. We must improve identification of materials and pay close attention to production methods and labeling practices so as to promote their safe use. Herbs have been used for thousands of years; from this broad empirical base we may conclude that many botanicals can be safely used by the general public. At the same time, we must remain watchful for new and unknown hazards. Both industry and government should participate in a process to collect and review such information.
6. There is growing need to ensure the quality of herbs, beginning with collection practices, handling and processing procedures, and the development of appropriate good manufacturing practices. Global harmonization of botanical standards is an important but daunting task that will be a subject of interest to the U.S. Pharmacopoeia as well as to the botanical industry. It is generally agreed that efforts to establish and follow appropriate quality standards is a high priority. Also, the loss of commercially important species due to over collection or unwise harvesting practices should be addressed with a view toward protecting endangered species.
7. The European botanical market is far larger than previously thought. The U.S. market is much smaller but growing quickly. The chief reason for this disparity appears to be a well-developed regulatory structure for botanicals and phytomedicines in Europe. Incentives to create proprietary assets in botanicals would stimulate research and sales. However, this may be difficult to accomplish under current law. The need for regulatory and legislative change should be addressed. The regulation of botanicals and phytomedicines remains the subject of great discussion in both Europe and the United States. The different regulatory models whereby herbs could be regulated include prescription drugs, over-the-counter drugs, traditional medicines, and dietary supplements. These models differ significantly, presenting a range of advantages and disadvantages. A collaborative and ongoing effort between the Food and Drug Administration and industry to develop regulatory approaches that protect consumers from unsafe or falsely labeled products while assuring information and access to beneficial products is urgently needed.

Summary of the Conference

LOREN D. ISRAELSEN

Clearly, this conference has been a historic undertaking, bringing together people from many different entities and organizations in industry, academia, and government to address the role of botanicals in American health care. The size and scope of the industry, we learned, is much larger and more diverse than we realized. People continue to seek health care and take botanicals for a wide range of motives, yet the medical profession knows very little about the actual use of these plants. In America, unlike Europe, doctors are not getting involved.

The efficacy of botanicals is an issue we must continue to assess by gathering and collecting relevant data and identifying the spectrum of options. Proving the utility and benefit of botanicals will work best if we can remain flexible and pragmatic as we go about it. It is a daunting task to be sure, because the ramifications extend to so many different constituencies. We may have succeeded in this conference in identifying the best way to continue that efficacy assessment in the context of American culture.

There seems to be a strong desire to continue to review and assess the safety of botanicals, with an emphasis on surveillance of the products as they are used and misused. We need to identify heretofore unknown hazards or risks and address them quickly and decisively once they are clarified. We do, however, recognize the traditional use and role of botanicals, and that there is a baseline of evidence to suggest that many can be used safely. Both industry and the Food and Drug Administration take the issue of safety seriously. We agree that botanical products must be manufactured to quality standards, appropriately labeled, and free of false claims in order to ensure consumer safety. One effect of legislation is a clear mandate to industry to become proactive and responsible, to develop models and methods to self-regulate, because there are severely limited resources and personnel available in the government.

In addition, it is clear that the quality of herbal products must be assured, beginning with collection and harvesting to handling and processing. We need to develop Good Manufacturing Practices that apply specifically to botanicals, which focus on special issues of microbiologic growth, misidentification, and possible adulteration. We also need to address the lack of qualified and specifically trained botanists. This is an important priority.

The global harmonization of botanical standards is an important task, but apparently a difficult one, given the wide range of different standards that exist throughout the world, and the U.S. Pharmacopoeia has a keen interest in addressing such issues. It is generally agreed that quality standards are a high priority that need to be addressed aggressively by the industry, academia, and the agency.

Finally, we see that the European market is far larger than we understood it to be, and that the U.S. market is also larger, but that collecting data on the actual scope of the industry is difficult. One challenge is to quantify who and what we are: This is one of the active projects of the American Herbal Products Association.

Among the choices we have, how do we best regulate botanicals—as prescription drugs, over-the-counters, traditional medicines, or as dietary supplements? How do we find and provide appropriate means to create access to these products, while ensuring that any claims made for them are appropriate to consumers and industry? Passage of the di-

---

Executive Director, Utah Natural Products Alliance, Salt Lake City, UT.

etary supplement law provides new choices and options, and we appreciate that it will take time and hard work to evaluate all of the challenges and opportunities it presents as well as options in the drug arena.

Collectively and collaboratively, among industry, government, and the scientific community, we must find the most appropriate way to ensure access to botanicals and to provide useful and meaningful information on their benefits. This remains one of our most urgent tasks. We appreciate the broad representation from the FDA and from the National Institutes of Health's Office of Alternative Medicine, which makes this conference a first in many regards. But it also probably marks the first of a number of discussions among all of these groups as we continue the dialogue.

We have asked many more questions than we have answered. That is precisely what the conference was designed to do and I believe it accomplished that. I look forward to an ongoing discussion, as we unravel the intriguing issues presented by the dietary supplement legislation and as the industry continues to assess how to respond. As I have said to a few people: "We've just gotten our 'green card'; now we have to figure out what to do with ourselves." Assuming we do that, we hope the agency will likewise address those same issues as quickly and expeditiously as it can, within the restraints of time and resources.

Index

A

Absinthium, 155
Acacia, 154
Achillea, 154
Aconite, 154
Acupuncture, use of, 189
African-American healers, 33–35
Agar, 160
Agency for Health Care Policy and Research, synthesis of evidence, 65–74
   combining evidence, 70–72, *71*
   consensus development program at NIH, 75–76
   databases, 65
   evidence, types of, 65–67
   expert opinion, 65–66
   individual study evaluation, 67–68, 68–69t
   literature searches, 66
   published evidence, 65
   summarizing evidence, 66–67, 67t
AGRICOLA, 56
Aletris, 154
Alfafa leaf, 29
Algorithms, for safety evaluations, standards, 84–85
Allium, 19, 154
Almond oil, 155, 164
Aloe, 17–18, 154
   commercial price of, 185
Alternative system for evaluation, of botanicals, 41–42
Althaea, 155
American religious groups, medical practices of, 33–35
Amish medical practitioners, 33–35
Amygdala amara, 164
Ancient, modern medical systems, relationship, 47
Ancistrocladus korupensis, 134–135
Angelica, 18–19, 155
Angustrura, 160
Anise hyssop, 186
Anisum, 164
Anthemis, 155
Anti-inflammatory agents, for arthritis relief, 49
Antibiotics, effect on otitis media, 67
Apocynum, 155
Application, new drug, cost of, 171
APRALERT, 56
Aralia, 155
Archer, J., writings of, 93
Arnica extract, 29
Arnicae radix, 155
Arthritis relief, 49–54
   anti-inflammatory agents, 49
Arum, 155

Asafoetida, 159
Asarum, 155
Asclepias, 155, 167
Asian herb shops, retail sales in U.S., 184
Asian medical practitioners, 33–35
Aspidium, 159
Aspidosperma, 156
Assafoetida, 163
Assays, standards harmonization, 150–151
Astragalus, 18
   commercial price of, 185
Atropine, 29
Avenae farina, 156
Ayurvedic medicine, 29, 33–35
Azedarach, 162

B

Balsamum peruvianum, 167
Balsamum toluifera, 167
Balsamum tolutanum, 167
Bayberry, 186
Belladonna, 156
Benzoinum, 167
Berberis, 156
Beverage herb tea, retail sales in U.S., 184
Bilberry, 29
Biofeedback, use of, 189
BIOSIS, 56
Bitter orange oil, 157
Black cherry, 186
Black cohosh, 186
Black hellebore, 95–96
Black mustard, 156
Black walnut, 186
Bloodroot, 186
Blue cohosh, 186
Boneset, 186
Botanicals
   alternative system for evaluation, 41–42
   approval of, as traditional medicines, regulatory models, 205–212
   defined, 5, 143
   dietary supplement legislation, 199–204
   economics of, 175–182, 183–191
   evaluation of, scientific context, 39–41
   historical use of, 90–99
   manufacture of, 143–144
   medicinal use of, 13–16
   modern usages, traditional, differences between, 90–91
   pharmaceuticals, costs compared, 186–187, 187t
   processing of, 143–145

   professional guidance of policy, need for, 30–31
   projects on, in United States, current overview, 189–190
   quality control, 115–168
   safety, 81–114
      historical perspective, 87–101
      information base for, 103–106
   standards
      international conference on harmonization of, 42
      scientific issues, 149–153
      worldwide harmonization of, 147–168
   use of, 5–79
      in United States, 17–25
      types, 27–31
Bougainvillea, 29
Brayers, 156
Bryonia, 156
Buchu, 156
Business Genetics Co., retail sales in U.S., 184

C

CA search, as database, 56
Calamus, 154, 186
Calendula, 156
Calumba, 158, 161
Cambogia, 160
Camphor, 156
Canada snakeroot, 186
CANCERLINE, 56
Canella, 156
Cannabis indica, 156
Capsicum oleoresin, 18, 156
Cardamon, 159
Carnauba wax, 158
Carota, 158
Carrageenan, 165
Cascara, 18, 29, 165, 186
   commercial price of, 185
Cascarilla, 158
Cassia acutifolia, 23
Cassia fistula, 157
Castanea, 157
Castor oil, 30, 165
Cataria, 163
Catechu, 154
Caulophyllum, 157
Cayenne, commercial price of, 185
CDC. *See* Centers for Disease Control and Prevention
Cedar leaf oil, 167
Centers for Disease Control and Prevention, 107
Cetraria, 157
Chamomile, 18, 29, 30
   commercial price of, 185
Chanberlayne, J., writings of, 93

Page numbers in *italics* indicate figures. Page numbers followed by "t" indicate tables.

Change, foundation for, 10–11
Chapparal, 186
Chelidonium, 157
Chicory peppermint, 29
Chimaphila, 157
Chinese medicine, traditional, 29, 33–35
　for eczema, 113
　medicine derived from, 45–47
Chirata, 167
Chiretta, 154
Chiropractic, use of, 189
Chlorophyll, 29
Chondrus, 157
Chrysarobin, 155
Cimicifuga, 157
Cinchona, 157
Cinnamomum saignoicum, 157
Cinnamon, 29
Cinnamon bark, 157
Cinnamon oil, 157
Circulation, nonprescription phytomedicines, retail dollars, 176
Citronella, 30
Clove oil, 159
Cloves, 29
Coca, 159
Colchici cormus, semen, 158
Cold, nonprescription phytomedicines, retail dollars, 176
Coles, W., writings of, 93
Colic root, 186
Collection, of raw plant specimen, 140
Colocynth, 157
Comfrey, 97
Commercial weight-loss programs, use of, 189
Commission of dietary supplement labels, 203–204
Common juniper, 186
Communication, regarding safety, in United States, 83–84
Conference on harmonization of standards, international, 42
Conium, 158
Contaminants, environmental, detection of, 127–131
Controlled trial, randomized, alternatives to, herbal efficacy, 59–64
Convallaria, 158
Copaiba, 158
Copper toxicity, 112
Coriander, 158
Corn oil, 168
Cornus, 158
Cost
　botanicals, 183–191
　health care, effect of regulations on, 169
　herbal medicines, comparative, 187, 187t
　new drug application, 171
　pharmaceuticals, *vs.* botanicals, 186–187, 187t
Cottonseed oil, 160

Cough, nonprescription phytomedicines, retail dollars, 176
Crataegus, 21
Crocus, 158
Cubeba, 158, 164
Culpepper, N., writings of, 93
Culver's root, 186
Curve, multiple-use, *124,* 124–125
Cusso, 160
Cydonium, 158
Cypripedium, 158

D

Databases, 55–57
　AGRICOLA, 56
　APRALERT, 56
　BIOSIS, 56
　CA search, 56
　CANCERLINE, 56
　EMBASE, 56
　Food Sciences and Technology Abstracts, 56
　Medicine, 56
　Medline, 56
　on-line databases, 55–57
　PHYTODOK, 56
　searches, examples of, 56–57
　TOXLINE, 56
Deer's tongue, 186
Delphinium, 158
Devil's club, 30
Dietary supplement. *See* Botanicals
Dietary supplement legislation, 199–204
　advance notice of proposed rulemaking, 203
　commission of dietary supplement labels, 203–204
　compendial specifications, 203
　conditions of use, 203
　dietary supplement, defined, 199–200
　directions, 203
　effective date, 203
　food additive status, exemption from, 200
　foods, dietary supplements deemed to be, 200
　good manufacturing practices, 203
　labeling, 202
　office of dietary supplements, 204
　percentage level claims, 202–203
　provisions of, 199–204
　publications, to promote products, 201–202
　safety requirements, 200–201
　statement
　　of agreements, 204
　　of nutritional support, 202
　stipulated legislative history, 204
　warnings, 203
Digitalis, 159
Digitoxin, 29
Dioscorides, 92
Diospyros, 159
Dodoens, D.R., writings of, 93

Domestication, in quality control of botanicals, 133–137
Dong quai, 18–19, 29
　commercial price of, 185
Dracontium, 159
Drying, of specimen, 140
Dulcamara, 166

E

Echinacea, 19, 29, 30
　commercial price of, 185
Economics of botanicals, 183–191. *See also* Cost
Eczema, Chinese herbal medicine, 113
Effective date, dietary supplement, 203
Elastica, 161
Elaterium, 159, 163
Elderberry, 186
Eleuthero ginseng, 23
Eleutherococcus senticosus, 23
EMBASE, 56
EMEA. *See* European Medicines Evaluation Agency
Energy healing, use of, 189
Environmental contaminants, detection of, 127–131
Ephedra, 21, 98–99
　cold care teas, 29
　commercial price of, 185
Ephedrine, 29
Equisetum, 98–99
Ergota, 158
Erigeron, 159
Eriodictyon, 159
Eucalyptus leaf, 29
Eucalyptus oil, 159
Euonymus, 159
Eupatorium, 159
European Medicines Evaluation Agency, 110
Evening primrose oil, 30
Exercise, use of, 189

F

FDA. *See* Food and Drug Administration
Fennel oil, 159
Fennel seed, 29
Feverfew, 19
　commercial price of, 185
Ficus, 159
Filix-mas, 156
Fish oils, 49
Foeniculum, 159
Folk remedies, use of, 189
Food and Drug Administration, 1, 107
　different standards within system, 41–42
　role of, 7–9
　standards of, 7–8
　status of, 7–9
Food Sciences and Technology Abstracts, 56
Food stores, retail sales in U.S., 184
Foxglove, 96
Frangula, 165

INDEX

Frasera, 159
Fringetree, 186
FSTA. *See* Food Sciences and Technology Abstracts

G

Galbanum, 160
Galen, 92
Galenical formulations, manufacture of botanicals, 144
Gambir, 163
Garlic, 19
  commercial price of, 185
  powder, 29
  tablets, 29
Gastrointestinal tract, nonprescription phytomedicines, retail dollars, 176
GATT. *See* General Agreement on Tariffs and Trade
Gelsemium, 160
General Agreement on Tariffs and Trade, 147
General purity limits, standards harmonization, 151
Gentian root, 29
Gentiana, 160
Geranium, 160
Gerard, J., writings of, 93
Geriatrics, immunostimulants, nonprescription phytomedicines, retail dollars, 176
German model, 10
Germander, 186
Germany, drug therapy in, 14
Gillenia, 160
Ginseng root, 29
Ginger, 19–20
  commercial price of, 185
Ginkgo, 20, 29
  commercial price of, 185
Ginseng, 20, 29, 186
  commercial price of, 185
  standardized, 29
Global toxicovigilance program, development of, 85
Glycyrrhiza, 21, 160
Goldenseal, 20, 29, 30, 186
  commercial price of, 185
Good botanical practices, 121–125
  ethnobotanical inquiry, 123
  herbarium specimens, preparation of, 121–123
  multiple-use curve, *124,* 124–125
Good manufacturing practices, 117
  dietary supplement, 203
Gordo lobo, 30
Gossypii cortex, 160
Gota kola, 29
Gotu kola, commercial price of, 185
Granatum, 165
Green, T., writings of, 93
Grindelia, 160
Guaiacum, 160
Guar gum, 158
Guarana, 164

Guidelines for Assessment of Herbal Medicines, 205–207
Gutta percha, 163
Gutta-percha, 161
Gynecology, nonprescription phytomedicines, retail dollars spent, 176

H

Haematoxylon, 160
Hamamelis Virginiana, 24
Handling, of raw plant materials, 139–142
Harmonization of botanical standards, worldwide, 147–168
Hawthorn, 21, 186
  commercial price of, 185
Health care providers, herbal use by, 33–35
Heart, nonprescription phytomedicines, retail dollars, 176
Hedeoma, 160
Helianthemum, 160
Heliotropium, 97
Hellebore, 160
Hemlock, 93–94
Henbane, 94–95
Hepatica, 160
Herbal abortifacients, 112
Herbal efficacy, randomized controlled trial, alternatives to, 59–64
Herbal materials. *See also* Botanicals
  medieval tests on, 92
Hesiod, 92
Heuchera, 160
Hippocrates, 92
Homeopathy, use of, 189
Hops, 21
  commercial price of, 185
Humulus, 21, 161
Hydrangea, 186
Hydrastis, 20, 161
Hyoscyamus, 161
Hypnosis, use of, 189

I

Identification, standards harmonization, 149–150
Ignatia, 167
Imagery, use of, 189
Immunostimulants, nonprescription phytomedicines, retail dollars, 176
Industry views, on plant monographs, current situation concerning phytomedicines, 195
International conference on harmonization, of standards, 42
Inula, 161
Ipecac, 157
Ipecacuanhua, 157
Ipomea, 161
Iris, 161

J

Jalapa, 159
Japanese medicine, 33–35

Joe-pye weed, 186
Juglans, 161
Juniper tar, 161
Juniperus virginiana, 161

K

Kamala, 162
Kampo prescription
  arranging clinical trial for, 45
  defined, 45
  evaluating, by modern methods, 45–47
Kino, 165
Korean medicine, 33–35
Krameria, 161

L

Labeling
  dietary supplement, 202
  in manufacture of botanicals, 145
  standards harmonization, 153
Labrador tea, 30
Lactucarium, 161
Lappa, 155, 161
Lavender, 29, 30, 162
Lead poisoning, 112–113
Legislation, of dietary supplements, 199–204
  advance notice of proposed rule-making, 203
    voided, 203
  commission of dietary supplement labels, 203–204
  compendial specifications, 203
  conditions of use, 203
  dietary supplement, defined, 199–200
  directions, 203
  effective date, 203
  food additive status, exemption from, 200
  food supplements deemed to be, 200
  good manufacturing practices, 203
  labeling, 202
  office of dietary supplements, 204
  percentage level claims, 202–203
  provisions of, 199–204
  publications, to promote products, 201–202
  safety requirements, 200–201
  statement of agreements, 204
  statements of nutritional support, 202
  stipulated legislative history, 204
  warnings, 203
Lemon grass, 29
Lemon oil, 158
Leptandra, 162, 168
Licorice, 21
  commercial price of, 185
Lifestyle diets, use of, 189
Linden flowers, 29
Linum, 162
Lobelia, 162, 186
Lovell, R., writings of, 93
Lupulinum, 161

Lycopodium, 162
Lycopus, 162

M

Ma huang herb, 21, 29
Macrobiotics, use of, 189
Maidenhari fern, 186
Maltum, 161
Manna, 159
Manufacture of botanicals, 143–144
   individual batches, tracking of, 145
   package labeling, 145
   shelf life, 144–145
   stability testing, 144–145
   vegetable drugs, extraction of, 143–144
Maranta, 162
Marketplace, effect of regulations on, 169
Marrubium, 162
Massage, use of, 189
Mastiche, 164
Matico, 155, 164
Matricaria, 18, 162
Mayapple, 186
Medieval tests on herbs, 92
Medline, 56
Megavitamin therapy, use of, 189
Melissa, 162
Menispermum, 162
Menopause, nonprescription phytomedicines, retail dollars, 176
Menstrual disorders, nonprescription phytomedicines, retail dollars, 176
Mentha x piperita, 22
Metals, standards harmonization, 151
Mexican-American curanderos, 33–35
Mezereum, 158
Microbial limits, standards harmonization, 152
Mid-wives, 33–35
Middle-Eastern doctors, 33–35
Milk thistle, 21–22, 29
   commercial price of, 185
Modern medical systems, ancient, relationship, 47
Modern usage of herbal materials, traditional, differences between, 90–91
Monarda, 163
Morphine, 29
Mortality curves, for various populations, 89
Mucuna, 163
Multiple-use curve, good botanical practices, *124,* 124–125
Murrha, 156
Myristica, 163
Myrrha, 158

N

NAFTA. *See* North American Free Trade Agreement
National Institute of Health, consensus development program, 75–76
Native American healers, 33–35
Native North American medicinal herbs, in commercial demand, 186, 186t
Natural foods
   retail stores, herb sales, 183–184, 184t
Naturopathic physicians, 33–35
NDA. *See* New drug application
Nectandra, 163
Neem oil, 30
New drug application, cost of, 171
New Jersey tea, 186
North American Free Trade Agreement, 147
North American medicinal herbs, in commercial demand, 186
Nutgall, 165
Nutmeg, 29
Nux vomica, 167

O

OAM. *See* Office of Alternative Medicine
Office of Alternative Medicine, 1
Oleoresins of cassia, 29
Oleum anisi, 161
Oleum bergamottae, 158
Oleum betulae, 156
Oleum cajuputi, 162
Oleum cari, 156
Oleum caryophylli, 157
Oleum chaulmoogra, 161, 167
Oleum chenopodii, 157
Oleum coriandri, 158
Oleum gaultheria, 160
Oleum juniperi, 161
Oleum myrciae, 163
Oleum pini pumilionis, 164
Oleum rosae, 165
Oleum rosmarini, 165
Oleum santali, 166
Oleum sesami, 166
Oleum theobromatis, 167
Oleum thymi, 167
Oleum tiglii, 158
Olive oil, 163
On-line databases, 55–57
Opinum, 163
Opium poppy, 96–97
Orange, 29
   peel of, 29
Oregano, 29
Oregon grape, 186
Origanum, 163
Osha root, 186
Otitis media, antibiotics, effect on, 67

P

Pacific yew, 186
Package labeling, in manufacture of botanicals, 145
Packing, of raw plant specimens, 140
Panax, 20, 163
Paprika, 29
Pareira, 157
Parkinson, J., writings of, 93
Parsley, 29
Passionflower, 186
Pau d'arco, commercial price of, 185
Peanut oil, 155
Pechey, J., writings of, 93
Pennyroyal, 186
Pepo, 158
Peppermint, 22, 162
   commercial price of, 185
   oil of, 29
Percentage level claims, dietary supplement, 202–203
Perpolitiones oryzae, 163
Persic oil, 164
Peruvian balsam, 163
Pervianum, 164
Pesticides, standards harmonization, 152
Petroselinum, 164
Pharmaceuticals, botanicals, costs compared, 186–187, 187t
Physostigma, 164
PHYTODOK, 56
Phytolacca, 164
Phytomedicines. *See also* Botanicals
   attitudes toward, 14–15
Phytotherapy, advantages of, 15
Picrotoxin, 155
Pilocarpus, 164
Pimenta, 159, 164
Pine cones, 29
Pine tar, 164
Pink lady slipper, 186
Pink root, 186
Piper, 164
Pipsissewa, 186
Pix burgundica, 154
Plant growth, contaminants introduced during, 129–131
   pesticides, 130–131
Plant monographs, industry views on, 195–197
Plantago, 22, 164
Pleurisy root, 186
Pliny the Elder, 92
Podophyllum, 164
Prayer, use of, 189
Prickly ash, 186
Prinos, 164
Processing, of botanicals, 143–145
   standards harmonization, 153
Production, in quality control of botanicals, 133–137
Professional guidance of policy, need for, 30–31
Projects on botanical medicines, in United States, current overview, 189–190
Proprietary assets, 171–172
Prunum, 164
Prunus virginiana, 165
Psyllium, 22
   commercial price of, 185
   retail sales in U.S., 184
   seed of, 29

INDEX

Publications, to promote dietary supplement products, 201–202
Pulsatilla, 155
Purity limits, standards, 151
Purple coneflower, 19, 186
Pyrethrum, 155
 flowers of, 30
Pyrrolizidine alkaloid, 97

Q

Quaking aspen, 186
Quality control, of botanicals, 115–168
Quassia, 164
Quercus, 165
Quillaja, 165

R

Randomized controlled trials, 39–40, 59–64
Ranunculus, 165
Raspberry leaf, 29
Rauwolfia serpentia, 165
Raw plant materials, shipping, handling, 139–142
Receipt, of raw plant materials, 139–142, 141–142
Red ceder, 186
Red clover, commercial price of, 185
Regulation of botanicals, need for, 16
Regulatory changes, 9–10
Regulatory models, for approval of botanicals, as traditional medicines, 205–212
Relaxation techniques, use of, 189
Reserpine, 29
Resina, 164
Respiratory tract, nonprescription phytomedicines, retail dollars, 176
Retail stores, natural-food, herb sales, 183–184, 184t
Rhamnus, 18, 165
Rheum, 165
Rhus glabra, 165
Rhus toxicodendron, 165
Rosa gallica, 165
Rose, 30
 hips, 29
 oil, 165
Rose geranium, 29
Roselle, 29
Rosemary, 30
Rottlera, 165
Rubber, 161
Rubia, 165
Rubus, 165
Rue, 165
Rumex, 165

S

Sabal, 166
Sabbatia, 165
Sabina, 161
Safety of botanicals, 81–114
 communication about, in United States, 83–84
 dietary supplement, 200–201
 historical perspective, 87–101
 information base for, 103–106
Safflower oil, 156
Sago, 165
Salvia, 166
Sambucus, 166
Sanctum, 160
Sanguinaria, 166
Santalum rubrum, 165
Santonica, 155
Sarsaparilla, 22, 166, 186
Sassafras, 166, 186
Saw palmetto, 22–23, 29, 186
 commercial price of, 185
Scammonium, 158
Schultz-Bip., 19
Scientific testing of plants, 118–119
Scilla, 167
Scoparius, 158, 166
Scopola, 166
Scullcap, 186
Scutellaria, 166
Searches, database, examples of, 56–57
Self-help groups, use of, 189
Senecio, 97
Senega, 164
Senna, 23, 29, 157
 commercial price of, 185
 laxative teas, 29
 leaf, 29
 pod, 29
Sennasides, 29
Serenoa Repens, 22–23
Serpentaria, 155
Sesame oil, 166
Sesami, 166
Shavegrass, 186
Shipping, of raw plant materials, 139–142
Siberian ginseng, 23, 112
 commercial price of, 185
Silybium Marianum, 21–22
Simaruba, 166
Sinapis alba, 166
Sinapis nigra, 166
Slippery elm, 23, 29
 commercial price of, 185
Smilax, 22
Solomons seal, 186
Spearmint, 163
Special purity limits, standards harmonization, 151
Specimen identification, 139–140
Spigelia, 166
Spikenard, 186
Spiraea, 166
Spiritual healing, use of, 189
Squill, 166
Standardization, scientific issues in, 149–153
Standardized ginseng, 29
Standards
 as future benchmark for product claims, 117–118
 harmonization of, international conference on, 42
Staphisagria, 158
Starch, 162, 166, 168
Statement
 of agreements, dietary supplement, 204
 of nutritional support, dietary supplement, 202
Statice, 166
Stillingia, 166
Stipulated legislative history, dietary supplement, 204
Stoneroot, 186
Storage, of raw plant materials, 140
 short-term, 139–142
Storax, 162
Stramonium, 158
Strophanthus, 167
Styrax, 162
Sumac, 186
Sumbul, 159, 167
Supplement legislation, 199–204
 advance notice of proposed rulemaking, 203
 commission of dietary supplement labels, 203–204
 compendial specifications, 203
 conditions of use, 203
 dietary supplement, defined, 199–200
 directions, 203
 effective date, 203
 food additive status, exemption from, 200
 foods, dietary supplement deemed to be, 200
 good manufacturing practices, 203
 labeling, 202
 office of dietary supplements, 204
 percentage level claims, 202–203
 provisions of, 199–204
 publications, to promote products, 201–202
 safety requirements, 200–201
 statement
  of agreements, 204
  of nutritional support, 202
 stipulated legislative history, 204
 warnings, 203
Sweet gale, 186

T

Tabacum, 163
Tamarindus, 167
Tanacetum, 19, 167
Tannic acid, 165
Tapioca, 157, 161
Taraxacum, 167
Tea roses, 29
Tea-tree oils, 29
Terebinthina, 154, 164
Terpene, 97–98
TGA. *See* Therapeutic Goods Act
Theophrastus, 92
Therapeutic Goods Act, 207

Tibetan medicine, 33–35
Tiliae flos, 167
Tolu balsam, 163
Tonics, nonprescription phytomedicines, retail dollars, 176
Tormentilla, 164
Toxicovigilance program, global, development of, 85
TOXLINE, 56
Tracking, of raw plant specimen, 140–141
Traditional Chinese medicine, 29
  doctors of, 33–35
  medicine derived from, 45–47
Traditional medicines, regulatory models for approval of botanicals as, 205–212
Traditional use of herbal materials, modern usages, differences between, 90–91
Tragacanth, 156
Transport, of raw plant specimen, 141
Trials, randomized controlled, 39–40
Trillium, 186
Triticum, 154
Turnsole, 97
Tussilago farfara, 97

U

Ulmus, 23, 167
Unani doctors, 33–35
Unconventional therapies, use of, 189
United Kingdom, surveillance, safety of herbal remedies, 111–114
United States, drug therapy in, 13–16
Urology, nonprescription phytomedicines, retail dollars, 176
U.S. botanical market, dimensions of, 27–30
  botanical products, categories of, 29–30
  categories of herbs, 28
  classification schemes, 28
  herbs
    as supplements, 28
    as traditional medicines, 28
  orthodox drugs, 28
  pharmacologic effects, 28
  range of botanical products, 28, 29–30t
  spices, 27–28
Uva passa, 168
Uva ursi, 155

V

Valerian, 23–24, 29, 168
  commercial price of, 185
Valerium, 23–24
Vanilla, 168
Veratrum, 168
Vernonia oil, 30
Viburnum opulus, 168
Viburnum prunifolium, 168
Vietnamese medicine, 33–35
Vincristine, 29
Viola, 168
Virginia snakeroot, 186

W

Warnings, on dietary supplements, 203
Wax myrtle, 186
Weight-loss programs, use of, 189
Wheat, 167
White oak, 186
White pine, 186
White willow, commercial price of, 185
WHO. *See* World Health Organization
Wild lettuce, 186
Wild quinine, 186
Wild yam, 186
Willow, 185, 186
Wintergreen, 186
Witch hazel, 24, 160, 186
  commercial price of, 185
Wold cranebill, 186
World Health Organization *Guidelines for Assessment of Herbal Medicines,* 103
Worldwide harmonization of botanical standards, 147–168

X

Xanthorrhiza, 168
Xanthoxylum, 159, 168

Y

Yellow ladyslipper, 186
Yerba buena, 30
Yerba santa, 30

Z

Zea, 168
Zeylonicum, 157
Zingiber officinale, 19–20